*Buddha Shakyamuni.*

*Guru Rinpoche.*

༄༅། །ཁབ་གསང་མཁན་འགྲོའི་སྙིང་ཐིག་གི

སྟོན་འགྲོའི་ཁྲིད་རིམ་ཐར་ལམ་སྣང་སྒྲོན

ཞེས་བྱ་བ་བཞུགས། ། །

པདྨ་ཀུ་རའི་སྐུ་བསྐུར་མཐུན་ཚོགས་ནས

སྐུ་བསྐུར་ཞུས།།

# *A* TORCH
# LIGHTING *the* WAY
# *to* FREEDOM

Complete Instructions on the Preliminary
Practice of the Profound and Secret
*Heart Essence of the Dakini*

## DUDJOM RINPOCHE,
## JIGDREL YESHE DORJE

*Translated by the*
Padmakara Translation Group

SHAMBHALA
*Boston & London*
2011

Shambhala Publications, Inc.
Horticultural Hall
300 Massachusetts Avenue
Boston, Massachusetts 02115
www.shambhala.com

The recitation text, Chariot of the Path of Union, is reproduced by kind permission of Editions Padmakara. A practice booklet, including the translation, phonetics, and the Tibetan text, can be obtained from Editions Padmakara, Le Plantou, 24580 Plazac, France. www.padmakara.com. e-mail: editions@padmakara.com.

9 8 7 6 5 4 3 2 1

FIRST EDITION
*Printed in the United States of America*
*Designed by Steve Dyer*

♾ This edition is printed on acid-free paper that meets the
American National Standards Institute z39.48 Standard.
♻ This book is printed on 30% postconsumer recycled paper.
For more information please visit www.shambhala.com.
Distributed in the United States by Random House, Inc.,
and in Canada by Random House of Canada Ltd

LIBRARY OF CONGRESS CATALOGING-IN-PUBLICATION DATA
Bdud-'joms 'Jigs-bral-ye-ses-rdo-rje, 1904–1987.
[Zab gsan mkha' 'gro'i sqin thig gi snon 'gro'i khrid rim thar lam snan sgron. English]
A torch lighting the way to freedom: complete instructions on the preliminary practice
of the profound and secret heart essence of the Dakini / Dudjom Rinpoche;
translated by the Padmakara Translation Group.—1st ed.
p. cm.
Translated from Tibetan.
Includes the English translation of the recitation text Zab gsan mkha'
'gro'i sqin thig gi snon 'gro'i nag 'don zun 'jug lam gyi shin rta.
Includes bibliographical references and index.
ISBN 978-1-59030-909-4 (hardcover: alk. paper)
1. Bdud-'joms 'Jigs-bral-ye-ses-rdo-rje, 1904–1987. Zab gsan mkha' 'gro'i sqin
thig gi snon 'gro'i nag 'don zun 'jug lam gyi shin rta. 2. Rdzogs-chen (Rqin-ma-pa)
I. Bdud-'joms 'Jigs-bral-ye-ses-rdo-rje, 1904–1987. Zab gsan mkha' 'gro'i sqin
thig gi snon 'gro'i nag 'don zun 'jug lam gyi shin rta. English.
II. Comiti de traduction Padmakara. III. Title.
BQ7662.6.B443313 2011
294.3'44—dc22
2011012953

The Padmakara Translation Group
gratefully acknowledges the generous support
of the MACH Foundation and Tsadra Foundation
in sponsoring the translation and preparation
of this book.

# Contents

List of Illustrations      xix
Foreword      xxiii
Acknowledgments      xxv

Preamble      1
    The three defects of the pot      3
    The six stains      4

## PART ONE

### How to Follow a Spiritual Friend, the Root of the Path

CHAPTER ONE: The Qualifications of Masters to Be Followed      9

CHAPTER TWO: The Qualifications of the Disciples Following a Master      23

CHAPTER THREE: How to Follow One's Masters      29
    I. Making offerings      30
    II. Regarding one's teachers as Buddhas      32
    III. Carrying out one's teacher's instructions      34
    IV. How to treat the teacher's belongings and entourage      35
    V. Conducting oneself purely in the teacher's presence      35
    VI. Particular points on serving one's teacher      38
    VII. Getting rid of pride      38
    VIII. Training in not asserting one's own independence      40

## PART TWO

### The Main Explanation of the Stages for Setting Out on the Path

*Section One: The General Preliminary Practice*      47

CHAPTER FOUR: The General Preliminary Practice for Each Session, Which Makes One a Fit Vessel      49

*Section Two: The Specific Preliminary Practice for the Yogas of
the Two Phases*                                                                    55

*Subsection One: The Common Preliminaries That Cultivate the
Field of One's Mindstream with the Four Practices for Turning
the Mind*                                                                          57

CHAPTER FIVE: Reflecting on the Difficulty of Finding the
    Freedoms and Advantages                                                        59
    I. Identifying the freedoms and advantages                                     59
    II. The way in which the freedoms and advantages are so
        difficult to obtain                                                        62
        A. The difficulty of finding the freedoms and advantages
           in terms of their cause                                                 62
        B. The difficulty of finding the freedoms and advantages
           in terms of a simile                                                    63
        C. The difficulty of finding the freedoms and advantages
           in numerical terms                                                      64
    III. Reflecting on the importance of finding the freedoms and
         advantages                                                                65
        A. Reflecting on how the freedoms and advantages constitute
           the support for accomplishing benefit and happiness                     66
        B. Reflecting on the superhuman qualities one will obtain                   66
        C. Reflecting on how much one stands to gain or lose                        67
    IV. Reflecting on the need to make full use of the freedoms
        and advantages                                                             68
        A. Reflecting on the need to be diligent in the Dharma by
           all means                                                               68
        B. Reflecting on the need to guard the mind, which is the
           root of the Dharma                                                      68
        C. Reflecting on the good qualities of the precious human body             69

CHAPTER SIX: Reflecting on Death and Impermanence                                  73
    I. Reflecting on the inevitability of death                                     73
        A. Reflecting on the inevitability of death by considering the
           universe and beings in general                                          73
        B. Reflecting on the inevitability of death by considering the
           diamond body and so forth                                               75
        C. Reflecting on the inevitability of death by investigating
           different examples                                                      76

II. Reflecting on the uncertainty of when one will die 78
  A. Since one's life span is uncertain, there is no certainty
    when one will die 79
  B. Since the causes of death are many and the causes for
    living are few, there is no certainty when one will die 80
  C. Since this body too is so frail, there is no certainty
    when one will die 81
III. Reflecting on the fact that when one dies nothing can
    help one 82
  A. Reflecting that one's body cannot help one 82
  B. Reflecting that one's possessions cannot help one 86
  C. Reflecting that one's relatives and friends cannot help one 87

CHAPTER SEVEN: Reflecting on the Defects of Cyclic Existence 95
I. Reflecting generally on the sufferings of cyclic existence 95
II. Reflecting specifically on the sufferings of the six classes
    of beings 98
  A. Reflecting on the sufferings of the three lower realms 98
    1. Reflecting on the sufferings of the hells 99
      a. Reflecting on the sufferings of the hot hells 99
      b. Reflecting on the sufferings of the cold hells 101
      c. Reflecting on the sufferings of the neighboring hells 103
      d. Reflecting on the sufferings of the ephemeral hells 104
    2. Reflecting on the sufferings of the hungry spirits 105
    3. Reflecting on the sufferings of the animals 107
  B. Reflecting on the sufferings of the higher realms 108
    1. Reflecting on the sufferings of humans 109
    2. Reflecting on the sufferings of the demigods 111
    3. Reflecting on the sufferings of the gods 111
      a. Reflecting on the sufferings of the gods of the world
        of desire 111
      b. Reflecting on the sufferings of the gods of the two
        higher worlds 112
III. Reflecting particularly on the nature of the three kinds
    of suffering 113

CHAPTER EIGHT: Reflecting on the Unfailing Law of Actions:
Cause and Effect 117
I. Reflecting generally on actions and their results 117
II. Reflecting specifically on categories 119

A. Reflecting on negative actions to be avoided    119
B. Reflecting on positive actions to be accomplished    126
C. Transforming indeterminate actions into positive ones    130
III. Summary of key points: the Four Truths    131
  A. The truth of the origin    131
  B. The truth of suffering    132
  C. The truth of the path    133
  D. The truth of cessation    133

*Subsection Two: The Uncommon, Special Preliminaries That
Sow the Seeds of the Profound Path in Five Stages*    137

CHAPTER NINE: Taking Refuge, the Entrance to the Path    139
I. General points to be understood    139
  A. Taking refuge, the entrance    139
    1. The reasons one needs to take refuge    139
    2. Identifying the object of refuge    141
      a. The causal object of refuge    141
        i. The refuge objects of the common vehicles    141
          (1) Worldly objects of refuge    141
            (a) Inferior refuges    141
            (b) Supreme refuges    141
          (2) Supramundane objects of refuge    142
            (a) Objects in which realization is manifest    142
            (b) Sources of inspiration    143
            (c) The absolute object of refuge    143
        ii. The particular refuge objects of the Mantra Vehicle    144
      b. The resultant object of refuge    144
    3. The duration for which one takes refuge    145
    4. The manner in which one is protected    146
    5. The ritual for taking the refuge vow    146
    6. The precepts of taking refuge    146
      a. The actual precepts    146
        i. Special precepts    146
          (1) Precepts with regard to things one must avoid    146
          (2) Precepts with regard to things one should do    147
        ii. General precepts    148
          (1) Not to forsake the Three Jewels, whatever one
            might stand to gain    148

(2) Not to seek refuge elsewhere, whatever
    happens 148
(3) To constantly remember the virtues of the
    Three Jewels and make offerings 148
(4) Remembering the benefits, to take refuge six
    times a day 149
  b. The causes of the refuge ceasing 149
7. The benefits of taking refuge 150
  a. The benefit that one becomes a Buddhist, a follower
    of the Buddha 150
  b. The benefit that one will not fall into the lower
    realms 150
  c. The benefit that one becomes a support for all vows 150
  d. The benefit that one will not be harmed by obstacles
    caused by humans or nonhumans 151
  e. The benefit that one will have few illnesses and a
    long life 151
  f. The benefit that the obscurations of deeds performed
    in the past will be purified 151
  g. The benefit that by completing its cause, the two
    accumulations, one will swiftly attain Buddhahood 152
B. The nature and categories of faith, which is what makes
one take the entrance of refuge 153
1. The reason one needs to develop faith 153
2. Categories of faith 153
  a. Vivid faith 153
  b. Eager faith 153
  c. Confident faith 154
3. How to cultivate faith 154
4. The causes and conditions that make faith
grow or decrease 155
  a. Using the causes that increase faith to make it grow 155
  b. Recognizing and eliminating the conditions that
    make faith decrease 156
5. The particular characteristics of faith 156
6. The fault in not having faith 157
7. The benefits of cultivating faith 157
II. Clarification of the points of the training in this case 158

CHAPTER TEN: Arousing the Mind Set on Supreme Enlightenment,
the Root of the Whole Path      169
I. General points to be understood      169
   A. The definition of the arousing of bodhichitta      169
   B. Categories      170
   C. The particular referents      170
   D. How bodhichitta is aroused      171
   E. The ritual for taking the vow      173
   F. Training in the precepts      173
      1. The actual precepts      173
         a. The precepts of bodhichitta in aspiration      173
            i. Using mindfulness, vigilance, and carefulness in
general      173
            ii. Adopting and giving up the eight white and
black actions in particular      174
         b. The precepts of bodhichitta in action      175
            i. Maturing oneself: training in the six transcendent
perfections      175
               (1) Generosity      175
                  (a) Material giving      176
                  (b) The gift of protection from fear      176
                  (c) The gift of Dharma      176
               (2) Discipline      176
                  (a) The discipline of refraining from negative
actions      176
                  (b) The discipline of gathering positive
actions      177
                  (c) The discipline of working for the benefit
of sentient beings      177
               (3) Patience      177
                  (a) Patience in remaining imperturbable in the
face of harm      177
                  (b) Patience in happily accepting suffering      178
                  (c) Patience in aspiring to a true knowledge
of reality      178
               (4) Diligence      178
                  (a) Armorlike diligence      178
                  (b) Diligence in application      178
                  (c) Diligence in benefiting others      179

(5) Concentration 179
   (a) The concentration that procures a feeling
      of well-being in this life 179
   (b) The concentration that gives rise to
      excellent qualities 179
   (c) The concentration that benefits sentient
      beings 180
(6) Wisdom 180
   (a) The wisdom of listening 181
   (b) The wisdom of reflecting 181
   (c) The wisdom of meditating 181
  ii. Maturing others: training in the four ways of
    attracting disciples 185
  iii. Incorporating the essential practice of the above
    two precepts: training the mind 186
 2. An explanation of the circumstances in which
  bodhichitta declines 188
G. The benefits of bodhichitta 189
 1. The benefit that bodhichitta is outstandingly greater
  than other forms of virtue 189
 2. The benefit that it is the root of Dharma 189
 3. The benefit that one's merit grows ever greater 190
 4. The benefit that one has immeasurable qualities 190
 5. The benefit that one becomes an object of the world's
  reverence 191
 6. The benefit that everything one undertakes is
  meaningful 191
 7. The benefit that all those with whom one is connected
  are linked to liberation 191
II. Clarification of the points of the training in this case 193

CHAPTER ELEVEN: Purifying Negative Actions and Obscurations,
Which Are Unfavorable Conditions on the Path: Instructions
on the Meditation of Vajrasattva 201
I. General points to be understood 201
 A. The reason one needs to purify negative actions 201
 B. The method for purifying negative actions 203
 C. The benefits of purification 207
II. Clarification of the points of the training in this case 209

CHAPTER TWELVE: Gathering the Accumulations, Which Are
  Favorable Conditions on the Path: The Way to Offer the Mandala   217
I. General points to be understood   217
    A. A general mention of the two accumulations   217
    B. Particular points on the mandala practice   218
        1. The reasons for making the mandala the main offering   218
        2. The nature of the offering   219
        3. The meaning of the word *mandala*   220
        4. Different ways of offering the mandala   220
        5. The special feature of the practice   221
        6. The various elements that are visualized in offering the
           infinite Buddhafield   222
        7. Considering one's aim in making such an offering   227
        8. The unique benefits   228
II. Clarification of the points of the training in this case   229

CHAPTER THIRTEEN: Training in Guru Yoga and Receiving
  the Teacher's Blessings, the Heart of the Whole Path   235
I. General points to be understood   235
    A. The reason one needs to be diligent, convinced that this
       is the essence of the path   235
    B. Different ways to practice   241
        1. General principles in making devotion and respect
           the path   241
        2. Specific points on the different stages of receiving
           blessings: the approach and so forth   244
        a. In general   244
        b. In particular   245
            i. Visualizing the object of prayer   246
            ii. Accumulating merit with the seven branches   246
                (1) Prostration, the antidote to pride   246
                (2) Offering, the antidote to miserliness   247
                (3) Parting from negative actions, the antidote to
                    hatred   248
                (4) Rejoicing, the antidote to jealousy   248
                (5) Exhorting the teachers to turn the Wheel of
                    Dharma, the antidote to bewilderment   248
                (6) Praying not to pass into nirvana, the antidote
                    to false views   249

(7) Dedicating to enlightenment, the antidote
to doubt 249
(a) The reason one needs to dedicate 249
(b) The method for dedicating 251
(i) What one dedicates 251
(ii) The goal to which one makes the
dedication 252
(iii) For whose sake one dedicates 253
(iv) The way to dedicate 254
iii. The meaning of the Vajra Guru mantra, the
essence of Guru Rinpoche 257
iv. Receiving the four empowerments 259
C. The benefits and purpose of exerting oneself on the path
in this way 260
II. Clarification of the points of the training in this case 261

*Afterword* 281
*Colophon* 283

Chariot of the Path of Union: A Recitation Text for the Preliminary
Practice of the Profound and Secret *Heart Essence of the Dakini* 285

Notes 303
Glossary 313
Bibliography 340
Index 347

# List of Illustrations

Buddha Shakyamuni (traditional painting)     i

Guru Rinpoche (painting by Orgyen Lhundrup)     iii

Key to Dudjom Rinpoche and his past and future
incarnations (designed by Lydie Berta)     xx

Dudjom Rinpoche and his past and future incarnations
(traditional painting after the prayer, *The Pearl Necklace*)     xxi

Vajrasattva (traditional painting)     200

The Mandala of the Universe (traditional painting)     216

Dudjom Rinpoche, Jigdrel Yeshe Dorje (photo courtesy
of Arnaud Desjardins)     234

Ekajati (from the Dudjom Tersar tradition)     355

Rahula (from the Dudjom Tersar tradition)     355

Dorje Lekpa (from the Dudjom Tersar tradition)     355

Shenpa Marnak (from the Dudjom Tersar tradition)     355

## COLOR PLATES

Refuge Tree of *Heart Essence of the Dakini* (traditional painting)
    facing page 196

Key to the Refuge Tree (designed by Lydie Berta)     facing page 197

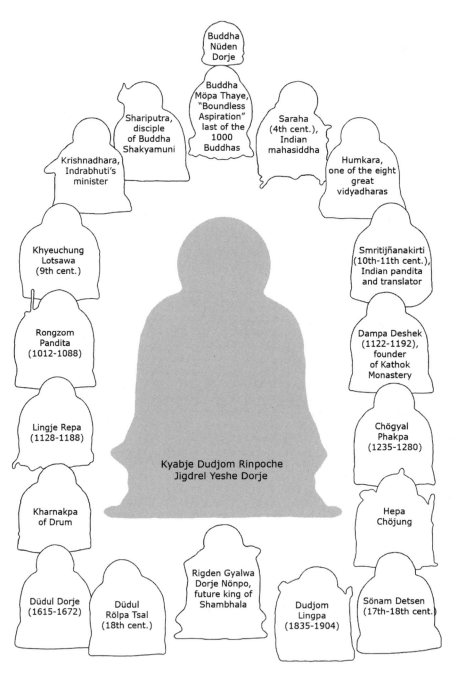

*Key to Dudjom Rinpoche and his past and future incarnations.*

*Dudjom Rinpoche and his past and future incarnations.*

# Foreword

Kʏᴀʙᴊᴇ ᴅᴜᴅᴊᴏᴍ ʀɪɴᴘᴏᴄʜᴇ ᴡᴀs ᴀ ɢʀᴇᴀᴛ ᴍᴀsᴛᴇʀ ɪɴ ᴡʜᴏᴍ peerless realization and accomplishment were combined seamlessly with deep and wide-ranging scholarship. Among the many ways in which he left his mark on the world, both in Asia and in the West, are his own writings, which fill twenty-five large volumes. His concern for the teachings covered the whole range of Buddhist traditions in Tibet, as is evident from the three volumes in which he lists the transmissions he received from all of them. The only motive underlying his concern was that the teachings—as the path by which all sentient beings can reach the same level of freedom as the Buddha—be preserved for the benefit of all.

Kyabje Dudjom Rinpoche himself explained many times that realization of the teachings of the Great Perfection depends solely on the practice of the preliminaries. This text contains his own detailed exposition of these essential preliminary practices. The *terma* tradition from which it comes (discovered by himself and his predecessor, Dudjom Lingpa) covers in one complete cycle all the stages of the path, starting with these preliminaries and continuing right up to the most sublime and profound practices of the Great Perfection. This is a very precious handbook, written with great compassion for anyone seriously interested in removing any obstacle between themselves and the total freedom of enlightenment.

I would like to express my gratitude to Kyabje Dudjom Rinpoche's wife, Sangyum Rinpoche Rigzin Wangmo, for bestowing on us the honor of translating this precious text into English, French, and other languages. It is through her blessings and encouragement that this translation has been possible.

I am most grateful, too, to Kyabje Dudjom Rinpoche's daughter, Semo Tsering-la, for her repeated encouragements; and to Soktse Rinpoche, and Yola Jurzykowski of the MACH Foundation, for their generous support. I would also like to thank Dungse Shenphen Rinpoche and all of Kyabje

Dudjom Rinpoche's children and lineage holders for continuing his peer-less lineage.

Finally, I would like to thank the Tsadra Foundation for its continued support of the Padmakara Translation Group.

*— Taklung Tsetrul Pema Wangyal Rinpoche*

# Acknowledgments

WE ARE DEEPLY GRATEFUL TO THE FOLLOWING LAMAS for their help in translating this text. Taklung Tsetrul Pema Wangyal Rinpoche initially went through the whole commentary for the benefit of those practicing in the traditional three-year retreat in Chanteloube, later overseeing the work of translation, answering innumerable questions, and clarifying many difficult points. Jigme Khyentse Rinpoche gave unstintingly of his time to answer questions and direct us to suitable reference works. Khenchen Pema Sherab Rinpoche shared his extraordinary learning in helping us unravel the intricacies of a number of obscure quotations. Many of their comments have been incorporated in the footnotes and endnotes.

We are indebted to the MACH Foundation, who generously funded the initial translation. Its completion, along with supplementary research on textual sources and notes, was made possible by a grant from the Tsadra Foundation.

The text was translated from the Tibetan by Stephen Gethin (who alone is responsible for any errors that may appear in this book), in collaboration with Patrick Carré and in consultation with John Canti, Wulstan Fletcher, and Helena Blankleder, all of the Padmakara Translation Group. We would like to thank Judith Wright, Kali Martin, and Paul Johanson, who patiently read through the translated text and sent us many useful comments. Finally, we would like to express our gratitude to Emily Bower, Sara Bercholz, Ben Gleason, and their colleagues at Shambhala Publications for their enthusiasm and expertise in transforming our manuscript into a finished book.

# A TORCH
# LIGHTING *the* WAY
# *to* FREEDOM

# PREAMBLE

OM SVASTI

Here is a complete instruction on the preliminary practice of the profound and secret *Heart Essence of the Dakini,* explained in a way that is easy to apply, and entitled "A Torch of Perfect Explanation That Lights the Way to Freedom."

Respectfully I submit obeisance to the Glorious Teacher inseparable from the Lake-Born Diamond Bearer,* who embodies the oceanlike, all-encompassing objects of refuge.

Never moving from emptiness, the expanse of peace,
Compassionately he takes existence through illusory manifestations.
To the all-pervading lord, the gracious Teacher,
Union Diamond Holder who does not dwell in extremes, I submit
    obeisance.
As they wander in the gloom of utter ignorance and a hundred evils,
Travellers in cyclic existence, while yearning for liberation,
Head directly for the dreadful abyss of the lower realms.
That they may swiftly and easily find comfort in the sublime grove
    of nirvana,
I shall light here a jeweled lamp of perfect explanation
To clearly illuminate the excellent path of the profound meaning.
Bestow your kindness that I may complete what I have begun,
That all connections it makes may be meaningful, and that it may
    benefit infinite beings.

Fortunate beings—you who seek these full instructions on the preliminary practice of the profound and secret path, *Heart Essence of the*

---

*Tsokye Dorje Chang (Tib. *mtsho skyes rdo rje 'chang*), i.e., Guru Rinpoche.

*Dakini*—come to the place in which the teaching is to be given. On arriving there, you should clean the room and erect a proper seat for the teacher, such as a lion- or jewel-throne. Put up an awning and curtained canopy, and arrange offerings such as incense, flowers, rows of lamps, and a gold or silver mandala, all beautifully set out and in the proper order. Welcome the teacher, going before him or her with incense and music, and show every courtesy and respect.

Everyone listening to the teaching should refrain from covering their heads, carrying weapons, wearing shoes, and any other such faults in physical conduct. Verbally, you should avoid chatting and laughing. And mentally, you should give up all attitudes that are influenced by the eight ordinary concerns and the afflictive emotions—finding fault in or looking down on the teacher, and so on. Instead, sit up straight with hands folded together, and cultivate great devotion and respect, keeping your mind concentrated and undistracted, for you should realize that to encounter a teacher and a sacred teaching like this is very difficult, and that to do so is extremely beneficial.

Conducting yourself respectfully, with care and cleanliness, present whatever material offerings you can.[1] For the sake of all sentient beings, and in order to request the teachings, fill space with all kinds of offerings—both those that are owned by someone and those that have no owner—and offer too your own body, possessions, and all the merit gathered in past, present, and future. With regard to everyone in the assembly, you must not feel attachment, aversion, or jealousy toward them, indulge in idle chatter, or say unpleasant things about them. Train yourself, rather, in having only pure perception. In short, adopt the right qualities described in the precious sutras and tantras, and without separating from the precious bodhichitta, sit in the teacher's presence listening to the teaching in the proper manner.

If you are the master giving the teaching, you should set an example by being clean and conducting yourself purely. Eschewing pride and contempt, any desire to be famous or special, and attachment to offerings, respect, and possessions, you should maintain the mind set on supreme enlightenment, thinking, "I shall acquire the eye of Dharma for all sentient beings. I shall light the lamp of primal wisdom. I shall do everything to ensure that the Buddha's teaching remains for a long time." Visualize yourself as the Universally Good Lake-Born Diamond Bearer* with his consort,

---

* Kunzang Tsokye Dorje Chang, referring to Guru Rinpoche in the form of Vajradhara

and, seated respectfully in front of him, tens of millions of gods, sages, knowledge holders, and other beings. Consider your speech as the sound of the Dharma, endowed with the sixty qualities, filling the whole universe; it dispels the darkness of ignorance in all sentient beings and they gain the power of memory as an entrance to the Dharma, along with confident eloquence and concentration. Avoid being sleepy, dull, or distracted, chatting meaninglessly, hinting at people's faults, speaking irrelevantly, and other such faults. You should teach at a moderate pace, neither too leisurely nor too hurriedly, with a clear, pleasant voice, in a relaxed and regular manner, teaching for a suitable length of time, without getting angry, so that those listening to the teaching do not become weary. In this manner, you should begin with the following instruction requesting the disciples to arouse bodhichitta and to adopt the right conduct for receiving the teaching.

Let us arouse the mind set on supreme enlightenment by thinking, "Oh! All sentient beings have been our mothers, and their number is as vast as space. To draw them out of cyclic existence, the great ocean of suffering, and set them by whatever means we can in the precious state of unsurpassable enlightenment, we shall properly receive the nectarous sublime Dharma and train correctly on the stages of the path."

As for your conduct when you are listening to the Dharma, in the *String of Lives* it is said:

> Sit on a very low seat,
> Cultivate the virtue of self-control,
> Look with joyful eyes,
> And drink the words like nectar;
> With a pure and unstained mind,
> Listen like a patient to the doctor:
> Make offerings and listen to the Dharma.

Accordingly you should listen properly, free of the three defects of the pot and the six stains.

### The Three Defects of the Pot

Whether or not you appear to be concentrating on the teaching, if you are dull and sleepy, or playing around, or distracted with your mind on other

---

("Diamond Bearer") and inseparable from the absolute-body Buddha Samantabhadra ("Universal Good").

things, you are like an *upside-down pot:* not a drop of the rain of nectar*
pouring down will go inside.

If each time you listen to teachings, you do not familiarize yourself
with them once the teaching is over by repeatedly thinking of them, you
will forget them and be like a *pot with a leaky bottom:* even if the rainwater
collects in it while it is on the ground, when it is picked up the water will
all leak out.

If you are influenced by afflictive emotions, and feel proud when you
hear the teachings again, you will be like a *pot containing poison:* it might
stay filled to the brim with rainwater, but it will be totally unfit for drinking.

Avoid these three and, as instructed in the *Middle Sutra of Transcendent
Wisdom,*

> Listen properly and well, and remember; then I will teach you.

or, in other words:

> Listen properly, without afflictive emotions;
> Listen well, without the mouth turned upside down;
> Remember, without the bottom leaking.

## The Six Stains

In the *Well-Explained Reasoning* it is said:

> It is a stain to listen with pride,
> With lack of devotion, or without interest,
> While distracted outwardly,
> Introverted, or discouraged.

These six stains are:

- to listen while feeling proud of some minor virtues one might have—one's
  ancestry, for instance;
- to listen without sincere respect and devotion to the master and the
  teaching;
- to listen without a genuine commitment to the path of Dharma;
- to listen with the mind distracted by external factors;

---

*I.e., the nectar of the teachings.

- to listen with the six senses excessively withdrawn so that one does not understand the words or the meaning of what is being explained;
- and to listen with a sad and weary mind.

Rid yourself of these and listen with the right kinds of qualities, as described in the *Sutra Requested by Subahu:*

> Consider the teacher proclaiming the Dharma as a priceless treasure.
> Consider the teaching as a wish-fulfilling jewel.
> Consider that to hear the teaching is extremely rare.
> Consider that to hold the teaching and reflect on it is most precious and beneficial.
> Consider that a discerning understanding of the Dharma is something you will not find in a hundred lifetimes.
> Consider that those who give up seeking the teachings have thrown away nectar and can only enjoy poison.
> Consider that those who listen and reflect will achieve their aims.

and so on.

So with a correct attitude and perfect mindfulness, meditate as follows: The place where we are is arrayed with the ornaments of all the Buddhafields and endowed with boundless good qualities, and on this ground is the building we are in—no ordinary building, but the Palace of Great Liberation, bedecked with the "jewels of the Essence of Space,"[2] a measureless palace formed from the self-radiance of primal wisdom,* utterly perfect in proportions and design. In its center, seated on a jeweled throne of indestructibility and on the anthers of the king of lotuses, is the teacher, in whom the compassion and activities of all the Buddhas of the past, present, and future are combined; who embodies the net of the magical display of primordial wisdom; whose activity is such that simply hearing the teacher's name brings liberation from cyclic existence and the lower realms; who is the sole glorious protector of samsara and nirvana. Visualize him or her as the Universally Good Lake-Born Diamond Bearer in person, with his consort.† From his mouth the words of the teaching stream forth in the form of rays of light with syllables made up of the vowels and consonants.

---

* Rather than being built of bricks and mortar like an ordinary building, it is made of light.
† Details for visualizing Tsokye Dorje Chang are given below on page 51.

Visualize the men listening to the teaching as the reddish-yellow Tikshna-Mañjushri,* holding an *utpala* flower upon which are a sword and a volume of the teachings. Visualize the women listening to the teaching as the goddess Tara, who is green and holds an *utpala* flower. The ears of both male and female listeners are sixteen-petaled blue *utpala*s, through which the words of the teaching enter, lightly dissolving³ into the lotuses in our hearts and dispelling the darkness of our ignorance. Consider that the lotus of knowledge blooms and that the meaning of the teaching is clearly understood and perfectly retained through the power of unforgetting memory.

———————

This is how the teacher requests the disciples to listen. As for the instructions to be studied, these fall into two general sections: how to follow a spiritual friend, the root of the path; and how, in so doing, to set out on the path. The first of these two parts is divided into three chapters: the qualifications of masters to be followed, the qualifications of the disciples following a master, and how to follow the master.

———

*Tib. *'jam dpal rnon po,* the supremely intelligent or sharp Manjushri.

## PART ONE

# How to Follow a Spiritual Friend, the Root of the Path

*The qualifications of masters to be followed*

*The qualifications of the disciples following a master*

*How to follow one's master*

# CHAPTER ONE

# The Qualifications of Masters to Be Followed

ORDINARY, CHILDLIKE BEINGS ARE INCAPABLE OF PROCEED-
ing even vaguely in the same direction as the perfect path by the strength
of their own minds, so they need first to examine and then to follow a
qualified diamond master. Diamond masters are the root that causes us to
correctly engage in the whole Buddhadharma in general and especially to
follow the path properly. They are knowledgeable and experienced guides
for inexperienced travellers setting out on a journey, powerful escorts for
those who are travelling to dangerous places, ferrymen steering the boat
for people crossing a river. Without them, nothing is possible. This is reit-
erated in countless scriptures. The *Sutra of the Arborescent Array* says:

> Omniscience depends on the instructions of a spiritual friend.

In the *Transcendent Wisdom* we read:

> Bodhisattvas who wish to attain perfect Buddhahood must first
> approach spiritual friends, follow them, and serve them.

And it is said:

> Without someone at the helm,
> The boat will never reach the other side.
> Even for one in whom all virtues are complete,
> Without a teacher, there is no end to existence.

What, then, are the qualifications of a spiritual friend? The general qualifications are stated in *Ornament of the Sutras:*

> Take as a teacher someone disciplined, peaceful, perfectly peaceful,
> Possessed of superior qualities, diligence, and knowledge of the
> texts;[4]

Who understands them fully, is skilled at explaining them,
Is full of love, and never tires of teaching.[5]

As this passage shows, teachers should be individuals who have perfectly tamed their minds by means of the three superior trainings—the training in discipline, the training in concentration, and the training in wisdom.[6] They should have great learning as a result of having extensively studied the three baskets—the Vinaya, Sutra-pitaka, and Abhidharma—which expound the essential points of these three trainings. They should have seen the way things truly are unmistakenly and be eloquent in conveying their own experience of it to their disciples, combining scriptural authority and reasoning. They should have no regard for veneration and should be governed, rather, by great compassion for beings stricken by suffering. They should be diligent, taking pains to achieve others' welfare. They should have the virtue of patiently putting up with difficulties, never tiring of explaining the teachings again and again.

In particular, with regard to those who are worthy to be masters who have perfected the path of the Diamond Vehicle, the *Fifty Verses on the Teacher* says:

> Steady, disciplined, intelligent,
> Patient, impartial, and free from guile,
> Knowledgeable in applying the mantras and tantras,
> Compassionate, well versed in the treatises,
> Having a thorough knowledge of the ten principles,
> Expert in drawing mandalas,
> And skilled in explaining the mantras—such masters are
> Extremely faithful and have disciplined their senses.[7]

Diamond masters are careful in controlling their bodies and are thus steady. Careful in controlling their speech, they are disciplined. They are supremely wise and intelligent. They are very patient in the face of being harmed, putting up with hardship, and meditating on the profound truth. They are impartial in their pure and superior intentions for all sentient beings. They do not craftily attempt to hide their own faults or make out that they have good qualities that they do not have: they are free of guile and their minds are well controlled. They are skilled in the use of mantras, substances, and medicines for performing the activities of pacifying, increasing, bringing under control, and wrathful subjugation, and are proficient in the principles of tantra. In their wish to free beings tormented by suffering, they are immensely compassionate, much more so than those who practice the Vehicle of Transcendent Perfections.* (Their imperative, in this context of the unsurpassable Mantra Vehicle, is that we strive for the level of Vajradhara in one lifetime, which in this degenerate age is so short. They cannot bear the fact that, when it takes those practicing the Vehicle of Transcendent Perfections three measureless great kalpas to attain Buddhahood and those practicing the lower tantras sixteen or seven lifetimes, beings will be tormented by suffering for that long. It is this need to put us on the path using urgent diligence and particularly powerful compassion that makes them so extremely loving and compassionate.) They are learned in the treatises of the inner sciences† and well acquainted with the ten principles.‡ They are skilled in drawing mandalas with colored powders and in explaining the path of the secret mantras to others. They have great faith, having great respect for and firm devotion to the Great Vehicle in general and to the Mantra Vehicle in particular. They have disciplined their body, speech, and mind by eradicating distractions with the wrong kinds of objects, and have thus brought their senses under control.

The *Net of Magical Display* says:

> One who is steady, disciplined, and intelligent,
> Patient, impartial, and free of guile;
> Who knows how to apply the secret mantras and tantras
> And can draw mandalas;
> Who is fully versed in the ten principles,
> Gives all beings the gift of freedom from fear,
> And takes perpetual delight in the Great Vehicle—
> Such a being is said to be a master.

The master Kunga Nyingpo§ describes the ten principles as follows:

> Mandalas and supreme concentration,
> Symbolic gestures, movements, sitting postures,[8]

---

*Tib. *phar phyin theg pa:* another name for the Vehicle of Characteristics based on the sutra teachings.
†Tib. *nang rig pa,* refers here to the uncommon Buddhist path, i.e., the Diamond Vehicle.
‡Tib. *de nyid bcu.* These are listed by Kunga Nyingpo in the quotation below.
§Sachen Kunga Nyingpo (1092–1158) was the son and successor of Khön Könchok Gyalpo, the founder of the Sakya tradition.

> Recitation, fire offerings, offerings to the deity,
> Activities and dissolution—
> These are well known as the ten principles.

Even more special than the above qualifications are those of a master who teaches the pith instructions. These are listed in the *Great Array of the Sublime:*

> Learned, free of mundane activities,
> Having reached the ultimate point of the absolute nature,
> And not deluded as to what is desirable—
> These are the marks of a master of the secret mantras.

The Great Master* says:

> The roots of the path are the diamond masters:
> From keeping their commitments, their conduct is pure;
> From listening, they are richly adorned; as a result of reflection,
>       they have discernment;
> Through meditation, they possess the signs of warmth and the
>       qualities of experience and realization;
> Applying compassion, they care for their students.

These points are widely taught in other sutras, tantras, and pith instructions and have been summarized into seven sets of qualifications by the Omniscient Dharma King,† which we shall now explain.

*The first set of qualifications.* On this he writes:

> Skillful in means, infinitely compassionate,
> And possessed of the wish-fulfilling treasure of the sutras and
>       tantras, they guide beings.
> Free of defects, and full of good qualities,
> Teachers in this degenerate age are the same as the Buddha in
>       person.
> Take them on the crown of your head with great devotion and
>       reverence.

---

* "The Great Master" (Tib. *slob dpon chen po*) is a widely used designation for Guru Padmasambhava.
† "The Omniscient Dharma King" (Tib. *kun mkhyen chos kyi rgyal po*) refers to Kunkhyen Longchen Rabjam (1308–1363).

Because they are well versed in the methods for accomplishing the great goal with little difficulty and are untiring in their compassion, they benefit others on an infinite scale. With their broad and flawless vision stemming from their immense learning in the teachings in the sutras and tantras—the sublime words of the Sugatas—they are a vast treasure store of the Dharma. With their boundless activities in steering beings upward, they draw them along the path to liberation. Unstained by negative actions of body, speech, or mind, they are free of all defects. They have perfected all the qualities that fulfill all their own and others' wishes and are like wish-granting gems. Nowadays, in these degenerate times, such teachers are the same as the Buddha in person, so take them on the crown of your head with the utmost devotion. As the *Sovereign Array of Sublime Qualities* advises:

> Fortunate child, you should rely on spiritual friends who are learned, unobscured, and steeped in compassion.

*The second set of qualifications.*

> Teachers who have naturally perfected all virtues
> Are of good family and have a sense of shame and decency; their
>     faculties are complete;
> They have immense loving kindness, compassion, and wisdom,
> Are learned, disciplined in body, speech, and mind, and very
>     patient.
> Honest and good-natured, they are without deceit.
> With a hundredfold devotion, take them as wishing gems upon
>     your crown.

Their "family" qualities come from their being born into a royal family or similar birth: they are very conscientious with regard to themselves, and are careful to avoid anything that others would consider shameful. As a result of the merit they have accumulated in former lives, their faculties are complete and perfect. Having been born into the family of the Great Vehicle, they are very loving and compassionate. Since they are learned in the Supreme Vehicle, their attitude is vast and open. Through the awakening of their deeds in training during their previous lives, they have been born with great intelligence. They have few dualistic concepts and afflictive emotions, and are therefore disciplined and patient. From having sought many different teachings, they possess numerous avenues of learning. Their body, speech, and mind are naturally disciplined; they are straightforward and have no deceitful intentions. They have abandoned ordinary, evil ways and are devoted to correct conduct. As we find in the *Compendium of the Buddhas' Wisdom,*

> Of noble family, they have a gentle mind, are inwardly
>     disciplined,
> Outstanding in their qualities, and detached.
> Their knowledge is inexhaustible,
> Their intellect immeasurably vast.
> Patient and forbearing, always straightforward,
> Sincere and free from deceitful behavior,
> They avoid frivolous entertainments and ordinary activities,
> Are never restless or distracted, and rely on solitude.
> Those who are all this are worthy and sublime.

*The third set of qualifications.*

> Sublime teachers, freed from existence,
> Have left their homeland far behind and turned their backs on
>     worldly ways.
> With little attachment to useless wealth and possessions, their
>     own or others',
> They are confident in the law of cause and effect, engaging in
>     virtue and shunning evil.
> Renouncing the things of this present life, they accomplish the
>     greater long-term goal.
> The Great Vehicle is truly theirs, so they act skillfully for the sake
>     of beings.
> Examine them, these glorious, marvelous Lords of Dharma,
> Then follow them untiringly and constantly, and never leave them.

They have severed all connections with their native land and left their country far behind. Recognizing the sufferings of cyclic existence, they have turned their backs on the ways of the world.* Having realized how unnecessary food and riches are, they have little attachment or desire for them. Because they have developed confidence in the law of cause and effect, they engage in positive actions and avoid negative actions. They see the things of this life as useless chaff and are therefore accomplishing

---

*I.e., activities that are concerned only with this life.

the great long-term goal. They have mastered the teachings of the Great Vehicle and know how to use skillful methods for benefiting beings. The *Compendium of the Buddhas' Wisdom* has this to say:

> These courageous and powerful beings have abandoned their homeland;
> They speak the truth and act in accord with the teachings.
> Like the lion, the king of animals,
> They examine things thoroughly; incomparable are their virtues.
> Skillfully they provide protection from suffering.

*The fourth set of qualifications.*

> Fortunate teachers endowed with immense wisdom—
> In them the whole sphere of knowledge in all the sciences is complete.
> Having listened and reflected extensively, they have mastered the words and meanings of philosophical doctrines;
> Their exalted view and conduct are beyond reproach.
> Possessing both the scriptures and reason, they do not invent or improvise.
> They have examined the minds and tendencies of their disciples and teach them the Dharma accordingly.
> Follow and respect these guides who lead you along the path to enlightenment,
> Who possess the discerning eye of wisdom and take you to the jeweled isle of liberation.

Through their general training in the arts and sciences,⁹ they have an unrestricted knowledge of these. And as a result of their specific study and reflection—these being the entrances to the Dharma—they have realized the words and meanings taught in all the vehicles. In particular, their exalted view and action have freed them from erroneous and inferior philosophical doctrines. Never deviating from the guidelines of scriptural authority and reasoning, they do not presume or improvise with regard to the teachings. Having examined the mental dispositions of their disciples, they introduce them to the appropriate teachings. They know how to distinguish what is Dharma and what is not, and thus how to eradicate demons and deviations. As we find in the *Sublime Sutra of the Arborescent Array*,

Those whom we call spiritual friends avoid evil and apply
themselves to virtue.
They teach us the authentic Dharma without any mistake, and
practice accordingly.
Possessed of the seven noble riches,* they strive for enlightenment,
and introduce others to it too.

*The fifth set of qualifications.*

Teachers who possess the blessings of the lineal transmission
Have delighted those who have come before them and hold the
lineage of the accomplished ones.
They have realized the treasure in their teacher's mind and hold
the instructions of the aural lineage.
They have seen their teacher's way of practicing and know how to
accomplish the twofold goal.
Through diligence in the practice, they have gained great clouds
of accomplishments;
Able to transform others' perceptions, they lead them on the path
to liberation.
The teachings of the sutras and tantras have come down to them
and their commitments are pure.
Take such learned and accomplished glorious protectors on the
crown of your head.

As a result of pleasing the spiritual friends who are their teachers, they
hold the lineage of accomplished beings. From probing their teacher's trea-
surelike mind, they possess the instructions of the aural lineage. Through
having seen how their predecessors have practiced,[10] they know how to
accomplish the twofold goal.† Through constant diligence in the practice,
they have attained the different kinds of accomplishment. Because the
blessings of former great beings have entered them, they have the ability to change others' perceptions, and through their knowledge of various skillful means they lead beings to liberation. They have mingled their
mindstreams with the Dharma and so the Three Jewels are complete in
them. Through the blessings of the Buddhas, the teachings of the sutras
and tantras have come down to them. As a result of their immense good

---

* See glossary, *seven noble riches.*
† The twofold goal: one's own goal and that of others.

fortune in the Secret Mantra Vehicle, they have kept the commitments of the transmissions they have received purely. In the *Magical Display of Indestructible Reality* we read:

> They have studied many teachings, have great wisdom,
> And have definite realization of the wisdom transmitted in the teachings.
> Never pursuing material gain,
> They are hardly discouraged by difficult practices,
> Have all the pith instructions, and transcend the path.[11]
> They know their disciples' potentials and can recognize the signs of progress.
> Endowed with bodhichitta, they have great compassion.
> They hold the lineage and know how to accomplish the teachings that have come down to them.
> They possess the treasure of the teachings; in them the river of blessings is complete.
> Having liberated their own mindstreams, they are diligent in benefiting others.
> These are the signs that they are teachers of the Secret Mantra Vehicle.

*The sixth set of qualifications.*

> Compassionate teachers who guide beings along the path
> Have trained in bodhichitta and constantly act to benefit others.
> Having received their teacher's blessings, they bless others' perceptions.
> They have experienced the view, meditation, action, and result, possess the signs of success in the practice,
> And have all the power and ability to dispel obstacles due to negative forces.
> Skilled in means, these supreme individuals who lead beings along the path to liberation
> Are the incomparable ornaments of the world: rely on them with respect.

Because they have trained in the precepts of the Great Vehicle, everything they do will be beneficial for others. As their teacher's blessings have entered them, they have the ability to transform others' perceptions. They have trained in the meaning of the true condition of things and thus obtained the signs of "warmth"—that is, of having gained experience of the view, meditation, action, and result. Because they have grasped the essential point of awareness, they can get rid of negative forces and obstacles. They know how to employ miraculous methods and can therefore gather under their influence those with wrong views. And being well versed in the means for helping others, they guide beings along the path. As it says in the *Highest Expression of Truth,*

> Steadfast in bodhichitta, skilled in means,
> Endowed with the signs of having realized the ultimate nature,
> Possessed of power, untrampled by obstacle makers,
> And blessed by having pleased the teacher—
> Such is a diamond master.

*The seventh set of qualifications.*

> Teachers who teach the ultimate essence
> Liberate all with whom they are connected and join them to the
>     profound path,
> Introducing them to the absolute body that dwells within, which is
>     the essence of the profound path.
> By means of the profound enhancing practices, they increase one's
>     experience and realization.
> Through their consummate realization they lead one to the ground,
>     the true condition of things;
> By means of the profound path of skillful means, they transform
>     everything into the path.
> Because they possess many instructions, they are adept at liberating
>     their disciples' mindstreams.
> These captains who can carry one across the river of cyclic existence
>     in this very life,
> These kingly doctors who fulfill all wishes,
> Are the most exalted of all beings, so rely on them with matchless
>     devotion.

Because of their boundless compassion, all the connections they make with beings are significant. As they know the gradation of the different vehicles, they establish beings on the path of liberation according to their aspirations. They know how to climb the path from the bottom, in stages, and thus it is that they induce beings of modest mental capacity to practice virtue. By means of the profound essential instructions of the path to liberation, they introduce them to directly seeing the absolute body that dwells within one. Through the profound enhancing practices that train one's skills, they make excellent qualities blaze forth more and more. As they have consummate realization, they give rise in their disciples to the experience and realization of the way things truly are. Because they have mastered the profound path of skillful means, they can transform anything into the path. They have many different kinds of advice and so are skilled in liberating beings' mindstreams. Because of their extensive insight, learning, and experience, they know how to eradicate obstacles and deviations. As they have reached the very pinnacle of realization, they can liberate every kind of mindstream. The *Tantra of the Sublime Wish-fulfilling Secret* has this to say:

> Learned, diligent in making others happy;
> Rich in knowledge of the ultimate teachings,
> Transforming everything into the path and adept at liberating
> others' minds,
> Skillful in destroying demons and deviations—
> Such are the qualities of that unsurpassed, essential being,
> the teacher.

The opposite of such teachers are "fault-ridden friends,"[12] who are not to be relied on. The *Fifty Verses* describes them thus:

> Lacking in compassion, short-tempered and aggressive,
> Conceited, full of attachment, undisciplined,
> And boastful: do not follow them.

And the Great Omniscient One* says:

> The wrong kinds of teacher have many faults: they have broken
> their vows and commitments,
> Have little loving kindness, compassion, wisdom, or learning,
> Are very lazy, indifferent, ignorant, and proud,
> Quickly angered, brutal, and grossly affected by the five poisonous
> emotions.

---

* "The Great Omniscient One" (Tib. *kun mkhyen chen po*) is another epithet of Kunkhyen Longchen Rabjam (1308–1363).

They pursue the concerns of this life and throw their future lives
to the wind.
Though they teach a semblance of Dharma, it is not Dharma,
and they are frauds.
Such teachers are like heaps of filth:
However many flies they may attract as disciples, keep well away.
They lead those who have faith in them along wrong paths toward
the lower realms,
So those who desire the path to liberation should never follow
them.

They have spoiled their vows and commitments, and have little compassion or learning. They are very lazy, proud, irritable, and crude, being
full of the five poisons. They go after the things of this life—followers,
possessions, and fame. Even if they stay in secluded places, they are in-
undated by a rain of distracting activities and afflictive emotions pouring down, and they throw their next lives to the wind. They criticize all
teachings and individuals different from theirs. Although they are full of
clever talk that sounds like Dharma, in fact they have confused the words
and the meanings, without any beneficial effect on their own minds, and
they are thus known as frauds. Even if they attract a large following of disciples—with little merit—like flies round a dunghill, they will lead those
who seek liberation and have faith in them to the lower realms. For this
reason, you must keep well away from such teachers. If the blind were to
try leading the blind, both would inevitably end up falling over a cliff. The
same is true of conceited fools expounding dry words—which they boast
as being the Dharma—to self-centered idiots: instead of liberating their
minds, they will bind them tighter with the fetters of wrong views and
turn them back from the path of liberation.

Again, in the *Sutra of the Buddha's Treasure* we find:

Ordinary enemies may deprive us of our lives and throw away our
bodies, but that is all: they do not make us fall into the lower realms.
Ignorant men, by introducing us to the wrong path, lead those pur-
suing virtue to the hells for thousands of kalpas. Should you ask
why, it is because they make use of substantial entities and characteristics and teach mistaken ways. Thus, I tell you, the greatest negative
action, worse than killing all sentient beings, is to teach a doctrine
that leads beings astray.

Sublime teachers who are rid of all the faults just described and who possess all the right qualities are, because of the times,* very hard to find—like the *udumbara*, the king of flowers.† Even if they should happen to come across such teachers for just a little while, sentient beings with impure perception see faults in them—as has happened many times, starting with Devadatta who saw faults in the Bhagavan. Moreover, most people nowadays have the same store of negative deeds and misfortune, and so they perceive faults as good qualities and good qualities as faults. They see even those who have not a single ability that accords with the Dharma, whether manifest or hidden, as sublime beings, and so on. Those who know how to check are rare indeed. In particular, with regard to giving the profound teachings on the actual condition of things, teachers who have no realization cannot make the ultimate experience and realization develop in their disciples' mindstreams. We should therefore take this point‡ as a basis and regard a teacher who has most of the right qualities as the equal of the Buddha. The reason for considering even those in whom six of the above sets of qualities are complete and who have most of the right qualities as sublime beings and for following them is described in the *Approach to the Absolute Truth:*

> Because of the age of strife, teachers have a mixture of faults
> and virtues:
> There are none with no negative aspects at all.
> Having carefully checked those who have more qualities,
> Disciples should put their trust in them.

---

* I.e., in this degenerate age.
† The *udumbara* flower is used in Buddhist teachings as a symbol of extreme rarity. See glossary.
‡ I.e., the fact of whether or not the teacher is a realized being.

# CHAPTER TWO

# The Qualifications of the Disciples Following a Master

THE *FOUR HUNDRED* SAYS:

> Impartial, intelligent, and having interest—
> Such listeners are said to be suitable vessels.

In other words, they have straightforward minds, with no tendency to partiality—they do not feel attachment to those in their own group or aversion for people in other groups.* They are intelligent, able to distinguish between words of truth (to be adopted) and those that are wrong (and to be rejected). They are deeply interested in the sublime Dharma and greatly respect and trust those who teach the Dharma. These are the basic qualities, to which the *Self-Arisen Awareness* adds the following particular ones:

> They have the strength of faith, great diligence,
> Great intelligence, and no clinging or attachment.
> They have great respect, and practice the secret mantras.
> Their minds free of discursive thoughts, they are undistracted.
> They keep the commitments, are diligent in the practice,
> And act in accordance with the teacher's words.

Good disciples have vivid faith—that is, great joy and keen interest with regard to the teacher and instructions; eager faith—a yearning for the result of the practice; confident faith that entertains no doubts;

---

*Tib. *rang phyogs* and *gzhan phyogs,* lit. "own side and other side." "Group," conceived in this context as friend or foe, could range from family and close friends to an entire nation or group of nations.

and consummate faith unaffected by petty circumstances. They are thus completely ready to receive blessings. They are firmly committed in their determination to accomplish unsurpassable enlightenment, and constant in their practice, never postponing it. As they have the intelligence and clarity to investigate the profound meaning of the way things truly are, experiences and realization come to them easily. They have little attachment and clinging to worldly happiness or possessions such as food and clothes. Since they have great respect for the teacher and the *yidam*, they are an open door by which blessings may enter. They have cleared all their doubts and hesitations regarding the path of the secret mantras and are therefore able to undertake the profound practices. Since their minds are not prey to ordinary thoughts to do with attachment, aversion, and bewilderment, they are not distracted. They keep their promises and do not transgress the root and branch commitments that they have accepted. They do not tire of practicing the profound path and never go against the teacher's instructions. As the Great Omniscient One says,

> Disciples with good fortune have great faith and wisdom,
> They are diligent, careful, mindful, and vigilant.
> They do not go against the teachings and keep their vows and
> 　　commitments.
> Their body, speech, and mind well controlled, they are very
> 　　compassionate and altruistic.
> Open-minded, cheerful, and generous, they have very pure
> 　　perception,
> Are stable, and have great devotion.

It is disciples with just such qualifications as these that one should accept to teach. Their opposites are bad disciples, whom we shall now consider.

## BAD DISCIPLES

These are described in the *Self-Arisen Awareness* as follows:

> They show no honor or respect,
> They pervert the secret mantras in their conduct,
> They have neither the qualities of family and lineage nor
> 　　a good character,
> Are quite unintelligent,
> Scorn kindness,

And make a meaningless mess of things.
Such disciples, unexamined, are the enemies of a teacher.

And the Omniscient One* says:

> On the other hand, disciples with bad fortune are the basis for
>     all faults.
> They have no faith, no sense of shame or decency, and little
>     compassion;
> Their family, nature, and behavior reflect their evil fortune.
> Their minds and actions are grossly affected by the five poisonous
>     emotions,
> They break the precepts, confusing Dharma and non-Dharma,
>     good and evil;
> They fail to keep their vows and commitments, and have no
>     antidotes.
> Extremely stupid and unintelligent, they are difficult to satisfy,
> Their anger and harsh words ever on the increase.
> These disciples follow the teacher with five wrong notions:
> Seeing the teacher as a deer, the teachings as musk,
> Themselves as hunters, their intense practice as a form of shooting,
> And the result—the accomplishment of the Dharma—as
>     something to be traded.
> Because they do not keep the commitments they will suffer in this
>     life and the next.
> Some begin unthinkingly without first examining the teacher;
> For the novelty of it, they talk about his good qualities, but later
>     they criticize.
> Others are two-faced, deceitful hypocrites,
> Slyly trying to get the better of the teacher's closest disciples.
> All this results in birth in the Hell of Ultimate Torment.

Such disciples of evil destiny† are vessels for numerous faults. They have little faith and hardly any shame with regard to themselves, decency with regard to others, or compassion. They are of an evil family[13] and bad-natured. They conduct themselves badly and have little fortune. Their minds and afflictive emotions are very gross. They break the precepts and

---

*"The Omniscient One" (Tib. *kun mkhyen*) once again refers to Kunkhyen Longchen Rabjam (1308–1363).
†Tib. *skal ngan,* lit. "bad fortune." See glossary, *fortune.*

confuse positive and negative actions. They do not keep their vows or commitments. They have no control over their afflictive emotions and are ignorant of the antidotes. They are not very intelligent and are difficult to please. They get angry and shout over trifles. They are naturally diligent in non-Dharmic activities. They betray the Buddha, disgrace the Dharma, and destroy the Sangha. When they seek teachings from the teacher, since their minds are not at all at peace, they harm and despise everyone, like hunters. They think, "Apart from the fact that I am receiving this particular transmission from him, the master has this fault and that defect—he's no better than an animal," and, wanting to be better than others in having heard the teaching, they treat it like musk. Before they have even finished receiving the teaching, they transmit it and sell it—as a favor to others, or because they despise it, or for the sake of some small reward. Such disciples will be unlucky in this life, and in the next life they will have to wander in the lower realms, as is explained in the commentary on the *Tantra That Establishes the Three Commitments:*

> Those who criticize a diamond master of the secret mantras,
> Who abuse the Dharma and exchange it for riches,
> And though they know the commitments, do not keep them
> Will, in this life, suffer from a short life span,
> The decline of their splendor and good fortune,
> And the punishments of the dakinis.
> In the next life, they will fall into the lower realms.

In the first place, teacher and disciple accept each other without each examining the other. Then, although the disciples, for the novelty of it, may show respect and make gifts to the teacher, they get angry over circumstantial trifles, crying insults and being rude. Even if they stay alone, they find fault in the slightest thing and discourage all the teacher's close disciples. Some disciples may praise their teachers in their presence and make a false show of devotion, but in their minds there is neither faith nor respect, and they are secretly using their artful ways to play them false. Because of all this, and because they criticize their teachers, the negative consequences are boundless, as the *Fifty Verses* shows:

> Who will endure the terrifying hells,
> The Hell of Ultimate Torment and others?
> Those who speak ill of the master:
> As has been well explained, it is there they will remain.

For this reason teacher and disciple must first examine each other thoroughly, and not begin anything without prior deliberation. As the same work points out,

> Since teacher and disciples
> Will break the commitments equally,
> The brave must first check the connection
> Between master and disciple.

If this is not apparent within a short time, then, as the explanatory tantra the *Diamond Necklace* says, they will need to check each other over a long period:

> Examine for up to twelve years.

Such examination must be carried out before any connection is made through empowerment or teaching. But once one has received an empowerment or teaching, even if one's teachers have broken their vows by committing all four radical defeats,* it is improper to examine them or lose faith, or do anything but regard them as objects of devotion and respect. As it is said,

> If you don't consider as your teachers
> Those from whom you've heard a single verse,
> It's as a dog you'll be reborn a hundred times,
> And as an outcaste you'll take birth.

---

* In other words, even if they have irretrievably broken the basic vows of monastic ordination, namely the vows to abstain from killing a human being, stealing, sexual intercourse, and lying.

# CHAPTER THREE

# *How to Follow One's Masters*

Having found a master with the right qualifications, how should we follow him or her? The Buddha taught that in order to be cured of the malady of afflictive emotions, we should rely on our teachers like patients relying on a doctor. To gain protection from the fear of difficulties, we should rely on them like common people relying on a king.* To escape from the narrow defile of birth and death, we should rely on them like travellers relying on a guide. To accomplish our own and others' welfare, we should rely on them like merchants relying on a ship's captain. To cross over the river of cyclic existence, we should rely on them like passengers in a boat relying on a helmsman. This is explained in the *Sutra of the Arborescent Array:*

> Fortunate child, think of yourself as a sick person, think of the teaching as medicine, think of your assiduous practice as the treatment, think of the spiritual friend as a skilled physician.
>
> Fortunate child, think of yourself as a common subject, think of the teaching as fearlessness, think of your assiduous practice as removing anything that could harm you, think of the spiritual friend as a king.
>
> Fortunate child, think of yourself as a traveller, think of the teaching as something that gives protection from fear, think of your assiduous practice as freeing you from every kind of danger, think of the spiritual friend as an intrepid guide.
>
> Fortunate child, think of yourself as a merchant, think of the teaching as something that gathers together your goods, think of

---

*A good king protects his subjects from difficulties such as being unfairly judged and punished; they go to him to be pardoned.

your assiduous practice as making a profit, think of the spiritual friend as a ship's captain.

Fortunate child, think of yourself as a passenger on a ferry, think of the teaching as the ferry, think of your assiduous practice as crossing the river to the other side, think of the spiritual friend as a skilled helmsman.

And,

Fortunate child, think of yourself in relation to the spiritual friend as being like the earth, which never wearies under all the loads it bears; like a diamond, which no adverse factor can alter; like a disciple who never ignores the advice he is given; like a servant who obeys everything he is told; like a bull with broken horns who has lost any sense of self-importance.

Of the many ways that have been taught for following a teacher, here we will consider eight headings, basing our explanation on that given in the *Fifty Verses on the Teacher:*[14] making offerings, regarding the teacher as a Buddha, carrying out the teacher's instructions, how to treat the teacher's belongings and entourage, conducting oneself purely in the teacher's presence, particular points on serving the teacher with one's body and speech, getting rid of pride, and not asserting one's own independence.

## I. Making offerings

It is important to follow your teachers by offering them all the things that are extremely difficult for you to give—your own child, spouse, body, and wealth:

If constantly following the master
With whom you have a sacred commitment
Means giving things impossible to give—
Your child, your spouse, and your own life—
What need to mention giving your wealth and possessions?

and,

With the utmost devotion, three times a day,
Offer mandalas of flowers, join your hands,
And make obeisance with your crown at their feet:
Thus honor the masters who teach you.

Three times a day, offer a mandala made of heaps of flowers if you have one ready, or, failing that, keep in mind the features of the outer, inner, and secret mandalas and offer these to the teacher. Having done so, prostrate three times. As the *Ornament of the Indestructible Essence* says,

> Wise diamond disciples
> Who seek complete happiness
> Should make offerings with minds full of devotion and respect.
> Those who fail to offer what they have intended
> Are doomed to ruin,
> Assured of rebirth in the hells and hungry-spirit realms.

In other words, if you do not offer things that please the teacher, or if you decide to make an offering and then do not do so, you will definitely be reborn as a hungry spirit and in the hells. Disciples should therefore make suitable offerings to their teachers, and the teachers, for their part, should be sure to accept the offerings in order to counter the disciples' craving. As we read in the *Tantra of Perfect Union,*

> When someone offers the teacher
> Something that is dear
> With a mind free of expectation,
> The teacher accepts it compassionately,
> And, to counter the disciple's clinging,
> Takes it with the intention to benefit him.

If you give offerings to your teachers in this way, you will definitely complete the accumulations* as if you had delighted all the Buddhas by constantly making offerings to them:

> Since they are the same as all the Buddhas,
> And because of your desire for the inexhaustible,†
> The smallest pleasing things
> Become extremely special.
> Offer them to your teachers:
> Giving them is the same as giving
> Constantly to all the Buddhas.
> It is by giving to one's teachers that one accumulates merit,

---

* The two accumulations of merit and wisdom.
† I.e., the inexhaustible qualities of Buddhahood.

> And through accumulation one achieves the supreme
>   accomplishment.

And the *Tantra of Supreme Wisdom* states:

> Greater by far than offerings made
> To all the Buddhas in a kalpa
> Is the mass of merit that comes when one anoints
> A single hair of the teacher's pores with just one drop of oil.

And so on.

## II. Regarding one's teachers as Buddhas

The diamond masters are Vajradhara in person, and you must follow them knowing that they are so, without any doubt or hesitation. As we read in the *Glorious Tantra of the Gathering of Secrets:*

> Fortunate child, regard the master as the adamantine enlightened mind of all the Sugatas and Bodhisattvas. Should you ask why, it is because the master is the same as the enlightened mind and inseparable from it.

From the adamantine absolute body or enlightened mind there arises the body of perfect enjoyment, and these are present as form, the latter's manifestation.* But beings are unable to see this, so as long as this is so, the teacher continues to appear in that ordinary body and works for the benefit of beings.

Similarly, the *Ornament of the Indestructible Essence* says:

> How do disciples with constant devotion to their teachers
> See the teacher?
> The teachers are the same as all the Buddhas,
> They are always Vajradhara.

Moreover,

> Do not think about the master and Vajradhara
> Regarding them as distinct entities.

You should therefore view your teachers as the embodiment of all the Buddhas, their eyes, limbs and so forth as the Close Sons (Kshitigarbha

---

*I.e., the absolute body and the body of perfect enjoyment are present in the body of manifestation.

and the others),* the hairs on their bodies as Arhats, their crowns as the Buddhas of the five families, their thrones as the guardians of the world, and the rays of light streaming forth from them as the infinite hosts of the eight classes of elemental spirits—"malignant" *yakshas*, smell-feeding *gandharvas*, and the rest—bound under oath as protectors, as described in the *Diamond Daka:*

> Their bodies are by nature the totality of Buddhas,
> Their limbs are Bodhisattvas,
> The hairs on their bodies, Arhats;
> The Buddhas of the five families are their crown;
> The worldly gods are their throne;
> Their rays of light are the Lord of Secrets,† king of the yakshas.
> With these and other qualities
> Should those who practice always view their form.

For this reason, simply stepping on their shadow has negative consequences as serious as demolishing a stupa. Stepping over their belongings—their shoes, seat, clothes, horse, eating bowl and other everyday articles, their umbrella, canopy, and so forth—is just as bad, so always be careful to avoid such things:

> For fear of the negative consequences,
> Equivalent to those of destroying a stupa,
> Never tread on even their shadow,
> Let alone their shoes, their seat, or mount.

And the *Vajrapañjara Tantra* says:

> The fool who steps upon
> The teacher's umbrella, shadow,
> Shoes, seat, or cushion
> Will fall from the human state onto razors.

It is said that just to step on the teacher's shadow is the same as a crime with immediate retribution‡ and leads to one's falling into the Hell of Ultimate Torment. Therefore, if it should happen that you cannot avoid doing so, you should visualize yourself using diamond power to glide

---

* The Close Sons, the Buddha's eight closest Bodhisattva disciples. See glossary, *Eight Great Close Sons.*
† Tib. *gsang ba'i bdag po,* another name for Vajrapani.
‡ See "The Five Crimes with Immediate Retribution," page 123.

unobstructedly underneath the object and recite "Om vajra bega krama hung." According to the tantras, this will prevent any fault being produced. Why is such an act so serious? Because the object is so special, as the *Compendium of the Buddhas' Wisdom* explains:

> Know that the teacher is more potent
> Than all the Buddhas in a thousand kalpas.
> The reason is that all the Buddhas
> In a kalpa, all without exception,
> Arise through reliance on teachers.
> Without teachers to precede them,
> There'd be no Buddhas, nor even the name.

## III. Carrying out one's teacher's instructions

It is important to carry out everything your teacher asks joyfully and respectfully. If you cannot do so, either because it is something inappropriate—contrary to the Dharma or whatever—or because you are unable, properly ask to be excused in a way that does not displease the teacher, and request permission. To abandon it thinking it does not matter, without asking the teacher's permission, will not do. It is said:

> The wise, with joyful mind,
> Make every effort to obey the teacher's word.
> If they are unable to do what they ought,
> They clarify their inability by speaking about it.

and,

> Therefore, make every effort
> To not transgress the teacher's word.

Even if your teacher asks you to do something improper, such as something that is contrary to the Dharma, you must carefully consider the reason you have been asked to do it, and why it is normally not allowed.[15] Then either carry it out or ask permission not to, in a way that does not displease the teacher. It is wrong to do otherwise and to disobey. As the *Display of the Perfected Wheel* says,

> If one does as they have said,
> Even if it is something wrong,

It will lead to ultimate good:
Why, then, question doing it?

## IV. HOW TO TREAT THE TEACHER'S BELONGINGS AND ENTOURAGE

As much as one values one's own life, so too should one value one's teachers' belongings. Have as much respect for your teachers' children, consorts, and families, of whom they are equally fond, as you have for the teachers themselves. And you should also treat their attendants affectionately, like friends:

> The teachers' belongings are like your life,
> And those they're fond of, like the teachers themselves,
> While those around them are like good friends:
> Meditate on this and constantly reflect.

The *Tantra of Secret Union* says:

> Those who covet the teacher's property
> Will remain hungry spirits for two kalpas.

And in the *Tantra That Drives Back Armies* we find:

> Those who angrily and resentfully upset
> Their teachers and their circle
> Will cook in the Hell of Ultimate Torment
> For kalpas as many as the atoms in the universe.

## V. CONDUCTING ONESELF PURELY IN THE TEACHER'S PRESENCE

### *Physical Conduct*

When your teachers get up, never stay lying down or sitting as if nothing had happened. Never lie around casually in their presence. Do not walk in front of them without obtaining their permission or unless there is a special reason. Do not take your place before your teachers reach the throne, and when they are seated on the bare ground, do not sit on a seat.[16] Do not put your hands on your hips in front of your teachers, twist your body back and forth, or lean against a pillar or wall. Do not massage or pull your finger joints in their presence. When you are seated, never have your back turned to the teacher, or stretch your legs, or wear anything wrapped round your head.[17] In your teacher's presence, never carry a stick or weapon without reason, and do not carelessly spit, blow your nose, or hawk up phlegm. Apart from on ritual occasions such as the feast offering, or with the teacher's permission, do not sing, dance, or play different kinds of musical instruments.

> Do not sit on their bed or walk in front of them,
> Wear your hair in a top knot,
> Sit on a seat, or place your hands on your hips
> In their presence.
> When your teachers wish to sit,
> Do not lie or sit.
> Always, whatever they do,
> Be ready to stand up and act perfectly.
> Do not spit and so forth,
> Stretch your legs when seated,
> Or walk around or argue
> In front of your teachers.
> Do not massage your limbs, dance,
> Sing, or play music.
> Those who are wise should not twist
> Or lean against pillars and the like,
> Nor crack and strain their knuckles.

But at night, when crossing a river, or where the way is dangerous, if your teachers ask you to do so, you may walk in front of them:

> At night, by a river or on a dangerous path,
> Having been instructed, go in front.

And the *Ornament of the Indestructible Essence* states:

> At night, when crossing a river,
> Or when in rocky defiles,
> In order to fulfill their instructions,
> To go in front will not be a fault.

Also, when you rise from your seat, you should do so respectfully, bowing down. It will not do to act otherwise, negligently and carelessly, as if it did not matter:

> Rise from your seat with head bowed,
> Sit down respectfully.

## Verbal Conduct

Avoid joking, laughing, or chatting idly and gossiping. Do not say or repeat lies, or things that slander or criticize others. Even if they are true, the person who says such things will reap very negative results. Why? Because to do so will affront and upset the teacher, and to upset the teacher for even an instant has boundless negative consequences. As it says in the *Three Stages,*

> Do not speak carelessly in the teacher's presence.
> If one angers even an ordinary person,
> One will fall into the ephemeral hells.
> Someone who transgresses the teacher's wishes
> Will cook for a billion kalpas
> In the pitch dark of the Hell of Ultimate Torment.

## Mental Conduct

As for your thoughts, do not covet your teachers' wealth and possessions, or have malicious thoughts with regard to their attendants, disciples, sponsors, and so forth, because any selfish clinging will displease them. For different reasons, your teachers may act gently or wrathfully and behave in an apparently ordinary manner, but never, even for the smallest of their acts, confuse their words with their intentions and think that what they are doing is wrong. Nor should you imagine a multitude of contradictions in the things they say at different times and in the most trivial things they do. As we find in the *Accomplishment of Wisdom,*

> Avoid dishonoring or coveting
> The teachers' belongings and followers, or their attendants.
> Their various deeds are a great magical display
> Skillfully benefiting beings.

Reject wrong views, finding fault in
The oceanic infinity of their wisdom and activities.

## VI. Particular points on serving one's teacher

When you offer your teachers water for washing or when you massage them, begin by performing three prostrations. Then when you have finished, again do three prostrations. Also, if you mention the teachers' names, rather than blatantly referring to them by name, you should speak of them with laudatory phrases such as "in the presence of the Great Knowledge Holder" or "the Sublime and Noble One" or "the Glorious Teacher."[18]

> When washing their feet or washing their body,
> Drying them, massaging them, and so forth,
> Begin by first prostrating to them,
> And likewise at the end, in whichever way seems best.
> When you utter their names,
> Add "Your Presence" to the name,
> And in order to inspire others to be respectful,
> Speak of them in honorific terms.

Moreover, prepare a seat for your teachers, and praise them with folded hands. When they arrive or depart, get up to welcome them or see them off. It is said in the Vinaya texts:

> As soon as you see the abbot, rise from your seat.

If you fail to do so, says the *Hundred Parables on Action*, you will be born a cripple for five hundred lifetimes. Whereas if you rise to serve your teacher, you will obtain the major and minor marks, as a commentary on the *Ornament of True Realization* points out:

> Those who escort and greet their teacher will bear the mark of the wheel on their hands and feet.

## VII. Getting rid of pride

In the morning, for example, first ask your teachers for instructions on what you should do today, and while they are giving them, listen undistractedly, with body bowed and hands joined. When they have finished, instead of going away without replying, take your leave, saying "I shall do as you say." Once you have completed the tasks they have given you, gently and politely inform them that you have done as they asked.

When you are next to them and you need to cough, yawn, sneeze, or laugh, cover your mouth to avoid being unsightly. Unless you cannot help doing otherwise, leave by walking backward with your hands joined until you are out of your teachers' presence.

While you are receiving teachings, sit humbly and avoid any show of pride, haughty demeanor, or behavior designed to draw attention to yourself. Dress properly, and request the teaching three times, kneeling and with your hands joined. In short, avoid contemptuous and careless behavior and the faults of apprehension and doubt. Like a newly wed bride,* you should be extremely controlled in your behavior and listen to the teachings with a proper combination of mindfulness, vigilance, and carefulness.

> Request advice from your teachers
> And tell them, "I will do as you say."
> With hands folded, undistractedly
> Listen to your teachers' instructions.
> If you do things such as laugh or cough,
> Cover your mouth with your hand.
> When you have completed your task,
> Inform them politely.
> In their presence, sit humbly,
> Be subdued in your manner and dress,
> And if you wish to receive teachings,
> Kneel down, join your hands together,
> And make your request three times.

and

> In everything you do to serve and venerate them,
> Keep your mind free of pride.
> Controlling yourself with a sense of shame and awe,
> Conduct yourself like a newly wed bride.
> All attempts to draw attention to yourself

---

*In traditional society, a newly wed bride takes pains not to vex her husband or her mother-in-law.

Must be abandoned in the teachers' presence;
Check yourself and renounce
Any other similar behavior.

## VIII. TRAINING IN NOT ASSERTING ONE'S OWN INDEPENDENCE

When your own teachers are staying in the same area,[19] you must first seek their advice for performing consecration ceremonies, giving empowerments, teaching the Dharma, performing fire ceremonies, and so forth. If they give their permission, you may proceed, but otherwise you should not do any of these. Never teach your teachers' disciples or your own in their presence. Do not let your own disciples rise from their seats, prostrate to you, or show you other signs of respect in the same place as your teacher is staying. Even if you have obtained your teachers' permission and give empowerments and so on in the same area as them, you should present any offerings you receive to your teachers. They in turn will accept whatever they wish of those offerings and then give back the rest and allow you to use them.

Consecrations, mandalas, fire ceremonies,
And gatherings of disciples
Are not to be done without permission
When the teacher is staying in the same area.

and

Your teacher's disciples are not your disciples,
Even your own disciples are not so in your teacher's presence.
So stop them paying you respect
By rising from their seats or prostrating to you.

and

Whatever you receive from "Opening the Eyes"*
Offer it all to your teachers.
Once they have accepted your offering,
You may use the rest as you please.

---

*"Opening the Eyes" (Tib. *spyan 'byed*) refers to painting a statue of the Buddha or a deity, of which the most important part is painting the eyes. The person who does this is often paid a fee for his work.

Moreover, when you have occasion to make an offering personally, do so with your head bowed and with both hands. You should do likewise when receiving something from your teachers.

> Anything they offer the master,
> And anything their teacher gives them,
> Wise disciples will offer and accept
> With both hands, and with head bowed.

It is said that such acts should be accompanied by prostrations. As we read in the *Tantra of Perfect Union,*

> Those who offer or receive
> Should first prostrate.

To sum up, maintain constant mindfulness and vigilance, and be diligent in following the spiritual friend sincerely, without hypocrisy. If your diamond brothers and sisters behave improperly, helpfully point out their mistakes to them and prevent them doing negative actions.

> Be diligent in your own conduct
> With mindfulness, forgetting nothing.
> And if your siblings go amiss in their conduct,
> You should correct each other good-naturedly.

If it should happen that because of ill health you have to do things like lie down, but without having obtained permission, you will not be at fault as long as you maintain a pure and correct attitude.

> For someone who is sick,
> Prohibited behavior even without permission—
> Failure to bow when serving the teacher—
> Will not have negative consequences for one who has
>     a positive attitude.

*A summary of all the above:*
Always be diligent in the ways to please your teachers and constantly avoid anything that might displease them:

> What need is there to say a lot on this?
> Do anything that pleases your teachers,
> Avoid everything that might displease them:
> Be diligent in both of these.

"Accomplishment follows from the master,"
The Diamond Holder himself has said.
Know this and please the teacher perfectly
In everything you do.

And the *Ornament of the Indestructible Essence* says:

All skillful means depend on
The diamond holders, the supreme teachers.
Do everything to please them accordingly;
To please them is to please all the Buddhas.

It is naturally very difficult for us beginners to see the teacher as having exhausted all faults and perfected all good qualities. When the teacher is actually present, conditions can easily make wrong thoughts come up, and they may be very strong. We might think, "This teacher is very short-tempered, he's so tight-fisted, he only likes new people . . ." You must resist such thoughts and think, "This is impossible, it is my own impure perception and way of seeing things." Part from* your disrespectful attitude immediately, or within four hours, or at least within twenty-four hours. The Great Omniscient One has said:

Constantly dwell on the teacher's good qualities,
Don't think of faults, and even if you see any, consider them as
 good qualities:
"They are surely my own perception, for the teacher has no faults."
Think this sincerely, and use the antidote of parting and restraint.

Moreover, should you have a disrespectful thought in a dream with regard to the teacher's conduct, you must part from it as soon as you wake up, as is explained in the *Display of the Perfected Wheel:*

If in the course of a dream
You see faults in the teacher,
Part from that the moment you awake.
Should you fail to part from it, it will grow into
The cause for rebirth in the Hell of Ultimate Torment.

---

*Tib. *bshags pa,* see glossary, *parting,* for an explanation of this term, formerly translated as "confession."

If you hear others speaking of faults in the teacher, do your best to find a way to stop them, and if you cannot do so, block your ears with your fingers and reflect on the teacher's good qualities. You should not keep the company of such people or relax with them. As the *Source of Nectar Tantra* says,

> If they criticize the diamond master,
> Stop them by peaceful means or wrathful.
> If you do not have the ability,
> Mindfully block your ears.
> Do not associate with them or talk to them;
> If you frequent them
> You will cook in the lower realms.

Nowadays there are many people who talk about the qualities of, say, a good dog: they extol its fine pedigree and loud bark, they claim how much fiercer it is than the most savage carnivores, and so forth; and they praise the excellence of their horses and cattle, saying how indebted they are to them. But when it comes to the excellent qualities of a master who teaches the Dharma, rarer than a star in the daytime, it seems, are those who think about all the qualities their teachers have and all the kindness they have shown. Point at yourself, now, and think carefully: we do not even have as much regard for our teacher as for our horses and cattle and dogs; how could we ever attain accomplishment that way? Reflect and call to mind even the smallest of your teachers' good qualities. Think of their kindness—even just a single verse of a scripture that they have transmitted to you, or a cup of tea, or simply an approving look. By thinking about this, not just once, but again and again, your devotion will grow. In this manner, work hard at the different ways to please your teachers: by serving them with material offerings, you will fill the measure of the two accumulations; by serving them with your body and speech, you will purify the obscurations of your body, speech, and mind; and, most importantly, by serving them with your practice, you will hold the teachings of the practice lineage. The benefits of so doing are described in the *Sutra Requested by Maitreya:*

> Know that all attainment—all the mass of perfect liberation and vision of primal wisdom of the Listeners, Solitary Realizers, and Unsurpassable Buddhas—all of it arises from having perfectly followed

a spiritual friend. Maitreya, you should also know that the benefit and happiness[20] of sentient beings all arises from one's own sources of good, and those too arise from the spiritual friend.

In the *Sutra Requested by Ratnacuda* we read:

> Child of the gods, by following and venerating a spiritual friend, you will see everything as a pure Buddhafield, you will obtain the supreme concentration of great compassion, you will never be without transcendent wisdom, you will bring sentient beings to full maturity, and all your hopes will be perfectly fulfilled.

And the Great Omniscient One says:

> As a result, unbiased pure perception arises,
> One is trained in loving kindness, compassion, and bodhichitta,
> Experiences and realization naturally grow,
> One acts on an infinite scale for others' good
> And accomplishes all their wishes in accordance with the Dharma.

And so on—all this is widely dealt with in numerous texts.

This completes a brief account of how to follow the spiritual friend, who is the root of the path.

## PART TWO

# The Main Explanation of the Stages for Setting Out on the Path

*Section One: The general preliminary practice for each session, which makes one a fit vessel*

*Section Two: The specific preliminary practice for the yogas of the two phases*

# The General Preliminary Practice for Each Session, Which Makes One a Fit Vessel

# The General Preliminary Practice for Each Session, Which Makes One a Fit Vessel

GENERALLY SPEAKING, WHICHEVER STAGE OF THE PRACTICE one is engaged in, it is most important to begin by making use of a pleasant, isolated place where nothing will happen to adversely affect one's concentration, such as people moving about or disturbances from noise. As the *Six Prerequisites for Concentration* points out,

> Like bangles on a young maid's wrist,*
> With many there are constant fights;
> With even two there will be rivalry:
> So I must remain alone.

There, not only should you give up all negative and neutral activities of body, speech, and mind, but also, until you achieve a little stability, you must even for the time being abandon positive actions if they adversely affect your concentration. Once you have stemmed the continuous flow of exhausting tasks, idle chatter, and thoughts and can rely on being free from these three faults (physical, verbal, and mental) related to concentration, make a firm resolve to devote yourself completely to the practice.[21] For this, it is important to have in mind the eight types of mental application that act as antidotes in eliminating the five faults, since they are indispensable accessories to putting the instructions into practice.

The five faults, as listed in *Distinguishing the Middle from Extremes,* are as follows:

---

* More than one bangle on her arm will jangle unpleasantly.

> Laziness, forgetting the essential instructions,
> Wildness or dullness,
> Nonapplication, and overapplication—
> These are said to be the five faults.*

In other words, these faults are:

- being lazy and uneager to practice;
- forgetting the words and their meaning with regard to what one is meditating on;
- being overpowered by wildness or dullness;
- not using the antidote when either of these two occur; and
- applying the antidote too strongly once one has overcome wildness and dullness.

The eight types of mental application that dispel these are described in the same text:

> Interest, effort,
> And their respective cause and result,
> Not forgetting the object of concentration,
> Considering whether one is distracted or dull,
> Actually applying the antidote that eliminates those,
> And, when they are pacified, letting things be.

There are four antidotes to laziness: wanting to meditate—interest; maintaining interest by diligence in exerting oneself; faith, which is the cause that gives rise to interest; and a perfectly trained and flexible, fit body, speech, and mind, which is the result of diligence. The antidote to forgetting the object of concentration is unforgetting mindfulness of the words and their meanings. Then there is vigilance, checking whether or not wildness and dullness are occurring; actual application of the antidote to eliminate these when they do occur; and nonapplication—leaving things be—as the remedy to applying the antidote too strongly, making eight in all.

Having got this clear, sit on a comfortable seat, soft and level. As the essential point for the body, sit in the seven-point posture of Vairochana†

---

*Wildness (Tib. *rgod*) and dullness (*bying*) are counted as a single fault. These two faults can also be translated respectively as distraction (or excitation or sensual incitement) and drowsiness.

† See glossary, *seven-point posture of Vairochana.*

or in any other comfortable posture with your back straight. As long as you are practicing the step-by-step instructions, apart from when you have to adopt any general or specific physical postures, never sit in an ordinary fashion, lying or leaning against anything. The reason for this is that the body is like a city, the channels are like the streets in it, the subtle energy in them is like a horse, and the consciousness is like a crippled rider. If movement is bound, the street junctions are blocked and it is impossible for the rider and horse trapped inside to move. And just as the scales a snake uses for locomotion[22] do not stand out unless one twists the snake, unless the body is forced into the posture, the mind will not stay still. If the right conditions are arranged in the body, realization will take birth in the mind. This is the first thing the teachers of the past have mentioned in the profound instructions.

Next, expel the stale air three times through the right nostril, the left nostril, and both together. Each time you so do, imagine all the negative actions, obscurations, illnesses, negative forces, and other adverse factors accumulated by all sentient beings in their beginningless series of lives all gathered together and being flushed out with the air through the nostrils, and that the whole inside of your body becomes pure as if thoroughly rinsed. This is like washing out a container before pouring some valuable substance into it.

After that, leave the mind in its natural state for a while, and when you have managed to lay a firm foundation for meditation that is not shaken by circumstances, first longingly arouse bodhichitta, thinking "I am going to practice this profound path for the benefit of all sentient beings filling space."

Now visualize in the space in front of you, on a level with the point between your eyebrows, in an expanse filled with brilliant rays and circles of rainbow light, a jeweled throne borne by lions, and on it a multicolored lotus, sun, and moon. Seated upon this is your gracious root teacher appearing in the form of the Lake-Born Diamond Bearer. He is clear blue in color, utterly beautiful on account of his having the major and minor marks of a Buddha, and adorned with silks and jewels. His two hands are crossed over, holding *vajra* and bell, and he is in union with his consort Tsogyal.* She is white tinged with red, and naked, and she holds a knife and skull, embracing him round the neck. He is seated with his legs crossed in the diamond posture. Visualize him as having an illusion-like

---

* Yeshe Tsogyal; see glossary.

wisdom body, apparent yet empty, considering you with great delight, as if he were actually present, and recite the visualization text:

---

In the sky in front of me, in an expanse of rainbow lights and
   circles,
Upon a jeweled lion throne, lotus, sun, and moon,
Is my incomparably kind root teacher
In the form of the Lake-Born Diamond Bearer of Oddiyana,
Clear blue, holding vajra and bell, in the attire of the body
   of perfect enjoyment,
United with his own radiance, the consort Great Bliss.
He is smiling happily, his body emanating rays of wisdom
   light.
He is the essential embodiment of all the infinite refuges.

---

Then generate intense, longing devotion, seeing your teacher as the Buddha in person, and with hands joined at your heart, pray one-pointedly:

---

To the teacher I pray,
To the teacher, all-pervading absolute body, I pray:
Bless me that the darkness of ignorance be dispelled.
To the teacher I pray,
To the teacher, body of perfect enjoyment, I pray:
Bless me that the radiant light may shine from within.
To the teacher I pray,
To the teacher, compassionate body of manifestation, I pray:
Bless me with realization as vast as space.
To the teacher I pray,
To the teacher, precious Buddha, I pray:
Bless me that the twofold goal may be accomplished
   spontaneously.

---

Imagine that as a result of your prayer, the teacher cannot help but be inspired and delighted; looking unable to resist any more, he moves to a point above the crown of your head. Immediately, teacher and consort melt into light, the essence of bliss, and enter you through the crown opening as a drop of ambrosial bodhichitta. It dissolves into the middle of your heart and your body, speech, and mind become inseparable from the teacher's three diamonds:

The strength of my devotion inspires and delights the teacher,
And with a show of unbearable happiness,
He comes above the crown of my head, and as a cloud of
  bodhichitta,
Confers the empowerment of the enthronement of wisdom:
In the great state of simultaneous realization and liberation
  I am blessed.

Recite this and imagine it, then rest in equanimity for a while in the state of awareness without fabricating or spoiling it.

This practice is an important preliminary for every session. It is necessary for reducing obstacles on the path and for making blessings enter swiftly.

# The Specific Preliminary Practice for the Yogas of the Two Phases[23]

*Subsection One: The common preliminaries that cultivate the field of one's mindstream with the four practices for turning the mind*

*Subsection Two: The uncommon, special preliminaries that sow the seeds of the profound path in five stages*

# The Common Preliminaries That Cultivate the Field of One's Mindstream with the Four Practices for Turning the Mind

*Chapter Five: Reflecting on the difficulty of finding the freedoms and advantages*

*Chapter Six: Reflecting on death and impermanence*

*Chapter Seven: Reflecting on the defects of cyclic existence*

*Chapter Eight: Reflecting on the unfailing law of actions: cause and effect*

# Reflecting on the Difficulty of Finding the Freedoms and Advantages

THIS CHAPTER HAS FOUR SECTIONS: IDENTIFYING THE freedoms and advantages, the reason they are so difficult to obtain, the importance of finding them, and reflecting on the need to make full use of them.

## I. IDENTIFYING THE FREEDOMS AND ADVANTAGES

The precious human body is the indispensable support for accomplishing enlightenment, and it has to have the following perfect features: the essence of the support, namely freedom, which is the opposite of the eight states of lack of opportunity; and its particular features, namely the five individual advantages, which are like ornaments, and the five circumstantial advantages which, as it were, illuminate and enhance those ornaments.

### THE EIGHT STATES OF LACK OF OPPORTUNITY

These are listed in the *Great Commentary on the Transcendent Wisdom in Eight Thousand Verses:*

> The hells, hungry spirits, animals,
> Barbarians, long-lived gods,
> Wrong views, the absence of a Buddha,
> And being dumb—these are the eight states that lack opportunity.

Those who are born in the three lower realms suffer too intensely and have too poor a physical support to have the opportunity to practice the

Dharma. The gods in the world of desire are distracted by their attachment to the pleasures of the senses and have little disillusionment, while the gods in the world of form and in the formless world are mostly perpetually high on concentration, so they too have no opportunity to practice the Dharma. There are also those who are born in worlds devoid of a Buddha, that is, in places to which no Buddha has come; those who, even though born in a world to which a Buddha has come, are barbarians in border regions where the Dharma has not spread; those who, even if born in a place to which the Dharma has spread, have wrong views and do not believe in past and future lives, in the fact that actions lead to results, or in the Three Jewels; and those who are born completely dumb* and are not intelligent enough to be able to undertake what is right and reject what is wrong.

These, then, are the eight states of lack of opportunity. Of them, the three lower realms and long-lived gods are nonhuman states, and the other four are human states in which there is no opportunity to practice the Dharma. To be free of these eight states of no opportunity constitutes freedom, as shown in the *Sutra of Precious Space:*

> The Bodhisattva Akashagarbha asked: "Bhagavan, how should one view the freedoms and advantages?"
>
> He answered: "When mind is buffeted by thoughts and thus distracted, this is 'having no leisure.' When the thoughts in the mind are stilled and it is at ease, this is 'freedom.'"

In the *Condensed Transcendent Wisdom* we read:

> By eliminating the eight states of no opportunity one will always find freedom.

## THE TEN ADVANTAGES

### *The Five Individual Advantages*

To be born a human, in a central land, with all one's faculties
   complete,
Without a conflicting lifestyle, and with faith in the Dharma,

---

* "Dumb" here refers both to mental dullness and the inability to speak.

in other words,

- in general, to have obtained a human body; and in particular:
- to have been born in a central land in which the Dharma is propagated;
- with all one's faculties—the five sense doors and so forth—complete, so that one is fit to understand what to adopt and what to avoid;
- without a conflicting lifestyle, in which one would commit, for example, crimes with immediate retribution;* and
- with faith in the Buddha, the source of everything that is virtuous, and in his excellent words, the sublime Dharma.

Since these five have come together in oneself and are favorable conditions for accomplishing the Dharma, they are referred to as individual advantages. To be free of the eight states of no opportunity and to have the five individual advantages is crucially important.

## The Five Circumstantial Advantages

A Buddha has come, he taught the Dharma,
His doctrine has endured, it has a following,
And they are kind-hearted and altruistic.

In other words,

- even though the coming of a Buddha in the world is even rarer than the flower of the *udumbara*, a Buddha has appeared in the world at this time;
- he taught the sacred Dharma, the way to liberation;
- his teachings have not disappeared but still endure;
- there are also individuals who follow and practice those teachings;
- they are able, moreover, to compassionately guide other beings.

Since these five are comprised in other streams of being and are favorable conditions for accomplishing the Dharma, they are referred to as circumstantial advantages. In the sutra we read:

"Advantage" is to know the nature of the mind, one's mind being thus endowed with the authentic truth.

---

* See "The Five Crimes with Immediate Retribution," page 123.

A human body like this, complete with the eighteen freedoms and advantages, is difficult to find: to obtain it is even more amazing than a blind pauper's finding the greatest of precious gems. For this reason, having obtained a precious human body after going round and round in the six realms of existence, you should be immensely joyful and make every effort to practice the sublime Dharma. A sutra that teaches the freedoms and advantages says:

> Just as it is for a blind man to find a precious gem at a crossroads, so it is for beings wandering in cyclic existence and blinded by the cataract of ignorance to find a human birth—a source of tremendous joy. Strive constantly, therefore, to accomplish the excellent Dharma.

And the Great Omniscient One says:

> Friends, to find the gemlike essence, the body with the freedoms
>     and advantages,
> From among the six classes of beings is extremely hard.
> Like a blind man finding a treasure of jewels,
> Rejoice and accomplish benefit and happiness.

## II. The way in which the freedoms and advantages are so difficult to obtain

There are three parts: the difficulty of finding the freedoms and advantages in terms of their cause, the difficulty of finding them in terms of a simile, and the difficulty of finding them in numerical terms.

## A. The difficulty of finding the freedoms and advantages in terms of their cause

Of all the sentient beings there are, in general few enough are humans, and this is particularly so in our world, the Land of the Jambu Tree.* More especially, those who have a human body and are spiritually inclined are so few as to be next to none. The reason for this is that those who commit negative actions, the cause of the lower realms, are very numerous,

---

*Tib. *dzam bu gling*, Skt. *Jambudvipa*. See glossary, *Jambudvipa*.

indeed infinite in number, while those who perform positive actions are extremely few. Rarer still are those who have observed sufficient discipline to act as the propelling cause for a faultless human body. This is why it is so difficult to find a human body, as the *Introduction to the Middle Way* affirms:

> And high rebirth derives from discipline alone.[24]

When one has the cause for higher rebirth, which is discipline and nothing else, and it is accompanied by an infinitely vast store of positive actions, and these are linked by pure prayers of aspiration, one will obtain the freedoms and advantages. But to accumulate so much merit is rare.[25] As Shantideva says,

> And yet the way I act is such
> That I shall not regain a human life!
> And losing this, my precious human form,
> My evils will be many, virtues none.
>
> Here is now my chance for wholesome deeds,
> But if I fail to practice virtue,
> What will be my lot, what shall I do,
> Bewildered by the sorrows of the lower realms?[26]

## B. The difficulty of finding the freedoms and advantages in terms of a simile

How difficult it is to find this human body with the freedoms and advantages is shown by the following simile, stated by the Protector Nagarjuna:

> Harder, harder still than that a turtle chance upon
> The opening in a yoke adrift upon the great wide sea
> Is rebirth as a human after rebirth as a beast;
> So heed the sacred Dharma, King, and make your life bear fruit.[27]

and in *The Way of the Bodhisattva:*

> This is why Lord Buddha has declared
> That like a turtle that perchance can place
> Its head within a yoke adrift upon the mighty sea,
> This human birth is difficult to find![28]

The scriptural source for these is the *Flower Chapter:*

> "It is difficult to find Bhagavan Buddhas appearing in the world. It
> is difficult too to find someone becoming human and accomplishing
> the perfect freedoms. Let me give you an example of this. Shariputra,
> say this great earth were to become a single ocean, and in it there
> was a yoke with a single opening, and also a blind turtle. On that
> huge ocean a wind called 'up-draughts and down-draughts' starts to
> blow. Now the blind turtle comes to the surface once in a hundred
> years, and one could say that the blind turtle rising to the surface
> once in a hundred years might put its neck through the single open-
> ing in the rapidly moving yoke. But to become a human being again
> after falling into the lower realms is not like that: for those who have
> fallen into the lower realms it is exceptionally difficult to become a
> human being."

So if it is hard to obtain just a human body, what is there to say about enjoying the freedoms and advantages and the sublime Dharma? As we read
in *The Way of the Bodhisattva,*

> The appearance of the Buddhas in the world,
> True faith and the attainment of the human form,
> An aptitude for good: all these are rare.
> When will they come to me again?[29]

And in the *Sutra Requested by Ratnacuda:*

> To see a Guide is very hard indeed,*
> To hear him speak the peaceful Dharma is also very hard,
> To be reborn a human, free and well endowed, is very difficult,
> To keep on finding discipline and faith is very hard as well.

## C. The difficulty of finding the freedoms and advantages in numerical terms

Among the different classes of beings, the beings in the three lower realms
are extremely numerous, indeed as infinite in number as the dust particles
on the earth. The beings in the higher realms are very few and are said
to be only as many as the dust particles on a fingernail. Of the beings

---

*Guide (Tib. *'dren pa*), i.e., a Buddha.

in the three lower realms, the least numerous are the animals, and yet there is an inconceivable number of animals that live in the depths, in the great oceans, while those that live scattered in different places fill everything—the ground, mountains, valleys, and the air. If you consider this, to be a god or a human is practically impossible. In the *Transmitted Distinctions Regarding the Vinaya* the Buddha taught:

> Monks, look at the beings in the lower realms: to subsequently attain the human state is extremely difficult.

Even if there are many who obtain a human body, rare are those who engage in the sublime Dharma. Even rarer are those who encounter the unmistaken path to liberation, because the majority are overpowered by karmic obscurations and beguiled by demons, and so there are many who enter mistaken and inferior paths. The *Sutra of the Arborescent Array* states:

> To encounter the perfect Dharma is extremely hard.

Moreover, even to have a meritorious thought for just an instant and think "I will do something virtuous" is difficult. Such a thought comes through the compassion of the Buddha, and it is as difficult for it to occur as for lightning to flash many times over a long period in the middle of a dark night. This is stated in *The Way of the Bodhisattva:*

> Just as on a dark night black with clouds,
> The sudden lightning glares and all is clearly shown,
> Likewise rarely, through the Buddhas' power,
> Virtuous thoughts rise, brief and transient, in the world.[30]

That you have at present found a human body like this, with an inclination to the Dharma, has happened through the force of previous merit. So now, when you have obtained the perfect physical support that is so hard to find, you should think, "In order to gain lasting happiness, I must do whatever I can to accomplish the sacred and perfect Dharma."

## III. REFLECTING ON THE IMPORTANCE OF FINDING THE FREEDOMS AND ADVANTAGES

There are three parts: reflecting on how they constitute the support for accomplishing benefit and happiness, reflecting on the superhuman qualities one will obtain, and reflecting on how much one stands to gain or lose.

## A. Reflecting on how the freedoms and advantages constitute the support for accomplishing benefit and happiness

If you are wondering what is the point in obtaining this human body that is so hard to find, the benefits of doing so are enormous. Not only is one easily able, temporarily, to accomplish all the happiness and perfections of the higher realms, but one can also accomplish the nirvana of the lower vehicles and unsurpassable enlightenment as well. Without obtaining a human body, there is no way one can achieve any kind of happiness in cyclic existence, let alone accomplish liberation. But by starting from the most insignificant positive actions and devoting one's efforts exclusively to the sublime Dharma, one obtains the manifold perfect qualities of higher rebirth and ultimate excellence. As it says in the *Jewel Garland,*

> If you constantly practice the Dharma,
> You will make the whole world
> And yourself happy,
> And this will be all to the good.
> With the Dharma you will always fall asleep happy
> And wake up happy.
> Inwardly you will be without fault, and so
> Even in your dreams you will see virtue.
> By wholeheartedly respecting your parents,
> Venerating the head of the lineage,
> Putting your wealth to good use, being patient, giving generously,
> Speaking gently, avoiding slander, and telling the truth—
> Observing these for one lifetime,
> You will reach the level of Indra
> And be Indra again and again.
> Bit by bit you will accomplish Buddhahood.

And in the *Sutra of the Arborescent Array* we read:

> Child of good family, whoever has the freedoms and advantages, on him will also fall the great and abundant rain of the Buddha's teaching, and he will acquire infinite other benefits.

## B. Reflecting on the superhuman qualities one will obtain

When the Buddha Shakyamuni attained the great enlightenment, the support he had was as the Lord of Mankind in our world of Jambudvipa, the excellent support of a body with the freedoms and advantages, and it was therefore called "better than the gods." The *Sutra of Manifest Enlightenment* explains:

> He did not attain enlightenment in the realms of the gods because gods are proud of their abode and therefore do not clearly realize the truth. Having seen that only the human state has the perfect qualities of the freedoms and advantages, he departed for Kapilavastu.*

It has been taught that the ultimate goal of the Secret Mantra Vehicle[31] too is swiftly accomplished through a human support, as we find in a tantra:

> Humans who are diligent
> In this marvelous kinglike Secret Mantra Vehicle
> Will attain its accomplishment in this very life,
> Not to mention the other powers achieved through the practice.

## C. Reflecting on how much one stands to gain or lose

By relying on the boat of the freedoms and advantages, now that one has it, one will cross the ocean of suffering that is cyclic existence. If one is extremely clever and expert in the means for extracting its essence—this jewel desired for the long term[32]—this hard-won gain will be of immense benefit, far more than when a pauper finds a wish-fulfilling jewel. If one fails to make proper use of it,[33] one's loss will be much more disastrous than if one were to return from an island of jewels empty-handed. As Chandragomin says:

> Having obtained it, one reaches the end of the ocean of birth.
> Since it helps plant the seed of supreme enlightenment, virtue,
> It is far superior in qualities to a wish-fulfilling gem.
> Who, having won the human state, would let it not bear fruit?

And in *The Way of the Bodhisattva* we find:

> Take advantage of this human boat.
> Free yourself from sorrow's mighty stream!
> This vessel will be later hard to find.
> The time that you have now, you fool, is not for sleep![34]

---

*Kapilavastu was the capital city of the Shakya kingdom in which the future Buddha's parents had their palace.

So reflect on this, thinking, "What a joy it is that I have now obtained a precious human body, that I am following a sublime teacher and practicing the profound instructions. I must do my best to make full use of it."

## IV. Reflecting on the need to make full use of the freedoms and advantages

There are three parts: reflecting on the need to be diligent in the Dharma by all means, reflecting on the need to guard the mind, which is the root of the Dharma, and reflecting on the good qualities of the precious human body.

## A. Reflecting on the need to be diligent in the Dharma by all means

Now that all the ideal conditions coincide—you have found the freedoms and advantages that are so difficult to find and so important once found, you are not afflicted by problems of health and the like, you are not subject to others' authority, and you have your own independence—it is important to be diligent in the methods for making full use of the freedoms and advantages. Not to make the effort would be even more foolish than a navigator going all the way to an island of precious jewels and then returning empty-handed, as the *White Lotus Sutra of Compassion* points out:

> To win perfect freedom, rid of the eight states of no opportunity, is nigh impossible. Take heed, therefore, and be diligent in practicing well, lest you regret it later.

And in *The Way of the Bodhisattva* we read:

> Thus, having found this moment of reprieve,
> If I now fail to train myself in virtue,
> What greater folly could there ever be?
> How more could I betray myself?[35]

## B. Reflecting on the need to guard the mind, which is the root of the Dharma

The whole of the Dharma depends on the mind, and the mind is dependent on the precious human body. This is an interdependent relationship of support and what is supported: the mind is the root of Dharma, and the freedoms and advantages are the support or accessory for this. For this reason one need train only in taming the mind, as Nagarjuna advises:

> The vital point is tame your mind, for mind's
> The root of Dharma, so the Buddha said.[36]

And the Great Omniscient One says:

> The Dharma depends on the mind,
> And that depends on the freedoms and advantages,
>     interdependently.
> Now that the many causes and conditions have come together,
> Tame your mind—that's the main point of Dharma.

The sufferings of fear and poverty that occur throughout this life and will occur in subsequent lives are the negative consequences of using your precious human body to indulge in pointless distractions, while all the happiness and good qualities of higher rebirth and ultimate excellence come solely from not wasting the freedoms and advantages. As we read in the *Sutra of the Arborescent Array*:

> Child of noble family, it has never occurred to those who wander in cyclic existence that their body ornamented with the freedoms and advantages is so difficult to find; because of their evil friends,* they continue to circle in cyclic existence and are tormented by the fire of suffering. But I, by reflecting on this supreme freedom,† have been completely liberated from existence. You too should do likewise.

## C. Reflecting on the good qualities of the precious human body

By listening, reflecting, and following the practice—these constituting the excellent door of the sublime Dharma—one tames one's mindstream, encourages others to do positive actions, and dons the great armor of liberation. To do so is what we call the "great victory banner of the Sage."[37] The victory banner of the Sage does not refer simply to one's style of dress

---

*Tib. *mi dge ba'i bshes gnyen*, the opposite of *dge ba'i bshes gnyen*, or spiritual friends.
† I.e., a precious human body.

but rather to one's diligence, irrespective of whether one assumes the appearance of a layperson or takes monastic ordination. Such diligence is what determines a "precious human body." In the *Sutra Requested by Shri Gupta* we read:

> Shri Gupta, when one studies by listening to many teachings, reflects on their meaning, practices by meditating without afflictive emotions, and moreover encourages others to do so, one is the fairest thing in the world, including the celestial realms. That is what we call making full use of the freedoms and advantages. That is what we call the precious human body.

The benefits of thus training your mind—reflecting deeply on how difficult it is to find these freedoms and advantages—are infinite, but they may be summarized as follows: You will cease to engage in the activities of this life, realizing that they are all pointless. Since your thoughts will be on future lives, whatever you do, you will act without contravening the law of actions and their results. With diligence blazing like fire, you will persevere in regularly listening, reflecting, and meditating. By abandoning unsuitable companions given to negative actions and always performing positive actions, you will follow virtue. Having cast aside any desire for the pleasures of cyclic existence, you will not waste your freedom,* and so when you die, you will depart with a joyful mind. As a result of having freed yourself of the demon of avarice and of having accumulated generosity (the provisions for the journey), wherever you are reborn, you will never be poor. Being without attachment to wealth, you will be content, and your body, speech, and mind will therefore be in constant accord with the Dharma. You will realize that nothing has any essence, and you will thus cut through the entanglements of attachment. By recognizing that everything is impermanent, you will not be distressed by conflicts and you will be naturally, sincerely virtuous. As a result of your seeing that nothing is really necessary, the wall of the eight ordinary concerns will collapse. By practicing the Dharma correctly, you will be drawn along the path to liberation and will swiftly accomplish Buddhahood.

So reflect thoroughly on the virtues of the precious human body, which is so hard to find and which, when found, is so beneficial. Understand that all appearances and perceptions limited to this life are short-lived and

---

*Tib. *dal,* i.e., the freedom one has to practice the Dharma.

without essence, like good and bad dreams in a single period of sleep, and forsake them. Then, in order to accomplish your long-term wishes—that is, what is important for future lives—you must now speedily put your efforts into making full use of the freedoms and advantages. If you fail to make the effort, even though you appear to have a human form, you will in fact be no different from an animal, with what is called a "mere human body"—a corpse even if you are not dead, insane even though not possessed by spirits, lifeless even though still breathing. Here is the advice the Great Master gave Gyalse Lhaje in the *Golden Garland of Pledges:*[38]

> Births in the higher realms are generally very scarce,
> But in comparison a precious human birth is much more rare.
> Even if you have gained a human body, it is nigh impossible to
>     obtain the Dharma.
> Son of my Speech, do not forsake the freedoms and advantages
>     and return empty-handed.

And,

> Difficult to find repeatedly, like the *udumbara*,
> So beneficial when found, like the wishing gem:
> Now that for once all the perfect conditions are ready,
> Use all your efforts to go beyond existence.

When you have a boat, you should cross the river. When you have an army of brave men, you should put down the enemy. When you have water, manure, warm weather, and moisture all together, you should sow as much seed as you can. So reflect: "Every time I have obtained the suitable support for accomplishing the extraordinary goal, it has so far been wasted. Now, rather than let the freedoms and advantages go to waste, I would rather die than not do everything I can to practice the sublime Dharma genuinely in order to nurture and prepare for my survival in future lives." Thinking, "That I might be able to do so, precious teacher, in you I put my trust!" arouse intense devotion and determination to be free, and pray one-pointedly as follows:

> NAMO. Glorious embodiment of all the Buddhas and Bodhi-
>     sattvas of the three times,
> Endowed with knowledge, love, and power,
> Sole abiding refuge, kind teacher and lord,

Dwell inseparably in the wheel of great bliss on the crown of
  my head.
As I pray to you, precious teacher,
Bless me, incomparably kind lord.

These freedoms and advantages are so difficult to find:
May I make full use of this significant human body.
As I pray to you, precious teacher,
Bless me, incomparably kind lord.

# CHAPTER SIX

# Reflecting on Death and Impermanence

THIS CHAPTER HAS THREE SECTIONS: REFLECTING ON THE inevitability of death, reflecting on the uncertainty of when one will die, and reflecting on the fact that when one dies nothing can help one.

## I. REFLECTING ON THE INEVITABILITY OF DEATH

There are three parts: reflecting on the inevitability of death by considering the universe and beings in general, reflecting on the inevitability of death by considering the diamond body and so forth, and reflecting on the inevitability of death by considering different examples.

## A. Reflecting on the inevitability of death by considering the universe and beings in general

If this support, with its freedoms and advantages, so extremely difficult to find, were something that, once obtained, never died, that would be fine. But it is not eternal—far from it—and you are certain to die. Everyone thinks, "I will die eventually," but up until the moment of death they go on hoping they will not die for a while. Obscured by this sort of wrong thinking, they pass the time being distracted by the things of this life. They put off accomplishing anything for the next life until later and are overpowered by laziness. This is why we have to meditate on impermanence. As the *Discourse on Impermanence* says,

> In front of everyone who is born,
> Waiting there, is death,
> And even I am not exempt.
> Practice Dharma, therefore, from this very day.

Generally speaking, the things we perceive as the world, the whole array of the universe with the beings it contains, are phenomena created simply through causes and conditions coming together, and for this reason there will eventually come a time when they perish and disappear, becoming one with space,[39] as we find in the *Sutra of the King of Concentrations:*

> One day this world appears,
> And once appeared, this world then disappears.
> As in the past, so it will be in the future.
> Know that thus it is with all phenomena.

And *Letter to a Friend* states:

> The ground, Mount Meru, and the oceans too
> Will be consumed by seven blazing suns;
> Of things with form not even ashes will be left,
> No need to speak of puny, frail man.[40]

As for the beings grouped together in the three worlds and the six realms,* on account of their individual past deeds, they may be large or small, happy or miserable, given to positive actions or negative ones, fortunate or unlucky, of high or low status—in short, they may have all kinds of good or bad experiences. Yet whether they have long lives lasting kalpas, short lives that are over in barely a moment, or lives of medium length that can be counted in years, months, and days, they all, every one of them, end up dying. No being is exempt from death. As Ashvagosha says,

> Of all those born upon this earth
> Or in the upper realms,
> Did you ever see, or hear, or even pause to doubt
> That some were born and have not died?

The whole of the three worlds of existence is impermanent, moving and dissolving like clouds in autumn that mass together one moment and disperse the next. Beings are born and die under the fickle control of their good and bad deeds, manifesting in all kinds of ways like the choreographic movements of a skilled dancer. People's lives race by, swift and brief, like a flash of lightning in the sky that vanishes in an instant, or like a stream cascading down a mountainside. Just as there is no turning back a river, which flows until it reaches its lowest point, nothing can stop the

---

* See glossary, *three worlds* and *six realms of existence.*

span of one's life running out: one is certain to die. As we read in the *Sutra of Extensive Play,*

> The three worlds are impermanent, like autumn clouds,
> Beings are born and die as if in a ballet,
> A person's life is like a flash of lightning in the sky,
> Like a mountain torrent, it rushes swiftly on.

## B. Reflecting on the inevitability of death by considering the diamond body and so forth

Look at the Buddhas who have come to this World of Forbearance—Vipashyi, Shikhin, Vishvabhu, Krakucchanda, Kanakamuni, Kashyapa, and Shakyamuni—who blazed with the light and majesty of the major and minor marks, like the full moon in autumn. They came with retinues of Listeners, Bodhisattvas, Brahmas, and other worldly protectors, as if surrounded by galaxies of stars. These radiant beings, their bodies shining with light, their voices clear and soft, their minds limpid and free of stain, were as firm and stable as diamonds, yet they all passed into nirvana, and even their teachings (apart from those of the Lord of the Shakyas) have gradually disappeared. Reflect on this and ask yourself: "Why should my body, which is as devoid of essence as a bubble, last forever?" In *Sayings on Impermanence* we find:

> If even the body of the Sugata, blazing with a thousand marks,
> Accomplished from hundreds of meritorious acts, is
>     impermanent,
> How will one's body, as undependable
> As a bubble that bursts, not certainly perish?
> Look at how the sun will set—the Buddha who came for
>     beings' sake;
> And the moon as well—the treasury of the sublime Dharma.
> And know that in all one's prosperity, one's retinue and wealth,
> There is nothing that is eternal.

The protectors of the world—Brahma, Ishvara, Vishnu, Indra, the Four Great Kings, and others—fill the world with great beams of light and are brighter than a thousand suns. Their majesty and merit are renowned through all the heavens and the earth. They are the lords of all worlds—subterranean, earthly, and heavenly—adorned with the greatest fortune. And yet for them too the time will come to die, as is written in the Vinaya scriptures:

> O monks, look at all these riches that fade and are essenceless. As I remember my past lives in cyclic existence, even though I was Brahma, Indra, the Four Great Kings, and other lords of beings an inconceivable number of times, I was never satiated, and I transmigrated and fell to the lower realms.

Furthermore, the gods, demigods, accomplished ascetics, and mantra holders* are also all bound to die, as the Vinaya scriptures affirm:

> Gods who have accomplished concentration, spirits who can take
>     human form,[41]
> Demigods, sages, and ascetics, refulgent with splendor
> And living for kalpas on end—if even they are impermanent,
> Need one mention human beings,
> Whose frail bodies will perish and disintegrate like bursting
>     bubbles?

Universal emperors with dominion over the four continents, kings, ministers, monks and nuns, brahmins, householders, and the rest—not a single being is exempt from death, as we read in the *Intentionally Spoken Chapters:*

> Emperors who possess the seven jewels,
> Kings and ministers,
> Monastics, brahmins, householders, and the rest—
> All these beings are impermanent:
> They are like beings in a dream.

## C. Reflecting on the inevitability of death by investigating different examples

In this world of ours, there has been change as the past age of complete endowment has progressed through the age of half-endowment and that of third-endowment to the present age of conflict, making four ages in all.[42] Within a human life span there is also change, through its four stages: the period of infancy, the period of childhood, the period of youth, and

---

* "Mantra holders" (Tib. *rigs sngags 'chang ba*) refers to beings who have attained common accomplishments and magical powers through the power of mantra (not necessarily Buddhist), and not only to practitioners of the Secret Mantra Vehicle.

the period of old age and infirmity. A single year too changes over its four seasons: spring, the season of plowing and sowing seed; summer, the season of new leaf growth and increased moisture; autumn, when the fruit is perfectly ripe; and winter, when the soil is dry and the stones are frozen. It is all impermanent. Impermanent too are all the beings—enemies, friends, and those that are neither—that we now see gathered in one place: a crowd of people assembled in a marketplace, for example, or at a crossroads, or in a guesthouse, which may seem permanent for a while, but quickly disperses.

It is not only others that are concerned. Think of when *you* were young—when your parents, family, livestock, guard dogs, and possessions were all gathered together in your house. It seemed then that they would be there forever, and because of your clinging you got involved in disputes and in trying to prevent this or achieve that.* Yet where are they now? Things are no longer the same: some have died, some have gone away, some have come together, others have separated. So wherever you stay, whoever you accompany, whatever work you do, there is only one thing to keep in mind: separation. Do not fight with or harm anyone, and do your best to tame your mind. The *Intentionally Spoken Chapters* says:

> Since everything that is gathered separates,
> Nothing is worth relying on.
> Therefore do not cling or be attached
> To people or to yourself.

Furthermore, think of old villages that have fallen into ruin in your early life, or in the meanwhile, or even before. They were once prosperous, happy, delightful places to be, yet they have ended up in ruins. Say to yourself: "Even my own house, valuables, and possessions are not exempt from such a fate; I will therefore abandon them. They are going to abandon me, so I will give them away while I am still free to do so, for the benefit of the Dharma. In giving them for the Dharma, I am sure to accomplish liberation." This is how to make the best use of your fluctuating possessions, which are devoid of essence.[43] As *The Way of the Bodhisattava* says,

> To think of giving all away
> Is the best way beyond all misery.[44]

---

* I.e., to prevent anything that threatened your family's well-being and achieve anything that furthered it.

In future you will be powerless to enjoy your wealth and possessions, so if, now that you are free to do so, you yourself give them away to create merit, you will benefit greatly. Even if you complete things according to the usual custom, leaving your possessions to others in your will when you die, there will be a little benefit. But other people's disagreements, as you lie there on your deathbed, over how your possessions are to be shared out will become a source of negative consequences for you. For this reason, those who have given up worldly life[45] and aspire to the Dharma should begin their practice by learning to have few desires. The masters of the past, who were both learned and accomplished, have said:

> With few desires, one joins the family of sublime beings.
> With no desires at all, one actually is a sublime being.
> Always train, therefore, in having few desires.

Reflect on how, even in this life, happiness in the earlier part of one's life changes to suffering in the latter part. Recognize that it is in the nature of things that fortunes decline, youth does not last forever, friends and relations separate, and that there is nothing one can rely on. In doing so, you should develop a feeling of total disenchantment related to the impermanent nature of things. As we read in the *Sutra of Extensive Play,*

> Men should know that the pleasures of the senses
> Are like the reflection of the moon in water,
> Like images in a mirror, echoes off a cliff, and optical illusions,
> Like the spectacle of a dance, and like dreams.

And the *Nirvana Sutra* says:

> Where things flourish, they will decline,
> Where there is gathering, there will be parting.
> Even youth is not eternal:
> Lovely complexions are robbed by disease.
> There is nothing at all that lasts forever.

## II. Reflecting on the uncertainty of when one will die

There are three parts: since one's life span is uncertain, there is no certainty when one will die; since the causes of death are many and the causes

for living are few, there is no certainty when one will die; and since this
body too is so frail, there is no certainty when one will die.

## A. Since one's life span is uncertain, there is no certainty when one will die

You might think: "Of course I will die in the end, but I won't die for a
while yet. What's all the hurry?" But the length of time beings live, apart
from those in Uttarakuru,* is generally quite uncertain, and this is especially true in our world, where beings' life spans are extremely unpredictable. In the beginning,† their lives could last an infinite number of years;
in the end it will be no longer than ten years. At present, whether one is
young, old, or middle-aged, one cannot be sure when one will die. As the
*Treasury of Abhidharma* puts it,

> Here it is unpredictable: at the end
> Ten years, in the beginning immeasurable.

And the *Intentionally Spoken Chapters* has this to say:

> From that very night
> When a person first enters the womb,
> His life is running out, it cannot be topped up;
> And there is no going back on what is past.
> In the morning, one sees many people;
> In the evening, some are no longer to be seen.
> In the evening, one sees many people;
> In the morning, some are no longer to be seen.
> Many men and women are there
> Who will die even in the prime of life,
> And one will say "They were so young!"
> But what guarantee is that for staying alive?
> Some will die inside the womb,
> Others while they are being born,
> Some just when they have begun to crawl,
> Some when they can get up and run,

---

*Uttarakuru, the northern continent in the Buddhist universe, where beings have definite
life spans.
† I.e., at the beginning of the present kalpa.

> Some when old, and some when young,
> Some are people in the prime of youth;
> One by one they will depart
> Like ripe fruit dropping from a tree.

As a result of the good deeds you performed in the past, you might live until you are sixty or seventy. But even so, it is impossible to calculate, starting from today and based on how many years have passed, how many more years you have to come. You might not even reach more than thirty or forty. These days, life expectancy has fallen under thirty years and is closer to twenty, so even if we have the time for our life to run its full course, it cannot last longer than that. At the end of a day we have breathed in and out 21,000 times. Thirty days make a month, twelve months make a year, and twelve years are termed a cycle;* and when, at the end of three cycles, it is time for us to die, it will seem as if no more than an hour has passed since we were born. Wherever we are, we see or hear of people dying suddenly. If we think about it, we are no different from them. We do not know which will come first, tomorrow or our next life, so it is important to completely cut the ties of involvement in the activities of this life. As we read in *The Way of the Bodhisattva,*

> "Today, at least, I shall not die."
> So rash to lull myself with words like these![46]

And the Great Omniscient One says:

> This life is impermanent like an earthenware vase.
> One cannot be sure which will come first:
> Tomorrow or the perceptions of the next world.
> So from today onward, practice the sublime Dharma!

### B. Since the causes of death are many and the causes for living are few, there is no certainty when one will die

What with all the external causes that can injure us (human beings, animals, negative forces, and the like) and dangers from the elements (fire, water, precipices, and so forth), along with the internal causes that affect the body (the 404 kinds of illness, for example), there is nothing we can rule out as a cause of death. Even if we rely on such things as food, clothes,

---

*A twelve-year cycle according to the Tibetan calendar system.

and medicine in the hope that they will keep us alive, we can never be sure that they will not serve to cause our death. Meditate, therefore, and tell yourself, "The evil factors causing death are swirling round me as if I were in the middle of a snowstorm. There's no knowing when I'll die." For as Nagarjuna points out,

> Many are the things that can cause death,
> While few are those that help one stay alive—
> And even they may serve to cause one's death.
> Therefore, practice Dharma constantly.[47]

And Padampa Sangye says:

> While you're busy being distracted, the demon of death will
>     catch you;
> People of Tingri, practice from this very moment onward.[48]

## C. Since this body too is so frail, there is no certainty when one will die

The force that keeps us alive is as impermanent as a bubble in a stream. It is as delicate as a dewdrop on the tip of a blade of grass. Life is like a candle in the wind: there are so many causes for dying and so few for staying alive. Our lives are as brief as a flash of lightning in the clouds. As we find in the *Jewel Garland,*

> We live amid the lords that cause our death,
> Like a lamp set in the middle of a dust storm.[49]

And in *Letter to a Friend:*

> With all its many risks, this life endures
> No more than windblown bubbles in a stream.
> How marvelous to breathe in and out again,
> To fall asleep and then awake refreshed.[50]

This quotation gives the measure of just how numerous the causes of death are and how extremely fragile we are: it is something of a miracle that one can wake up without dying in one's sleep, and that one does not die in the interval between breathing out and breathing in again. It is just as if one were carrying a guttering lamp on a site blasted by gales: there is no knowing, from one minute to the next, when it will go out. There is no time to take things easy and to think "I'll practice the Dharma later." So rather than putting it off until next year, practice this year. Rather than putting it off until next month, practice this month. Rather than putting it off until tomorrow or the next day, practice today. Life is like water poured into one's cupped hands and trickling out between one's fingers: without one's knowing, it has all run out. As the master Saraha says:

> Those who think "As today, likewise tomorrow,"
> Who are attached to wealth and prosperity,
> Are like a pair of cupped hands full of water,
> Leaking imperceptibly, O good people.

And in *The Way of the Bodhisattva* we read:

> Never halting, night or day,
> My life drains constantly away,
> And from no other source does increase come.
> How can there not be death for such as me?[51]

In the beginning when we were young, being immature, we did not practice the Dharma. At the end when we are old, though people might say it is a good time to practice the Dharma, we will be physically and mentally depleted and unable to make any progress. And in the half of our lives in between, we are overtaken by sleep. Moreover, we are overwhelmed by all sorts of pointless distractions, whether we are sitting or moving around, and we therefore have scarcely any opportunity to practice the Dharma. So develop the certainty that all the tantalizing enjoyments of this life are devoid of essence, like the happiness experienced in a single dream, and put all your efforts into accomplishing the sublime Dharma.

### III. REFLECTING ON THE FACT THAT WHEN ONE DIES NOTHING CAN HELP ONE

There are three parts: reflecting that one's body cannot help one; reflecting that one's possessions cannot help one; and reflecting that one's relatives and friends cannot help one.

### A. Reflecting that one's body cannot help one

When the time actually comes for you to die, even if you are young and good-looking, and have a perfect physique, it will not help you. Even if your body is huge, many leagues high, it will not be of any use. Even if you are so strong that you can lift Mount Meru onto your lap, it will not help you. Similarly, although you may be infinitely knowledgeable and skilled, physically and verbally, in magic, the arts, sciences, and crafts, none of these will help you at the time of death. And in any case, you will have to depart leaving behind this body that you were born with. As *The Way of the Bodhisattva* says,

> This flesh and bone that life has knit together,
> Will drift apart, disintegrate,
> And how much more will friend depart from friend?[52]

At present, we constantly cling to what we call our body as "me" and "mine," offering it food and clothes, and serving and pampering it. We are put out by the smallest unpleasant thing others may say about it, so that we answer back and try to protect it from being hurt. But as we find in the same text,

> My body is like something briefly lent.[53]

When the Lord of Death overpowers us and our body and mind separate, this body will be either buried under rubble or under the earth, to perish and be eaten by grubs, worms, and the like. Or consigned to the water, to be carried away by a river and eaten by fishes and so forth. Or left in a charnel ground to be devoured by vultures and carnivorous beasts. Or abandoned, to be eaten by dogs, or to decompose and rot, food for swarms of flies and grubs. Or consumed in a fire, our bones reduced to powder. There is no other alternative. What is the use, therefore, of having accumulated all sorts of negative actions for the sake of this body when it will not help us at the moment of death? The fact is that all our deeds and afflictive emotions related to attachment, aversion, and so on have been accumulated in dependence, above all, on this body. Thus, killing and hating—that is, considering people as enemies—happen principally in relation to this very body. For example, when someone says something unpleasant to us and we get angry, it is only because of this body, at which that person utters those words, that we get angry. If it were not for the body, the thought "This is my enemy" could never occur. If the sound of the wind or an echo were to swear at us, we would not get angry.

This body has made you suffer in the past, and in the future, too, it will make you accumulate deeds that will result in your being born and dying again and again in cyclic existence and the lower realms. So reflect on this repeatedly, telling yourself: "This body cannot help me in any way."

The *Sutra of Advice to the King* explains this at length:

> Great King, let us take an example. Imagine that from the four directions, four great mountains—solid to the core, indestructible, unfissured, extremely hard, and quite undamaged—their huge masses touching the sky, were to fall back onto the earth. All the plants and trees—trunks and boughs and branches, leaves and all— along with all the animals and other living creatures, would be completely pulverized. It would not be an easy matter of using speed to run away, or strength to push them back, or wealth to pay a ransom, or special substances, mantras, and medicines to avert them.
>
> Great King, in the same way, there are four great dangers that will occur. What are these four? They are old age, sickness, death, and decline. Great King, old age will destroy your youth. Sickness will destroy your good health. Decline will destroy your prosperity. Death will destroy your life. It will not be an easy matter of using speed to run away from them, or strength to push them back, or wealth to pay a ransom, or special substances, mantras, and medicines to remove them.
>
> Great King, let us take an example. Imagine the king of animals, the lion, going into the midst of a herd of antelope and seizing one. It can dominate the animals as it pleases. In its terrible and powerful jaws, that antelope will be rendered helpless.
>
> Great King, in the same way, when the Lord of Death impales you on his torch, your pride will desert you, you will have no protector, no refuge, no relatives to defend you, no friends. Your joints will become lax, your flesh and blood will dry up, your body will be stricken by illness, you will be parched with thirst, your countenance will change, your arms and legs will flail about. Unable to accomplish any task, your strength will fail you. Your body will be stained with spittle, snot, urine, and vomit. Your sense organs—eyes, ears, nose, tongue, body,\* and mind—will cease to function. You will hiccough and emit rasping sounds. The doctors will give you up, and all your medicines, snacks, food, and drink will seem to abandon you. You will be about to depart elsewhere and will lie on your bed

---

\* The body is the organ of touch and physical sensations.

for the last time. You will sink into the continuous cycle of birth, aging, and death that has no beginning. With still a little vitality left, and full of terror at the Lord of Death, you will be overpowered by your misfortune. The movements of your breath will cease, your mouth will gape, your nostrils flare, and your teeth will be clenched. You will wish you could practice some charity.* As a result of your deeds, you will go from one existence to the next. Utterly alone, you will have no one to accompany you as you leave this world behind and go to the world beyond. You will make the "great change of abode."† You will enter a great darkness, fall into a great abyss, pass into an environment that is eerie and oppressive, travel through a great wilderness, be carried away in a great ocean, blown by the wind of your past deeds, proceeding onward with no place to halt or rest. You will go onto a great battlefield, be seized by terrible negative forces, and banished into space. Your father and mother, brothers and sisters, and sons and daughters will gather round you and, as you breathe your last, they'll say, "Let's divide up his fortune." Their hair in disarray, they will weep: "Alas, my father!" "Alas, my mother!" "Alas, my child!" Your only friends will be your deeds of generosity, ascetic practice, and the Dharma. And apart from the Dharma, you will have no other refuge, no other protector, no other friends to support you.

Great King, at that time the Dharma will be an island, a shelter, a protector, and a guide. Great King, at such a time, as you lie on your bed, you will have a taste of the experiences of the next life. If you are going to go to the lower realms, you will start to be frightened by your surroundings. At that time nothing but the Dharma will provide any refuge.

Great King, you protect your body so carefully, but however well you cherish it, you will die. Even if it has every kind of good attribute and you nurture it by satisfying it for years with plenty of good food and drink, when you are on your deathbed, given up by the doctors and abandoned by everything, you will die in mental anguish.

Great King, though you wash your body like this, anoint and perfume it, and drape it with sweet-smelling flowers, have no doubt,

---

* Realizing that you will not be able to take your possessions with you, you will wish that you could use them charitably in order to gain some merit.
† Tib. *skyas 'degs,* lit. "to move house," a figurative term for dying.

it will smell bad. Great King, you may clothe it with fine garments of silk and Benares muslin, but on your deathbed you will die wearing soiled clothes, and depart alone and naked. Great King, you might take delight in various forms of sensual enjoyment, but they will all be forsaken, and you will die deriving no satisfaction from sensual pleasure.

Great King, your home may be filled with incense, flowers, silken hangings, rugs and cloths of all kinds, and cushioned couches to right and left on which to recline, but do not doubt that you will be abandoned in a great charnel ground full of crows, foxes, and nauseating human corpses, your lifeless body left lying on the ground.

Great King, you may be mounted on the backs of elephants and horses, and take delight in the sweet sounds of different musical instruments. With victory banners and parasols raised, you proceed, watched and glorified by kings, ministers, and friends. But before very long, you will die in your bed and be borne by four people, your father, mother, brothers, and so on holding their hands aloft and beating their breasts, overwhelmed by grief. Taken out through the southern gate of the city you will be buried in a wasteland, or devoured by crows, vultures, foxes, and the like, and your bones burned in a fire, or thrown into a river, or buried underground, whichever is the case. Reduced to dust by the wind, sun, and rain, you will decompose, scattered in every direction.

Great King, thus are all compounded phenomena impermanent, thus are they inconstant.

Reflect deeply on this again and again, and having recognized that none of the activities of this life can help you, make an effort day and night to practice the sublime Dharma.

## B. Reflecting that one's possessions cannot help one

At the time of death, our dwelling place is of no use to us. Even if it is a measureless palace in the god realms, we will have to leave it behind and depart. We might hide somewhere impregnable, but there is nowhere that can help us, as we read in the Vinaya scriptures:

> Wherever one is, there is nowhere
> That is not struck by death:

Neither in the air, nor yet in the ocean,
Neither in the gods' abodes, nor even in a hidden valley.

The wealth we have accumulated will not help. The gods' precious attributes and possessions, the universal monarch's dominion, and the treasuries of the rich will all have to be left behind, as the Vinaya scriptures explain:

When a tree falls down,
What use are the twigs and leaves?
Likewise, when a person dies,
What use are possessions?

Food, clothes, and the other things we enjoy will not help. The gods' sweet nectar, their finest clothes of five-colored silk, the most delicious human foods "with a hundred tastes," the finest satin and cotton—in short, the whole variety of beautiful forms, pleasant sounds, sweet scents, delicious tastes, and stuff that is soft to touch—none of these will help us when we die. As we find in the *Sutra of Extensive Play,*

Constantly these beings are caught and snared
By lovely forms and beautiful sounds, sweet smells,
The most delicious tastes, delightful sensations, and death.
Like a monkey caught in a hunter's net,
To those who delight in the senses much harm will come,
With fear, with constant enmity and afflictive emotions,
Like a sword's sharp edge and the leaves of a poisonous plant.

And in *The Way of the Bodhisattva* we read:

Though we be rich in worldly goods,
Delighting in our wealth for many years,
Despoiled and stripped as though by thieves,
We must go naked and with empty hands.[54]

## C. Reflecting that one's relatives and friends cannot help one

At death, the relatives and friends with whom we are connected will be of no help to us. We may have won the friendship of the universal monarch, be surrounded by five hundred young goddess consorts, have a thousand godling children playing. Our nephew and uncle might be the lords of the gods, our clan might consist of demigod soldiers, our subjects may be the four continents and the celestial realms, and our riches might include the seven precious attributes.* Our paternal uncles may be Brahma and Indra, our friends the gods of the realm of the Four Great Kings, and we might have a thousand celestial servants to serve us. But none of them can keep us alive, provide help, prolong our life, escort, or accompany us. We will have to depart alone, like a hair plucked out of butter,† and proceed along the narrow defile of the intermediate state with no one to accompany us. As we find in the *Sutra Requested by Putri Ratna,*

> When the hour of death arrives
> Neither your parents, nor your relatives,
> Nor your children will protect you,
> Neither your youth nor your strength.

And in the *Sutra of Extensive Play:*

> At death, the move from here to somewhere else,
> Destitute, one parts from those one loves.
> Once dead, there's no return, nor meeting them again,
> Like falling leaves, like a river flowing on.

Physical courage and agility are of no use: at the time of death we have to depart with nothing to help us. The most able suggestions cannot help: there is no chance of talking or arguing one's way out. Courage and skill will not help: there is no way one can fight one's way out. An athlete's speed will not help: there is no chance to escape. A beautiful face will not help: there is no seducing death. Intense activity will not help: this is not the moment for starting anything. Craft and cunning will not help: there is nowhere one can slip away to. One has to go alone. As we read in the Vinaya scriptures,

> Here, even mighty long-lived gods
> Living in their lofty abodes,
> Their lives exhausted, will grow weak,
> So who today can escape from death?
> Even heroes and champions cannot protect one.

---

*The seven precious attributes of royalty, beginning with the precious wheel, are described on pages 224–25.
†None of the butter sticks to the hair.

Kings, renunciates, and ascetics,
Activities, diligence, determination,
Vast retinues, and intelligence
Have no power to free one from death.

Powerful friends and allies cannot help us. Even such mighty beings as Brahma, Indra, Ishvara and Vishnu, great sages, and Narayana are not exempt from death. "Malignant" *yakshas* and ogreish *rakshasas*, demons, serpentine *nagas*, and the like cannot escape it. Medicine, science, divination, crystal-gazing,* and other methods cannot help us escape. The power of such things as secret mantras, charms, magic, and clairvoyance will not help. Male gods, Dharma protectors, and dakinis cannot provide a refuge. We will die without any help from the power of elixirs, special substances, or medicines. Again the Vinaya scriptures say:

Might and power they have, their fame spreads far and wide—
Brahma, Indra, and Vishnu,
Rahu, the Kauravas and Pandavas†—
But even they are powerless to stop death.
From He Who Puts an End to All‡ neither medicines,
Nor all the activities of mantras, nor soldiers,
Neither gods, nor guardians, nor magical rituals,
Neither wealth, nor relations can protect one.

Making use of the numerous illustrations and arguments mentioned above, in everything you do—moving around, walking, lying down, sitting, and so forth—think only of death, and recognize everything you see, hear, and think of as impermanent by nature, as an example of impermanence, and as a goad reminding you of impermanence, following the words of *The Way of the Bodhisattva:*

This should be my one concern,
My only thought both night and day.[55]

---

* In Tibet, such means for seeing the future made use of mirrors, the surface of lakes, and so on rather than crystals.
† Brahma and Vishnu are the creators of the world according to the Hindu tradition; Indra is an all-powerful god in Indian mythology. Rahu, the maker of darkness, is a demon who swallows the sun and moon, thereby causing eclipses. The Kauravas and Pandavas are warring clans that figure in the famous Indian myth Mahabharata.
‡ Tib. *mthar byed pa,* i.e., the Lord of Death.

And those of the Great Omniscient One:

> As you walk, every step you take is impermanent—an incitement
> to move toward Buddhahood.
> When you are sitting, staying is impermanent—an incitement to
> remain in the unchanging state.
> When you rise, standing is impermanent—an incitement to arise
> into the state of evenness.
> Eating, drinking, and everyday activities are impermanent—an
> incitement to eat the food of concentration.
> Dwellings are impermanent—an incitement to reside in the palace
> of evenness, the absolute body.
> Drawing in your limbs is impermanent—an incitement to
> withdraw from compounded activities.
> Stretching out your limbs is impermanent—an incitement to vastly
> extend your vision beyond this world.
> Lying down is impermanent—an incitement to take rest in the
> way things truly are.
> When you travel, the way is impermanent—an incitement to set
> out on the path to enlightenment.
> Fearful enemies are impermanent—an incitement to vanquish your
> enemies, afflictive emotions.
> The words you say are impermanent—an incitement to recite
> mantras and the scriptures.
> Agricultural activities are impermanent—an incitement to
> constantly abide by the teachings.
> Food and drink are impermanent—an incitement to make
> offerings to the mandala of the deity.
> Wealth and possessions are impermanent—an incitement to
> accumulate the seven noble riches.
> Power and fame are impermanent—an incitement to constant
> humility.
> Pleasure is impermanent—an incitement to accumulate merit and
> wisdom.
> Sentient beings are impermanent—an incitement to place them on
> the path to enlightenment.
> The causes of sudden death are impermanent—an incitement to
> seize the citadel of deathlessness.

Washing and grooming yourself are impermanent—an incitement
to use the four powers to purify your defilements and
obscurations.

The five afflictive poisons are impermanent—an incitement to
realize spontaneous primal wisdom.

The world you perceive is impermanent—an incitement to purify
your perceptions as a Buddhafield.

The sound of fame is impermanent—an incitement to proclaim
the melodious sounds of the Dharma.

Thoughts and memories are impermanent—an incitement to
develop the wisdom of elimination and realization.

## THE FAULT IN NOT MEDITATING ON IMPERMANENCE

Failure to reflect on impermanence will have the following negative consequences. Having been dominated exclusively by the things of this life, all
we are likely to have achieved is some profit, fame, attachment, aversion,
laziness, hoarded wealth, discouragement, disputes, and some short-lived
Dharma practice—but nothing else. And we will not be liberated from
cyclic existence very quickly that way. If even ordinary tasks cannot be
accomplished by doing them only occasionally, when one has the time,
there is no need to mention accomplishing liberation and enlightenment.
We have to apply ourselves with great diligence for a long period of time
until we attain Buddhahood. Think about how enlightened beings like
Dipamkara and Shakyamuni were. They began as sentient beings just like
us, but by the strength of their diligence, they became Buddhas. We have
never given rise to diligence, and so we are still wandering in cyclic existence. Countless Buddhas have come in the past and subsequently passed
into nirvana, but we were not the objects of their healing activities and
at present, on account of our actions, we continue to wander endlessly in
cyclic existence. It is important to reflect on all this and be guided on the
path to liberation now, in this present life. This life is like a short-term
loan, so reflect on impermanence and apply yourself sincerely to practicing
the essential Dharma, for it is said in *The Way of the Bodhisattva:*

> From this day forth, if I now fail to strive,
> I'll fall from low to even lower states.
> Striving for the benefit of all that lives,

Unnumbered Buddhas have already lived and passed away.
But I, by virtue of my sins, have failed
To come within the compass of their healing works.
And this will always be my lot
If I continue to behave like this,
And I will suffer pains and bondage,
Wounds and laceration in the lower realms.[56]

## The Advantages of Meditating on Impermanence

The benefits of meditating day and night just on death and impermanence are said to be boundless. One sees that everything that appears is perishable and thereby gains a deep sense of nonattachment to outer objects. The fire of diligence in the performance of positive actions is set ablaze. One begins to feel an uncommon and heartfelt fear of the sufferings of cyclic existence. From recognizing that at the time of death nothing can help one, one gives up the activities of this life. One uses one's body, speech, and mind to practice the Dharma, without taking even a moment of ordinary leisure. One sees how actions mature as results, and this gives rise to determination to be free and disenchantment. As one knows that the time of death is unpredictable, one does not count on anything. Numerous virtues that one did not have before are born in one's mindstream. One stops believing things are eternal. One does not have attachment to friends and relations or hatred for enemies. One is constantly diligent in performing positive actions. One understands that life is a delusion. One completes the two accumulations of merit and wisdom, and so on. The *Nirvana Sutra* says:

> Of all the various kinds of cultivation, reaping the autumn crop
>     is the best;
> Of all footprints, that of the elephant is the biggest;
> Of all thoughts, that of impermanence and death is the greatest:
> It stops all thoughts involved with the three worlds.

The Great Master says:

> To obtain the freedoms and advantages is scarcely possible, but
>     even if you do,
> There's no knowing when you'll die, for death, like lightning's play,
>     is unpredictable.

With each day, each hour, life is running out,
So don't defer the practice, Child of my Speech.

Nagarjuna writes:

> As if your hair or clothes had just caught fire,
> Abandon all to put a stop to this,
> And do your best to not be born again:
> No greater goal or need is there than that.[57]

And Padampa Sangye:

> If first you finish what you have to do, you'll never get to Dharma;
> People of Tingri, while you're thinking of it, practice straight
> away.[58]

So reject all the superficial things of this world as though it were so much spit in the dust and practice the perfectly pure, sacred Buddhadharma according to the instructions of the Buddhas and Bodhisattvas. Thinking, "That I might be able to do so, precious teacher, in you I put my trust!" earnestly recite the following prayer.

---

> The perceptions of this life are just temporary conditions, like
> a dream:
> May I be deeply mindful of impermanence and death.
> As I pray to you, precious teacher,
> Bless me, incomparably kind lord.

---

# CHAPTER SEVEN

# Reflecting on the Defects of Cyclic Existence

THIS CHAPTER HAS THREE SECTIONS: REFLECTING GENERALLY on the sufferings of cyclic existence; reflecting specifically on the sufferings of the six classes of beings; and reflecting particularly on the nature of the three kinds of suffering.

## I. REFLECTING GENERALLY ON THE SUFFERINGS OF CYCLIC EXISTENCE

As we have seen, we are sure to die, and we are powerless to continue living. But things do not stop with death: we have to take birth again, and as long as we are reborn, it cannot be anywhere other than in cyclic existence. As we read in the Vinaya scriptures,

> Driven by ignorance, craving, and becoming, all beings—
> Humans, celestial beings, and those in the three lower realms—
> Circle foolishly in the five realms,
> Going round and round like a potter's wheel.

And:

> The three worlds are ablaze with the sufferings of old age
>    and sickness;
> Here the fire of death rages, and there is no protection.
> Beings never have the intelligence to escape from cyclic
>    existence,
> Round and round they go like bees caught in a jar.

Here, in the six realms, our tainted positive and negative actions cause us to circle, taking one rebirth after another, and this is why we speak of cyclic existence.* Moreover, even though we want to be happy, we never accomplish the positive actions that lead to happiness. And though we want to avoid suffering, we persistently indulge in its cause, negative actions, and we therefore experience their result, suffering, in all its various forms. Even then we seem incapable of fear, and voluntarily accept suffering. We are like thieves who have had their hands cut off for stealing and who again commit a robbery, for which the punishment this time will be beheading. As *The Way of the Bodhisattva* puts it,

> For beings long to free themselves from misery,
> But misery itself they follow and pursue.
> They long for joy, but in their ignorance
> Destroy it, as they would their foe.⁵⁹

How is it that they "destroy joy"? Because of their attachment to the five objects of desire,† their afflictive emotions increase in strength and lead them into suffering. Moths are attracted by the light of a lamp and are thus burned by their desire for beautiful forms. Deer are drawn to their death by the sweet sound of the flute.‡ Bees try to suck the honey from a flower and die when they get stuck or the flower closes on them. Fish are lured to their death by the taste of the bait on the tip of the angler's hook. And elephants die when their desire for coolness induces them to plunge into a lake. In songs from the *Treasury of Songs of Realization* we read:

> Every single being is beguiled by the gestures of existence.

and,

> "Oh!" says the Archer, speaking of the ignorant:
> "Regard them as being like fish, moths,
> Elephants, bees, and deer."⁶⁰

From the five objects the afflictive emotions arise, and because of these we wander endlessly in cyclic existence. There is not a single one of all these sentient beings with whom we have not been related in turn as father or mother, or related through enmity, friendship, or indifference. If one were to try to number the ancestral maternal line of a single being by rolling

---

* The Tibetan word *'khor ba* that translates the Sankrit word *samsara* means "wheel."
† Tib. *'dod pa'i yul lnga,* the objects of the five senses: forms, sounds, smells, tastes, and physical sensations.
‡ Flutes used by hunters to lure their prey.

pilules the size of juniper pips from the earth and counting them, saying "This one is this being's mother, that one is her mother," one could go on counting until all the earth were used up. But there is no end to counting the ancestral line of each being's mothers, as the Buddha explained in a sutra, whose meaning is conveyed in the following verse by the Protector Nagarjuna:

> To count one's mother's lineage with pills
> Like juniper pips in size, the earth would not suffice.[61]

Thus, from time without beginning until now, there is no form of suffering that one has not experienced in cyclic existence. This is explained in the *Close Mindfulness Sutra:*

> O Monks, you should be weary of the world of existence. Why? Because in all the time you have been going round and round in beginningless cyclic existence, the bodies you have left behind from your rebirths as an ant, if all added together, would make a pile far higher than the king of mountains, Sumeru. The tears you have wept exceed all the water in the four oceans. The quantity of boiling molten copper, blood, lymph, pus, and nasal mucus that you have drunk an infinite number of times when you were a hell being or a hungry spirit is greater than the four great rivers that flow into the oceans from the four continents. The heads, eyes, limbs, fingers, and toes that you have had severed on account of your desires exceed in number all the molecules of earth, water, fire, and wind in universes numerous as the grains of sand in the River Ganges.

Moreover, in all the time you have spent in this wheel of existence, there is not a single place—no region of land, water, mountain, island, or space—that you have not been to. There is no joy you have not experienced in your countless lives as gods, as serpentine *naga*s, "malignant" *yaksha*s, smell-feeding *gandharva*s, monstrous *kumbhanda*s, gangrenous *kataputana*s,* Brahmas, Indras, and universal monarchs. And when the result of your former positive actions was exhausted and you returned to the lower realms, there was no form of suffering that you did not experience. How terrifying! In the *Sutra of Perfect Renunciation* we read:

---

* These five refer to different kinds of nonhuman beings and spirits, not necessarily malignant, that feature in Indian mythology and who, because of their powers, may have experienced certain kinds of happiness. They are described in detail in *Wikipedia*.

When the Guide, the Lord of Lions, died
And transmigrated from the Tushita heaven,
He spoke the following words to the gods:
"Abandon all carelessness."
All the many joys of the gods
Come from the positive actions that are their cause.
Be grateful, therefore, for those acts.
The merit you have accumulated will be exhausted here
And, after suffering unhappiness,
You'll fall into the lower realms.

In a dream, one might be the lord of gods and humans with riches, mansions, and an abundance of everything one could enjoy. But when one wakes up, there is nothing left. It is as *The Way of the Bodhisattva* says:

All that I possess and use
Is like the fleeting vision of a dream.
It fades into the realms of memory,
And fading, will be seen no more.[62]

Accordingly, because it is the nature of things to change when we die, we cannot count on any of the superficial happiness of cyclic existence. So reflect, thinking, "In this present life, I must do whatever I can to obtain liberation from the great ocean of suffering that is cyclic existence and attain lasting happiness in perfect Buddhahood."

## II. REFLECTING SPECIFICALLY ON THE SUFFERINGS OF THE SIX CLASSES OF BEINGS

This section is divided into two parts: reflecting on the sufferings of the three lower realms, and reflecting on the sufferings of the higher realms.

## A. Reflecting on the sufferings of the three lower realms

Our roaming through the city of cyclic existence is limited to the happy states of the higher realms and the evil states of the lower realms. These are related to the propelling effects of white and black deeds. Deeds are not, however, something independent, for they are connected to the person who performs them. So we have to ask ourselves, "What sort of suffering am I going to experience when I am reborn in the lower realms as a result of the negative actions I have accumulated?" As the Glorious Protector Nagarjuna says,

> Daily think of the hells,
> With their extremes of heat and cold.
> Think of the hungry spirits, too,
> Emaciated by hunger and thirst.
> Observe and think of the animals
> Who suffer so much from stupidity.
> Give up the causes of these and practice the causes of bliss.

These lower realms will now be described accordingly.

## *1. Reflecting on the sufferings of the hells*

There are four parts.

### a. Reflecting on the sufferings of the hot hells

## THE PARTICULAR PLACE

The land is of burning iron, with mountains, gorges, and ravines, constantly blazing with flames a cubit high, and molten copper and lava flowing over it. Everywhere there are fiery trees of burning steel. Savage birds and carnivorous beasts abound, and the terrifying executioners who guard hell. One is completely surrounded by walls of burning metal and trenches of fire. It is said that the fires of the hells are hotter than the fire in the period of destruction at the end of a kalpa, and that as one descends, each hell is four times hotter than the one above it.

Beings in the intermediate state who are going to be born there have a feeling as of cold from being driven by wind and rain. When this happens, they see the hot hell where they will be and, thinking that it is warmer there, are attracted and race toward it. The moment they arrive there, they take birth in the hell as if waking from sleep. Since they have very sensitive minds, and soft, tender bodies, even the smallest ordeals there cause exceedingly great pain, both physically and mentally.

## THE PARTICULAR SUFFERINGS

*The Reviving Hell.* Beings in this hell, as a result of their past deeds, find themselves holding a variety of sharp weapons. Their bitter hatred and mutual enmity make them strike out, causing each other such extreme pain that they faint and fall to the ground, whereupon they are revived by a voice from the sky—"Revive!"—or by a cold wind, and they experience the same intense suffering as before. So it continues until their deeds are exhausted.

*The Black-Line Hell.* Here the guardians of hell draw numerous black lines—four, eight and so on—on their victims' bodies, and then cut them up, carving along these lines with saws and splitting them with axes. The pain this causes never ceases.

*The Crushing Hell.* Those born in this hell suffer from having their bodies piled together by the guardians of hell and pushed between iron mountains shaped like the heads of goats, sheep, lions, tigers, and other animals, where they are then pressed, causing blood to flow out of all their openings. Again they are bunched together and pounded like sesame with huge steel hammers and pestles, and struck and crushed by a hail of burning iron boulders.

*The Screaming Hell.* In terror, they try to find somewhere comfortable, and, seeing an iron house, they go in. No sooner have they done so than the door shuts and they are burned everywhere—outside and inside—by blazing fires. However much they weep and cry for help, they are unable to find a refuge, and so their agony continues.

*The Great Screaming Hell.* The beings here are burned in the same way as in the preceding hell, but in this case in a double iron house, one inside the other, so that the suffering they go through is all the more intense.

*The Hell of Heat.* Here their bodies are cooked like fish in blazing iron cauldrons many leagues deep. They are impaled on fiery steel stakes from the anus to the top of the head, burning all their entrails and making flames shoot out of all their openings and pores, and thrown onto the burning iron ground to be pounded with blazing iron hammers.

*The Hell of Intense Heat.* The bodies of the beings in this hell are impaled from the anus to the shoulders and the top of the head on blazing steel tridents so that flames shoot out from all their openings. Their bodies are wrapped in incandescent sheets of metal and, upside down in boiling iron, copper, and brine, they are cooked like rice, destroying all the flesh and leaving only their skeletons. These are spread out on the iron ground, only to be cooked once more when the flesh grows back.

*The Hell of Ultimate Torment.* From the iron ground, fire blazes forth in all directions, burning the whole body—skin, flesh, sinews, bones, and marrow. Their bodies burn so fiercely that they are indistinguishable from the fire, like the wick in a candle flame, and they are only recognizable as sentient beings from the cries they emit. They are roasted on iron grates with glowing embers and forced to climb up and down huge mountains of incandescent iron. Their tongues are drawn and stretched out on the burning iron ground and then nailed down with pegs. They are flayed and then laid on their backs on the burning iron ground. Their mouths are forced open with tongs, and metal lumps and molten copper poured in, burning the whole of their mouths, gullets, and intestines and coming out again at the other end. There is no way to endure these and the other sufferings in this hell.

## THE PARTICULAR SPAN OF LIFE

How long the beings live in these hells is described in the *Treasury of Abhidharma:*

> Fifty years in human terms
> Make just one day for the lowest
> Of the gods in the realm of desire,
> And there they live five hundred years.
> For each realm above, these two quantities are multiplied by two.

and

> In the six hells, Reviving and the others, respectively,
> One day equals a lifetime as a god in the world of desire.

Fifty human years are equivalent to one day for the gods in the realm of the Four Great Kings, and the gods there live for five hundred years on their own scale. This is equivalent to an entire day in the Reviving Hell, whose inhabitants, on that basis, live five hundred years. For each hell beneath it, the numbers of years each increase by a factor of two, and the calculations in terms of days are also doubled, so that calculating the span of life involves two sets of multiplication by two.[63]

### b. REFLECTING ON THE SUFFERINGS OF THE COLD HELLS

## THE PARTICULAR PLACE

The cold hells are completely pervaded by intense darkness, unlit by sun, moon, or any other source of light, and by extreme cold, with glaciers and frozen crevasses, gales, and snowstorms. These hells are named after the physical and vocal afflictions caused by the cold, which is said to become seven times more intense from one hell to the next one below it. Beings in the intermediate state who are going to be born there feel as if they are being burned in a fire, at which point they see the cold hells, to which they are attracted, and race toward them, thus taking birth there.

## THE PARTICULAR SUFFERINGS

*The Hell of Blisters.* Beings here suffer from being blasted by icy winds and blizzards, which cause their bodies to be completely covered with blisters, making them shrivel up.

*The Hell of Burst Blisters.* The intense cold in this hell causes the blisters to burst into running sores, from which worms with sharp mouthparts emerge, so that the beings there suffer from their skin being ripped open, and blood and lymph oozing out and congealing.

*The Hell of Lamentation.* The beings here moan, uttering just the smallest sounds of one syllable in whispers.

*The Hell of Groans.* This hell is even colder: its inhabitants, unable to utter a word, emit tiny, whispering sounds of pain through their teeth.

*The Hell of Chattering Teeth.* The cold is greater than ever, and the beings there shiver without uttering a sound, their teeth chattering.

*The Hell of Utpala-like Cracks.* The cold is so much more intense that the skin turns blue and cracks, splitting into five or six sections.

*The Hell of Lotuslike Cracks.* The skin changes from blue to red and splits into ten or many more sections.

*The Hell of Great Lotuslike Cracks.* This is the ultimate extreme of cold: the skin contracts and turns vivid red, splitting into hundreds or thousands of sections. There is no enduring the pain experienced here.

## THE PARTICULAR SPAN OF LIFE

The length of beings' lives in these hells is described in the *Treasury of Abhidharma:*

> Take a seed of sesame every hundred years
> From a *jang* of sesame until the store runs dry:
> That's how long they live in the Hell of Blisters.
> Multiply by twenty to know the life span in the others.

In other words, the length of time beings live in the Hell of Blisters is the time it would take to empty a *jang* measure filled to the brim with sesame seeds if one were to take out one sesame seed every hundred years (a *jang* being a vessel used in Magadha, with a capacity of eighty *khal*).* The life spans in the hells beneath it are calculated in each case by multiplying that in the previous hell by a factor of twenty.[64]

## c. Reflecting on the sufferings of the neighboring hells

The *Treasury of Abhidharma* describes these as follows:

> After the eight there are sixteen more,
> In their four directions:
> They are the pit of hot embers, the swamp of putrefying corpses,
> The razor road and so on, and the river.

In each of the four directions of the eight hot hells, there are four neighboring hells, the pit of hot embers and so on, making sixteen in all. Beings may arrive there from the main hot hells or be born there directly. In whichever direction they flee, they sink up to their knees, trapped in a pit of hot embers. As soon as they put a foot down in it, their flesh and skin are burned, but as soon as they lift it again, they are restored. Even if they escape from there, their bodies sink into an utterly foul-smelling swamp of putrefying corpses, whereupon sharp-mouthed worms like needles bore through their skin and flesh, eating them right down to the bone. Even if they escape from there, they arrive on a road full of sharp razors: as soon as they step on it their feet are cut to pieces, and the moment they raise a foot, it is restored.

Next (the "and so on" in the above quotation), even if they escape from that, they come to the forest of swordlike leaves. As they sit down in its shade, the swords, stirred by the wind of these beings' past deeds, fall on them like rain, cutting their entire bodies, and they collapse, only to be attacked and devoured by packs of dogs.

Should they manage to escape from that, they are pursued by savage beasts. Seeing the grove of iron *shalmali* trees they flee toward it, but as they climb up and fall down again, their bodies are perforated like sieves by sharp, sixteen-inch thorns pointing up and down, and they are ravaged by steel-billed crows and similar birds that gouge their eyes out and peck away their flesh.

---

*A *khal* is equal to about 30 pounds or 20 measures of 2 pints (40 pints). A *jang* would therefore contain a little over one ton.

Once they have broken free from that, tormented by heat, they see a flowing river and race toward it, only to tumble into a scalding river of brine. As they sink into its depths, their flesh separates away, revealing the white of the bones. When they rise to the surface again, their flesh grows back and once again they sink down. Even though they want to run away, the guardians of hell are there on the banks, wielding weapons, and will not let them escape. From time to time they haul them out with hooks, lay them on their backs, and ask them what they want. When they reply, "I do not know, I cannot see, but I am hungry and thirsty," the guardians pour blazing lumps of metal and boiling molten copper into their mouths. These are just some of the torments in this hell.

Of the above hells, the road of razors, the forest of swordlike leaves, and the *shalmali* trees are grouped together as a single hell, so that there are four neighboring hells altogether.*

The span of life in these hells is not described definitely, but since one has to stay many hundreds of thousands of years in each of them, it is in any case a long period of terrible suffering.

### d. Reflecting on the sufferings of the ephemeral hells

There are no definite locations for these hells—they include the neighborhood of the principal hells, seashores, regions underground, the surface of the earth, rivers, and so on. The sufferings there include being burned by fire, being frozen and split, being slain and eaten by killers, enjoying happiness during the day and being tormented at night, and vice versa. The span of life is not definite. Examples of these hells occur in the *Story of Shrona* and the *Story of Sangharakshita*.†

---

The causes for taking birth in these places of such suffering are none other than one's own negative deeds, so it is important to be fully dedicated to giving them up. If you fail to do so, as will be explained, the result of the many negative actions you have accumulated in the past, and will still accumulate, will be such that there can be no more than the tremulous to

---

*I.e., the pit of hot embers, the swamp of putrefying corpses, the road of razors (plus forest and *shalmali*), and the river.
† These stories from the *Bodhisattvavadana-kalpalata* are partly retold by Patrul Rinpoche in *The Words of My Perfect Teacher*, pages 70–71 and 72–74.

and fro of your breath between this life and the hells. How can it be right, therefore, to remain in a happy frame of mind? As Shantideva says,

How can you remain at ease like this
When you have done the deeds that lead to hell?[65]

And in *Letter to a Friend* we read:

The very instant that they cease to breathe,
The wicked taste the boundless pains of hell.
And he who hearing this is not afraid
In every way is truly diamond hard.
If you take fright from seeing pictures of the hells,
Or when you hear or think or read about those realms,
Or make some sculpted figures, need we say
How hard to bear the ripened fruit will be?[66]

and:

For one whole day on earth three hundred darts
Might strike you hard and cause you grievous pain,
But that could never illustrate or match
A fraction of the smallest pain in hell.[67]

## 2. Reflecting on the sufferings of the hungry spirits

The hungry spirits mostly live more than five hundred leagues beneath our world, but there are some who are scattered, distributed throughout the earth, mountains, and rivers. The *Close Mindfulness Sutra* mentions thirty-six kinds of hungry spirits, but these can be condensed into three categories: hungry spirits with external obscurations, those with internal obscurations, and those with obscurations related to food and drink.

### HUNGRY SPIRITS WHO SUFFER FROM EXTERNAL OBSCURATIONS

These hungry spirits are afflicted by hunger and thirst, and they therefore have dried-up, emaciated mouths and bodies, scrawny necks and limbs, and shaggy hair. They run everywhere looking for something to eat and drink, but never find anything. Even if they see, far in the distance, piles of food, rivers, or orchards laden with fruit, as soon as they reach them, they see the food vanish without trace, the rivers dry up or turn into pus and blood, and the fruit trees wilt and lose their fruit. Or, if that does not happen, they are obstructed by large numbers of men brandishing weapons and keeping guard. And so they suffer.

## HUNGRY SPIRITS WHO SUFFER
### FROM INTERNAL OBSCURATIONS

The sublime Nagarjuna describes these as follows:

> Some, their mouths like needles' eyes, their bellies
> Huge as mountains, ache from want of food.
> They do not even have the strength to eat
> Discarded scraps, the smallest bits of filth.[68]

Even if they find something to eat or drink, it will not go into their mouths, though if it does, the food is dispersed inside their cheeks and the drink dries up in their poisonous mouths. Should they manage to swallow a little bit, it does not get past the throat, and any that does is not enough to fill the stomach. They are thus tormented by their inability to eat or drink.

## HUNGRY SPIRITS WHO SUFFER
### FROM OBSCURATIONS RELATED
### TO FOOD AND DRINK

Any food and drink they do ingest bursts into flames, blazing away and burning all their entrails. The so-called filth eaters have to eat food that is bad and only causes them distress—unclean, foul-smelling things like excrement, urine, pus, blood, spittle, and snot, or poison or glowing embers.

———

For all these different hungry spirits there is the unbearable misery of constant hunger and thirst. Since they do not have clothes, they are burned by heat and numbed by the cold. In spring, the moon burns them; in winter, the sun feels cold. The clouds in summer rain down fire. They are worn out from constantly hunting for food, and as they grow weaker, their joints dislocate and burst into flames. As they are all each other's enemies, they live in fear of being bound, beaten, and killed, and, with no one to trust, they run away in terror. These and other severe torments have to be experienced for long periods of time.

Their particular span of life is, in the words of the *Treasury of Abhidharma,*

> Five hundred, where a month is a day.

In other words, they live for five hundred years, one of their days being equivalent to a whole human month.

*Letter to a Friend* gives another explanation:

> For five, ten thousand years they will not die.[69]

That is, for some hungry spirits the life span is five thousand years, while for others it is ten thousand.

The causes of their misery are such things as stinginess and preventing others from being charitable, so we should exercise care and concentrate on adopting what is right and avoiding what is wrong.

## 3. Reflecting on the sufferings of the animals

Animals are divided into those that live in the depths and those that live scattered in different places.

*Animals that live in the depths* are those in the great oceans. Since they have no dwelling to provide protection, they are carried along by the waves, drifting at random. Each is food for the other, the smaller animals being gulped down by the larger ones, and the larger animals having their bodies bored into and eaten by the smaller ones. The serpentine *naga*s suffer from being burned daily by hot sand and preyed on by the eaglelike *garuda*s. They are all thus perpetually fearful of something hostile appearing, and suffer unbearable distress.

*Animals that live scattered in different places* are those in the realms of gods and humans. Nondomesticated animals are constantly tormented by the fear of something hostile appearing and their minds are never at ease. They are preyed on by birds and carnivores, and are helpless to resist being killed by humans. Domestic animals suffer from having their hair pulled out* and their noses pierced, and from being castrated, burdened with heavy loads, beaten and exploited, and killed for their meat, blood, hide, and bones. Moreover, their stupidity and ignorance result in their suffering generally from bewilderment in that they do not know what to do and what not to do. In this respect, and in such things as hunger, thirst, heat,

---

* For example, the soft belly hair of the yak, used as wool, is pulled out rather than shorn.

cold, and exhaustion, their misery rivals that in the hells and hungry-spirit realms. As we read in *Letter to a Friend,*

> For animals there's multifold distress—
> They're slaughtered, tied up, beaten, and the rest.
> For those denied the virtue that brings peace
> There's agony as one devours another.
> Some are killed just for their pearls or wool,
> Their bones and blood and meat, or skins and fur,
> And other helpless beasts are forced to work,
> They're kicked or struck with hands, with whips and goads.[70]

Their span of life is said to be:

> For animals, a kalpa at the longest.

That is, those with the longest lives can live for up to a kalpa; those with shorter lives do not have fixed life spans.

———

How should one reflect on the sufferings of the lower realms? Examine your own feelings. If you find it difficult now to stand putting your finger in the fire for just a second, or sitting naked in an icy hollow in the dead of winter, or going without food and drink for a few days, or merely being stung by a bee or bitten by a flea or louse, imagine how you would endure the torments of the hells or the hungry-spirit and animal realms. Doing so should inspire in you a feeling of fear and total disenchantment, and a strong determination to gain definite liberation, so that your precious human life is made truly meaningful.

## B. Reflecting on the sufferings of the higher realms

By accumulating positive actions consistent with ordinary merit* on the paths for beings of modest, medium, or great capacity, one takes birth respectively as a human being, as a god in the world of desire, or as a god in the higher worlds, and one enjoys the temporary happiness of such rebirths. You might think, therefore, that since there is no chance of happiness in the lower realms, you should put your efforts into trying to attain the higher realms. But just as a fire, whatever its size, cannot but burn, cyclic existence is by nature suffering, whether you take a high or low

———

*See glossary, *positive actions consistent with ordinary merit.*

rebirth, and it therefore contains nothing worthwhile. It is important to understand that it is not only the lower realms that constitute suffering, but the higher realms as well. To do this we reflect on the sufferings in the human, demigod, and god realms.

## *1. Reflecting on the sufferings of humans*

### BIRTH

To begin with, and until the pregnancy reaches term, we have to stay in the cramped confines of our mother's womb, scarcely tolerating the darkness, the evil smell, and the changes in temperature. Then, when we are born—upside down—it is as if we were being drawn through a wire extruder. When we are touched, it is like being whipped with briars. When we are wiped clean, it is as if we were being flayed alive. When we are taken onto our mother's lap, we feel like a little bird being carried off by a hawk. Such are the sufferings of birth.

### OLD AGE

As we age, our complexion fades, and we lose our good looks and take on a dark blue ashen color. Our senses become dulled, while our body becomes bent and our limbs crooked. The flesh withers, the skin becomes loose. Our face is a mass of wrinkles, our hair turns white, and our teeth fall out. As we become physically weaker, we find it difficult to get up, we stagger as we walk, we collapse when we sit down, and when we speak we cannot articulate. As our senses degenerate, our eyesight dims, we become hard of hearing, and our food loses its flavor. Our enjoyment of things diminishes, so that we cease to derive pleasure from sensual delights such as food: a little less food leaves us feeling hungry, while a little more gives us indigestion. Nobody likes us.

### ILLNESS

When we are sick, we suffer infinite pain and distress resulting from imbalances of the four elements due to our previous deeds and present circumstances. Aching and physically weakened by illness, we are no longer free to enjoy things we like, such as food and drink, or sleep. We are obliged to resort to unpleasant medicines, treatments, regimens, and so forth, and wonder apprehensively whether we are going to die.

## DEATH

At the time of death, nothing—neither medicines, nor treatments, nor special rituals—can help, and we will have no choice but to leave behind all the wealth, fame, power, following, and friends we have worked so hard to obtain, and even the body we have cherished so much. As our vital force is severed, we will go through intense suffering and die.

---

These four great rivers of suffering are common to all human beings, but they are not the only ones we have to experience, for there are also specific sufferings that occur interspersed between these four.

*The suffering of not getting what we want*—things such as happiness, riches, power, and pleasure in this life that we fail to achieve even though we sacrifice our bodies and lives and go through all sorts of difficulties to do so.

*The suffering of misfortune befalling us*—things we do not want, such as hunger and thirst, heat and cold, involvement in disputes and lawsuits, being the subject of rumors, or being punished by the authorities.

*The suffering of separation from beloved relatives and what is pleasant*—happiness and comfort, wealth, entourage, companions, relatives and friends, and the like.

*The suffering of encountering hated enemies and what is unpleasant*—sickness, negative forces, obstacles, enemies, robbers and bandits, fires, floods, and savage beasts of prey.

In short, both rich and poor suffer greatly. For the rich, the greater their wealth and circle of attendants, the more they must suffer protecting it all. For the poor, there is the misery of deprivation, for they never manage to acquire the food, clothes, and other things they need, however much they look for them. As we read in the *Series of Lives,*

> The first is afflicted by guarding it,
> The second is exhausted looking for it.
> Whether they are rich or poor,
> Nowhere will there be any joy.

And the *Four Hundred* says:

> At best there is mental anguish,
> In most cases it is physical.
> By both these forms of suffering
> Is the whole world daily crushed.

These quotations merely illustrate what we can all too plainly see for ourselves.

## 2. Reflecting on the sufferings of the demigods

In general, the jealousy that the demigods experience when they see the splendor, abundance, and perfection of everything in the gods' realms causes them constant, unbearably intense anguish. In particular, from time to time they go to war with the gods, and because their merit is weaker, they go through terrible suffering as they are killed, or struck, dismembered, and torn apart. During these battles, as long as the gods do not have their heads or waists severed, their injuries heal again even if a vital organ is struck, whereas the demigods, like humans, die if a vital organ is hit. It is said that the reflections of the dead demigods appear in the lake called All-Appearing on top of the ground of gold, and so their families are stricken with grief even before the soldiers return.

Demigods are mostly evildoers and therefore have no interest in the Dharma. The few who are induced to aspire to the Dharma are so obscured by the fully ripened effects of their previous actions that they do not have the good fortune to be able to distinguish right from wrong.

## 3. Reflecting on the sufferings of the gods

This consists of reflecting on the sufferings of (a) the gods of the world of desire and (b) of the two higher worlds.

### a. REFLECTING ON THE SUFFERINGS OF THE GODS OF THE WORLD OF DESIRE

At first, the gods of the world of desire are seduced by the pleasures of carefree indulgence in sensual enjoyment and fail to see their lives trickling away. But when the time comes for them to die, they lose their beautiful complexions, their seats no longer feel comfortable, their flower garlands grow old, stains appear on their clothes, and perspiration, formerly absent, breaks out on their bodies. These five portents appear seven gods' days before they die, so the anguish they go through in dying is enormous and long lasting. During this time their own goddesses and attendants abandon them and go off to spend their time with other gods, causing them great sorrow. In particular, despite their attachment to the splendor and pleasure of their celestial state, they know they cannot help but be separated from them. They also know that once they have died, it is all but impossible to be reborn in the celestial realms again, and that even if a few of them are reborn as human beings, the majority will be reborn in the lower realms and will have to experience terrible suffering there for long periods of time. This knowledge and their subsequent fall are unbearably painful for them, as we read in the *Close Mindfulness Sutra:*

> Falling from the gods' abodes,
> Their agony is most intense.
> The denizens of hell do not endure
> A mere sixteenth of such great misery.

And in *Letter to a Friend:*

> Indra, universally revered,
> Will fall again to earth through action's force.
> And he who ruled the universe as king
> Will be a slave within samsara's wheel.[71]

Furthermore, when they see the majesty and abundant pleasures of gods with greater merit, the ones with less merit become depressed and intimidated. For the weaker gods, there is the distress of being driven out of their homes by the stronger ones. The gods in the realm of the Four Great Kings and the Heaven of the Thirty-Three, in particular, quarrel and fight with the demigods, and they suffer horribly when they are cut and torn, or killed, by their weapons.

### b. REFLECTING ON THE SUFFERINGS OF THE TWO HIGHER WORLDS

In the form and formless worlds there is no manifest suffering of suffering, but the gods there are never exempt from the suffering of everything composite.* Because the ordinary beings† in these realms become, as it were, intoxicated with concentration, they do not make any progress in increasing their good qualities. Once they have tasted the flavor of concentration, they dare not be parted from concentration as an experience,[72] and as a result, their concentration fades and they die. In particular, when

---

* The suffering of suffering and the suffering of everything composite are described below in the next section.

† Tib. *so skye,* ordinary individuals as distinct from Bodhisattvas on the first and higher Bodhisattva levels who have attained the sublime path (*'phags lam*).

the propelling action* they performed in a previous life is exhausted, the ordinary beings in these realms again take birth in the world of desire. Although they have had an apparently blissful experience in their earlier meditation of worldly concentration and now in the concentrations of the form and formless realms, when the propelling force for this tainted bliss is spent, they will again fall into the lower realms without any idea where they are going, like an arrow being shot into the sky. *Letter to a Friend* says:

> A Kamaloka god, one gains such bliss,
> As Brahma, bliss that's free from all desire;
> But know that after that comes constant pain:
> As firewood one feeds Avici's flames.[73]

So, wherever we are born in the three worlds of cyclic existence, there is suffering. Whatever the place, it is a place of suffering. Whoever accompanies us is a companion in suffering. Whatever we experience, it does not go beyond the experience of suffering. As is stated in the *Sublime Continuum,*

> Just as in excrement there are no good smells, for the five kinds of
>     beings there is no happiness;
> Their sufferings are like the ever-continuing sensation of fire,
>     weapons, caustic salts, and so forth.[74]

That is what we have to understand.

### III. REFLECTING PARTICULARLY ON THE NATURE OF THE THREE KINDS OF SUFFERING

Generally speaking, there are two aspects to the sufferings of cyclic existence: cause and effect. The cause concerns gods and humans who, despite having retinues, wealth, and everything they could possibly want, are permeated (in thought) by nonvirtuous intentions and engage (in deed) in negative actions. The effect concerns the three lower realms and, in the higher realms, poverty, affliction by physical ailments and mental anguish, and so on. This suffering can be summarized as three kinds: the suffering of suffering, the suffering of change, and the all-pervading suffering of everything composite.

---

* Propelling action (Tib. '*phen pa*): the deed that results in a particular rebirth, in this case the meditative concentration practiced in a previous life that has resulted in rebirth in the form or formless world.

*The suffering of suffering* covers all painful sensations such as heat, cold, hunger, and thirst. It is illustrated by the image of poison poured into a wound and is mainly experienced in the three lower realms.

*The suffering of change* comprises all pleasant perceptions, from long life, wealth, and so on up to the bliss of concentration. It is illustrated by the example of having a fire to heat one when one is cold and is mainly experienced by humans and the gods of the world of desire.

*The all-pervading suffering of everything composite* refers to the perpetuating aggregates,* which are the basis of both of the above kinds of suffering. It is the foundation of all suffering and is exemplified by a person parched with thirst drinking salty water. From it, birth, aging, and all other forms of suffering appear in stages. Entirely neutral sensations are thus given the name "suffering of everything composite." This kind of suffering is mainly experienced in the realms of the four concentrations† and is what is referred to by the following quotation from the sutras:

> Whatever perceptions there may be, they are all suffering.

Unless we are free from this kind of suffering, there will be no liberation from the other two. It is the trunk that has to be cut: there is no point in hacking away at the branches and leaves. As the *Analysis of Actions* says:

> The suffering of existence is like a pit of fire, with no chance of getting cool. It is as terrifying as being surrounded by ferocious beasts and savages. It is like a king's jail, from which there is hardly any possibility of escape. Like the waves of the ocean, it recurs again and again. Like the deadly black aconite, it destroys the vital force of happy states.

So whatever kind of rebirth we take—high or low—in these three worlds of cyclic existence, we suffer as if ill and unceasingly wracked by pain. There is no chance of being happy even for a second. We should therefore feel deeply disillusioned with cyclic existence, thinking, "From now on, I must seek definite freedom, as if I were escaping from a dark dungeon." As the Great Master says,

---

*Tib. *nye bar len pa'i phung po*, explained as the tainted aggregates that are produced from taking hold of past deeds and afflictive emotions and that lead to taking hold of future deeds and afflictive emotions. cf. glossary, *aggregates*.

† That is, by gods in the twelve realms of the four concentrations, in the world of form.

However much effort you put into worldly activities, they are
  never finished;
Put your efforts into the Dharma and the job will be quickly done.
Activities concerned with cyclic existence, however good, bring
  ruin in the end;
The result of practicing the sublime Dharma can never be spoiled.
From time without beginning, we have made a habit of deeds,
  afflictive emotions,
And habitual tendencies, continuously storing them in our stream
  of being:
As a result, we wander in cyclic existence, deluded by our
  perceptions.
As to when we will be liberated, who can say?[75]
Even if we think of the Dharma as we are dying, it will be far
  too late:
Medicine is of no use to someone who has been beheaded.
For this reason, wholly acknowledge the sufferings of cyclic
  existence,
And to truly climb the road to peace,
Care for all beings with love and compassion
And meditate on the union of compassion and emptiness.

Unless we mentally forsake all the superficial activities of this life, however many years we spend trying to accomplish the Dharma, it will never be the real thing. So, recognizing that the whole of cyclic existence is meaningless,[76] relinquish all your endless projects and use every possible means to practice the perfectly pure, sublime Dharma. Thinking, "That I might be able to do so, precious teacher, in you I put my trust!" recite the following prayer:

The three worlds of cyclic existence are by nature suffering,
So may I eradicate all attachment and clinging.
As I pray to you, precious teacher,
Bless me, incomparably kind lord.

# CHAPTER EIGHT

# Reflecting on the Unfailing Law of Actions: Cause and Effect

THERE ARE THREE SECTIONS: GENERAL REFLECTION ON actions and their results, specific reflection on categories, and an explanation, in summary, of the Four Truths.

## I. REFLECTING GENERALLY ON ACTIONS AND THEIR RESULTS

We might think that although it is true that life is impermanent and we will die (as was explained above), we won't have to take birth again—after all, is it not said,

> Like wind-blown ashes from a fire,
> What is there to be reborn?

Or even if we are to be reborn, are not the happiness and suffering of cyclic existence and its higher and lower states produced by an external creator, or perhaps independently, rather than by our deeds? Will our positive and negative deeds not simply be wasted?* Do we really need to practice the Dharma?

But the truth is, the relationship between cause and effect is unfailing, and the results of actions ripen on the doer. How this happens is explained in the *Hundred Parables on Action:*

> Marvel! The world is created from deeds.
> Happiness and suffering are produced by deeds;

---

*All these erroneous ideas are those of various non-Buddhist philosophical schools.

They come from the gathering of conditions.
It is our deeds that produce our pleasure and pain.

And further:

Even after a hundred kalpas,
Beings' deeds are never lost.
When the time and conditions are right,
They will ripen as their respective results.

And the *Sutra on the Analysis of Actions* states:

Parrot, the son of the brahmin householder To'uta, asked: "Oh,
Gautama, what are the causes and conditions by which beings have
long or short lives, good or poor health? Why are they handsome or
ugly, powerful or weak, of noble or humble origins, wealthy or poor,
intelligent or dull?"

The Buddha replied: "Son of a brahmin, sentient beings are the
product of their deeds. The lot they enjoy is that of their deeds. The
place they are born in is decided by their deeds. They are dependent
on their deeds and are thus distinguished as sublime, base, or middling; as of high or low status; as good or bad. Beings have all sorts
of deeds, all sorts of views, all sorts of experiences. Because of the
negative actions associated with these, they take birth in the hells,
or as hungry spirits, or as animals. Because of their positive actions,
they will be born among gods and humans."

Accordingly, the result of positive actions is happiness and the result of
negative actions is suffering. We therefore need to undertake the former
and give up the latter, for the manner in which positive and negative actions ripen as their respective results is said to be inconceivable. Whether
positive or negative, even though an action may be insignificant at the
moment it is performed, at the moment of its full maturation, its result
will have greatly increased until it has become a hundred, a thousand, or
even an infinite number of times greater, like a grain of barley or some
other seed growing and spreading. Unless the deeds we have accumulated
are annulled by antidotes, it is impossible for them to be used up until
their results have matured. So it is extremely important to take the adoption of virtue and avoidance of negative actions seriously. As the Great
Master said,

What's the use of winning happiness in this life through
  evil deeds
That will lead to misery in many lives to come?
This life is short, a mere few months or years,
And there's no telling how long one's future lives will last.
The way, therefore, to make your other lives happy and free
  of pain
Is to take up virtue and abandon negative deeds.

## II. REFLECTING SPECIFICALLY ON CATEGORIES

There are three parts: reflecting on negative actions to be avoided, reflecting on positive actions to be accomplished, and transforming indeterminate actions into positive ones.

## A. Reflecting on negative actions to be avoided

Negative actions comprise:

*Naturally shameful deeds:** these are actions that produce negative consequences for anyone who commits them. They include the root and lesser afflictive emotions (the three poisons, and pride, jealousy, miserliness, and the rest) that can motivate negative activity, and all the nonvirtuous actions motivated by these defilements and perpetrated by the body, speech, and mind.

*Shameful deeds that violate edicts:* these are actions that produce negative consequences for someone if they go against any vows that that person has taken.

All the sufferings in cyclic existence arise from and are caused by these negative actions. Although they are of many different kinds, as far as we are concerned in adopting virtue and giving up evil, the most important of them can be roughly summarized as ten in number, as the *Treasury of Abhidharma* declares:

Summarizing them roughly,
With regard to both positive and negative deeds
The path of action is explained as tenfold.

---

* See glossary for a definition of *shameful deeds.*

## THE THREE NEGATIVE ACTIONS
## OF THE BODY

### *Taking Life*

Taking life involves the wish to kill, the act of killing without mistaking the intended victim, and not abandoning one's murderous intentions until death ensues.

### *Taking What Is Not Given*

This involves such acts as stealing someone else's property or depriving them of it without it being given, in either case with a wish to obtain it for oneself.

### *Sexual Misconduct*

Sexual misconduct refers to sexual relations:

- with an inappropriate partner—a woman who is committed to someone else, someone related to one by fewer than seven degrees of consanguinity, a prostitute who has been hired by another person, someone who is the ward of his or her parents, of the state, or of some other guardian, or someone observing a vow of celibacy;
- at an inappropriate time—when the partner is unwell, distressed, pregnant or menstruating, or underage, and so on;
- in an inappropriate place—in front of a stupa, in a temple, on top of bricks or broken earthenware, or on a hard, uneven surface that hurts one's partner, and so on;
- or by an inappropriate route—using any passage other than the vagina.

These concern laypeople, but for someone who has taken a vow of celibacy, sexual relations of any kind constitute sexual misconduct.

The *Treasury of Abhidharma* says:

> Taking life is to kill another
> Intentionally and without mistake.
> Taking what is not given is to appropriate
> Another's property by force or stealth.
> Sex with improper desires
> Comprises the four kinds of sexual misconduct.

## THE FOUR NEGATIVE ACTIONS
## OF SPEECH

### *Lying*

When one lies, one deceitfully twists things round and knowingly says something untrue, and the other person understands what one has said.[77] This is not confined to speech: physical gestures can also be lies.

### *Sowing Discord**

Sowing discord involves wanting to divide two people who get on well, saying things that trouble the other person, and his or her grasping what one means.

### *Harsh Speech*

With harsh speech, one directly says things within someone's hearing that affect him or her deeply—recounting that person's faults, for example—and the person absorbs what one has said.

### *Worthless Chatter*

Worthless chatter comprises negative speech other than the first three kinds. It includes flattery; singing and acting; conversation about war, business, love, and so forth; and conversation involving wrong philosophical views.

About these, the *Treasury of Abhidharma* has this to say:

> Lies are words that pervert the truth
> And whose meaning is actually understood.
> Divisive speech is that spoken with a poisoned mind,
> Intent on splitting other people.
> Harsh words are those one does not like to hear.
> All speech influenced by afflictive emotions is worthless
>    chatter.

---

*Tib. *phra ma,* also translated as "divisive speech."

# THE THREE NEGATIVE ACTIONS OF MIND

## Covetousness

Covetousness involves a deep-seated wish and desire to make someone else's house, property, entourage, servants, and suchlike one's own.

## Harmful Intent

Harmful intent is a deep-rooted wish to harm another person and cause them pain.

## Wrong Views

Wrong views involve holding the firm belief that there is no truth in the law regarding actions and their effects, that there are no previous and future lives, that the Three Jewels do not exist, and so on.

This is stated in the *Treasury of Abhidharma* as follows:

> Covetousness is perverse attachment to others' property.
> Malice is hatred of sentient beings.
> The view that there is no virtue
> And no evil is wrong view.

———————

These ten have been described here in terms of the complete course of the action,\* but you should also definitely avoid any acts similar to the ten negative actions, for example, killing unintentionally, by mistake. As it is said,

> With attachment, aversion, and bewilderment—
> Actions thus engendered are negative.

———————

\* The complete course of an action is one in which all the elements are present. To obtain the fully ripened effect of killing, for example, the victim has to be identified, there has to be the intention to kill, the act of killing must be carried out, and it must result in the victim's death. Nevertheless, even an incomplete action has an effect, albeit less than that of the complete action. To think of killing someone, even if one does not finally do so, will still have negative consequences, as will an unsuccessful attempt to kill someone. Similarly, for negative speech to be complete, the person to whom it is directed must understand and absorb what has been said. For further explanation, see *The Words of My Perfect Teacher,* page 104, and *Treasury of Precious Qualities,* pages 53–56.

In particular, criticism of anything connected with the Dharma—the sublime doctrine, the spiritual friend who teaches it, and so forth—is said to be related to wrong view and has immeasurably negative consequences, as stated in the *Transcendent Wisdom in Eight Thousand Verses:*

> Subhuti, those who accumulate actions that deprive them of the Dharma fall headlong, to be reborn in the lower realms. They suffer in the great hell where beings' torments are unsurpassed.

And in the *Sutra of the Miracle of Decisive Pacification* we read:

> For many, many kalpas too,
> One's body—five hundred leagues in size,
> And on that body five hundred heads,
> And in those heads, in every one,
> No fewer than five hundred tongues,
> And on each tongue a giant plow
> With full five hundred shares, no less,
> Burning their blazing furrows there—
> All this because of evil deeds, of being critical.

Then there are the five crimes with immediate retribution and the five crimes that are almost as grave. These are determined by the objects on which they are perpetrated.*

## The Five Crimes with Immediate Retribution

To kill one's father; to kill one's mother; to kill an Arhat; to create a split in the Sangha; and, with evil intention, to cause a Tathagata to bleed.

## The Five Crimes That Are Almost as Grave

To destroy a stupa, to kill a Bodhisattva, to rape a female Arhat, to kill someone training on the path, and to appropriate the property of the Sangha.

---

*The objects against which the five crimes with immediate retribution are directed are so important that, after death, a person who has committed any of them is immediately reborn in the hell realms without passing through the usual intermediate state between rebirths.

After that, there are twenty-four serious faults and perverse acts that include shameful deeds in violation of edicts. They are determined by both their objects and the acts themselves.

## The Sixteen Serious Faults

The four serious faults entailing reversal are: to take the head of the row of scholars,* to accept the homage of a fully ordained monk, to eat the food of someone doing intensive practice,[78] and to appropriate a mantra practitioner's ritual materials.

The four serious faults entailing impairment are: to break a promise, to impair the vows of the Listeners,† to impair the Bodhisattva precepts, and to impair the commitments of the Secret Mantra Vehicle.

The four serious faults entailing contempt are: out of ignorance, to show contempt for the Buddha's body; out of pride, to show contempt for the good qualities of wise and learned persons; out of jealousy, to show contempt for words of truth; and out of partiality, to attempt to prove or disprove particular philosophical tenets.

The four serious faults entailing scorn are: to condone causing a Tathagata to bleed (one of the five crimes with immediate retribution), to condone wrong views (one of the ten negative actions), arbitrarily to condemn one among equals, and to make ungrounded accusations.

## The Eight Perverse Acts

These are described as follows:

> Maligning the good, praising the bad,
> Disturbing the minds of the virtuous,
> Stopping the faithful accumulating merit,
> Forsaking the teacher, the deity, and Dharma kindred,
> And separating from the sacred mandala—these eight
> Are said to be the eight perverse acts.

---

*I.e., to assume a higher rank than one has.
†I.e., any of the vows of individual liberation. See glossary, *individual liberation*.

## *The Results of Negative Actions*

The results of these negative actions can be divided into three: the fully ripened effect, the effect similar to the cause, and the environmental effect.

### The Fully Ripened Effect

The relative gravity of negative actions depends on specific factors such as their motivation, object, time, and frequency. Thus, the worst negative actions result in rebirth in the hells, less serious ones result in rebirth as a hungry spirit, and the least serious lead to rebirth as an animal, with the respective experiences of suffering described in the previous chapter. The *Close Mindfulness Sutra* states:

> The fully ripened effect of the least serious negative actions is rebirth among animals. That of more serious ones is rebirth among the hungry spirits. That of the worst ones is rebirth in the hells.

### The Effect Similar to the Cause

#### EXPERIENCES SIMILAR TO THE CAUSE

Taking life results in one's having a short life. As a result of stealing, one will be short of possessions. Sexual misconduct results in one's having numerous enemies. From lying, one will often be criticized and belittled. As a result of sowing discord, one will quarrel with one's companions. Because of one's harsh speech, everything one hears will be unpleasant. On account of worthless chatter, one's words will lack authority. As a result of covetousness, one's wishes will never be accomplished. Harmful intentions will result in one's always being afraid. Wrong views will result in one's being stupid and confused. This is stated in the *Jewel Garland* as follows:

> Take life, and you will have a short life,
> Take what is not given, and you'll be deprived of wealth,
> Commit adultery, and you'll have enemies,
> From telling lies, you will be much criticized,
> By sowing discord, you'll be parted from your friends,
> Speak harshly, and you'll hear unpleasant things,
> From worthless chatter, nothing you say will command respect,
> Covet things, and all your hopes will be shattered,

Harbor malice, and fear will be your lot,
From holding wrong views, you'll meet wrong views.[79]

### ACTIONS SIMILAR TO THE CAUSE

Having performed certain actions in past lives, one subsequently takes birth as a being who enjoys and indulges in those deeds, as is explained in the *Hundred Parables on Action:*

> From making a habit of negative actions and behavior, one again takes birth adopting negative actions, indulging in negative deeds, and following negative ways.

### The Environmental Effect

This is the effect that ripens as one's environment. It includes the following effects. As a result of one's having taken life, grain will be less nourishing, medicines less effective, and so on. As a result of one's having stolen, the harvests will fail. Sexual misconduct will result in a clammy environment thick with dust, mist, and rain. From lying, one will end up in filthy, foul smelling surroundings. As a result of sowing discord, the country around one will be a barren wilderness broken up by ravines. As a consequence of harsh words, the plains will be arid, thorny, and infertile. Worthless chatter will result in the four seasons being disrupted. As a result of covetousness, grain will be meager and of poor quality. Harmful intent will lead to delicious, nourishing food becoming bitter and unnourishing. On account of wrong views, grain will be scarce or completely unobtainable. The effect similar to the cause and the environmental effect occur unpredictably, either in the same life or in subsequent lives.

## B. Reflecting on positive actions to be accomplished

Positive actions refer in general to antidotes, which are inconceivable in number—the 84,000 teachings and so forth—but they can be summarized very roughly as consciously rejecting the ten negative actions described above and then acting out that decision to reject them by physically and verbally turning away from them. There are therefore ten such actions, determined by what they accomplish and how they are accomplished. The three physical positive acts are to protect beings' lives, to give generously without attachment, and to observe pure conduct.* The four verbal positive acts are to tell the truth, to reconcile parties in disagreement, to speak gently and good-naturedly, and to talk about others' good qualities. The three mental positive acts are to be satisfied with what one has, to think lovingly of others, and to have confidence in the law of cause and effect. The Buddha himself spoke of ten positive actions, as we find in the *Middle Sutra of Transcendent Wisdom:*

I too have abandoned the taking of life . . .

and so on. And in the *Jewel Garland* we read:

Not to take life, to avoid stealing,
To keep away from others' wives,
To observe perfect restraint as regards lying,
Sowing discord, harsh words, and worthless chatter,
And to abandon attachment, malice,
And the view of nihilism[80]—
These comprise the tenfold path of positive action.

As well as these, there are ten positive actions determined in relation to the training in the precepts. *Distinguishing the Middle from Extremes* describes them thus:

Copying the scriptures, making offerings, charity,
Listening, reading, memorizing,
Teaching, reciting,
Reflecting, and meditating—
These ten activities
Yield boundless stores of merit.[81]

As to a common method for applying all these to oneself, there are the ten transcendent perfections—generosity and so on.

You should be eager to perform these positive actions—never disdain even the most insignificant of them. In this respect, what do we mean by rejecting the ten negative actions consciously? It entails recognizing the fault in doing them and thus never ever feeling any desire to perform them. As for physically and verbally turning away from them, this is not only a question of never committing the ten negative actions generally. It may

---

* "Pure conduct" (Tib. *tshang spyod*) is frequently used to imply celibacy.

happen that as far as your present circumstances are concerned, you have a lot to gain from doing them, without any effort involved. Nevertheless, you should remind yourself that you have consciously rejected them and thus be incapable of undertaking such actions. In avoiding the seven physical and verbal negative acts, you must have both of these two aspects;* avoiding the three mental acts simply entails giving them up mentally.

To think of negative actions as wrong constitutes the decision to avoid them. The knowledge that they are wrong is undeluded relative knowledge. It is the antidote to them, and the essence of discipline. If our decision to avoid negative actions is very powerful, even if sleepiness, dullness, distraction, and so forth intervene, we will recognize the circumstances in which we could perform negative activities and will thus be prevented from doing them. This happens through the force of the seed, that is, the power of our former decisions to avoid negative actions. Thus, the ten positive actions include that seed, the decision to avoid the ten negative actions.

To sum up, not only should you make the decision to avoid negative actions, but you should also wholeheartedly practice all kinds of physical and verbal actions that have a virtuous motivation—physical acts like prostrations, circumambulations, offerings, and general activities for the benefit of the Dharma and beings; and verbal acts like reciting praises and mantras, and anything you might say for the sake of the Dharma and beings. And as far as the mind is concerned, you should earnestly give rise to any naturally virtuous states of mind such as faith, devotion, determination to be free, love, compassion, bodhichitta, and meditation. As it is said,

> Without attachment, aversion, or bewilderment,
> Actions thus engendered are positive.

## The Results of Positive Actions

The results of these positive actions can be divided into three: the fully ripened effect, the effect similar to the cause, and the environmental effect.

### The Fully Ripened Effect

Positive actions may be powerful, less powerful, or weak, depending on whether or not, in their preparation, actual execution, and conclusion,

---

*I.e., mental rejection and physical and verbal restraint.

they have been backed by a positive attitude. It is taught in the sutras that the most powerful positive acts result in rebirth as a god in the higher worlds, less powerful ones as a god in the world of desire, and weak ones as a human being; while acts that are positive but performed with an impure attitude, for example, result in rebirth as a demigod.

## The Effect Similar to the Cause

This is the opposite of the effect similar to the cause described earlier for the ten negative actions, as we find in the *Jewel Garland:*

> A long life, riches, and no enemies,
> Praises, great renown, and pleasant words,
> Words that are respected, wishes accomplished,
> A happy frame of mind, a burgeoning intellect—
> These are the ten effects of virtue similar to the cause.

## The Environmental Effect

The same text describes this as follows:

> Nourishing grains and effective medicines, good harvests,
> Pleasant surroundings, level land, fertile fields,
> The grass and trees grow, the seasons are timely,
> The grain is fat, food delicious, and fruits luxuriant.
> Such are the environmental effects of the ten positive acts.

And,

> Through these practices, one is liberated
> From the hells, and the hungry-spirit and animal realms.
> One will obtain abundant happiness, glory, and dominion
> Among gods and human beings.
> Concentrations, boundless attitudes, and formless meditations
> Will lead one to experience the bliss of Brahma and others.

An action that is performed with a positive attitude throughout its preparation, actual execution, and conclusion can only be a wholly positive action, and it can therefore only give happiness as its fully ripened effect. On the other hand, actions that are negative in their intention and positive in their application (for example, acts of charity performed out of a desire for public esteem) and actions that are positive in their intention and negative in their application (for example, beating someone or saying unpleasant things to him with a desire to help him) produce a mixture of happiness and suffering. Train, therefore, in accomplishing only wholly positive actions, without getting discouraged or weary, like a farmer at work. Train in virtuous activities on a vast scale, courageously and without losing heart, like a brave man going into battle. Train without respite, like a whirling firebrand going round and round.*

## C. Transforming indeterminate actions into positive ones

Indeterminate actions are ones that are not motivated by a positive or negative attitude, and whose result cannot be predicted as happiness or suffering. They include acts such as moving about and eating. Whichever of these we do, they have no real benefit and merely serve to pass the time. It is therefore important to transform them into positive actions. So infuse all your actions of body, speech, and mind with bodhichitta, thinking: "When I am doing things like eating and drinking or walking, they do not produce any result: they will not lead me to gain liberation from cyclic existence. They are pointless. What a waste! Now I will definitely transform them into something virtuous." As we read in the *Four Hundred,*

> For those who have the Bodhisattva's intention,
> All their actions, whether positive or negative,
> Are turned to perfect virtue.
> Why? On account of that intention.

And in *The Way of the Bodhisattva:*

> Henceforth a great and unremitting stream,
> A strength of wholesome merit,
> Even during sleep and inattention,
> Rises equal to the vastness of the sky.[82]

So rather than continuing to be an external observer, turn the vital force of your practice inward and make whatever you do positive and beneficial, carrying it right through to the end.

---

* I.e., like the continuous circle of light that is seen when someone whirls a firebrand or torch around in the dark.

### III. Summary of key points: the Four Truths

"Truth" means something that does not deceive. There is what we call the "truth of cyclic existence," which is that the appearances we perceive as the three worlds are results arising interdependently from their causes (actions and afflictive emotions): they appear through the unfailing power of the law of cause and effect. And there is what we call the "sublime truth," which is that through one's efforts aimed at enlightenment, one will unfailingly, as the result of that cause, attain the state of perfect liberation. Everything in samsara and nirvana can generally be included in the Four Truths, and there is nothing anyone seeking liberation needs to practice that is not included in these Four Truths. They concern the origin, suffering, the path, and cessation.

## A. The truth of the origin

Although the actual condition of the ground, which is beyond expression, being indescribable and inconceivable, is emptiness, we fail to recognize that state on account of innate ignorance. And because of the ignorance of artificial imputations, we make distinctions and consider the aggregates to be a self. This is delusion. Once we start considering the aggregates to be a self, attachment arises in relation to things that agree with us, aversion arises in relation to things that do not agree with us, and bewilderment arises in relation to things that neither agree nor disagree. In dependence on these three poisons, the five poisons come into being. These are what we call "thoughts based on total affliction" and from them all actions are produced, just as from the earth in summer, which is the source of all that grows. Actions are of many different kinds, but those that propel us in cyclic existence can be condensed into three: nonvirtuous acts, virtuous acts, and unwavering acts.* Of these, the first throw us into the lower realms, the second take us to happy states in the world of desire, and the third lead us to the two higher worlds. The different categories of these actions have been explained above. When afflictive

---

*Unwavering act (Tib. *mi gyo ba'i las*): an action, in the form of a profound state of meditative concentration (but devoid of bodhichitta), that invariably results in rebirth in the world of form or the formless world. The results of meritorious or positive actions (*bsod nams*) and nonmeritorious or negative actions (*bsod nam ma yin pa*), on the other hand, are dependent on conditions and therefore it is not possible to say with certainty exactly how they will ripen.

emotions, which are the root of cyclic existence, arise in one's mind, therefore, it is very important to seize hold of the antidote and to repulse them. As Padampa Sangye says,

> When afflictive emotions arise, if you do not bring the antidote
>    to bear,
> People of Tingri, you'll have lost the whole reason for the Dharma.

## B. The truth of suffering

While the origin or cause is actions related to the afflictive emotions (the three and five poisons), their result is wandering in the three worlds of cyclic existence, constantly weakened and tormented as we ceaselessly experience the deeds and sufferings of the six classes of beings. In the *Transmitted Distinctions Regarding the Vinaya* we read:

> There's no sweet fragrance in a swamp of filth,
> No happiness, likewise, in the six realms.
> No coolness is there in a pit of blazing coals,
> And nowhere in existence is there any joy.

In short, although the nature of all beings' minds is clear light, which is the essence of Buddhahood, it has become obscured by the adventitious stains of incorrect thinking. Motivated by thoughts of this kind, beings indulge in tainted deeds, thus producing the aggregates, constituents, and senses-and-fields of cyclic existence,* as explained in the *Sublime Continuum:*

> Improper use of the mind
> Gives rise to actions and afflictive emotions.
> From the water of actions and afflictive emotions
> The aggregates, constituents, and senses-and-fields arise.[83]

And the different positive and negative actions produce the aggregates in the respective higher and lower realms, as is stated in the *Jewel Garland:*

> From negative actions come all suffering,
> And likewise all the lower realms.
> From positive acts come all the higher realms
> And constant happiness.

---

*That is, they produce the psychophysical components and experiences that make up beings' perceptions in cyclic existence. See glossary for explanations of these terms.

Remind yourself, therefore, of the defects of cyclic existence described earlier so that you feel a strong inclination to perform positive actions, and thus inspired, try to practice them as much as you can, for as *The Way of the Bodhisattva* says,

> If my acts are good, sincerely intended,
> Then no matter where I turn my steps,
> The merit gained will honor me
> With its resulting benefits.[84]

## C. The truth of the path

While the causal condition for the path is the Buddha-nature,* the dominant condition is the sublime teacher, because the path comes about through practicing his or her teachings, and realization of the ground *as it is* depends on the teacher. The actual practice of the path depends on the individual; the path itself is virtue that combines skillful means and wisdom and serves as the gateway to liberation. It is said in the sutras:

> Wisdom accompanied by skillful means is the path.
> Skillful means accompanied by wisdom is the path.

And in the Abhidharma texts we find:

> The path, in brief, is to fully recognize suffering, to abandon the origin of suffering, to realize cessation, and to follow the path of meditation.

It is by energetically and single-mindedly training in the general and specific stages of the path that comprise the Buddha's doctrine, matching them to one's own individual capacity, that one will gradually travel the paths of accumulation, joining, seeing, and meditation, all the way to the end. For the actual attainment of the result depends on practice.

## D. The truth of cessation

The ground in which everything in cyclic existence ceases is emptiness. This is the actual condition of all phenomena, the absolute nature,

---

*Tib. *rigs,* lit. "family" or "potential," meaning in this context the Buddha-nature (Tib. *de gshegs snying po,* Skt. *tathagatagarbha*) present in every sentient being.

thusness, completely free of all conceptual extremes such as existence, nonexistence, and so on. Since the absolute nature, the state of emptiness, pervades all other phenomena, the absolute nature and phenomena are not separate entities. But since the uncompounded absolute nature and compounded phenomena are incompatible in their characteristics, neither are they a single entity. The unchanging absolute space that transcends the extremes of eternalism, nihilism, and so forth, is emptiness. By practicing the path that leads to the realization of that emptiness, all paths motivated by the truth of the origin—namely the three and five poisons—cease and one attains the result, the cessation of the suffering aggregate and the suffering related to it.* In short, the afflictive emotions and their seeds that cover awareness fade and subside into the absolute space and are thus eliminated. This state of elimination† is the primal wisdom of emptiness, the ground of cessation: it is the extraordinary truth of cessation, and what we call the attainment of liberation and nirvana. Thus it has been taught that the nature of the truth of suffering is the truth of cessation, and that the nature of the truth of the origin is the truth of the path; cessation and the path, elimination and realization, are said to be essentially inseparable.

Let us illustrate this with an example. Indulging in unwholesome food and behavior that make one ill is the origin. Being tormented by the aches and pains of illness is suffering. Being careful about one's diet and behavior and following the treatment is the truth of the path. Curing the illness and returning to good health is the truth of cessation.

Here, now, is an analogy of this example: Miserliness and preventing others from being charitable is the origin. Poverty and deprivation is suffering. Making offerings and gifts of charity is the truth of the path. And being consequently rid of future suffering from poverty is the truth of cessation. This is how you should understand and apply the process of cause and effect.

———————

Having thus reflected on the manner in which causes unfailingly give rise to effects, you should perform all kinds of positive action and abandon all forms of negative action. Never do anything harmful, whether on your own account or anyone else's. Even for the sake of your teachers or the

———————

* The suffering aggregate (Tib. *sdug bsngal gyi phung po*) refers to the body.
† Tib. *spangs pa,* also "riddance," that is, the elimination of all factors obscuring or preventing enlightenment.

Three Jewels, it is wrong to do negative actions: it is not they who will receive the fully ripened effect of such deeds as their allotted fate, as *Letter to a Friend* tells us:

> Perform no evil, even for the sake
> Of brahmins, monks and gods, or honored guests,
> Your father, mother, queen, or for your court.
> No share they'll take of its infernal fruit.
> Although performing wrong and evil deeds
> Does not at once, like swords, create a gash,
> When death arrives, those evil acts will show:
> Their fruit, whatever it may be, will be revealed.[85]

Now, to turn away from negative deeds, strengthen your positive actions, and thus accomplish liberation, there is nothing anyone else can do to take your place or help you out. It is you alone who have to give up negative actions and undertake positive ones, as *Letter to a Friend* says:

> Freedom will depend on you alone
> And there is no one else, no friend can help.
> Bearing study, discipline, and concentration,
> Bring diligence to the Four Noble Truths.[86]

So, applying all the teachings on the workings of cause and effect to your own stream of being, practice adoption and avoidance correctly, and thus do whatever you can to make this life meaningful. Thinking, "That I might be able to do so, precious teacher, in you I put my trust!" pray earnestly as follows:

> Positive and negative actions ripen unfailingly:
> May I be skillful and disciplined in adopting good and
>     shunning evil.
> As I pray to you, precious teacher,
> Bless me, incomparably kind lord.

If we fail to acquire some genuine feeling for these four common preliminary practices, all the practice we do in the generation and perfection phases of the main practice will do no more than reinforce the eight ordinary concerns, and the Dharma will be of no benefit. Nowadays we all boast that we are Dharma practitioners, but we have not severed our attachment to the things of this life, we have not turned our minds away from cyclic existence, we have not relinquished even the smallest of our desires—for friends and relations, entourage, servants, food and clothes, pleasant conversation, and the like. As a result, any positive activities we undertake are not really effective. Our minds and the Dharma go different ways. We manage to find fault in others while failing to consider our own defects. We become puffed up with pride at the smallest good quality in ourselves. Our minds are distracted by honors and entertainments. We get involved in pointless conversations and all sorts of different activities. We count up months and years of practice without any diminution in our afflictive emotions. We think we can combine the Dharma and worldly goals, but we end up not being successful at anything at all. Right from the start, we have been completely impervious to any determination to be free.

The learned and accomplished beings of the past used to say that the preliminaries are even more profound than the main practice. What they meant was that the root of Dharma depends on relinquishing the things of this life. So rather than looking outside ourselves, we should make an effort to blend our minds and the Dharma inside. Then, when a few good qualities related to the Dharma appear within us, we will understand how profound these instructions are, and our confidence in the Dharma will grow. At that time, we will remember our teacher's compassion and kindness, and devotion will automatically well up in us. It is thus that all the qualities of the path will spontaneously and effortlessly emerge.

This completes the brief explanation of the four practices that cultivate the field of one's mindstream and turn one's thoughts away from cyclic existence.

# The Uncommon, Special Preliminaries That Sow the Seeds of the Profound Path in Five Stages

*Chapter Nine: Taking refuge, the entrance to the path*

*Chapter Ten: Arousing the mind set on supreme enlightenment, the root of the whole path*

*Chapter Eleven: Purifying negative actions and obscurations, which are unfavorable conditions on the path*

*Chapter Twelve: Gathering the accumulations, which are favorable conditions on the path*

*Chapter Thirteen: Training in Guru Yoga and receiving the teacher's blessings, the heart of the whole path*

# CHAPTER NINE

# Taking Refuge, the Entrance to the Path

THIS CHAPTER ON HOW TO GO FOR REFUGE, THE ENTRANCE
to all paths, has two sections, the first mentioning a few general points to
be understood, and the second consisting of instructions on the points of
the training in this case.* The former is further divided into a presentation
of refuge, the entrance; and the nature and categories of faith, which is
what makes us take that entrance.

## I. General points to be understood

### A. Taking refuge, the entrance

This section has seven parts: the reasons one needs to take refuge, identifying the object of refuge, the duration for which one takes refuge, the
manner in which one is protected, the ritual for taking the refuge vow,
the precepts of taking refuge, and the benefits of taking refuge.

### *1. The reasons one needs to take refuge*

The master Vimalamitra says:

> Out of fear and mindfulness of the qualities we go.[87]

The reason one needs to go for refuge is that one is subject to fear. When
one has nothing to fear and is free to make one's own choices and decisions, one obviously does not need to seek protection from anyone.

---

*The second section in this and each of the following chapters describes the specific
details of the practice according to *Heart Essence of the Dakini.*

However, since time without beginning we have been lost in the darkness of ignorance, imprisoned in the fearful dungeon that is cyclic existence, and from this nothing except the Three Precious Jewels is able to protect us. So it is in order to be protected from such fear that we go for refuge, keeping in mind their qualities in having the power to protect us.

There are three kinds of individuals who go for refuge. Beings of modest capacity take refuge as if to acquire an escort, through fear of the lower realms and a desire to obtain, as a result, the happiness of the higher realms. Their principal motives are this fear and desire. The "family" to which such individuals belong includes Buddhists and non-Buddhists, whether or not they adhere to a particular philosophical school.

Beings of middling capacity take refuge out of fear of cyclic existence and a desire to attain, for themselves alone, liberation in the blissful state of nirvana. In addition to fear and desire, their principal motive is faith. They belong to the families of Listeners and Solitary Realizers.

Beings of greater capacity take refuge because they are afraid of samsara and nirvana, and because they wish to attain the nondwelling state beyond suffering.* In addition to fear, desire, and faith, their principal motive is compassion. They belong to the family of the Great Vehicle.

As we read in the *Lamp for the Path,*

> Know that those who strive,
> By any means, and for their own sake,
> Simply to be happy in cyclic existence
> Are beings of the lowest capacity.
> Those who turn their backs on happiness in cyclic existence
> And draw away from evil deeds,
> Who merely strive for their own peace,
> Are known as middling beings.
> Those who, through the suffering they have understood
>      in themselves,
> Yearn for the complete exhaustion
> Of all the suffering of others—
> Such beings are supreme.

There is another reason for taking refuge, as Lord Atisha points out:

---

*Tib. *mi gnas pa'i myang 'das,* the nirvana that is beyond the extremes of samsara and nirvana (or "existence and peace").

All may have the vows
Excepting those who have not taken refuge.[88]

In other words, the refuge is the indispensable basis for all vows. Buddhists and non-Buddhists are classified as such according to whether or not they have taken refuge, and without having taken refuge there is no way one can be freed from cyclic existence.

## 2. Identifying the object of refuge

There are two kinds of refuge object: causal and resultant.

### a. THE CAUSAL OBJECT OF REFUGE

The causal object of refuge has two aspects, namely the refuge objects of the common vehicles and the particular refuge objects of the Mantra Vehicle.

### i. The refuge objects of the common vehicles

These comprise worldly and supramundane objects of refuge. The former are divided into inferior objects and supreme objects of refuge.

### (1) Worldly objects of refuge

### (a) Inferior refuges

Inferior refuges include inanimate things such as mountains and fortresses, powerful nonhuman beings such as gods, and rulers and other influential human beings. Because they are unable to protect us from cyclic existence, they are inferior objects of refuge, for they themselves have not gained freedom from the prison of cyclic existence. As we read in the sutras,

> People who are fearful and afraid
> Mostly seek refuge in mountains,
> Forests, and trees.
> These are not the best refuge,
> For by relying on such refuges
> One will not be freed from all kinds of fear.

### (b) Supreme refuges

These refer to the Three Jewels taken as objects of refuge by worldly people who merely want to be protected from fear and to better their lot.

## (2) Supramundane objects of refuge

The objects of refuge for those who strive for complete liberation are the Three Jewels. The Three Jewels have the power temporarily to protect us from the fears of cyclic existence and ultimately to establish us in ultimate excellence, and they are therefore an infallible refuge, for as the Great Master has said,

> Samsaric lords, however good, will let us down.
> As objects of refuge, the Three Jewels will never fail.

The Three Jewels are identified differently according to the different categories of greater and lesser vehicles. Here, in the unsurpassable tradition of the Great Vehicle, there are three categories of object: objects in which realization is manifest, those that are sources of inspiration, and the absolute object of refuge.

## (a) Objects in which realization is manifest

These are:

- the Jewel of the Buddha who embodies the four bodies and five wisdoms, who is endowed with the two purities* and is the ultimate fulfillment of the twofold goal.
- the Dharma of realization and transmission—the cessation and path included in the truth of untainted complete purity, and the Excellent Words that express it as perceptible words and letters.†
- the Sangha—the true Sangha of sublime Bodhisattvas on the great levels,‡ children of the Buddha endowed with the qualities of realization and liberation; and the surrogate Sangha of beings following the Great Vehicle on the paths of accumulation and joining and of sublime Listeners and Solitary Realizers following the Basic Vehicle.

---

*The two purities are original purity (*rang bzhin ye dag*), which is the Buddha-nature in all beings, and purity from all adventitious stains (*blo bur phral dag*). Only a Buddha has this second purity as well.

† The Dharma of realization is the subject that is described by the Dharma of transmission, i.e., the Buddha's teachings.

‡ Tib. *sa chen po*, the three pure Bodhisattva levels: the eighth, ninth, and tenth.

## (b) Sources of inspiration

- all fashioned images representing the Buddha, for example, drawings or paintings and statues;
- books containing the Dharma, the Buddha's teaching, in the form of letters;
- and the Sangha of ordinary beings following the path—the lesser Sangha of lay practitioners and intermediate ordinees,* and the so-called greater Sangha of fully ordained monks, four such taken together being called an assembly of the Sangha. There is also the Sangha of knowledge holders comprising those, whether monks or lay practitioners, who are following the path of the Mantra Vehicle and abide by the commitments. Whichever discipline they observe, these are all fields† by which beings may acquire merit.

## (c) The absolute object of refuge

The ultimate refuge is the Buddha alone. Neither of the other two is the ultimate refuge, for the following reasons. Once one has seen the truth, the teachings that make up the Dharma of transmission have to be discarded. The Dharma of realization in the minds of Bodhisattvas, Listeners, and Solitary Realizers is subject to improvement and is therefore impermanent and deceptive. As for the Sangha, since its members are themselves still on the path to be trodden, they do not have the ultimate qualities; and since they are unable to eliminate their latent tendencies and the obscurations particular to their respective levels without depending on the Buddha, they still have fear. As we read in the *Sublime Continuum,*

> One will be abandoned, one is deceptive by nature,
> And one does not have and is still afraid. For these reasons
> The two kinds of Dharma and the assembly of sublime beings
> Are not the highest, everlasting refuge.
> Ultimately, the refuge of beings
> Is the Buddha alone, because,

the Buddha being none other than the body of truth,

---

*Tib. *dge tshul,* Skt. *shramanera.* An intermediate ordination between lay followers who take the four basic vows and fully ordained monks and nuns. See glossary, *intermediate ordinee.*
† See glossary for an explanation of the term "field" (Tib. *zhing*).

the Capable One embodies the teachings
And that is the final goal of the community too.[89]

## ii. The particular refuge objects of the Mantra Vehicle

According to the tradition of the Diamond Mantra Vehicle there are, in addition to the above, the particular Three Jewels: the teacher, the object from whom one receives blessings; the *yidam*, from whom one receives accomplishments; and the dakinis and Dharma protectors, who are charged with accomplishing the activities. Furthermore, we distinguish the teachers as the embodiments of all Three Jewels (their bodies as the Sangha, their speech as the Dharma, and their minds as the Buddha), the *yidam* deities manifesting in their peaceful and wrathful forms as the nature of the Buddha in the body of perfect enjoyment and body of manifestation, their tantras as the extraordinary Dharma, and the dakinis and Dharma protectors as the special Sangha. In this way, we take them as our refuge. The Great Master expresses it thus:

> The Lord Teacher, root of blessings,
> Yidam deity, source of accomplishments,
> Dakinis, who perfectly grant the blessings.*

## b. THE RESULTANT OBJECT OF REFUGE

One's own mind, which is the union of emptiness and clarity, embodying the essential nature, natural expression, and compassion, present from the very beginning, is the nature of the Three Jewels. In order to realize that, one adopts the causal refuge or, most importantly, rather than looking for refuge elsewhere (for it is spontaneously present within oneself), one settles naturally in the uncontrived, unchanging state of one's own mind without adopting or rejecting anything. This is the resultant refuge. The *Accomplishment of Wisdom* says:

> The mind free of anything to be purified and anything
>    to be attained is the Buddha,
> Its unchanging nature, free from stains, is the Dharma,
> Its qualities, spontaneously complete and perfect, are
>    the Sangha.
> For this reason it is the nature of one's own mind that
>    is supreme.

---

*In other words, they fulfill the activities.

Regarding the etymology of the term "Jewels" in this context, the word "Jewel" (*ratna* in Sanskrit) was translated* as "rare and supreme" on account of its preciousness and its six analogous features, as presented in the *Sublime Continuum:*

> Because they occur rarely, are flawless,
> Have power, are an ornament for the world,
> Are supreme, and do not change,
> They are indeed rare and supreme.[90]

These six features analogous to those of a jewel are explained as follows:

- The Three Jewels' occurrence is rare because beings in the world who have not given rise to sources of good will not come across them even in many, many kalpas.
- They are immaculate because they are entirely unstained by faults.
- They are powerful† because they possess inconceivably powerful qualities such as the six kinds of preternatural knowledge,‡ and can therefore dispel the troubles of the world.
- They ornament the world because they are the source of all beings' positive wishes.
- They are supreme, superior to counterfeit jewels, because they have supramundane qualities.
- They are unchanging, unaffected by circumstances such as praise or criticism, because theirs is the uncompounded absolute nature.

The Three Jewels' excellent qualities can also be found in greater detail in texts such as the *Sutra Remembering the Three Jewels.*

## 3. The duration for which one takes refuge

Beings take refuge for different lengths of time. In general, worldly people take refuge until they have achieved their own minor goals, for this life or the next. Listeners and Solitary Realizers take refuge for as long as they live. In our case, that of the Great Vehicle, we take refuge until we attain enlightenment, as we read in *The Way of the Bodhisattva:*

> Until the essence of enlightenment is reached.[91]

---

* I.e., translated by the early translators, from Sanskrit to Tibetan.
† A jewel's power lies in its hardness and ability to cut through other stones.
‡ See glossary, *six kinds of preternatural knowledge.*

### 4. The manner in which one is protected

The Buddha protects us as the ultimate refuge and guide. The Dharma protects in serving as the path, because practicing what the Buddha taught frees us from fear. The Sangha protects us in acting as a companion leading the way. In the Secret Mantra Vehicle, the teacher performs all the activities of the Three Jewels and is therefore the embodiment of all Three Jewels, as the *Tantra of the Emergence of Chakrasamvara* says:

> The Teacher is the Buddha, the Teacher is the Dharma,
> Likewise, the Teacher is the Sangha:
> The Teacher is the glorious Diamond Being.

### 5. The ritual for taking the refuge vow

Initially one takes the vow from a spiritual friend, who is a pure object. Subsequently one takes refuge as the need arises and danger prompts one to do so, and six times a day, in either case visualizing the object of refuge in front of one and taking refuge.

### 6. The precepts of taking refuge

There are two parts: the actual precepts and the causes of the refuge ceasing. The actual precepts are divided into special precepts and general precepts, of which the former comprise precepts with regard to things one must avoid and precepts with regard to things one should do.

#### a. THE ACTUAL PRECEPTS

#### i. Special precepts

##### (1) Precepts with regard to things one must avoid

Having taken refuge in the Buddha, you should not put your hopes in worldly gods and rely on them as a refuge or pay homage to them. However, this does not preclude simply making offerings to them on occasion in order to entrust them with certain activities related to the Dharma.

After taking refuge in the Dharma, you must avoid doing anything harmful to beings, either in thought or in deed, such as beating them or tying them up. Instead you should be loving toward them.

Once you have taken refuge in the Sangha, you must not keep the company of those who hold non-Buddhist views or of people who, even if they claim to be Buddhists, have negative views and no confidence in the Three Jewels.

On this point the *Nirvana Sutra* says:

> Those who take refuge in the Buddha
> Are true followers of virtue:[92]
> They never take refuge
> In other gods.
> Those who take refuge in the sublime Dharma
> Are free of malice and harmful thoughts.
> Those who take refuge in the Sangha
> Will not keep the company of those who hold wrong views.

### (2) Precepts with regard to things one should do

If even a fragment of a Buddha image, half a verse of the sacred scriptures, or a yellow patch from the robe of a Sangha member[93] must be treated respectfully, it goes without saying how one should treat any other aspects of the Three Jewels. So having taken refuge in the Buddha, you must respect, and never disdain, a representation of the Buddha, whatever it is like. As we read in *Letter to a Friend,*

> The wise will always venerate
> Any Buddha statues, even made of wood.[94]

Once you have taken refuge in the Dharma, you must respect all books containing the Buddha's teachings and their commentaries, and avoid such things as criticizing them with sectarian intentions. The *Ear Ornament Sutra* declares:

> In the final period of five hundred years
> I will be present in the form of scriptures.
> Consider them as identical to me
> And show them due respect.

After taking refuge in the Sangha, you must respect not only pure monks and upholders of the three baskets but also anyone who retains merely the signs of ordination, and avoid any disdain or prejudice with regard to them. In the *Sutra That Inspires an Altruistic Attitude* we read:

> You who dwell among those who desire good qualities,
> Do not try to find fault in others.
> "I am especially sublime, I am the best!" —

> Do not develop such thoughts.
> Pride like this is the root of all carelessness,
> So never disrespect any monk as your inferior.

## ii. General precepts

These are fourfold: not to forsake the Three Jewels, whatever one might stand to gain; not to seek refuge elsewhere, whatever happens; to constantly remember their virtues and make offerings; and remembering the benefits, to take refuge six times a day.

### (1) Not to forsake the Three Jewels, whatever one might stand to gain

Do not forsake the Three Jewels for any reason, however important, whether to save your own life, for a kingdom, or for a reward. Doing so might procure a little comfort in this life, but nothing more, whereas by taking refuge in the Three Jewels you will accomplish all the virtues of higher rebirth and ultimate excellence. As we read in the Vinaya scriptures:

> Never forsake the Three Jewels to save your life, for a kingdom, or even just as a joke.

### (2) Not to seek refuge elsewhere, whatever happens

Whatever mishaps befall you—illness, unhappiness, and so on—place your trust exclusively in the Three Jewels and do not look for other, worldly, solutions. As Vimalamitra says,

> Now, whatever happens to you,
> Do not look for any other protector or refuge.[95]

You might wonder, in that case, whether it is wrong to resort to such things as ceremonies, mantra recitations, scripture recitations, prayers, and medical treatment when one is ill. But there is no fault in doing so, for these things are branches of the Jewel of the Dharma: they are not to be disdained but, rather, assiduously applied.

### (3) To constantly remember the virtues of the Three Jewels and make offerings

Forever calling to mind the excellent qualities of the Three Jewels, whatever you are doing, train in serving the Three Jewels. Wherever you are going, prostrate to the Buddha in that direction. Remembering the

Three Jewels' kindness, train in constantly making offerings to them, even offering them the first part of anything you eat or drink. Again, Vimalamitra says:

> With constant remembrance, offer
> Food of the best quality.[96]

### (4) Remembering the benefits, to take refuge six times a day

Keeping in mind the benefits of taking refuge, you should be sure to go for refuge six times—three times in the day and three times by night—or three times, or at the very least, once a day. On this point, Vimalamitra says:

> Constantly recite the refuge prayer,
> And encourage this, six times a day.[97]

Do as much as you can to induce other people as well to take refuge—your relatives, entourage, servants, and so on.

### b. THE CAUSES OF THE REFUGE CEASING

When one accomplishes the essence, attaining enlightenment as a Buddha, the time limit declared in the refuge ritual has expired,* so enlightenment is a nominal cause for abandoning the refuge. The causes for abandoning the refuge, in the true sense of the term, are: giving rise to wrong views and forsaking the Three Jewels; and being unable to keep the refuge precepts and giving back the vow.

Breaking a few of the precepts, for instance by paying homage to other gods, is known as "debasing the vow," and the negative consequences are numerous. One will be like a member of a corrupt dynasty and cease to be counted as a Buddhist. One will be like a merchant betrayed by his escort, and whatever one does, one will be afraid. Like a fresco on a wall falling to ruin, all one's vows and precepts will be easily destroyed. Like poor folk at the bottom of the social ladder with no friends for support, one will be easily oppressed by all kinds of violence. One will be like a common lawbreaker: having broken one's promise, one will be reborn in the lower realms. So, reflecting on the faults in breaking the precepts, regret and part from your breaches, resolving not to repeat them in future, and take the precepts again. This will restore your refuge vow.

---

*When one takes refuge, one says "Until the essence (or heart) of enlightenment is reached, I go for refuge . . ."

## 7. *The benefits of taking refuge*

There are seven benefits of taking refuge: one becomes a Buddhist, a follower of the Buddha; one will not fall into the lower realms; one becomes a support for all vows; one is not harmed by obstacles caused by humans and nonhumans; one has few illnesses and a long life; obscurations of actions performed in the past are purified; and one will swiftly attain Buddhahood through the completion of its cause, the two accumulations.

### a. THE BENEFIT THAT ONE BECOMES A BUDDHIST, A FOLLOWER OF THE BUDDHA

By renouncing the ways of non-Buddhists, who rely on Brahma and others for refuge, and taking the Three Jewels as one's object of refuge, one will be included in the ranks of Buddhists, as the wise have declared, for it is said:

> The difference between Buddhists and non-Buddhists is the refuge.

### b. THE BENEFIT THAT ONE WILL NOT FALL INTO THE LOWER REALMS

Taking refuge bars the entrance to the lower realms and places one, throughout one's series of lives, in the blissful states of the higher realms and liberation. It is said that the son of a god who was going to be reborn as a pig was prevented from doing so when he took refuge, as is related in the *Tale with a Sow,* which declares:

> Those who have taken refuge in the Buddha
> Will not go to the lower realms.[98]

### c. THE BENEFIT THAT ONE BECOMES A SUPPORT FOR ALL VOWS

Taking refuge reinforces our intention to attain nirvana, this being the reason for our taking vows, and it is therefore the basis of all vows, as the *Seventy Stanzas on Refuge* explains:

> A lay practitioner's going for refuge in the Three
> Is the root of the eight vows.*

---

* By taking refuge in the Three Jewels one becomes an *upasaka* (lit. "follower of virtue") or lay Buddhist practitioner. Without this basic vow of refuge, it is impossible to proceed to any of the eight forms of Buddhist ordination, those of male and female *upasakas* (who, in addition to the refuge vow, can take up to five vows, beginning with the vow

### d. THE BENEFIT THAT ONE WILL NOT BE HARMED BY OBSTACLES CAUSED BY HUMANS OR NONHUMANS

The manner in which taking refuge dispels all kinds of fear and danger is described in the *Supreme Victory Banner Sutra:*

> Monks, wherever you are—in solitary places, cemeteries, empty wastes, and the like—take refuge in the Three Jewels and you will be free from fear, suffering, and hair-raising experiences.

And in the *Essence of the Sun Sutra* we find:

> Beings who go for refuge in the Buddha
> Cannot be killed by ten million demons.
> Even if they have broken their vows and their minds are disturbed,
> They will surely go beyond birth.

### e. THE BENEFIT THAT ONE WILL HAVE FEW ILLNESSES AND A LONG LIFE

It is said that as a result of taking refuge, one will be less affected by illnesses related to past deeds and obstacles, and one will live a long life of abundance and splendor, as we find in *Ornament of the Sutras:*

> Against all kinds of negative actions,
> Aging, illness, and death
> The Buddha gives complete protection.
> Because he protects from all kinds of harm,
> From the lower realms and wrong paths,
> From the view of the transitory composite,* and from
>     lesser vehicles,
> He is the supreme refuge.[99]

### f. THE BENEFIT THAT THE OBSCURATIONS OF DEEDS PERFORMED IN THE PAST WILL BE PURIFIED

Every single one of the obscurations from deeds accumulated in the past will diminish and be exhausted. And even those who have committed

---

not to kill), of male and female intermediate ordinees (*shramaneras*), of fully ordained monks and nuns (*bhikshus* and *bhikshunis*), of woman novices or probationer nuns, and of holders of the twenty-four hour (*upavasa*) vow.

*The fundamental erroneous view in which the five aggregates (see glossary), which are transitory and composite, are regarded as being a permanent, unitary "I" and "mine."

crimes with immediate retribution (as did Devadatta, Ajatashatru, and others) will, by taking refuge in the Three Jewels, be liberated from the lower realms, as has been related in the scriptures.[100]

### g. The benefit that by completing its cause, the two accumulations, one will swiftly attain Buddhahood

In the soil of faith, watered by the rain of the two accumulations, the seed of the enlightened potential grows and ripens into the harvest of Buddhahood, as the *Nirvana Sutra* tells us:

> Those who take refuge in the Three
> Will acquire the supreme accumulations of merit
>     and wisdom,
> Propagate the Buddha's teaching in the world,
> And thereby attain Buddhahood.

And when the Buddha said, in the *White Lotus Sutra of Compassion,*

> Those who have entered this my doctrine, even lay practitioners or those who assume the appearance of monks, will in this same Excellent Kalpa attain the full nirvana without residue in the absolute space, without a single exception,

he was referring to beings who have taken refuge. Again in the *Sutra of the Immaculate* he said:

> If the merit of taking refuge were to possess form, it would fill the whole of space and still there would be more.

And in the *Condensed Transcendent Wisdom:*

> If the merit of taking refuge were to take form,
> The three worlds would be too small to contain it.
> How could one ever measure that treasure of water,
> The great ocean, in cupfuls?

There is no end to the explanations the Buddha gave on this. Taking refuge will create the dependent connection through which you will gradually come to accomplish ultimate Buddhahood, turn the Wheel of the Dharma, and gather around you a vast Sangha of Nonreturners.

## B. The nature and categories of faith, which is what makes one take the entrance of refuge

There are seven parts: the reason one needs to develop faith, categories of faith, how to cultivate faith, the causes and conditions that make faith grow or decrease, the particular characteristics of faith, the fault in not having faith, and the benefits of cultivating faith.

### 1. The reason one needs to develop faith

The root of taking refuge and of every other kind of virtuous practice is faith, and faith alone. So right from the start, it is very important to train in cultivating faith. As the *Jewel Garland* points out,

> Because one has faith, one relies on Dharma;
> Because one has wisdom, one has perfect understanding.
> Of these two, wisdom is the chief,
> But faith it is that must come first.[101]

And the *Sublime Continuum* says:

> The absolute truth of the self-arisen state
> Is to be realized through faith.[102]

### 2. Categories of faith

The essence of faith is a clear, untroubled mind, aware of what should be adopted and what should be avoided. And for this there are three categories: vivid faith, eager faith, and confident faith.

#### a. VIVID FAITH

This is the clear, fresh state brought about by the feeling of joy and devotion untainted by guile that results from seeing or hearing of the wondrous qualities of sublime beings. Like the water-purifying gem that renders turbid water limpid, it clears away all negative thoughts.

#### b. EAGER FAITH[103]

With this kind of faith, one yearns to be rid of the sufferings of cyclic existence; one yearns to attain liberation and enlightenment. And to those two ends, one is eager to give up what is wrong and adopt what is right.

Eager faith induces us to devote ourselves to the sublime Dharma in much the same way that a desire for wealth is what makes people pursue riches.

### c. CONFIDENT FAITH

Confident faith implies confidence that cyclic existence and its causes are to be eliminated, confidence that nirvana and its causes are to be adopted, and confidence that indeterminate states are pointless. Just as confidence in a future harvest induces a farmer to till the soil, confidence that the sublime Dharma will never fail us gives us the necessary conviction to practice without doubting and hesitating.

### *3. How to cultivate faith*

Unless we have faith, however many other good qualities we might have, they will not be of much use to us—as though we were very beautiful, but blind. So we have to make an effort to develop faith—by meditating on impermanence four times a day, by reflecting minutely on actions and their effects, by reflecting on the positive aspects of everything, by reflecting on how rare the Dharma is, by thinking of our teacher's kindness, by thinking of our spiritual brothers and sisters with pure perception, and by thinking of the excellent qualities of the Buddha. It is important to consider that other people are—all of them—marvelous, and to be free of partiality and notions of high or low status, thus making a habit of faith and taming your own mind.

The Omniscient Dharma Lord* said:

> Unless you do all you can to develop faith,
> You will never attain perfection,
> But will wander constantly in cyclic existence.
> Therefore, whomever you are following,
> Make every effort to cultivate faith.

In the first place, you should be shrewd in seeking a teacher and the teaching—begin by examining the sublime beings. Once you have found a teacher, train yourself in following him or her with devotion. For this there are ten aspects. Your devotion should be unchanging, like Mount Meru. Like the sun, it should not wax or wane. It should be like the ocean,

---

* "The Omniscient Dharma Lord" (Tib. *kun mkhyen chos rjes*) refers to Longchen Rabjam.

without surface or depth.* Like a mother it should never complain or expect to be thanked. It should be like space, without boundary or center; like the string of a bow, neither too taut nor too slack; like a boat or bridge, untiring and uncomplaining; like a great river, flowing unceasingly; like the sky, never prey to circumstances such as being influenced by others or scolded. And like the string of a prayer flag, it should be respectful, supple and adaptable, and embellished with reverence.

What are the signs that we have cultivated faith? We reject the deceptive appearances of cyclic existence like someone with nausea seeing food. We ache with devotion and longing for the teacher, like a small child yearning for its mother. We throw ourselves enthusiastically into study and reflection, like a thirsty person longing for water. We treasure our precepts like a poor person who has found some gold or a turquoise. We delight in practicing virtuous activities like a merchant travelling to an island of gold. Our faith and interest in all the different vehicles are like those of a keen shopper arriving at a market. It is when these signs occur that the Dharma has tamed our mind and the teachings and the individual have not gone different ways.

### 4. The causes and conditions that make faith grow or decrease

This section is divided into two parts: using the causes that increase faith to make it grow; and recognizing and eliminating the conditions that make faith decrease.

#### a. USING THE CAUSES THAT INCREASE FAITH TO MAKE IT GROW

How can we increase our faith and devotion?

• By sincerely following a sublime being, a qualified teacher;
• by relying on special companions who have blended their minds with the teachings;
• by studying the profound sutras and tantras;
• by reflecting undistractedly on death;
• by reading or listening to stories that illustrate the law of cause and effect;
• and by doing longer sessions than before of meditation and practice on the profound teachings.

---

*Tib. *kha gting med pa,* i.e., the same throughout, in all circumstances.

As the *Sutra of the Inconceivable Secrets* says:

> Because of faith, one does not engage in negative activities, and one performs the activities praised by the sublime beings.

Train in each of the above so that your devotion increases daily.

## b. Recognizing and eliminating the conditions that make faith decrease

It is said that when we begin practicing the sublime Dharma, negative forces create obstacles, and their "blessing" causes our faith to diminish. Signs that the demons have entered us are that we find fault in the spiritual friend, our teacher; we see defects in Dharma practitioners in general; we keep the company of ordinary people; we have less diligence in the practice; we indulge in pleasure heedlessly, without any moral principles; and our devotion and respect for the Three Jewels fades.

How can these be prevented? Reflecting on the excellent qualities of the teacher, the Three Jewels, and your spiritual companions, develop pure perception and respect for all who practice the Dharma. Tell yourself that seeing bad in other people is a sign that you yourself are impure: it is as if you were jaundiced and perceived conch shells as yellow. Remind yourself of the defects of the pleasures of the senses, and avoid befriending ordinary people. Recognize that a decrease in faith is a demon. As we read in the *Transcendent Wisdom:*

> Mara the demon comes in front of beginners and diverts even the devoted. He turns back even those practicing the activities of the Bodhisattvas.

## 5. *The particular characteristics of faith*

What are the particular characteristics of having faith? When one has faith, one is like a fertile field, in which the shoot of bodhichitta will sprout and grow. Faith is like a great ship crossing the river of cyclic existence. It is like a reliable escort protecting us from our enemies, the afflictive emotions. Like a good mount taking us to the land of liberation. Like a wish-fulfilling jewel accomplishing everything we desire. Like a mighty hero annihilating all that is nonvirtuous.

Faith is thus a sublime quality, and for this reason it is the first of the seven noble riches. People who have faith are especially exalted, and yet they are extremely rare, as the *Sutra of the Precious Lamp* points out:

Faith gives birth to delight in the Buddha's teaching,
Faith points the way to the city of happiness and excellence.
Faith banishes lack of opportunity, it is the best of all freedoms.
Faith turns one from the path of the demons,
Faith is what makes one attain Buddhahood.
Among the hosts of ordinary beings,
Rare are those who have such faith in the Dharma.

## 6. The fault in not having faith

People who lack faith are deprived of the good fortune of being able to practice the Dharma, and their not having faith is therefore an immeasurable defect. Just as a rock on the bottom of the ocean will never appear on the surface, without faith it is impossible to reach the dry land of liberation. Just as a ferry without a helmsman will never reach the other shore, without faith it is impossible to traverse the great river of suffering. Without faith, it is as impossible to nurture good qualities in one's being as it is for someone with no hands to pick up anything even if he were to find himself on an island of gold. Without faith, it is impossible for the shoot of bodhichitta to grow, for nothing can ever sprout from a burned seed. Without faith, one is like a blind person who finds himself in a temple: it is impossible to see the light of the Dharma. Without faith, however clever one is, one is trapped in the deep pit of cyclic existence: everything one does becomes an action that leads to cyclic existence, and it is impossible to ever attain the freedom of enlightenment. As the *Sutra of the Ten Qualities* puts it,

> From roasted seeds
> No greenery will sprout.
> In those who have no faith
> No virtue will appear.

## 7. The benefits of cultivating faith

There are boundless virtues in cultivating and increasing one's faith. It is the foundation for all virtuous practice. It clears away all the sufferings of cyclic existence and is the first step on the path to liberation. As a result of your faith, the Buddhas and Bodhisattvas will constantly keep you in mind. You will have a sense of shame, a sense of decency,* and wisdom. In

---

* Sense of shame, sense of decency. See glossary.

all your lives, as soon as you are born, you will meet a sublime teacher, the sacred teachings, and spiritual companions, and you will thus be able to practice the Dharma. You will be protected by those gods who delight in virtue. Falling asleep peacefully, in your dreams too you will have pleasant visions of encountering your teacher and the Three Jewels and practicing the Dharma, and you will wake in a happy frame of mind. You will accomplish all your wishes and die peacefully, guided by the Buddhas and Bodhisattvas. You will have none of the terrifying experiences of the intermediate state. You will be reborn wherever your aspirations lead you, and uphold the lineage of the Three Jewels. Swiftly, you will attain Buddhahood. Such are the infinite benefits of having faith, as we read in the *Sutra of the Precious Lamp:*

> Though for kalpas one might venerate beings
> Numerous as the atoms of the universes in the ten directions,
> Bringing them every kind of happiness,
> In comparison, nothing is more sublime
> Than the merit of faith in this Dharma.

## II. Clarification of the points of the training in this case

In a secluded place, sit on a comfortable seat, and with your body at ease in the correct posture and your mind utterly relaxed, meditate on the following visualization.

Consider your environment is a vast pure Buddhafield. The ground is even, giving slightly when trodden underfoot and springing back when one lifts one's foot. Through a landscape of rivers flowing with nectar, of wish-fulfilling trees and fresh meadows with many-colored flowers, saffron crocuses, and green grass, different species of sleek-coated, intelligent,[104] contented deer stroll peacefully. Here, in short, all the characteristics of a Buddhafield are perfect and complete; it is utterly beautiful and delightful.

In the center of this is the immaculate lake Dhanakosha, with its eight perfect qualities,* its waters full of celestial birds emitting their lovely calls. The shores are covered with pebbles of precious stone and gold sand. In the

---

*The eight perfect qualities of the water in lake Dhanakosha are described in a quotation on page 223.

middle of the lake is the single stem of a lotus made of precious substances, with five branches—one in the center and four arching over in the four directions like a parasol, the leaves on the tops of the branches spreading in the ten directions and filling the whole of space. They are bent under the weight of their abundant and perfect flowers and fruits, bedecked with all kinds of beautiful ornaments—golden chains spread from one branch to another, garlands of flowers and many-colored silk hangings, jeweled filigree ornaments, and gold and silver bells and tinklers—from which, with the slightest movement of the wind, the sound of the Dharma clearly resonates.

In the heart of the central branch is a broad, lofty throne of jewels supported by eight great lions, and in the middle of that is a multicolored lotus with a thousand petals. On its full cluster of anthers are cushions of sun and moon piled one upon the other.

Seated on this is the full embodiment of all the Buddhas of the three times, your own gracious root teacher, in the form of Guru Nangsi Zilnön.* He is white in color, tinged with red, like a conch coated with red varnish, and has the youthful beauty of an eight-year-old. His face is semi-wrathful,† his complexion radiant. He holds his right hand in the threatening gesture on his right knee, and in it a golden five-pronged *vajra.* In his left hand, in the gesture of meditation, he holds a skull-cup full of nectar, with a long-life vase. He is wearing, one on top of the other, the white secret diamond garment, the dark blue long-sleeved gown of the Mantra Vehicle, a red monastic robe with gold decorations, and a brocade cloak the color of power.‡ On his head is the resplendent Deerskin Hat decorated with a vulture's feather and various silks. In the crook of his left arm he holds his princess consort§ concealed in the form of a *khatvanga.*¶ With his two feet in the royal ruling posture,** he manifests in an expanse of brilliant, shimmering rays of rainbow light. Visualize him facing you, thinking of you and all beings with a loving, joyful heart.

---

*Nangsi Zilnön (Tib. *snang srid zil gyis gnon pa*), he who prevails over appearances and existence, whose majesty overawes all of existence. A particular form of Guru Rinpoche.
† His mouth is kind and gentle, but his eyes glare.
‡ I.e., red, the color of the activity of magnetizing or bringing under power.
§ Tib. *yum lha lcam,* refers here to Mandarava (see glossary).
¶ A symbolic trident, described on page 262.
** Tib. *gyal po rol pa'i stabs,* the posture of royal ease, with the right leg half extended and the left bent in.

Above the crown of his head, seated upon a lotus, sun, and moon, is the All-Pervading Lord Gyurme Ngedön Wangpo* in the form of a diamond holder observing the three vows.† His body is white in color, with a tinge of maroon, and he looks a little old. He wears a *pandita's* hat‡ on his head and is dressed in monk's robes and a brocade cloak. His right hand makes the gesture of supreme giving, his left holds a skull-cup brimming with nectar. In his belt is a *phurba*§ made of meteoric iron, and he is sitting cross-legged.

On his crown is Dudjom Lingpa, he who has imbibed the vital instructions,¶ his body dark red in color, his beard reaching down to the level of his heart. Wide-eyed, he stares straight ahead. His long locks are tied up in a knot on his crown, "marked" with a book; the rest hangs down loosely over his shoulders. He is wearing a maroon silk gown and a white cotton shawl.** He has conch-shell earrings, and the sword of wisdom tucked into his belt. His right hand imposingly holds aloft a *vajra,* his left rolls a meteoric-iron *phurba*. He is sitting with his left leg slightly stretched, in the royal ruling posture.

Above him is the dakini Yeshe Tsogyal, white in color, tinged with red. She plays a skull-drum in her right hand, while her left hand, in the gesture of meditation, holds a skull-cup full of nectar. She has the dress of a yogini—the silk skirt and headscarves, ornaments and necklaces of jewel and bone, and so forth—and is seated in the half-lotus posture.††

Above her is the Mighty Conqueror Padmasambhava, in the dress of a great Indian *pandita*. He holds a *vajra* in his right hand at the level of his heart, and in his left hand, in the gesture of meditation, a skull-cup and long-life vase. A *khatvanga* rests in the crook of his left arm. He is seated in the royal ruling posture, with his left foot slightly stretched out.

Above his head is the knowledge holder Shri Singha, light blue in

---

*Gyurme Ngedön Wangpo, Pokhong Tulku, one of Dudjom Rinpoche's root teachers in this lineage.

†Tib. *sum ldan rdo rje 'dzin pa,* a diamond holder who holds the vows of individual liberation, the Bodhisattva vows, and the Diamond-Vehicle vows.

‡A pointed hat (colored red in this tradition) with three braid rings and long flaps over the ears.

§A ritual dagger of triangular cross-section.

¶Tib. *khrag 'thung,* lit. "blood drinker," meaning that he has absorbed all the pith instructions that constitute the vital essence of the path of the Great Perfection.

**Respectively *dungma* (Tib. *'dung ma*), a long sleeved gown; and *genjar* (Tib. *'gan shyar*), the white shawl with red edges worn by tantric practitioners.

††With the right leg slightly stretched out.

color and wearing a red *pandita*'s hat, a blue undergarment, and the three monastic robes. He is leaning with his right hand on the ground to the side of him; his left hand on his knee touches the ground in front. He sits with his feet in the half-lotus posture.

Above him is the master Mañjushrimitra.* His body is dark yellow in color and he is dressed as an accomplished scholar-practitioner, like the previous master.† His right hand is in the gesture of giving protection; his left hand, in the meditation gesture, holds a jewel. He sits in the ruling posture with his right foot slightly stretched out.

Above his head is the body of manifestation Garab Dorje,‡ his body white in color, with the attributes of a supreme body of manifestation—the crown protuberance§ on his head, and so on. He holds both hands at his heart center in the Dharma teaching gesture and sits with his feet in the Bodhisattva's posture.¶

Above him is the body of perfect enjoyment Vajrasattva, brilliant white in color and wearing the dress of the body of perfect enjoyment. He holds a *vajra* in his right hand at his heart and a bell in his left hand resting on his hip. He is seated with his feet in the diamond posture.

Above his head is the absolute-body Samantabhadra. He is brilliant blue in color and naked, sitting in the diamond posture with his hands in the meditation gesture, in union with his consort, Samantabhadri, who is brilliant white.

Visualize all of them shining majestically in the expanses of their own light—canopies of rainbow lights and circles. Furthermore, in the air around the lineage teachers seated one above the other, visualize:

• the Buddhas of the five families of Conquerors and all the other Buddhas of the body of perfect enjoyment in their peaceful and wrathful forms, the twelve teachers of the Great Perfection,** and other masters of the mind lineage of the Conquerors, filling space;

---

* Mañjushrimitra is also often referred to by his Tibetan name, Jampel Shenyen (*'jam dpal bshes gnyen*).

† I.e., Shri Singha.

‡ Unlike the other Indian masters in the Nyingtik lineage, the master Prahevajra or Pramodavajra is more commonly known by his Tibetan name, Garab Dorje.

§ Tib. *gtsug gtor,* Skt. *ushnisha,* the prominence on the head of a Buddha, one of the thirty-two major marks.

¶ His right foot is stretched out, his left leg bent in. This is the most common posture associated with Tara, for example.

** See Dudjom Rinpoche, *The Nyingma School of Tibetan Buddhism,* pages 134–38.

- the Lord of Secrets* and other Buddhas who manifest as the chief Bodhi-sattvas remaining on the final stage of the tenth level, the Five Excellent Ones of Sublime Nobility,† the fortunate King Ja,‡ the dakini Wheel of Bliss,§ the Eight Knowledge Holders who held the transmissions,¶ the Twenty-One Wise Adepts, and other masters of the symbol lineage of the knowledge holders;
- and the Six Ornaments of Jambudvipa, the Eighty Great Accomplished Beings (Mahasiddhas), the Twenty-Five Disciples, the hundred emanational Treasure Discoverers, and all the other hundreds of thousands of beings who attained the level of supreme accomplishment in the hearing lineage of individuals.

Imagine them all like the gathering clouds at the top of a snowy mountain.

Who are the masters of the mind, symbol, and hearing lineages here? Those from Samantabhadra down to Vajrasattva or Vajrapani are the masters of the mind lineage. Those from Garab Dorje down to the Great Master** constitute the symbol lineage. And those from the Lord, Subject, Companion,†† and others down to our root teacher are the masters of the hearing lineage. In the present case the lineage is a treasure lineage, which also contains three distinct lineages: the prophesied lineage of the oral transmission, the lineage of empowerment and aspiration, and the lineage of teachings entrusted to the dakinis. These three, which are complete in the great emanational treasure discoverer,‡‡ together with the authentic lineage of transmission or realization through the transfer of blessings, are included in our root teacher.

---

*Tib. *gsang ba'i bdag po,* an epithet of Vajrapani; see glossary.

† The Five Excellent Ones of Sublime Nobility (Tib *dam pa'i rigs can dra ma lnga*) were a god (*grags ldan mchog skyong,* Skt. Yashasvi Varapala), a *naga* (*klu rgyal 'jog po,* the naga king Takshaka), a *yaksha* (*skar mda' gdong,* Ulkamukha), a *rakshasa* (*blo gros thabs ldan,* Matyaupayika) and a human being (the Licchavi *dri med grags pa,* Vimalakirti).

‡ A disciple of Vimalakirti and the master of the younger Indrabhuti, he was a major holder of the lineages of Mahayoga and Anuyoga.

§ Tib. *bde ba'i khor lo.*

¶ Tib. *bka' babs kyi rig 'dzin brgyad,* namely: Vimalamitra, Humkara, Mañjushrimitra, Nagarjuna, Padmasambhava, Dhanasamskrita, Rambuguhya-Devachandra, and Shanti-garbha. See Dudjom Rinpoche, *The Nyingma School of Tibetan Buddhism,* pages 475–83.

** Tib. *slob dpon chen po,* i.e., Guru Rinpoche, Padmasambhava.

†† Tib. *rje 'bangs grogs gsum,* namely King Trisong Detsen (the Lord), the translator Vairo-tsana (the Subject), and the dakini Yeshe Tsogyal (the Companion).

‡‡ I.e., Dudjom Lingpa.

Next, visualize the four branches spreading in the four directions, and on each of them a broad, lofty lion throne with tiered cushions of lotus, sun, and moon. On the front branch is the specific Jewel of the Buddha, the mandala of Vajrakumara (or whichever deity you consider to be your root *yidam*) with his consort, surrounded by all the *yidam* deities of the four or six tantra sections.

On the right-hand branch is the universal Jewel of the Buddha, the Victorious Lion of the Shakyas, surrounded by the thousand Buddhas of this Fortunate Kalpa and the other Buddhas of the three times and ten directions, all in the form of supreme Buddhas in the body of manifestation, attired as renunciates.

On the left-hand branch is the universal Jewel of the Sangha: the Eight Great Close Sons (the sublime Avalokiteshvara* and the others) surrounded by the Bodhisattvas who make up the Sangha of the Great Vehicle; and the Sublime Beings (the Sixteen Great Sthaviras† and other Listeners and Solitary Realizers who have attained Arhathood) who make up the Sangha of the Basic Vehicle.

On the rear branch, encased in a vast lattice of light, is the sublime Jewel of the Dharma—the Twelve Branches of Excellent Speech common to all vehicles, and the infinite tantras specific to the Mantra Vehicle—in the form of countless sacred volumes stacked into a huge, majestic mass like the side of Mount Meru, resonating with the spontaneous hum of the vowels and consonants.

In between all these and all around on the outside, visualize the specific Jewel of the Sangha—the assemblies of dakas and dakinis who guard the sacred places and lands, the dakas and dakinis who act as local protectors, and the hosts of Dharma Protectors included in the three tantras— awesome, powerful, and skillful, and endowed with the eye of wisdom, all massing together like summer mist.

Develop the complete certainty that all the objects of refuge are constant in their compassion and equal in their realization, arising as nothing other than the manifestation of the great primal wisdom, the union of bliss and emptiness that is your root teacher's mind.

---

The universe with its beings is a delightful pure Buddhafield,
In its center, the stainless, lovely lake of Dhanakosha.

---

* Avalokiteshvara; see glossary.
† The Sixteen Sthaviras; see glossary.

In the middle is a jeweled lotus, petals unfurled,
With five branches, and on the pistil of the central branch
The embodiment of all the Buddhas, the teacher
    Thöthrengtsel
In the form of Nangsi Zilnön, He Whose Majesty Overawes
    Appearances and Existence,
Glowing with the splendor of the major and minor marks,
    majestic in an expanse of rays of rainbow light.
Above his head are the teachers of the knowledge holders'
    lineages—
The mind, symbol, and hearing lineages,
The prophesied lineage of the oral transmission, the lineage
    of empowerment and aspiration,
The lineage of teachings entrusted to the dakinis, and the
    authentic lineage of realization:
All are present, one above the other.
The branches of the lotus spread out in the four directions,
    and upon them,
To the right, is the Conqueror, King of the Shakyas,
Surrounded by the thousand Buddhas of the Buddhafields
    of the Fortunate Kalpa
And all the other Victors Gone to Bliss of all the times and
    directions.
To the rear, in the interstices of a beautiful lattice of five-
    colored lights,
Is the Excellent Speech, the sublime Dharma of transmission
    and realization, in the form of books,
Resonating with the sweet sounds of the vowels and
    consonants.
To the left are the Eight Bodhisattvas, Close Sons,
And around them, the Sublime Beings, the Sixteen Great
    Sthaviras, and so on—
All the Sanghas of Bodhisattvas, Listeners, and Solitary
    Realizers.
In front is Vajrakumara and his consort
Surrounded by the hosts of peaceful and wrathful yidam
    deities of the four or six tantra sections
And the dakas and dakinis of the three places.
Outside, all around and in between,

Are all the infinite hosts of loyal protectors of the three
    tantras,
Gathered like massing clouds.
All of these possess the activity of stirring the depths of cyclic
    existence
With the wisdom of knowledge, love, and power:
They are present as leaders guiding all us beings
And thinking of us with great compassion.

Visualize them like this, directing their thoughts toward you. Then, in their presence, imagine your present father on your right, your mother on your left, your enemies and those who make obstacles for you in front, and your relatives and circle of friends behind you, with all around all the sentient beings who pervade space—those for whom you feel animosity, those with whom you are friendly, and those in between—a huge crowd like dust on the surface of the earth. With you leading the chant, you all show respect physically by joining your hands in the fashion of a lotus bud on top of your heads, you express your respect verbally by the sonorous recitation of the clear, melodious words of the refuge prayer, and you express your respect mentally by the firmness of your devotion and confidence as you think: "Whether I fall sick, whether I am in pain, whether I die or live, whatever happens to me, favorable or unfavorable, pleasant or painful, good or bad, from now on until I reach the heart of enlightenment I will have no other refuge, no other hope than you. Teacher, Three Jewels, in you I put my trust! Lead me this very moment out of the terrible ocean of cyclic existence, I beg you!" In this manner, make an effort to integrate your thoughts with the refuge prayer, and recite it a hundred, a thousand, ten thousand, a hundred thousand times, or more:

NAMO. I and the infinitude of those who have been my
    parents, numerous as space is vast,
Until the heart of enlightenment is reached,
Take refuge in the teacher, the Three Jewels.
Hold us with your love without separating from us for an
    instant.

At the end of the session, visualize white rays of light—the nectar of blessings—issuing forth from the hearts of the objects of refuge as from a hundred thousand newly risen moons shining simultaneously. They touch all of us sentient beings, purifying every one of our physical, verbal, and mental negative actions and obscurations. Our bodies become a mass of light which then dissolves into the objects of refuge. The retinues of the objects of refuge are gradually absorbed into the principal deities, which in turn dissolve into the teacher. The root teacher becomes a mass of light and vanishes like a rainbow into the expanse of the sky. Rest in equanimity in the uncontrived state of mind.

---

> From the objects of refuge a boundless nectarous stream
>     of blessings
> In the form of brilliant white rays of light issues forth.
> They dissolve into me and everyone else and purify the
>     obscurations of body, speech, and mind.
> In an instant we melt into light and dissolve into the objects
>     of refuge.
> The surrounding objects of refuge melt in stages and are
>     absorbed into the main deity;
> The main deity is absorbed into the absolute space beyond
>     concepts.

---

At the close of the session, seal the practice with prayers of dedication and aspiration before continuing with your everyday activities.* In the evening when you go to sleep, do not dissolve the object of refuge but imagine yourself going to sleep with your head directed toward it[105] and fall asleep meditating with devotion. This is an additional instruction.

---

When we take refuge, it is not enough to simply repeat the words. We have to have total confidence in the Three Jewels. If you are confident in them, it is quite impossible for the Three Jewels' compassion to not have the power to protect you. It might not avert some bad deeds that unavoidably have to be experienced in this life, making the Three Jewels' compassion seem temporarily to have run out, but as long as your faith remains unchanged, in the long term you will definitely have their protection.

Nowadays we get discouraged at the smallest mishap and think the Three Jewels have no compassion. This is a sign that we do not have heartfelt confidence. If the Three Jewels do not appear to be showing any compassion in our present circumstances, it is merely that we have not

---

*Tib. *spyod lam.* See glossary, *everyday activities.*

prayed to them properly. Although most of the graded path of the sutras and tantras is included in the refuge, we talk loftily of emptiness without having in any way integrated the practice of refuge with our minds. This is a deviation toward the great abyss of mistaken paths. So never, even slightly, engage in the negative action of giving up any teachings related to the Three Jewels,[106] and without ever forsaking the refuge even if your life is at stake, be diligent in one-pointedly putting the refuge prayer into practice.

# CHAPTER TEN

# Arousing the Mind Set on Supreme Enlightenment, the Root of the Whole Path

THERE ARE TWO SECTIONS: GENERAL POINTS TO BE UNDER-stood, and the points of the training in this case.

## I. GENERAL POINTS TO BE UNDERSTOOD

These are seven in number: the definition of the arousing of bodhichitta, categories, the particular referents, how bodhichitta is aroused, the ritual for taking the vow, a teaching on training in the precepts, and an explanation of the benefits.

## A. The definition of the arousing of bodhichitta

According to the *Ornament of True Realization,*

> The arousing of bodhichitta is the wish,
> for others' benefit,
> To attain perfect Buddhahood.

It is the wish to attain perfect enlightenment in order to establish all sentient beings on the level of Buddhahood. Its cause is threefold: faith in the Buddha, compassion for sentient beings, and learning of the benefits of bodhichitta. The contributory factor that helps bring about bodhichitta is having the courage and superior motivation to take upon oneself alone the great burden of the welfare of all beings, without exception. In essence it is the wish to be capable of liberating all beings by attaining perfect enlightenment.

## B. Categories

Bodhichitta can be classified in various ways, with four categories based on the different levels of the path, from the ordinary individual's level of earnest aspiration up to Buddhahood, twenty-two categories indicated by similes, and so on.* However, the most widely known and easily understood are the two categories based on their characteristics. These are:

- bodhichitta in aspiration, which is the wish to attain Buddhahood and is analogous to wanting to go somewhere; and
- bodhichitta in action, which is diligence in the two aspects of bodhichitta, being the means for accomplishing Buddhahood, and is analogous to actually going.

*The Way of the Bodhisattva* describes them as follows:

> Bodhichitta, the awakened mind,
> Is known in brief to have two aspects:
> First, aspiring, *bodhichitta in intention;*
> Then, *active bodhichitta,* practical engagement.
> As corresponding to the wish to go
> And then to setting out,
> The wise should understand respectively
> The difference that divides these two.[107]

## C. The particular referents

"To arouse bodhichitta," declares the *Bodhisattva Levels,* "is to focus on enlightenment and to focus on sentient beings." In other words, bodhichitta focuses, on the one hand, on seeking the primal wisdom of the Great Vehicle, and, on the other, on the four boundless attitudes.†

---

*The four categories are bodhichitta practiced through aspiration, bodhichitta of the utterly pure attitude, fully ripened bodhichitta, and bodhichitta totally free from all obscurations, related respectively to the paths of accumulation and joining, the first seven Bodhisattva levels, the three pure Bodhisattva levels, and the level of Buddhahood. The twenty-two similes are set forth in the *Ornament of True Realization* and also relate to different stages on the Bodhisattva path. See *Treasury of Precious Qualities,* pages 159–61.
† Tib. *tshad med bzhi,* boundless love, compassion, joy, and impartiality, as explained in the next section.

## D. How bodhichitta is aroused

Arousing bodhichitta embodies aspiration and action, combining the mind turned toward enlightenment and the compassion that supports it.

### BODHICHITTA IN ASPIRATION

From our own experience, which is that we do not want to suffer in any way and we very much want to be happy, we can infer that those who have been our parents—that is, all the beings in the six realms—are no different in having the same desires. It is therefore up to us, and us alone, to bring about their physical and mental well-being and help them create the merit that leads to happiness, and to make sure they are free from suffering and from the actions and afflictive emotions that lead to suffering. For this we arouse bodhichitta in aspiration by means of two pledges:

• a pledge to the cause, focusing with the four following attitudes on all beings filling space: *love*—the desire to take responsibility for them when we recognize that all beings have been our mothers; *compassion*—on account of which we cannot bear to abandon them, knowing that they are suffering on the road of existence; *joy*—the delight we feel when they achieve the happiness of higher rebirth and ultimate excellence; and *impartiality*—the absence of attachment to those close to us and aversion to those who are not;
• a pledge to the result, the intention to bring them all to Buddhahood.

These four attitudes are called boundless because they focus on all the realms of beings filling the furthest reaches of space, with no distinctions and no limit to their number.

How they are classified as such is explained in the *Sutra of the Sublime Essence:*

> When love and the other three are not backed by bodhichitta and are merely causes of happy existences, they are what we call the four abodes of the pure.* When these four are permeated with bodhichitta and create the cause for going beyond suffering, they are the four boundless attitudes.

---

*Tib. *tshangs pa'i gnas pa bzhi,* Skt. Brahmavihara; see *Treasury of Precious Qualities,* page 151 and note 112.

There are four contributory conditions that give rise to these:

- the causal condition, the natural potential present within us;*
- the dominant condition, namely, the spiritual friend;†
- the objective condition, which refers to their respective manifest objects;‡ and
- the immediately preceding condition, which entails seeing the benefits of the four boundless attitudes and the disadvantages of not having them.

As for the different ways in which the four boundless attitudes arise:

- in relation to sentient beings, they arise as the four conceptual boundless attitudes;
- in relation to the absolute nature, with the realization that they are by nature unborn, they arise as four states devoid of concepts.

With regard to their order, the sutras and tantras concur. The *Middle Sutra of Transcendent Wisdom* states:

> A Bodhisattva Mahasattva should meditate on great love, great compassion, great joy, and great impartiality.

And the *Hevajra Tantra* declares:

> First, meditate on love,
> Second, meditate on compassion,
> Third, meditate on joy,
> And finally, on impartiality.

## BODHICHITTA IN ACTION

Bodhichitta in action comprises the *intention* to strive for perfect Buddhahood oneself, in order to bring beings who fill the whole of space to Buddhahood, and the *execution* of that intention by training in the six transcendent perfections. This was widely taught by the Buddha, as, for example, in the following quotation from the sutras:

---

*I.e., the Buddha-nature, Skt. *tathagatagarbha*.
† I.e., the person who teaches the four boundless attitudes.
‡ The objects of the four boundless attitudes—beings and their sufferings, for example.

Subahu, for a Bodhisattva Mahasattva to swiftly realize perfect enlightenment, he must continuously train, all the time, in these six transcendent perfections.

## E. The ritual for taking the vow

The different rituals that come from the tradition of the profound view, the tradition of the vast activity, and the special tradition of the Mantra Vehicle involve taking the vow either from a spiritual teacher who has transformed his mind with bodhichitta, knows how to train in bodhichitta, and is able to guide others; or by using a support of the Three Jewels,* or by visualizing them in front of one.

## F. Training in the precepts

There are two parts: the actual precepts, and an explanation of the circumstances in which bodhichitta declines. The actual precepts are divided into two: the precepts of bodhichitta in aspiration and those of bodhichitta in action. Training in aspirational bodhichitta has two aspects, general and particular.

### *1. The actual precepts*

#### a. THE PRECEPTS OF BODHICHITTA IN ASPIRATION

#### i. Using mindfulness, vigilance, and carefulness in general

The most important point in the training is to guard one's mind from the whole host of afflictive emotions. If one loses mindfulness, vigilance†, and carefulness, one's positive activities will decline, and negative actions will instantly occur. For this reason, in everything we do throughout the six periods of the day, we should make every effort to guard our minds. Using unfailing mindfulness to familiarize ourselves with the sublime Dharma, and vigilance as a sentinel to recognize whether or not our actions are beneficial, we should think: "I have entered the sublime Dharma and am undertaking the training of a Bodhisattva, so I must never be like ordinary people." As Shantideva has said,

---

*For example, a statue or image of the Buddha, a volume of the Buddhist scriptures, and so on.
†Tib. *shes bzhin,* more completely translated as "vigilant introspection."

> All you who would protect your minds,
> Maintain your mindfulness and vigilance;
> Guard them both, at cost of life and limb,
> I join my hands, beseeching you.[108]

Moreover, with regard to ourselves we should have a sense of shame and give up afflictive emotions, while with regard to others we should have a sense of decency and guard ourselves from negative actions. These two are the essence of carefulness. As long as we observe carefulness, we will be able to accomplish everything that is good; without it we will accomplish nothing. As we find in the *Sutra of the King of Concentrations,*

> Everything that counts as virtuous practice—
> Generosity, discipline, patience, and the rest—
> The root of it all is carefulness.

And in *Letter to a Friend:*

> Carefulness is the way to deathlessness,
> While carelessness is death, the Buddha taught.
> And thus, so that your virtuous deeds may grow,
> Act carefully, constantly and with respect.[109]

### ii. Adopting and giving up the eight white and black actions in particular

The four black actions we should avoid are:

- To deceive teachers and others who are worthy of veneration by lying to them.
- To create regret in others when there is no reason for regret.
- To maliciously criticize someone who has aroused bodhichitta.
- To behave slyly and deceitfully with regard to sentient beings.

The Great Omniscient One says:

> To deceive those worthy of veneration, to create regret
>     without reason,
> To openly say unpleasant things about sublime beings,
> To act with craft and cunning among beings—
> These are the four black actions: give them up!

The four white actions we should undertake are:

- To not consciously tell lies.
- To place everyone on the profound path of the Great Vehicle.
- To respect and praise sublime beings.
- To act with superior intentions with regard to sentient beings.

On these he says:

> To follow sublime beings and praise their qualities,
> To encourage beings to practice pure virtue,
> To consider Bodhisattvas as one's teachers,
> And, with superior motivation, to bring about benefit
>     and happiness for beings—
> These are the four perfect white actions: rely on them!

## b. THE PRECEPTS OF BODHICHITTA IN ACTION

There are three parts: maturing oneself by training in the six transcendent perfections; maturing others by training in the four ways of attracting disciples; and training the mind, incorporating the essential practice of the above two precepts.

### i. Maturing oneself: training in the six transcendent perfections

Having taken up the discipline of bodhichitta, one now trains in the Bodhisattva activities, principally the six transcendent perfections, as described in *Letter to a Friend:*

> Generosity and discipline, patience, diligence,
> Concentration and the wisdom that knows thusness—
> Those measureless perfections, make them grow,
> And be a Mighty Conqueror who's crossed the ocean
>     of existence.[110]

Of these six, the first is generosity.

### (1) Generosity

The essence of generosity is to completely give away one's possessions with a mind free of attachment. Its function is to get rid of other people's poverty. It should be motivated by the thought of striving for perfect enlightenment for the benefit of others. There are three kinds of generosity, depending on what it is that one gives.

### (a) Material giving

Material giving involves freely giving away the different parts of one's body (inner gifts) and all one's wealth and possessions (outer gifts), avoiding the four improper aspects of generosity and adopting the four proper aspects—these four referring to one's intention, the gift itself, the recipient, and the manner of giving.[111] We should give in particular to the four fields.* In this, both the intention and the deed should be perfect, with no trace of stinginess, as if we were merely giving a piece of grass.

### (b) The gift of protection from fear

This is to use whatever means are appropriate and within our power to protect those who are in danger from the authorities, savage beasts of prey, enemies, robbers, fire, water, illness, negative forces, and the like, thereby relieving them of their fear.

### (c) The gift of Dharma

So that others have faith and we do not ourselves degenerate, we should practice the sublime Dharma by giving up improper actions with our body, speech, and mind and adopting proper ones. In this way we become worthy of being a spiritual friend, and the others are pleased and develop respect, thus bringing about the right conditions for disciple and teaching to come together. At that time, with our minds free of personal considerations, we should be skillful in the different means for expounding the teachings of the Greater or Lesser Vehicle to those who seek the Dharma, matching the instructions with the disciples' capacities and thereby setting them on the most appropriate path.

### (2) Discipline

The essence of discipline is embodied in the four virtues—in short, in taking vows and keeping them.[112] Its function is to reduce the torments of evil. It should be motivated by a real interest in training the mind, inspired by determination to be free, together with a parallel resolve to abandon negative actions. The precepts are divided into three.

### (a) The discipline of refraining from negative actions

This involves: keeping all the precepts perfectly (the common vows of the seven kinds of ordination for individual liberation,[113] the uncommon

---

* See glossary, *four fields*.

Bodhisattva vows that originate from the traditions of the Two Charioteers,* and the extraordinary vows of the Mantra Vehicle) and cutting
the stream of actions, negative in their intention and in their execution,
that constitute shameful physical, verbal, and mental deeds by vowing to
refrain from them in the future.

### (b) The discipline of gathering positive actions

Gathering positive actions means doing whatever one can to accumulate
tainted positive actions related to physical and verbal acts unsupported
by wisdom and, most importantly, untainted positive actions related to
mental concentration backed by wisdom.

### (c) The discipline of working for the benefit of sentient beings

The *Bodhisattva Levels* describes eleven ways—helping others usefully, and
so on[114]—in which a Bodhisattva benefits beings, but these can be summarized as assessing one's motivation to do whatever one can physically,
verbally, and mentally solely for other beings' welfare, and then carrying
out any actions one can to actually help others.

### (3) Patience

The essence of patience is to think nothing of good or bad, to be free from
trying to accomplish the one and get rid of the other. Its function is to
remove the anguish of being angry and in conflict. The point of patience is
to train so that our altruistic attitude is immovable and irrepressible in the
face of those who hurt us with their ingratitude and so forth.[115] Patience
is of three kinds.

### (a) Patience in remaining imperturbable in the face of harm

If you get angry with those at whose hands you and your relatives have
been struck and beaten, or suffered theft, robbery, criticism, and abuse,
you should remember the following and other verses[116] that show the fault
in losing one's temper:

> All the good works gathered in a thousand kalpas,
> Such as deeds of generosity,
> Or offerings to the Blissful Ones—
> A single flash of anger shatters them.

---

* The Two Charioteers are Nagarjuna and Asanga.

As well as this, make use of the five ideas and the nine considerations[117] to develop patience, thinking nothing of such harm.

### (b) Patience in happily accepting suffering

However much you suffer in the physical, verbal, and mental hardships that you undergo for the sake of accomplishing enlightenment through the Dharma, apply yourself joyfully and enthusiastically without losing interest. Just as it is necessary to employ drastic treatments to reduce the suffering in serious illnesses, one needs enormous courage to stop the battle of cyclic existence and conquer the enemies that are the afflictive emotions.

### (c) Patience in aspiring to a true knowledge of reality

This kind of patience entails aspiring to understand inconceivable subjects like the qualities of the Three Jewels, and, in particular, not being afraid of the ultimate absolute state, the profound actual condition of things, free from concepts and devoid of the two kinds of self; rather, you should have confidence in it and reach a full understanding of it.

### (4) Diligence

The essence of diligence is enthusiasm for positive activities and absence of laziness. Its function is to make the power of virtue grow. Its cause is one's enduring previous good deeds, which lead to vast courage being awakened to virtuous ends. There are three categories of diligence.

### (a) Armorlike diligence

Thinking, "From now on, and until every single being has been brought to the level of unsurpassable enlightenment, I will not abandon my efforts even for an instant," we should don the armor of a Bodhisattva against ever being discouraged by such things as how long that will take, or how difficult it will be to accomplish.

### (b) Diligence in application

This is to persevere—all the time, night and day, without letting up for an instant—in getting rid of afflictive emotions, performing positive actions, and working for the welfare of others by means of constant application and devoted application, without ever giving up, turning back, indulging in pride, or feeling one has done enough.

## (c) Diligence in benefiting others

If we are to benefit sentient beings directly or indirectly, it must be done with a joyful attitude, without ever getting discouraged even if we have to spend kalpas on end in the lower realms.

## (5) Concentration

The essence of concentration is to remain one-pointedly focused on virtue.[118] Its function is to reduce afflictive emotions.

Concentration requires preparation. Because this ordinary mind of ours, along with its movements, is the root of all harm and suffering, the aim is to achieve a happy, peaceful state in which thoughts are reduced. We must therefore begin by bringing about the causes of concentration (distancing ourselves physically from distracting activities and mentally from discursive thoughts, and being content, with few desires), avoiding the five faults, and relying on the eight types of mental application.* As for the actual concentration, this is of three kinds.

## (a) The concentration that procures a feeling of well-being in this life

This is a state of concentration common to worldly spiritual paths and is achieved by employing the nine methods of settling the mind.[119] It is characterized by freedom from discursive thought, blissful mastery of one's body and mind, and a lack of conceit and of attachment to experiences. Since this is the foundation on which all kinds of good qualities grow, we should make it the basis of our concentration. Each of the four concentrations† is divided into a preparatory stage and the actual concentration.

## (b) The concentration that gives rise to excellent qualities

To achieve the actual concentration of the first and higher concentrations, it is necessary to accomplish profound mundane insight,‡ through seven factors that are kept in mind.[120] For this, one mainly practices sustained calm in formal meditation and profound insight in the postmeditation

---

* For the five faults and the eight types of mental application that remedy them, see pages 49–50.
† The four states of concentration or *dhyanas* (Tib. *bsam gtan bzhi*) associated with the world of form.
‡ Tib. *'jig rten pa'i lhag mthong*, mundane *vipashyana* or profound insight (see glossary), mundane in the sense that it is not yet associated with the realization of emptiness that gives freedom from cyclic existence.

period, and by fully accomplishing the ten powers of perceptual limitlessness, eight kinds of perceptual domination, eight perfect freedoms, and so
on common to the paths of the Listeners and Solitary Realizers,[121] and the
extraordinary, infinite methods for perfect freedom and absorption that
are beyond the scope of the Listeners and Solitary Realizers, one completes
the paths of accumulation and joining.

### *(c) The concentration that benefits sentient beings*

Next, from the path of seeing onward, one attains the concentration of the
sublime beings, which is known as the untainted concentration or *Virtuous
Concentration of the Tathagatas.* The power of this kind of concentration
enables one to perform miraculous deeds on an infinite scale, benefiting
beings in eleven ways and so forth.[122] One thereby enters the field of activity of the Tathagatas, as the *Sublime Continuum* explains:

> The way Bodhisattvas in their postmeditation
> Perfectly liberate beings
> And the way all the Tathagatas do so
> Are, for people in the world, the same.[123]

In practicing all these transcendent perfections, up to and including
concentration, we should reinforce them with the wisdom devoid of the
concepts of subject, object, and action; we should be free of attachment
and expectation, and at the end we should perform the dedication free of
concepts. As a result, the transcendent perfections will grow greater and
be truly endowed with emptiness and the pure means of compassion.

### *(6) Wisdom*

The essence of wisdom is intelligence that perfectly discerns the nature of
all phenomena. Its function is to clear away the gloom of the two kinds
of obscuration. Although true wisdom is inherent to Buddhahood, its
cause—or "surrogate" wisdom—can be cultivated with discriminating intelligence. How this is done is described by Nagarjuna as follows:

> To make transcendent wisdom grow,
> Listen and reflect, and once you have these two,
> Meditation will arise from them;
> Thence unsurpassable accomplishment will be gained.

There are thus three kinds of wisdom.

## (a) The wisdom of listening

This involves mastering the words and meanings of all branches of knowledge. When we speak of "wisdom" here—whether the secular knowledge of language and logic, arts and medicine, or the spiritual wisdom that concerns a knowledge of the Excellent Words (the Buddha's teachings) and the treatises that elucidate their meaning—it is a case of the cause being named after the result.* We should therefore study extensively so as to not be ignorant in any of these disciplines.

## (b) The wisdom of reflecting

What we have listened to is not to be simply accepted with blind faith. We must use such means as the evidence of scriptural quotations, reasoning based on the evidence of things, and irrefutable proof to thoroughly examine the expedient and ultimate teachings, and the implied and indirect teachings, and thus elicit and reflect on their intended meaning, so that we come to a definite conclusion about them.

## (c) The wisdom of meditating

Reflection leads to certainty, and the knowledge we have gained has now to be correctly applied to our own minds. In particular, we should make an experience of what we have learned about the view by meditating on it, for the view is not merely a verbal or intellectual exercise to be left as such, but something to be truly realized as the unmistaken vision of the way things truly are.

---

## THE DEFINING CHARACTERISTICS OF THE SIX TRANSCENDENT PERFECTIONS

Anything a Bodhisattva undertakes in his or her training falls within the scope of the six transcendent perfections and is endowed with four distinguishing features, accompanied by the corresponding intention to accomplish infinite good. These four distinguishing features are:

• It is devoid of anything that runs counter to the respective transcendent perfection.

---

*The wisdom of listening (Tib. *thos pa'i shes rab*), even though it is called "wisdom," actually refers to the cause of wisdom, i.e., the listening that results in wisdom.

- It is supported and permeated by wisdom, in that it is free of any concept of subject, object, and action.
- It fulfills its function in bringing about others' welfare.
- It brings beings to ultimate maturity on any one of the three levels of enlightenment.

## CATEGORIES

Generosity and the other five of the six transcendent perfections can each be subdivided into six aspects:

- the generosity aspect, which is to introduce other beings to that particular transcendent perfection;
- the discipline aspect, which is to avoid anything that runs counter to it;
- the patience aspect, which is to be unmoved by difficulties in practicing it;
- the diligence aspect, which is to be joyful and make effort in practicing it;
- the concentration aspect, which is to keep the mind one-pointedly focused on the virtuous goal of that particular perfection; and
- the wisdom aspect, which is to practice these without any concept of subject, object, or action.

There are thus thirty-six subdivisions in all. These and other categories are explained in detail in the *Sutra of the Fortunate Kalpa.*

## WHY THERE ARE SIX TRANSCENDENT PERFECTIONS

From the point of view of attaining the higher realms and eliminating afflictive emotions, the number of transcendent perfections has been fixed at six. And in *Ornament of the Sutras* we read:

> Abundant wealth and perfect body,
> Perfect entourage and execution—within the higher realms;
> Never influenced by afflictive emotions,
> And unmistaken in everything one does.*

---

* *Ornament of the Sutras,* XVII, 2. By practicing the first four transcendent perfections one gains rebirth in the higher realms: generosity results in one being wealthy, discipline in having a celestial or human body, patience in a harmonious entourage, and diligence in the ability to complete anything one has begun. Practicing the last two perfections results in the qualities described by the last two lines of this quotation, and the attainment of enlightenment.

With regard to achieving one's own goal by working for others' benefit, their number is also six. In the same text we find:

Removing poverty, avoiding any form of harm,
Bearing injury, and not discouraged by work,
Making others happy, and giving clear explanations—
   because of these
Others' aims are fulfilled, and this is one's own aim.*

If we consider the transcendent perfections in relation to the three trainings, they again number six. Again, *Ornament of the Sutras* declares:

In terms of the three trainings,
The Buddha has clearly explained six transcendent perfections:
Three in the first, two in the last two,
And one included in all three.[124]

As a result of generosity one is free from attachment to possessions, and from this, one becomes perfectly disciplined. As a result of that, one possesses the four principles of a renunciate,† and this constitutes patience. These three transcendent perfections are thus the cause, the essence, and the special feature of the superior training in discipline, and in this respect they belong to that training. Concentration belongs to the superior training in concentration, and wisdom belongs to the superior training in wisdom. Diligence is an accessory for all three trainings.

## WHY THE SIX TRANSCENDENT PERFECTIONS ARE IN A PARTICULAR ORDER

The six transcendent perfections are classified in order in relation to three criteria:

• since each perfection arises from the preceding one, they are classified in order of cause and result;

---

* *Ornament of the Sutras*, XVII, 4. "Making others happy" refers to the powers of clairvoyance and other powers achieved through concentration, these being used to fulfill beings' hopes. As a result of wisdom one is able to explain the Dharma.
† The four principles of a renunciate (Tib. *dge sbyong*, Skt. *shramana*) are: not to return abuse with abuse, not to get angry even if someone is angry with one, not to strike anyone even if one has been struck, and, even if one's faults are exposed, not to find fault in return.

- since discipline is superior to generosity, and so on, they are classified in order of superiority;
- and since each is more subtle and difficult to realize than the preceding one, they are classified in order of subtlety.

As *Ornament of the Sutras* explains,

> Because, in dependence on the preceding one, the next one arises,
> And they are respectively inferior and superior,
> And because they are respectively gross and subtle,
> They are taught one after the other.[125]

## HOW THE SIX TRANSCENDENT PERFECTIONS ARE PRACTICED

Give generously without any expectation regarding the ripened effect of your deed. Keep your vows without aspiring to the higher realms. Meditate on patience with regard to everyone, impartially. Be diligent in amassing every kind of excellent quality. Practice the concentration in which form-lessness is dispelled. Practice wisdom inseparable from skillful means.
As *Ornament of the Sutras* says,

> Generosity without expectation,
> Discipline without aspiring to higher rebirth,
> Patience with all, in every respect,
> Diligence in gathering all good qualities,
> Likewise, concentration that is not the absorption of the
>     formless realm,
> And wisdom possessed of skillful means—
> Those who are steadfast in these six perfections
> Have the correct application.[126]

## DEFINITIONS

The same text gives:

> That which removes poverty,
> That which obtains coolness, that which bears anger,
> That which connects one to what is supreme, that which keeps
>     the mind focused,
> And that which knows the ultimate—thus they are explained.[127]

Getting rid of poverty is what we call generosity. Cooling the heat of the afflictive emotions and providing protection from it is discipline. Bearing anger is patience. Preparing oneself for Buddhahood is diligence. Holding the mind on a single point is concentration. Recognizing the nature of the ultimate truth is wisdom.

_____

When we put the six transcendent perfections into practice, it has to be with six supreme elements:

- The supreme support is to have bodhichitta.
- The supreme substance* is to engage in the six transcendent perfections wholly, not partially.
- The supreme purpose is to apply them to the welfare of all sentient beings.
- The supreme means is to permeate them with wisdom, free from the three concepts.
- The supreme dedication is to dedicate them to unsurpassable enlightenment.
- The supreme purity is to use them as the direct antidote for the two obscurations.

### ii. Maturing others: training in the four ways of attracting disciples

Once we have fully matured our own mindstreams by training in the precepts of bodhichitta in action, as we have just seen, we need to bring others to maturity, and the principal method or practice for achieving this comprises the four ways of attracting disciples. *Ornament of the Sutras* lists them in order as follows:

> *Generosity* is held to be the same.
> Teaching them, practicing them oneself,
> And inducing others to practice them are termed
> *Speaking pleasantly, acting accordingly,* and *giving appropriate advice.*†

_____

*Tib. *dngos po,* lit. "thing" or "matter," refers to the transcendent perfections themselves.
† *Ornament of the Sutras,* XVII, 73. The first of the four ways is generosity, which is qualified as "the same," meaning that it is the same as transcendent generosity described earlier. The other three, listed in the last line of this quotation, are defined in the second and third lines.

It goes on to explain their purpose and significance:

> Since they are the methods for bringing them benefit,
> For making them comprehend, for making them engage,
> And similarly for making them continue the practice,
> The ways of attracting disciples are to be known as four.[128]

How these are practiced is shown in the *Heaped Lotuses:*

> Gracefully summoning with the beckoning hand of generosity,
> And receiving with pleasant conversation,
> Reassure by acting according to the teaching,
> And give good advice according to need.

First of all, gracefully summon those who would be suitable as disciples and who are not yet included among your disciples by giving them appropriate material gifts. Once you have brought them into your circle, draw them onto the perfect path with pleasant, virtuous conversation that suits their way of thinking and appeals to them. In order that they do not then turn away again but set out on the path and develop a real interest, reassure them by acting in accord with the teachings you have given. And by introducing your disciples to the teachings of the different vehicles that suit their particular natures and capacities, give them advice for the long term, encouraging them on the path. These four include both material gifts and the gift of Dharma, and by means of these two we can bring beings temporary benefit and connect them to the glorious state of ultimate bliss.

### iii. Incorporating the essential practice of the above two precepts: training the mind

The entire practice of a Bodhisattva can be summarized as three essential points:

- the causal mind training, which is to meditate deeply on love and compassion;
- the main training, which is to take the vow of bodhichitta in each of the six periods of the day and night; and
- training in conduct, which is to dedicate one's positive actions to the welfare of other beings, and to exert oneself in the practice of sending happiness and receiving suffering, for as Shantideva says:

Those desiring speedily to be
A refuge for themselves and others
Should make the interchange of "I" and "Other,"
And thus embrace a sacred mystery.[129]

Accordingly, it is most important to follow the profound mind training of exchanging oneself and others. The reason for this he indicates by stating the following truth:

All the joy the world contains
Has come through wishing happiness for others.
All the misery the world contains
Has come through wanting pleasure for oneself.[130]

and its contrary:

If I do not interchange
My happiness for others' pain,
Enlightenment will never be attained,
And even in samsara, I shall have no joy.[131]

As to how one should exchange oneself and others,

Give the others victory and gain,
Take upon yourself defeat and loss.

This means imagining yourself gladly, willingly, unhesitatingly taking on the whole burden of beings' misery—its cause (all the actions and afflictive emotions that the entirety of parent-beings filling space have accumulated since time without beginning), and the experiences of suffering that result— and completely giving all those beings, one by one, the whole of the merit you have accumulated in your series of lives and the resulting experiences of physical well-being and mental happiness. As we read in the *Seven-Point Mind Training,*

Train to give and take alternately;
Mount them both upon your breath.

This will be described below in the section on the points of the training.

Whatever happens to you—whether you are in good or poor health, happy or miserable, at the top of the social ladder or at the bottom—don the great armor that renders you impervious to circumstances. Making compassion the basis of your practice, hit the essential point of relative bodhichitta; and by arousing it, making it stable, and increasing it more and more, train in realizing the sublime actual condition of things that is absolute bodhichitta.

## 2. An explanation of the circumstances in which bodhichitta declines

What makes bodhichitta in aspiration decline?

- Losing heart, thinking, "Someone like me will never be able to benefit others";
- laziness, from failing to see the benefits of the path and seeing only how difficult the practice is;
- engaging in the Listeners' path thinking that it is better than the Great Vehicle, and thereby abandoning bodhichitta.

As for the conditions that make bodhichitta in action decline, these are:

- losing bodhichitta in aspiration, that is, the very foundation of bodhichitta in action;[132]
- the occurrence of a root downfall, for that would run counter to bodhichitta;
- giving up bodhichitta by returning the vow.

Whichever the case, the negative consequences of letting bodhichitta decline are as follows:

- the merit one has accumulated in the past will be weakened, so that in future lives one will never be happy, nor encounter the Great Vehicle;
- for having broken one's promise, one will become an object of universal contempt;
- because this is such a serious fault, one will wander for long periods of time in the lower realms.

So be mindful and vigilant, and the moment your bodhichitta degenerates, part from the fault in the presence of a support and so on,* and renew the vow of bodhichitta just as you did in the vow ritual. That way your

* "And so on" here indicates that the parting should include the four powers: the power of the support, regret, action as an antidote, and the power of restoration or resolution. See pages 203–5.

bodhichitta will be restored. Some people claim that there is a limit to the number of times one can do this, but this is not the case, for it is said that whenever the positive thought of refraining from wrong arises, the Bodhisattva vow takes birth. As we find in *The Way of the Bodhisattva,*

> Deciding to refrain from every harmful act
> Is said to be transcendent discipline.[133]

## G. The benefits of bodhichitta

There are seven benefits: its superiority over other virtues, the fact that it is the root of the whole Dharma, the fact that it increases one's merit, its vast qualities, and the facts that one becomes an object of the world's reverence, that everything one undertakes is meaningful, and that all those with whom one is connected are linked to liberation.

### 1. The benefit that bodhichitta is oustandingly greater than other forms of virtue

From the very moment we arouse bodhichitta, even the most terrible negative actions are instantly destroyed. No other positive act is as powerful as this, for as *The Way of the Bodhisattva* points out,

> Virtue, thus, is weak; and always
> Evil is of great and overwhelming strength.
> Except for perfect bodhichitta,
> What other virtue is there that can outshine it?[134]

### 2. The benefit that it is the root of Dharma

Bodhichitta is the seed of everything that is excellent. Even while one is circling in existence, it will result in much happiness; and it is the sole cause of nirvana, supreme enlightenment. We can read in the *Sutra Requested by Brahma:*

> Brahma, because the superior motivation, bodhichitta, is the root of the whole Dharma, it is like a seed. Why is this? Just as from a seed there comes the shoot, the leaves, the flowers, and the fruit, from the superior motivation there comes the experience of much happiness among gods and humans and, furthermore, the attainment of omniscience.

### 3. The benefit that one's merit grows ever greater

For those who have aroused bodhichitta and not let it degenerate, not only are wisdom and skillful means combined during formal meditation, when they are in a state of no-thought, but even in ordinary situations in which they are not thinking—when they are asleep or unconscious, for example—an unbroken stream of merit arises. We are not talking here about a source of good consistent with ordinary merit which, like the plantain tree, bears fruit once and then is spent, but rather of merit that produces the fruit of happiness until the essence of enlightenment is reached: it is inexhaustible, growing more and more, like a great wish-fulfilling tree. *The Way of the Bodhisattva* describes it thus:

> For when, with irreversible intent,
> The mind embraces bodhichitta,
> Willing to set free the endless multitudes of beings,
> At that instant, from that moment on,
> A great and unremitting stream,
> A strength of wholesome merit,
> Even during sleep and inattention,
> Rises equal to the vastness of the sky.[135]

and,

> All other virtues, like the plantain tree,
> Produce their fruit, but then their force is spent.
> Alone the marvelous tree of bodhichitta
> Constantly bears fruit and grows unceasingly.[136]

### 4. The benefit that one has immeasurable qualities

Arousing bodhichitta results in an immense profusion of excellent qualities, among them, holding the infinite teachings of the Buddhas, understanding numerous teachings, and being blessed by the Buddhas. And it is a supreme offering to the Buddhas. The *Sutra of the Inconceivable Secrets* says:

> If the merit of bodhichitta
> Were to take form
> It would fill the whole of space,
> And still there would be more.

And in the *Sutra of the Arborescent Array* we read:

> In short, there is as much excellence and abundance of good quali-
> ties in arousing bodhichitta as all the excellence that the Victorious,
> Virtuous, Transcendent Buddhas possess: it is as vast as the firma-
> ment, as vast as the absolute space.

### 5. *The benefit that one becomes an object of the world's reverence*

Someone who possesses bodhichitta becomes an object of great reverence by the whole world,[137] including the gods, as *The Way of the Bodhisattva* shows:

> Should bodhichitta come to birth
> In those who suffer, chained in prisons of samsara,
> In that instant they are called the children of the Blissful One,
> Revered by all the world, by gods and humankind.[138]

### 6. *The benefit that everything one undertakes is meaningful*

Everything someone who possesses bodhichitta does, whether neutral or
positive, becomes a source of good consistent with liberation, for even if
the act is not backed by the actual thought of bodhichitta at the time, once
one has taken the vow of bodhichitta, provided one has not degenerated
it, all one's actions are permeated by bodhichitta. Everything such a person undertakes, therefore, is bound, ultimately, to be beneficial.[139] We can
read in the *Sutra of the Arborescent Array:*

> Child of good family, everything that someone who has aroused the
> supreme bodhichitta undertakes with his body, speech, and mind
> has meaning: it has a single flavor in that it is always and exclusively
> positive.

### 7. *The benefit that all those with whom one is connected are linked to liberation*

Because Bodhisattvas are such important "fields," people who, from lack
of faith, get angry with them and do them harm will have to experience
the lower realms, at least temporarily. But despite this, in the end, because of those Bodhisattvas' compassion, they will definitely reach the

end of cyclic existence and be liberated. As for those who do have faith in them, their merit will grow more and more powerful, and they will thereby swiftly attain enlightenment. The *Pagoda of Precious Jewels* states:

> Even those who do evil to a Bodhisattva, resulting in their going to the lower realms, will subsequently, because of that Bodhisattva's great efforts, find freedom and be set in unsurpassable enlightenment.

And *The Way of the Bodhisattva* says:

> I go for refuge to those springs of happiness
> Who bring their very enemies to perfect bliss.[140]

To sum up, in the forty-fourth chapter of the *Sutra of the Arborescent Array* we find a description of how boundless the merit and other benefits of bodhichitta are. Having taken the vow of bodhichitta from Mañjushri, Sudhana wished to request the precepts, and in order to do so travelled south. He arrived in a southern land on the shores of the ocean, at the palace called "Endowed with the Essence Ornamented by Vairochana," in which Maitreya was teaching the Dharma to a following of many hundreds of thousands of Bodhisattvas. Seeing him from a distance of five hundred leagues, Sudhana felt raptures of joy and prostrated to him. When Maitreya saw him, he placed his right hand on Sudhana's head and delightedly sang his praises to the assembled Bodhisattvas:

"Look, at Sudhana, he of pure intent,
Born of enduring riches,
Seeking the practice of supreme enlightenment,
He has come before me, the wise one."

and,

"Have you travelled well, you in whom compassion and love have
    arisen?
Have you come to the vast mandala of Maitreya?
Have you travelled well, you the sight of whom brings perfect peace?
Have you not tired of performing the deeds of a Bodhisattva?"
    and so on.

Thereupon, Sudhana, with his hands folded, said to him: "Noble One, now that I am fully engaged in unsurpassable enlightenment, I beg you, since I do not know, to show me how to wholeheartedly undertake the activities of a Bodhisattva."

To this Maitreya replied: "Fortunate child, you have been guided by a spiritual friend. Why is this? Fortunate child, bodhichitta is like the seed of all the Buddha's teachings. In making everything that is virtuous in all beings grow, it is like a field. In consuming everything that is evil, it is like the fire at the end of the kalpa. In bringing to exhaustion all negative actions, it is like the underworld. In fulfilling all wishes, it is like the king of wish-fulfilling jewels. In drawing beings out of the river of cyclic existence, it is like a hook. It is like an offering tree in the world of gods, humankind, and demigods. It fulfills all aspirations, like the bounteous vase."

And having actually described almost two hundred and fifty benefits, ending with the similes of elixirs and jewels, he concluded, "Thus, bodhichitta possesses these and infinite other benefits."

For a detailed account you should consult the sutra itself.[141]

## II. CLARIFICATION OF THE POINTS OF THE TRAINING IN THIS CASE

Relax physically, verbally, and mentally, and reflect as follows: "Just as one could never fix the dimensions of space even if one were to take measurements in the ten directions, there is no measure to the size and dimensions of the universe. And there is nowhere in the universe, not a single interstice, that is not filled with sentient beings belonging to the six realms. Throughout our series of past lives—and there is no saying when they began—I and all those beings have been wandering in cyclic existence and have been reborn countless times. Each time we took birth, we had a body. And for each of those bodies there was a father and mother. There is not a single one of all those sentient beings who has not been my father or mother—and not only once: every one of them has been my parent an incalculable number of times. On each occasion they have shown me nothing but kindness.

"Take this present life, for example. To begin with, when my body was developing in my mother's womb, she endured physical exhaustion, her beautiful complexion faded, it was difficult for her to stand or sit, her senses were dulled, and she could not eat and drink the things she liked. Then, when she gave birth to me at the end of all those months, all her joints except her jaws were stretched apart, and she had to take half a step into the land of the dead; yet she still unhesitatingly took me on her lap—I, who resembled a worm in a swamp of filth. Whatever the situation, whatever she did—like wiping up my excrement with her loving hand—she cherished and cared for me. She would have died rather than have her little child get sick. She gave me everything she had—all her property and possessions—but she never regretted it or held it over me. So it has been with my parents in all my past lives, who have truly cared for me, with great kindness. There is no difference between them and my present parents—they are all just as closely related to me.

"Now, all of them are groping in the gloom of ignorance, their minds crazed and deranged by afflictive emotions. Bereft of the eye of wisdom that sees what to adopt and what to avoid, they have no spiritual friend to act as a guide leading them in their blindness. Having cast aside the staff of merit, and with their legs—means and wisdom—broken, how will they ever escape from the abyss of cyclic existence? They want to be happy, but, ignorant of the means for achieving that, all they manage to accomplish are the very things that lead to suffering. What they practice runs counter to what they really want, and because of such deeds they are perpetually miserable, indulging in the causes of suffering and experiencing suffering as the result. How pitiful they are, these kind old mothers."

Reflecting in this manner, cultivate compassion to the point that you feel your heart about to burst or you feel a physical sensation of horror at others' suffering. Simply developing compassion, however, is not much help to all those beings. So think, "I have to draw them out of cyclic existence, the ocean of suffering, and swiftly place them on the level of liberation, unsurpassable perfect Buddhahood. At present I am incapable of doing that; I must therefore, in this very life, attain Buddhahood so that I can. In order to do so, I will practice the different stages of the profound path." Recite the following verses to remind yourself of your motivation:

All beings filling space have been my parents.
They wish for happiness, yet all they achieve is suffering.
How pitiful they are, wandering in cyclic existence with no
    chance of escape.
I must do everything I can to free them.
To that end I will drive myself with undistracted effort
And see the profound yoga through to completion.

For the actual practice of bodhichitta, appealing to the objects of refuge as your witness, make the following powerful aspiration: "Just as the Buddhas and Bodhisattvas in the past cultivated the aspirational bodhichitta and then trained in the active bodhichitta, so too will I, motivated by the four boundless attitudes, for the benefit of all beings who have been my parents, arouse the mind of supreme enlightenment and train in stages on the path of the six transcendent perfections." Along with this, recite from the depth of your heart the following verse, a hundred, or a thousand times or so:

---

Heed me, Protectors and your Children:
With the four boundless attitudes I will wholeheartedly take
   up the good of beings;
Holding bodhichitta, I will train in the six transcendent
   perfections.
May the twofold goal be spontaneously and gloriously
   fulfilled.

---

Concentrate especially on giving and taking. As you breathe in, imagine that all the negative actions, obscurations, and sufferings of all beings are gathered into a black mass, which enters your nostrils and dissolves into your heart, thus freeing beings forever from negative actions and suffering. As you breathe out again, imagine that all your own happiness and positive actions go out through your nostrils in a brilliant white stream, like rays of moonlight, and dissolve into all beings so that they immediately attain Buddhahood. Meditate on this joyfully. Along with this, recite at length any suitable prayers of aspiration, for example:

When I am happy, I dedicate it to the accumulation of virtue:
May space be filled with benefit and happiness.
When I am suffering, may it be the ripening of everyone's
   suffering,
May the ocean of suffering dry up.

Meditate for a long time with intense bodhichitta. At the end, dissolve the refuge tree as before* and rest in evenness in the state in which there are no concepts of beings as the object for which you arouse bodhichitta, of yourself as the agent arousing it, or of an attitude as the method by which it is aroused.

---

The essence of relative bodhichitta is compassion, and it is in dependence on this that absolute bodhichitta is born. As Padampa Sangye said,

---

* I.e., in same way as the dissolution at the end of a session of refuge practice.

Unless compassion arises, realization will not take birth.
Fishes swim in water, not on dry land.

By relying on relative bodhichitta, great compassion, we will realize the way things truly are without any mistake, and when that happens we will automatically achieve an unfabricated bodhichitta directed toward beings who have no realization, and we will be able to put our body, speech, and mind to service in benefiting others. So if we find ourselves having only selfish thoughts and no altruistic thoughts, it is that our bodhichitta has gone fundamentally wrong. It is therefore very important to meditate on considering others as equal to ourselves, and on exchanging ourselves and others.

Sentient beings are identical to us in all wanting to be happy. We are all the same in not wanting to suffer. And we are also all the same in our ultimate nature—in that we have no intrinsic existence. Moreover, since there is only one of me, whereas other beings are very numerous, not only are we equal but other beings are more important. For this reason, this wish to bring all beings to Buddhahood is not to be left as a merely intellectual idea; it must be something that you definitely apply to your own mind. To make progress in this, you must cease to consider yourself important, but consider any sentient being, even if it is only a single one, as extremely important. Thus you should be only too willing to devote yourself exclusively to helping others, in both your thoughts and deeds, joyfully undertaking even very painful ordeals for their sake, if you know it will make them happy. By thinking of others' welfare even when you are moving about, walking, lying down, or sitting, you will be training in accumulating merit and wisdom on a vast scale, these being the means for making bodhichitta grow.

Because we are ordinary beings, faults and downfalls that transgress the Bodhisattva vow often occur, so we must be certain to part from them and renew our vow—in the best case, in each of the six periods of day and night; in the middling case, at the beginning and end of the four sessions; and at the very least, once a day and once a night.

Should it happen that negative forces make you ill or injure you, people speak ill of you, or your afflictive emotions become very intense, pile up on top of such situations all the undesirable things that happen to beings. If you find yourself in painful circumstances, recognize that it is because of your past deeds and instead of getting depressed, take on others' suffering. If you find yourself in happy situations, dedicate your wealth and influence

*Refuge Tree of* Heart Essence of the Dakini.

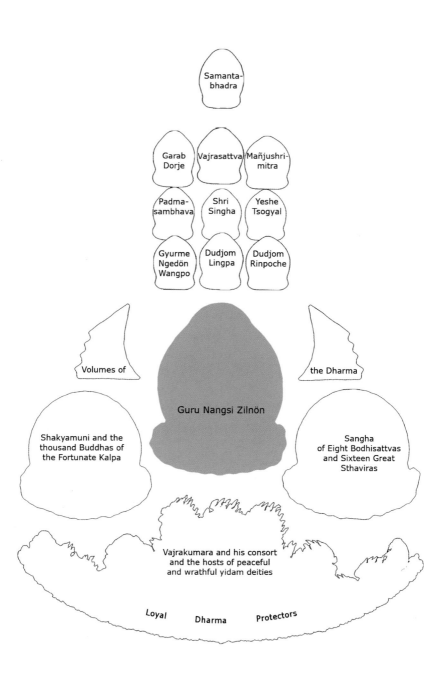

Samanta-
bhadra

Garab
Dorje

Vajrasattva

Mañjushri-
mitra

Padma-
sambhava

Shri
Singha

Yeshe
Tsogyal

Gyurme
Ngedön
Wangpo

Dudjom
Lingpa

Dudjom
Rinpoche

Volumes of

the Dharma

Guru Nangsi Zilnön

Shakyamuni and the
thousand Buddhas of
the Fortunate Kalpa

Sangha
of Eight Bodhisattvas
and Sixteen Great
Sthaviras

Vajrakumara and his consort
and the hosts of peaceful
and wrathful yidam deities

Loyal

Dharma

Protectors

*Key to the Refuge Tree.*

to virtuous ends; do not remain idle, but spur yourself to performing positive actions physically and verbally, and pray that all beings may be happy. Whatever unpleasant things happen to you—falling ill, getting depressed, getting involved in disputes, suffering loss or defeat—rather than feeling resentful of others, put the blame on yourself, thinking "This is simply my reward for considering myself more important."

Enemies, friends, and those who are neither are all supports for the mind training: they help us purify our negative actions and obscurations, so reflect on how grateful you should be to them. Do not do or say things in the hope that others will recognize how selfless you are. Keep your conduct absolutely pure, in accord with the Vinaya texts. Do not talk about others' faults. Any faults you see in others you should recognize as your own impure perception. Avoid trying to expose people's hidden flaws, speaking harshly, reciting wrathful mantras aimed at nonhuman beings, and the like. Do not pass on to others difficult tasks that have fallen to you, nor blame others for things that are your own fault. It is wrong to feel glad when those who are not on the same side as you are defeated, to think well of an enemy's death, or, when others fall ill, to wish that the riches and honors will come to you. Instead of being concerned about whether you feel good or bad, or about what people say about you, meditate on bodhichitta and give up the sort of sporadic practice that comes from lack of conviction.

With regard to those for whom it is hard to feel compassion—enemies, obstacle makers, and the like—meditate with special force. The practice you do is for your own benefit, so however much hardship it has entailed, do not boast about it to others. Instead of retaliating when people point out your faults, insult and humiliate you, criticize you, hit you, or beat you, meditate on compassion. Do not demonstrate exhilaration or displeasure over trivial things. If you cannot put up with the smallest harm done to you, and you do not manage to do the slightest thing to help others, you have lost sight of the point of bodhichitta, so train your mind in considering others as equal to yourself and in exchanging yourself and others.

To sum up, the purpose of all the teachings in the Great and Lesser Vehicles can be condensed into a single point: to subdue self-clinging.* As we practice, therefore, we should be reducing our self-cherishing. If it does not act as an antidote to the ego, our whole practice of Dharma will be pointless. Whether or not the practice we do is actually the Dharma

---

*Tib. *bdag 'dzin,* the belief in a truly existent self.

depends entirely on this, which is why it has been said that this is the scale on which those who practice the Dharma are weighed. Of course, other people who see you may testify to your being an authentic Dharma practitioner, but ordinary, worldly people cannot know what is hidden in your mind. You might feel pleased at having done one or two good deeds, but the real signs of having trained one's mind in bodhichitta are that one is not ashamed of oneself and that one is always in a happy frame of mind, whatever difficult or painful situations one finds oneself in, because rather than getting depressed about them, one takes them as aids to the practice. Nevertheless, while these may be indications that one has really gone to the heart of the teachings, they do not mean that one does not need to train further. So, until you attain Buddhahood, train in the precepts to make bodhichitta grow more and more.

*Vajrasattva.*

# Purifying Negative Actions and Obscurations, Which Are Unfavorable Conditions on the Path: Instructions on the Meditation of Vajrasattva

THIS CHAPTER COMPRISES TWO SECTIONS: GENERAL POINTS to be understood, and the points of the training in this case. The first is divided into three parts: the reason one needs to purify negative actions, the method for purifying them, and the benefits of purification.

## I. GENERAL POINTS TO BE UNDERSTOOD

### A. The reason one needs to purify negative actions

Since time without beginning, throughout our whole series of lives in cyclic existence, we ordinary beings have been accumulating the two kinds of obscuration, along with habitual tendencies, and we now have a great many of them in our stream of being. Because of them, the path to liberation and omniscience is obstructed, and, in particular, during the main practice, experiences and the wisdom of realization are prevented from forming properly in our minds. These interruptions and obstacles are the result of our past negative actions and downfalls related to vows. Furthermore, it is said that from breaking the Secret Mantra Vehicle commitments, many unpleasant things will happen to us in this life, we will meet with obstacles on the path, and we will go directly to the Diamond Hell, as we read in the tantras:

> The diamond ogre will suck the blood from your heart,
> You'll have a short life, with much illness, the loss of your wealth,
>     and fear of enemies;

And in the truly horrendous Hell of Ultimate Torment,
For ages you'll endure the most unbearable pain.

So because of the enormous benefits and risks involved, should the slightest breach occur, it must be parted from* immediately.

Actions motivated by the three poisons comprise mental actions, which are not given physical or verbal expression directly, and physical and verbal actions, which are actually expressed. For all actions, though, it is the thought that comes first. As it is said,

Because it makes the world go dark,
Mind is the root of the poisons.

All through our beginningless series of lives, we have unknowingly and imperceptibly gathered a mountainous burden of negative actions and downfalls, including the different kinds of negative actions described earlier in the chapter on cause and effect, the host of faults and downfalls that we have committed in transgressing the three kinds of vow,† deeds and downfalls we have induced others to do, those we have rejoiced at and praised, and so on. Added to all these are the negative actions and obscurations we have accumulated in this present life on account of most of our thoughts and deeds being exclusively influenced by the three poisons. Thus it has come about that we have never managed to escape from the sufferings of cyclic existence.

Now, if we keep these faults secretly hidden away, the seed of the negative actions will combine with the water and manure of deceit, and they will grow bigger and bigger. But if we recognize them as faults and without hiding them, we declare them to someone else, they will cease to grow and will become weaker. This is what we call "sealing the action with the truth."‡ Negative actions can be purified by intensely regretting and parting from them, and if we are diligent in this, we will have no difficulty in purifying our negative actions and downfalls completely. Such purification entails, on the one hand, an acknowledgment ("I have committed such-and-such a fault") and, on the other hand, a parting, with our minds in a state of longing caused by intense regret. Full of wonder and respect

---

*Tib. *bshags pa*, see glossary for an explanation of the term "parting," formerly translated as "confession."
† Tib. *sdom pa gsum*, the vows of individual liberation, Bodhisattva precepts, and Mantra-Vehicle commitments.
‡ Tib. *bden pas mtha' bsdoms pa*. Because of the truth, the action is finished with.

for those who do not have such faults, and ashamed and disheartened by the faults you have committed, declare them sincerely, praying from the depth of your heart, "Look on me with your compassion and purify these actions." All this is what is meant by "parting." If you part from them with heartfelt regret, there are no actions that cannot be purified by virtue of the essential fact that they are without intrinsic existence. As we find in the sutras,

> He who did, for many kalpas long,
> The greatest and most terrible evil deeds,
> Will, by parting fully from them once,
> Be cleansed of every single one.

And in *Letter to a Friend:*

> Those who formerly were careless
> But then took heed are full of beauty,
> As is the moon emerging from the clouds,
> Like Nanda, Angulimala, Darshaka, and Udayana.*

## B. The method for purifying negative actions

We read in the *Sutra of the Teaching on the Four Powers:*

> Maitreya, if a Bodhisattva possesses four powers,[142] all the negative deeds he has gathered will be completely overwhelmed. What are these four? They are regret, action as an antidote, the power of restoration, and the power of the support.

Accordingly, to part from negative actions one must have all four powers. When they are all present, even a heap of negative actions as high as Mount Meru will be purified by parting from them genuinely once.

### THE POWER OF THE SUPPORT

While the Three Jewels, the Three Roots, and all the infinite Buddhas are certainly the best support in general, here the particular support

---

* *Letter to a Friend,* 14. Nanda was unable to practice virtue on account of his attachment to his wife, and his taking monastic vows was motivated solely by the promise of future delights in the celestial realms. Angulimala killed 999 people, whose fingers he strung in a garland (hence his name, which means "Finger Necklace"). Darshaka (also known as Ajatashatru) murdered his father. And Udayana killed his mother. But by regretting and changing their ways, they were each able to attain a high level of realization.

is he who is praised as the Teacher Vajrasattva.* On the absolute level, the Bhagavan Glorious Vajrasattva is the great embodiment of the infinite adornments—the body, speech, mind, qualities, and inexhaustible activities—of all the Buddhas of the past, present, and future; he is the perfect essence of the single family of the Great Secret. On the relative level, when he first aroused the supreme bodhichitta, he made the following prayer: "Simply from hearing my name, may beings who have committed crimes with immediate retribution[143] and those who would fall into the Great Diamond Hell as a result of their Mantra Vehicle commitments having become deteriorated, broken, disintegrated, and torn apart† be immediately purified of their negative actions and obscurations. May I remain in the midst of those wrongdoers and, dispelling all their obscurations, bring them to the highest liberation." The strength of this pledge was such that he instantly purifies the greatest negative actions and downfalls, even those that are extremely difficult to purify.

His very essence, his mantra, is known as the Hundred Syllables of the Tathagatas. By changing a few of the names, it becomes the hundred syllables of infinite deities, such as the Heruka mantra,[144] and Vajrasattva is therefore praised in numerous tantras and transmissional texts as the Great All-Pervading Lord of all the Buddha families, both with regard to the deities and the mantras. He is the supreme heart essence, the treasure that all who have entered the Mantra Vehicle and follow the pith instructions hold in common.

This, then, is the power of the support—to visualize the Teacher Vajrasattva truly present, to take refuge in him with one-pointed respect, and, never forsaking bodhichitta, to reflect on the meaning of the mantra.

### *The Meaning of the Hundred-Syllable Mantra*

The mantra is a prayer evoking Vajrasattva's promise. Here are the words with their equivalent meanings.[145]

---

* "Teacher Vajrasattva" (Tib. *bla ma rdo rje sems dpa'*) refers to Vajrasattva inseparable from one's root teacher.

† Tib. *nyams chag zhig ral*. These refer to increasing degrees of transgression of the Diamond-Vehicle commitments in terms of the length of time they have remained unpurified. Where such transgressions have not been confessed and purified after three years, the commitments are said to have been irreparably "torn apart" and cannot then be purified.

| | |
|---|---|
| OM | Most highly praised, |
| VAJRASATTVA SAMAYAM | Vajrasattva! The sacred link between us— |
| ANUPALAYA VAJRASATTVA | Guard it closely. O Vajrasattva, |
| TENOPATISHTHA DRIDHO ME BHAVA | May you remain firmly with me. |
| SUTOKAYO ME BHAVA | May you completely satisfy me.[146] |
| SUPOKAYO ME BHAVA | Make me blossom fully. |
| ANURAKTO ME BHAVA | May you always be loving toward me. |
| SARVA SIDDHIM ME PRAYACCHA | Bestow on me all accomplishments. |
| SARVA KARMASU CHA ME | In all my actions |
| CHITTAM SHREYAH KURU | Make my mind most virtuous. |
| HUNG | (The vital seed syllable of Vajrasattva.) |
| HA HA HA HA | (Syllables indicating the four boundless attitudes, the four empowerments, the four joys, and the four bodies.) |
| HO | (A laugh of pleasure at those.) |
| BHAGAVAN SARVA TATHAGATA | O Victorious, Virtuous, and Transcendent One—of all the Tathagatas, |
| VAJRA MA ME MUŃCHA | You are the diamond—do not forsake me. |
| VAJRI BHAVA | Make me a diamond holder. |
| MAHA SAMAYASATTVA | O great being of the commitment, |
| AH | May I be inseparably united with you. |

## THE POWER OF ACTION AS AN ANTIDOTE

This entails performing positive actions as antidotes to negative ones. In this case it refers to the essential points of visualizing the deity, reciting the mantra, concentrating on the negative actions and obscurations being washed away, and so on.

## THE POWER OF REGRET

This is to give rise to intense remorse for the negative actions one has performed in the past—as if one had taken poison.

## THE POWER OF RESTORATION OR RESOLUTION

This is the firm resolution to refrain from negative actions in the future, even if one's life is at stake.

These last two powers are complete when at the end of reciting the mantra, one verbalizes one's parting, in verse or as prose, with such prayers as "In ignorance and confusion . . ."* Even if one cannot do this, giving rise to true regret and recognizing the fault in future wrongdoing will automatically produce the resolution to refrain.

There is not one of us who has not entered the door of the Secret Mantra Vehicle.† And once we have done so, if we do not subsequently keep the commitments, we will go to hell; if we do keep them, we will attain Buddhahood. There is no other destination than these two. The Secret Mantra Vehicle commitments are very subtle, numerous, and difficult to keep. Even Lord Atisha[147] said that after he had entered the Mantra Vehicle, he committed fault after fault in rapid succession. So for us who have few antidotes, weak mindfulness, and no vigilance (we do not even know the different categories of vows, nor the point at which we break the precepts), there can be no doubt that breaches of our vows are falling on us like rain. We should therefore do the practice of Vajrasattva every day and recite the hundred syllables twenty-one times. By doing so, our downfalls will be blessed and their fully ripened effect will be prevented from growing greater. And by reciting the hundred-syllable mantra one hundred thousand times, all our downfalls will be eradicated, as the *Ornament of the Essence* says:

> Clearly visualize Vajrasattva
> Enthroned on a white lotus and moon:
> By reciting twenty-one times
> The hundred syllables according to the ritual,
> Downfalls and the like will be blessed
> And therefore not grow greater.
> Thus the greatest accomplished beings have taught,
> So do this practice constantly.
> If you recite it one hundred thousand times,
> You will become the very embodiment of total purity.

Even if, for your own part, you have managed—through your stability in the generation and perfection phases, your mindfulness and vigilance, and so forth—to keep faultless commitments, there are others who may have

---

* See the prayer "O Protector, in ignorance and confusion . . ." on page 212.
† The entrance to the Secret Mantra Vehicle is empowerment, and in Tibet almost everyone had received one or more empowerments from a teacher.

broken the root commitments, and by mixing with them in conversation, joining with them in the same activities, and even drinking the water from the same valley as they, you will get the faults of transgression by association and of incidental transgression.[148] As the tantra says,

> I have kept the company of transgressors, fulfilled their wishes,
> Given teachings to them and to those unsuitable.
> I have thought nothing of those who've broken the commitments
> And have in turn been tainted by their defilements and faults.

It is also said:

> Like one drop of sour milk
> That turns all the milk sour,
> One degenerate practitioner
> Spoils all the other practitioners.

Breaches of Mantra-Vehicle commitments are easy to purify if we part from them properly. The teachings say that if a single root downfall of the vows of individual liberation occurs and is concealed, it is impossible to repair, like a shattered earthen pot. Root downfalls of the Bodhisattva vow are like broken objects made of a precious metal: they can be repaired with the help of someone else, namely a spiritual friend. Faults and downfalls in the Secret Mantra Vehicle are like slight dents in a precious metal object: one can completely purify them oneself, using the deity, mantra, and concentration as supports. As long as one parts from them immediately, they are easy to purify, but the longer one waits, the more the fault grows, and the harder it becomes to part from it. After three years, they cannot be purified, even if one attempts to part from them.

## C. The benefits of purification

This meditation and recitation is the internal cleansing method of the unsurpassable Secret Mantra Vehicle, so it is entirely appropriate to apply it at the beginning of all one's sessions. In any case, if one recites the hundred syllables one hundred and eight times in a single session, concentrating without any distraction and without adulterating the recitation with ordinary speech, all one's past negative actions, obscurations, and deteriorations and breaches will definitely be purified—as Vajrasattva himself has promised in the *Tantra of Stainless Parting:*

The quintessence of the mind of all the Sugatas purifies all deteriorations, breaches, and conceptual obscurations. Known as the hundred syllables, it is the king of all purifications by parting. To recite it
one hundred and eight times at one sitting repairs all deteriorations
and breaches and saves one from falling into the three lower realms.
Practitioners who recite it as a daily practice will, even in this very
lifetime, be guarded and protected by the Buddhas of past, present,
and future, who will think of them as their most excellent children.
And at their death, there is no doubt they will become chief of all
the Sugatas' heirs.

The boundless benefits of this practice are also described in numerous
texts, among them the *Tantra of the Three Verses on the Wisdom Mind:*

> Those who meditate on Vajrasattva
> And recite the mantra perfectly
> Will purify all their negative actions
> And become the same as Vajrasattva.

and the *Tantra of the Song of Vajrasattva,* which declares:

> The self-arisen essence, the hundred-syllable mantra,
> Is the seed of all the Buddhas.
> It destroys all deteriorations and breaches.

and,

> For those who hold the hundred syllables
> Untimely death will not occur,
> Nor will illness and misery befall them.
> For those who hold the hundred syllables
> There'll be no poverty or pain.
> Their enemies will disappear,
> And all their wishes will be fulfilled.
> Those who hold the hundred syllables
> And want a child, will have a child;
> If they seek riches, riches they'll obtain;
> And when they're homeless, they will find a home.
> If you wish to prolong your life,
> You should hold the hundred syllables:
> Even if you've come to this life's end,
> You'll easily live three hundred years.

In this life you will be happy,
At death you'll go to the Blissful Realm.*
Dakinis, elemental spirits, and those that possess and resurrect
    the dead,
Spirits that cast defilement, negative forces, and those that
    destroy memory
Can do no harm
To holders of the hundred syllables.
And even beings with great downfalls
Will surely see the Buddhas.
By reciting the Secret Mantra Vehicle's hundred syllables
The stupid will become intelligent,
And the ill-fated will have good luck;
Calamities and misery will be no more.
Even those burdened by the five crimes with immediate effect†
Will be purified by reciting the hundred syllables.
In those and subsequent lives,
They will become universal monarchs and the like.
Finally they will devote themselves to liberation
And attain Buddhahood.

## II. Clarification of the points of the training in this case

Begin by arousing bodhichitta, thinking "In order to purify all the negative actions, obscurations, faults, and downfalls that I and others have accumulated since time without beginning in our series of lives in cyclic existence, I will begin the meditation and recitation of the Teacher Vajrasattva."

For this, consider that your own body is in its ordinary form, and that above the crown of your head is a thousand-petaled white lotus, its stalk four fingers' breadth long, with the root planted in the crown opening on the top of your head. On top of the flower's fully developed cluster of anthers is a full-moon disc. Visualize upon it a clear, bright white syllable HUNG, from which inconceivable rays of five-colored light

---

*Tib. *bde ba can,* Skt. Sukhavati, the Buddhafield of Amitabha.
† The five crimes with immediate retribution (Tib. *mtshams med lnga*); see above, page 123.

radiate, making offerings to please the Buddhas and Bodhisattvas in the ten directions, and purifying all sentient beings of their negative actions and obscurations. The light rays are gathered back and dissolve into the HUNG, which transforms into your kind root teacher in the form of the Bhagavan, Glorious Vajrasattva. His body is as white as a conch, clear like a crystal, and brilliant as the sun. He has a radiant face, attractive and smiling, and is effulgent with the splendor of the major and minor marks. He is one-faced and two-armed: his right hand holds a five-pointed *vajra* at the level of his heart; with his left hand on his hip holding a bell, he embraces his consort. He is seated cross-legged in the diamond posture. His dark blue hair is tied up with a jeweled ribbon and ornamented with a crown jewel. He is bedecked with the five silken garments (an upper garment of gold-embroidered white silk, a multicolored skirt, a many-colored tasseled headdress, a two-colored blue silk sash,* and a long dancing shawl) and the eight jewel ornaments—a crown, earrings, a necklet, a short necklace (reaching down to the breast), bracelets, anklets, a girdle, and a necklace (reaching down to the navel).

On his lap, in union with him, is his self-radiance, the consort Vajra-topa, who is white, has the youthful appearance of a sixteen-year-old, and is adorned with the five symbolic ornaments. She is embracing him, her hands round his neck holding a curved knife and a skull, and her feet entwined round him in the lotus posture. Both of them display the nine modes of expression of the peaceful deities—supple, lithe, entwining, graceful, youthful, clear-eyed, lustrous,† giving out a sense of grandeur, and radiantly majestic. Endlessly emanating infinite rays of light, they are the essence of bliss and emptiness inseparable.

In Vajrasattva's heart is a fully bloomed, eight-petaled white lotus, and in the middle of its anthers, a full-moon disc. On top of that, visualize a five-pointed white, clear crystal *vajra*, in an upright position, and in the center of its hollow hub an upright white syllable HUNG, encircled by the letters of the hundred-syllable mantra, starting from the front and turning to the right, shining like mercury and spontaneously emitting the sound of the mantra.

Next, full of regret for all the negative actions and downfalls you have accumulated in your series of lives since time without beginning, and firmly vowing not to repeat them in the future even if your life is at stake,

---

*The belt is blue outside and red inside.
† This refers to the skin, which is bright and not pale.

think of the Teacher Vajrasattva above your head as the essence of all the Buddhas of past, present, and future, and generate such boundless devotion to him that tears well up in your eyes. Then recite the hundred syllables, concentrating on the mantra garland in his heart as if you were reading it, and, most importantly, reciting it as a prayer: "O my teacher, Vajrasattva, in you I put my trust!" As you recite, an endless, nectarous stream of blessings flows down, glistening like mercury. Pouring down through the bodies of the deity and his consort, it emerges from the point of their union, swirls down the lotus stem, enters you through the crown opening, and fills the whole of the inside of your body. Every illness in the form of pus, blood, and lymph, all kinds of negative forces in the form of animals and insects, and every one of your negative actions and obscurations in the form of liquid smoke and liquid charcoal—all are rinsed out like particles of dirt being flushed away by water pouring down a drainpipe. Trickling through the two lower orifices and all the pores of your skin, they percolate down to nine levels underneath the earth, to the male and female beings with whom you have incurred deed-related debts in past lives and who seek to avenge themselves on your flesh, flowing into their mouths until they are completely satiated. Consider that your body and mind are filled with untainted bliss.

---

Above my crown, on a lotus-and-moon seat,
Is the Teacher Vajrasattva, the color of crystal,
Smiling peacefully, youthful and radiant with the major and
    minor marks.
His right and left hands—means and wisdom—hold a vajra
    and a bell;
He sits cross-legged, in the complete attire of the body of
    perfect enjoyment.
On his lap is Topa, holding knife and skull, and embracing
    him.
In his heart is a moon disc with a HUNG surrounded by the
    mantra garland,
From which a stream of ambrosial bodhichitta flows down
    through the point of union,
Entering me by the crown opening and completely filling my
    body.
All deteriorations and breaches, negative actions, and
    downfalls are purified.

Om vajra sattva samaya manu pala ya
Vajra sattva tenopa tishtha dridho me bhava
Sutokayo me bhava
Supokayo me bhava
Anu rakto me bhava
Sarva siddhim me prayaccha
Sarva karma sucha me
Chittan shreyam kuru hung
Ha ha ha ha ho
Bhagavan
Sarva tathagata vajra mame muñcha vajri bhava
    maha samaya sattva ah

Recite the mantra assiduously as many times as you can—one hundred, a thousand, ten thousand, a hundred thousand times, or more. At the end of the session, fold your hands together and pray as follows:

O Protector, in ignorance and confusion
I have transgressed and deteriorated the commitments.
My Teacher and Protector, give me refuge!
O supreme Diamond Holder,
Embodiment of great compassion,
To you, lord of beings, I go for refuge.
I acknowledge and part from all my deteriorations and
    breaches of the root and branch commitments of body,
    speech, and mind.
I beg you, cleanse and purify all the stains of my negative
    actions, obscurations, faults, and downfalls.

As result of your prayer, your body becomes transparent, inside and out, like a heap of crystal, devoid of flesh, blood, bones, dirt, and foul matter. The whole inside is white, completely filled by the stream of nectar. All your negative actions and obscurations have been purified and cleansed. Imagine that

Vajrasattva smiles with pleasure and grants your prayer, saying: "Fortunate child, all your negative actions, obscurations, faults, and downfalls are purified!"

Immediately, Vajrasattva and his consort melt into white light and dissolve into you. You yourself are completely transformed into Vajrasattva with his consort as visualized earlier—all imagined in a flash. From the vital seed syllable in the heart surrounded by the quintessential mantra of six syllables, rays of light emanate, filling space.

| | | | |
|---|---|---|---|
| | sa | | |
| ་ | tva | hūṁ | vajra |
| | oṁ | | |

All impure perceptions resulting from attachment are purified, together with habitual tendencies. Consider that the whole universe outside becomes the Unexcelled Buddhafield of Manifest Joy; all the beings in it become none other than Vajrasattva. From their mouths the sound of the mantra resounds like the buzzing of bees from a bees' nest that has been broken open.

> All negative actions and obscurations are purified; I become
>     like a heap of crystal.
> Again, Vajrasattva melts into white light
> And blends into me, and I become Vajrasattva.
> All that appears and exists is viewed as purified, as the
>     infinite display.
> OM VAJRA SATTVA HUNG

Recite this mantra as much as you can. At the end, the universe and beings visualized as a Buddhafield and deities all melt into light and dissolve into you. You yourself then dissolve into the vital seed syllable in the heart. This again dissolves in stages from the bottom up into the *nada,** and the *nada* in turn vanishes into the state of emptiness, the nonconceptual clear light. Rest in evenness as long as you can, completely relaxed in the inexpressible state of great bliss, pure from the very beginning, free of all concepts of an object to be purified and a subject that purifies. Then, when you rise out of that state, dedicate the merit with such prayers as,

---

\* *nada,* the uppermost tip of the *bindu* or circle forming the top of the syllable HUNG.

> By the merit of this
> May I swiftly accomplish the nature of Vajrasattva,
> And, not leaving out a single being,
> May I establish them all in his level.

Then continue with your everyday activities.

Until you have signs that you have purified your negative actions and obscurations, it is important to be completely concentrated on the visualization and to do the recitation without distraction. As the Great Master said,

> If you are distracted, with your mind elsewhere,
> Even reciting for a kalpa will bring no result.

What are the signs of success in this practice? Meditational experiences or dreams in which you vomit or purge, are washing, are dressed in white, cross a wide river, fly through the sky, see the sun and moon rising, and so forth, are signs that you have purified negative actions. Dreams or experiences in which dirt, pus, blood, and lymph come out of your body are some of the indications that you have purified illnesses. Those in which minute animals such as ants emerge show that you have expelled negative forces. In particular, you may have real, direct experiences of clear awareness, of physical lightness, and of spontaneous devotion and determination to be free.

In general, if you have genuine confidence in the law of cause and effect, there is no way that you will not feel regret for your negative actions, and when this is so, your parting from faults too will be authentic. From purifying your mindstream in this way, you will certainly have more and more good experiences, and your realization will increase. Nowadays, however, we are not fundamentally interested in purifying our obscurations and do not make the effort. Even if we do, we follow the prayers and rituals merely as a duty, but without real, heartfelt confidence or shame and regret. This is why the qualities of experience and realization are as rare as stars in the daytime. So never underestimate the importance of this method for purifying obscurations, and make every effort to practice it so that it is truly effective.

*The Mandala of the Universe.*

# Gathering the Accumulations, Which Are Favorable Conditions on the Path: The Way to Offer the Mandala

THERE ARE TWO SECTIONS: GENERAL POINTS TO BE UNDERstood, and the points of the training in this case. The first of these is divided into two: a general mention of the two accumulations, and particular points on the mandala practice.

## I. GENERAL POINTS TO BE UNDERSTOOD

### A. A general mention of the two accumulations

The sublime Nagarjuna has said:

> From all such seeds
> The fruit appears as a likeness of its cause.
> What clever person could ever prove
> The existence of a fruit without a seed?

All phenomena exist through the relationship of cause and effect, so the view in which the two truths* are inseparable is of fundamental importance. Completing the two accumulations together creates the cause that will produce the absolute body and form body as the result. As the *Jewel Garland* points out,

> Stated briefly, the form body
> Arises from the accumulation of merit.

---

* The two truths are relative truth and absolute or ultimate truth.

Stated briefly, the absolute body,
O King, is born from the accumulation of wisdom.[149]

It is the accumulation of wisdom (which is included in sustained calm and profound insight as compatible causes) that is the cause for attaining the ultimate result, the absolute body, and that in turn depends on achieving the accumulation of merit. It is said in a sutra:

As long as one has not completed the supreme twin
    accumulation,
One will not realize supreme emptiness.

Furthermore,

Innate absolute wisdom can only come
As the mark of having accumulated merit and purified
    obscurations,
And through the blessings of a realized teacher.
Know that those who rely on other means are fools.

## B. Particular points on the mandala practice

There are eight parts: reasons, nature, the meaning of the word, different ways of offering, the special feature of the practice, the various elements that are visualized, considering one's aim, and the unique benefits.

### *1. The reasons for making the mandala the main offering*

In general, there is an infinite variety of ways to accumulate merit, and they are all included in the practice of generosity and the other transcendent perfections. However, the offering of the mandala, which is easy to perform and very effective, is the best of all offerings by virtue of the exceptional vastness of its field, attitude, and constituents, and by virtue of its purity. Its vastness lies in the fact that (1) the field to which one envisages making the offering is not limited* but comprises all the Three Jewels and teachers in the ten directions and the three times; (2) the attitude is impartial, for one is striving for unsurpassable enlightenment and one's thoughts therefore include all sentient beings filling the whole of space; and (3) the constituents of the offering are unrestricted, their

---

*The offering is not restricted to only a few persons.

arrangement and form as a Buddhafield that one mentally creates and then offers being as boundless as space. As for the mandala offering being extremely pure, this is because throughout its preparation, actual practice, and conclusion, it is untainted by such things as the self-centeredness and conceit that can occur, for instance, in making other material offerings. As Lord Atisha says:

> Of all the methods for accumulating merit using one's hands, none have greater merit than the mandala.

In particular, we read in the *Approach to the Absolute Truth:*

> In the three breaks between sessions, observing extreme purity,
> Wash your mouth, hands, and feet,
> Then take some perfect flowers and before the teacher
> Perform the perfectly round mandala of the Victorious Ones.

By offering the mandala when we meet our glorious, sublime teachers, when they turn the Wheel of Dharma, and even when we think of them, we will please all the Buddhas and complete our own accumulation of merit and wisdom, thus creating an auspicious connection. For these and many other important reasons, the mandala is acclaimed as being by far the best of all forms of offering.

## 2. The nature of the offering

The mandala and offering piles are merely symbolic. In the sutra tradition, we fully imagine all the Buddhafields in the ten directions, represented by a billion universes each made up of Mount Meru and the four continents, filled with clouds of all kinds of offerings, and we offer these to the teacher and the oceanlike infinity of the Three Jewels. In the Mantra Vehicle, on the other hand, we recognize the nature of the fundamental way things truly are. Everything that appears outwardly as the universe arises from the true way of being that is the inner diamond body, and both of these (outer and inner mandalas) are spontaneously present in the alternative mandala,[150] the mandala of the deity. These three (outer, inner, and alternative) arise as the display of the absolute mandala, the union of emptiness supreme in all aspects and unchanging great bliss. Outer, inner, and alternative offerings are therefore made within a single offering, the absolute offering of the Diamond Buddhafield that is the play of bliss-emptiness arising in all different forms.

## 3. *The meaning of the word* mandala

The word *mandala* refers to a surrounding environment with a central heart, or to something that holds an arrangement of ornaments. In the present context it has the sense of a Buddhafield, for it symbolizes the universe and beings, the support and the supported, all complete and perfect.

## 4. *Different ways of offering the mandala*

Of the two kinds of mandala that are described, the accomplishment mandala and the offering mandala, it is the latter that we shall discuss here.* In the Ancient Translations' tradition of the Secret Mantra Vehicle, the most widely known mandala is the one with seven piles, representing Mount Meru, the four continents, and the sun and moon. There are other traditions, with eleven, fifteen, and thirty-seven piles, and ones that are even more elaborate. In particular, the texts of the Great Perfection's pith instructions speak of the mandala of the body of manifestation, which is the one that has just been mentioned, the mandala of the body of perfect enjoyment with eight piles, and the mandala of the absolute body with five piles. In the original Indic texts related to the New Translations, there are numerous rituals for the mandala offering, including those of the masters Sucharita and Nishkalankashri, but the most important one, described by the great masters Buddhaguhya, Kambala, and others, uses twenty-three piles—Mount Meru, the four continents with their subcontinents, the seven attributes of royalty, the treasure vase, and the sun and moon. Mañjushrikirti and Nishkalankavajra also used mandalas of essentially twenty-three piles, but with the difference that the former substituted one's own body for the treasure vase while the latter offered all kinds of treasures such as sapphires. Jetari taught a mandala with seventeen piles. From these and other traditions there evolved a large number of different practices here in Tibet. Of these, the followers of the Kalachakra offer mandalas with nine piles and twenty-five piles, obtained by adding Rahu and Ketu† to the seven- and twenty-three-element mandalas respectively. In both cases, details such as the disposition of Mount Meru and the con-

---

*The accomplishment mandala is described below in the section "Clarification of the points of the training in this case."
† Tib. *sgra can dus me,* Skt. Rahu and Ketu, two figures in Indian mythology representing the ascending and descending lunar nodes that give rise to eclipses.

tinents follow the Kalachakra tradition. Other traditions have mandalas with more or fewer elements, but they all share the arrangement of Mount Meru and the continents common to both sutras and tantras, and they are therefore accepted as being in agreement with the third chapter of the *Treasury of Abhidharma.*

Nowadays the detailed mandala that is best known and most widely used in all the different schools is the thirty-seven-element mandala said to have been composed by Chögyal Pakpa Rinpoche. It consists of the twenty-three piles to which have been added the four particular attributes of the four continents, the eight offering goddesses (the Lady of Charm and so on), and the canopy and victory banner. This is the mandala that is most practiced.

## 5. *The special feature of the practice*

In order to complete the extraordinary accumulations, we need to perform the offering ritual, and the special feature of this is the importance of purity. The material from which the mandala base is made should ideally be gold or silver; the next best would be copper or steel, while at the worst, it could be stone or wood. The piles offered should ideally be of precious stones; next best would be different kinds of grain, and at the worst, white cowry shells. In any case, we should offer the best we can afford, arranged very beautifully. The materials for the piles are to be soaked with scented water* to symbolize that the offering is moistened with bodhichitta. To bring about favorable circumstances, namely freedom from faults, carefully wipe dust off the base. Sprinkle on it scented water to which the purifying ingredients from a cow have been added† (this symbolizes the spontaneous accomplishment of excellent qualities), and then dispose the piles in order without making any mistakes. All in all, observe cleanliness and respect—physically, verbally, and mentally—as you make the offering.

---

* In practice, scented water refers to saffron water.

† Tib. *ba byung.* According to Kriya tantra, five ingredients collected under specific circumstances are especially pure: they are the milk, butter, cheese, urine, and dung of a red cow, born at an auspicious moment, and which has just calved for the first time. These have to be obtained during a lunar eclipse by a fully ordained monk who has been ordained fifteen years, kept his vows perfectly, and now renews his vows before milking the cow.

## 6. *The various elements that are visualized in offering the infinite Buddhafield*

Begin by holding up the offering mandala base in your left hand. With a handful of flowers in your right fist, remove dust by wiping the mandala base clockwise three times while reciting the hundred-syllable mantra. As you do so, consider that all the obstacle-creating negative actions, obscurations, illnesses, and negative forces that you and all beings have accumulated in your mindstreams throughout your beginningless series of lives are being purified. Then, as you recite OM VAJRA BHUMI AH HUNG . . . and so on, consider that the mandala base becomes the mighty golden ground, immensely broad, its surface as even as the palm of the hand, and that the scented water that you place in the middle is the ocean, containing water with the eight perfect qualities.* This is sufficient, without one's having to visualize the mandalas of wind, fire, and water under the ground.

Next, as you recite OM VAJRA RE KHE . . . and so on, create the iron mountain, disposing the grain counterclockwise in a circle round the edge of the disc and considering that it forms the periphery, the Horse-Headed Mountain Range, a fiery ring of iron mountains. At this stage, as one re-cites HUNG, one can place a drop of saffron water or a flower in the middle for protection, but this does not happen in this tradition for practicing the mandala. Similarly, although one can generate the visualization of Mount Meru and the other elements from their respective seed syllables, here, Mount Meru, the continents, and the rest are each visualized in the same instant that each pile is set out, one by one.

In the center of the ocean is **Mount Meru** with its four steps.† It is square in shape, with its top surface broader and opening out. Its eastern side is made of crystal, the south of lapis lazuli, the west of ruby, and the north of gold, all blazing with light, so that the ocean, sky, and continents on each side take on their respective hues. Mount Meru is surrounded by seven golden mountain ranges disposed like screens in a square around it—Yugandhara, Ishadhara, Khadiraka, Sudarshana, Ashvakarna, Vina-taka, and Nimindhara[151]—each range being half the height of the previous one.‡ These mountain ranges are separated from each other by the Seas of

---

*The eight perfect qualities are listed in the quotation below.
† The items in boldface in this section, beginning with Mount Meru and ending with the victory banner, correspond to the thirty-seven piles in the mandala.
‡ The first range of mountains, Yugandhara, is a quarter of the height of Mount Meru.

Enjoyment, whose waters have the eight perfect qualities described in the Vinaya scriptures:

> Cool, sweet, light, and soft,
> Clear and odorless,
> Soothing on the stomach when drunk,
> And not irritant to the throat—
> Such is water that has the eight perfect qualities.

They are filled with wish-fulfilling jewels and the other multifarious riches that belong to the *nagas*.

Outside the seven golden mountain ranges are the **four great continents,** whose colors correspond to those of the four sides of Mount Meru. In the east is Purvavideha, which is semicircular in shape. To the south is the triangular Jambudvipa. In the west is Aparagodaniya, which is round. In the north is Uttarakuru, which is square.[152] To the right and left of each of these four continents are the **eight subcontinents:** Deha and Videha in the east, Chamara and Aparachamara in the south, Shatha and Uttaramantrina in the west, and Kurava and Kaurava in the north. They have the same color and shape as their respective main continents and are half their size.

The eastern continent is full of **mountains of** diamonds, lapis lazuli, sapphires, emeralds, pearls, gold and silver, crystals, and other **precious minerals.** The southern continent is covered with a great forest of **wish-fulfilling trees** from which everything one could want or need falls like rain. The western continent swarms with herds of elephants and **cows** from whose every hair flows an inexhaustible supply **of everything one could desire.** The northern continent is filled with **crops that need no cultivation:** they yield a hundred flavors and a thousand powers, dispelling all illness, negative forces, hunger, and thirst.

Now, with regard to the particular offerings, the *Gathering of the Glorious Ones* states:

> The wise completely fill this universe
> With the precious wheel.
> Because it grants the accomplishments they desire,
> Those with wisdom offer it every day.

and so on. This refers to the practice that the learned masters do at this point. When a universal monarch appears in the world, the riches of his royal state that come into being through the power of his merit comprise seven precious attributes, as is explained in the *Sutra of Extensive Play,* the *Sutra of Perfect Renunciation,* and the Vinaya scriptures. First of these is the precious wheel.

**The precious wheel** is composed (it is produced spontaneously rather than fashioned by a wheelwright) of the finest of celestial materials—gold and other such substances. Both wheel and hub are perfectly round, with a thousand spokes supporting the multicolored rim. Among its many extraordinary attributes, it can travel high in the sky, one hundred thousand leagues in a single day, and enable one to have dominion over all the continents.

**The precious jewel** is an eight-sided lapis lazuli the size of a tall person's thigh, transparent and luminescent, shining brightly both night and day and lighting up everything for a whole league around. As well as these three particular properties, it also possesses other virtues, among them the capacity to produce water with the eight perfect qualities when one is thirsty and the power to prevent anyone within a distance of a hundred leagues from falling ill or dying prematurely.

**The precious queen** is of royal birth and, in form and complexion, beautiful to behold. Her mouth carries the fragrance of *utpala,* while her every pore smells of sandalwood. Her skin is a delight to touch, as if she were clothed in the finest silk, warm when it is cold and cool when it is hot. She pursues virtue and is entirely free of negative actions. Being rid of the thirty-two weaknesses of womankind,[153] she is full of excellent qualities.

**The precious minister** has four sets of virtues. He is learned, clear-minded, and intelligent. As a result of his ability to see treasures many leagues distant with his divine eye, great quantities of precious gems are produced effortlessly and inexhaustibly. He obeys his king's commands and carries them out. Since he knows the king's wishes, he accomplishes them without being asked, and without ever harming others.

**The precious elephant,** with seven appendages (four legs, tail, penis, and trunk) touching or reaching down to the ground, has a huge, handsome body, steadfast and a joy to look at. White like a water lily, it can fly through the air, and is overcome with joy on seeing the king. Furthermore, it has eight other virtues: it is clairvoyant; it is obedient; its seven appendages are perfectly placed; it is victorious over the enemy's forces; it can give battle in water, on dry land, and in the sky; it can go round our world in a single day; it takes the king wherever he wants to go without being goaded; and the crown of its head is ornamented by a gold victory banner and covered with a cap of gold lacework.

**The marvelous and precious horse** has eight special qualities. It is the beautiful color of a peacock's neck. It is perfectly built. It can go round the whole earth and back as the day breaks, or go three times round our world in a day. It is free of physical disease and weaknesses. It has a jewel headpiece and other excellent marks. It can fly through the air. When the king is mounted on it, it behaves respectfully. And it possesses the miraculous power of magical manifestation.

**The precious general** has eight special qualities, which include the following virtues: He is knowledgeable, clear-minded, and a good analyst. He carries out the king's wishes without being instructed. He has everything it takes in terms of courage and skill. For his own part, he has rejected unvirtuous conduct. And with respect to others, not being attached to flattery and praise, he performs his duties correctly. Able to measure up his opponents, he knows when to advance or retreat. Therein lies his strength and glory as a vanquisher of enemies.

These, therefore, are the seven precious attributes of royalty. Then there is the **Excellent Treasure Vase** that yields a never-dwindling supply of diamonds, sapphires, emeralds, gold and silver, and so forth.

Next comes the outstanding offering that fills the Buddhas with untainted pleasure and bliss and is common to all yogas—the eight goddesses. The **Lady of Charm** is white, standing with her diamond-fisted hands on her hips. The **Lady of Garlands** is yellow, holding up garlands of flowers and jewel ornaments. The **Lady of Song**, who is white tinged with red, holds a *vina* and performs songs and melodies with the seven tones and other musical devices.* The **Lady of Dance** is multicolored, performing many different dance steps. The **Lady of Flowers** is white and holds a bouquet of *utpala*s and other flowers. The yellow **Lady of Incense** bears a censer diffusing the fragrance of aloe, sandalwood, and other incenses. The **Lady of Lamps** is pink, holding up a jeweled lamp as bright as the sun and moon. The green **Lady of Perfume** uses a conch shell to sprinkle pure water mixed with camphor, saffron, and other ingredients. All eight appear supple, lissome, sinuous, graceful, beautiful, smiling, and bewitching. They are bedecked with all kinds of silks and jewel ornaments.

In addition to all these, in the sky above the eastern continent is the mandala of the **sun**, its basic constituent made from the precious stone fire crystal, encircled by a golden aura; it is fifty-one leagues across. In the sky above the western continent is the disc of the **moon**, its basic constituent

---

* The seven tones are the seven notes (*swara*) of the Indian musical scale.

made from the precious stone water crystal, encircled by a silver aura; it is fifty leagues across. These are both special possessions of the gods. In the sections above the southern and northern continents are the white **umbrella** ornamented with numerous precious stones and a jewel as a top ornament, the handle being of gold; and the extraordinary **banner,** insignia of universal victory, with its top ornament, jeweled handle, and fluttering silks.

The top of Mount Meru has the following layout. In the middle is the city Lovely to Behold, with the Mansion of Victory, and in the four cardinal directions, the four pleasure groves, the Grove of Many Kinds of Chariots and so on. At the four intermediate points are four turrets. To the northeast is the All-Gathering Place[154] and in front of it the stone slab Amolika. To the southwest is the Assembly Place where the Gods hear the Excellent Law.

Above these,* one above the other in the sky and supported by clouds of jewels, are the Heaven Free of Conflict, the Joyous Realm, and the other worlds of the gods, with all their boundless riches. Interspersed between these different levels are:

- the eight auspicious symbols: the precious umbrella, the golden fish, the vase, the lotus, the right-spiraling white conch shell, the eternal knot, the victory banner, and the wheel;
- the eight auspicious objects: mirror, vermillion powder, white conch shell, bezoar, *durva* grass, *vilva* fruit, curd, and white mustard seed;
- the seven semiprecious articles: precious bedclothes, throne, cushion, sword, shoes, snakeskin, and robe;
- the six excellent medicines and numerous other kinds of medicine that cure disease;
- substances associated with "taking the essence" and accomplishment;
- different kinds of substances that prolong life, such as ambrosia and the excellent vase;
- swords, books, *vina*s, cymbals, and other articles that promote wisdom and fame;
- rainbow lights and rains of flowers, pools of scented water, lotus groves, emanated birds and deer, and other marvelous offerings;

---

* I.e., above Indra's Heaven of the Thirty-Three on the top of Mount Meru that has just been described.

- the five sense delights—beautiful forms, sounds, smells, tastes, and physical sensations;
- great numbers of sons and daughters of the gods as venerating attendants;

and so on—all the things that contribute to the glory, riches, and happiness of gods and humans, with nothing lacking, filling the universe to overflowing. And, just as you offer one such universe, in the same way you should offer the infinite universes in the ten directions, completely filled with every kind of special offering.

In short, offer infinite clouds of offerings, as many as there are atoms in the universe, like those manifested and displayed in the life stories of the Buddhas and Bodhisattvas on the great levels through the power of their aspirations and prayers, with no limit to size or measure, impregnating it all with a vast, pure aspiration to offer without interruption for as long as cyclic existence endures.

## 7. Considering one's aim in making such an offering

The master Ashvagosha says:

> All these sources of good that I have accomplished
> I dedicate as the cause of the state beyond the world,
> Without thoughts related to cyclic existence, or hopes
> Of any resulting fame, praise, or happiness, celestial or human.

Unless all our meritorious actions are backed by the skillful means of compassion and the wisdom of emptiness, they will merely become causes of cyclic existence resulting in cyclic existence. So it is extremely important that our actions be exclusively backed by the wisdom that realizes the profound meaning. As we find in *The Way of the Bodhisattva*,

> When something and its nonexistence
> Both are absent from before the mind,
> No other option does the latter have:
> It comes to perfect rest, from concepts free.[155]

When we do not have in mind any characterizing thoughts, nor even think of emptiness, which is absence of characteristics, but remain, without remaining,* in the state of emptiness—the ultimate nature that

---

* I.e., without any concept of remaining or particular effort to do so.

transcends both things with characteristics and the mental image of absence of characteristics—the accumulation of merit becomes perfectly pure, as indicated in *Introduction to the Middle Way:*

> Giving, void of giver, gift, receiver,
> Is called a perfection that transcends the world.[156]

The object to which you are offering the Buddhafield, the things you are offering, and you yourself, the offerer, are from the beginning devoid of real existence or characteristics, so rest in evenness in the natural state completely free of elaboration, without any concept of subject, object, and action. Offering in this way, as an unceasing manifestation of the merely illusory appearance aspect of interdependent arising, will become an unsurpassable source of good, in which generosity and the other transcendent perfections are performed with the eye of wisdom and the two accumulations are united.

## 8. *The unique benefits*

From the point of view of actually making the offering, a cloud of offerings like this constitutes the accumulation of merit, while from the point of view of its being backed by wisdom free from concepts, it constitutes the accumulation of wisdom. Even if we make a materially small mandala offering, our special visualization and attitude serve as skillful methods to increase it, and we will therefore gain infinite merit. Among the numerous explanations on this point, the *Mandala Sutra* states:

> Generosity in adding cow's dung and urine,*
> Discipline in cleaning,
> Patience in removing insects,
> Diligence in the endeavor one applies,
> Concentration as one thinks of these,
> Wisdom in very clear visualization—
> These are the six transcendent perfections
> That make the Capable One's mandala the perfect deed.

and,

---

* See note above, on page 221.

For those who do this practice physically,
A golden complexion will be theirs;
From every kind of sickness they'll be free.
Far superior to gods and humans,
They'll have the splendor of the moon,
An abundance of precious stones and gold.
And in the very best of households they'll be born,
In royal or Buddhist families.

And Kamalashila says:

From the merit of offering the four continents,
One will pacify every one of the four demons.
From the merit of offering the subcontinents,
One will possess the four boundless attitudes.
By offering the seven precious attributes,
One will obtain the seven noble riches.
Through the merit of offering the great treasure vase,
One's wealth will grow inexhaustible.
From the merit of offering the sun and moon,
One will gain clarity in mind, view, and meditation.
From the merit of offering precious things,
One will gain the self-arisen wisdom.
With a single mandala that possesses these six offerings,
The accumulation of merit is inconceivable.
Practice it, therefore, with diligence.

## II. CLARIFICATION OF THE POINTS OF THE TRAINING IN THIS CASE

Prepare the accomplishment mandala, while doing the visualization, by wiping it clean three times, sprinkling it with the purifying ingredients from a cow and scented water, and arranging upon it five piles. Place it on the altar in front, on which a cloth has been spread. If you have them, arrange the five offerings around it.* This should act as the support for your concentration, representing the field of accumulation, which you should visualize as in the refuge practice:

---

*The five offerings are flowers, incense, lamps, perfume, and food.

> The mandala is a delightful pure Buddhafield,
> In its center . . .

If you do not have an accomplishment mandala, or when you are offering the mandala in your daily practice, you may simply visualize the object of offering in the sky in front of you.

Next, hold up the offering mandala in your left hand and dispose the piles according to the visual transmission[157] that you have received in a practical demonstration of how to make the offering, using them as a support for your visualization, as follows: Outwardly, offer the "container and contents"—that is, the universe, consisting of the mighty golden ground and on it Mount Meru, the four continents, the sun and moon, and so forth, and the inconceivable riches of gods and humans completely filling it—multiplying the whole by one thousand million to make what we call "a third-order universal system of a billion worlds." In this manner, offer all the countless universes filled with clouds of offerings in the manner of Samantabhadra,* and in addition, all your own and other beings' bodies, possessions, parents and relatives, and sources of good—offering all this without holding back.

Inwardly, offer your own body, comprising the five aggregates, the five constituents, and the six senses-and-fields,† spontaneously present as a mandala. Visualize your body as the source of everything precious comprising the universe and its contents—for example, your skin as the golden ground, your blood as the scented water, your spine as Mount Meru, your four limbs as the four continents, the right (*roma*) and left (*kyangma*) channels‡ as the sun and moon, and the vital essence (bodhichitta) as all the wealth of gods and humans.

On the secret level, imagine the ground consciousness, which is the cause of samsara and nirvana, as the golden ground. Sprinkle it with the scented water of compassion inseparable from bodhichitta. Offer your own naturally arisen, radiant awareness, the precious bodhichitta, represented by Mount Meru; and arising from it, the four boundless attitudes,

---

*Infinite clouds of offerings miraculously multiplied by the power of concentration in the same manner as the Bodhisattva Samantabhadra. See *The Words of My Perfect Teacher,* page 321.

†Tib. *skye mched drug.* The six senses-and-fields (Skt. *ayatanas*) refer here to the inner senses-and-fields, that is, the six sense organs.

‡The two most important channels in the subtle body after the central (*uma*) channel.

the four joys, the four wisdoms, and so on represented by the four continents and subcontinents; and means and wisdom united, represented by the sun and moon. In short, offer this spontaneously accomplished mandala of the absolute expanse, which is naturally pure from the very beginning, like an extremely clear mirror, and reflected on its surface, great clouds of offerings filling the very ends of space, appearing as the display, unobstructed in any way, of awareness, the spontaneous primal wisdom, unchanging great bliss. Offer it all, imagining it like the offering miraculously emanated by the Bodhisattva Gaganagañja through the power of prayer.

With this in mind, begin by offering the detailed thirty-seven-element mandala as many times as you can. Then, continue with just the seven-pile arrangement symbolizing Mount Meru, the four continents, and the sun and moon, earnestly making the offering and reciting the prayer as many times as you can—one hundred, a thousand, ten thousand, or a hundred thousand times:

---

OM AH HUNG. The glorious infinite array of the billionfold
World of Forbearance,
Along with my body, possessions, merit, and sources of good,
All perfectly arranged as this beautiful mandala,
I offer to the Three Jewels in order to complete the two
accumulations.

---

As you do so, pray that you and all other beings may complete the two accumulations and purify the two obscurations. At the end, consider that light radiates from the accomplishment mandala visualized as the object of offering, touching you and all beings, so that we complete the two kinds of accumulation. The deities melt into light and dissolve into you. Rest in evenness for a while in the state free of concepts of subject, object, and action. After that dedicate the merit:

---

As a result of these positive actions, may all beings
Complete the accumulations of merit and wisdom,
And attain the two supreme bodies,
Which come from merit and wisdom.

---

Exert yourself in this practice until you get a sign that you are completing the accumulations, either in experiences or in dreams—for example, that you are sitting on a lion throne, wearing a crown, or that a lot of people are paying homage to you. In between sessions, be diligent in the many different methods for accumulating merit—performing prostrations, making offerings, and so on.

---

When genuine realization of the profound, actual condition of things occurs, the whole of the accumulation of merit and wisdom and the purification of obscurations is included. However, without the backing of previous accumulation, genuine realization cannot happen; those who have both the backing of previous accumulation and enduring past deeds are very few indeed. Even supposing that someone who has entered the gateway of the Dharma and acquired some faith has some habitual propensity for virtue in his or her stream of being, that propensity cannot be awakened just like that, for it is difficult for a tiny spark to get a fire blazing without the right conditions. As long as the root of virtue is not awakened, there will not be any progress in our experiences and realization. So it is by generating the special accumulations anew that the conditions for awakening our propensity for positive actions and immediately maturing our stream of being are created, and that great waves of experience begin to occur. For this reason, as long as we have inner faith and wisdom, there is an inconceivable number of different ways to accumulate merit, so we need not think that we have nothing to offer or that the conditions are not right. Simply offering the seven branches with bodhichitta leads to an accumulation of merit and wisdom as vast as space. Just one hand* raised in salutation to the Three Jewels is said to bring ten benefits, including a fine physique and a large entourage. Examples of this kind are very numerous and are clearly explained in the sutras.

The accomplished masters in the past made the accumulation of merit their principal practice—there are many stories that show this. But nowadays we are basically not interested in the need to complete the accumulations. Even if we are slightly interested, we have little devotion and diligence, and so we do not manage to do any practice for accumulating merit. We leave the supports of the Buddha's body, speech, and mind† to get covered in dust. We recklessly stuff them under our own tattered hats and clothes, and even walk over them. Though we have an altar and offer-

---

* If one is only able to raise one hand, rather than two as in the traditional salutation, this is nevertheless highly meritorious.
† For example, statues or paintings, books, and stupas respectively.

ing bowls, we leave them to grow dusty—it is more essential for us to clean and polish our own bodies. We have never offered a single flower to the Three Jewels with the thought of emptiness and an attitude of compassion. Not once have we recited the seven branches properly—yet we still say we do not have any merit. How could we have any merit? When it has been taught that in order to acquire merit one has to perform the accumulations, what merit could there be in offering lies to the Three Jewels? "I'm empty-handed, destitute of merit, I've nothing else to give,"* we declare, though we do not lack for gold, silver, fine silks, horses, and cattle. So saying, we keep the good food to eat ourselves and offer inedible ingredients to fill a tiny offering bowl with grain, or to make a small butter lamp or a food offering no bigger than a finger. And we then claim we have made an enormous offering! It is really most important to be diligent in accumulating merit with whatever you can afford, so make every effort to do so.

---

* *The Way of the Bodhisattva*, II, 7. By quoting Shantideva out of context (as a monk, Shantideva could truthfully say that he had nothing to offer), we are compounding our miserliness with hypocritical lies.

*Dudjom Rinpoche, Jigdrel Yeshe Dorje.*

# Training in Guru Yoga and Receiving the Teacher's Blessings, the Heart of the Whole Path

THERE ARE TWO SECTIONS: GENERAL POINTS TO BE UNDER-
stood, and the points of the training in this case. The first of these is
divided into three: the reason one needs to be diligent, convinced that this
is the essence of the path; different ways to practice; and the benefits and
purpose of exerting oneself on the path in this way.

## I. GENERAL POINTS TO BE UNDERSTOOD

### A. The reason one needs to be diligent, convinced that this is the essence of the path

> All the perfection and good qualities
> In the Buddhas and Bodhisattvas,
> Arhats, Listeners, Solitary Realizers,
> And ordinary beings beginning the path
> Come from reliance on their predecessors.

As this quotation from the *Root Tantra of the Assembly of Knowledge Holders*
points out, in general, all the excellent qualities of the Great and Lesser
Vehicles come from relying on a spiritual friend. In particular, in the profound Secret Mantra Vehicle the accomplishments all come from following a teacher—they cannot happen otherwise. Unless one has obtained an
empowerment from the teacher, one will not have the good fortune to even
hear the Secret Mantra Vehicle teachings. And even once one has received
empowerment, one cannot get to know the ordinary and extraordinary
pith instructions without their being revealed by the teacher. To practice
the Mantra Vehicle in any other way leads to the crime of unauthorized

use of the teachings, to the result of the practice being wasted, and other extremely serious faults. For these reasons, any accomplishment, however great or small, will only be obtained by pleasing the teacher and receiving his blessings. Even when you request a practice for accomplishing some minor purpose,* you should please the teacher with offerings and the like. By doing so, you will achieve your goal without difficulty. But if you fail to do so, there will be negative consequences, as has been widely described in the tantras, in the oral tradition, and in stories of the past.

Still more particular is the view of the coemergent absolute truth, the way things truly are, which is the inconceivable absolute nature beyond all description or illustration. This can only be introduced by means of the teacher's pith instructions or transmitted through the blessings of the authentic lineage. It cannot be pointed to in any other way. This is why we read in the tantras:

> Inborn, it cannot be expressed by others,
> One will not find it anywhere.
> Revealed by the teacher with timely skill,
> It is known as a result of one's own merit.

And this is mentioned again and again in the original scriptures and their commentaries. Saraha, for instance, says:

> When the teacher's words enter your heart,
> It is like seeing you have a treasure in the palm of your hand.

And Nagarjuna writes:

> One who tumbles from a lofty peak
> May think "I must not fall" but fall he will.
> One to whom a teacher has kindly given the beneficial
>     transmission
> May think, "I don't want to be set free," but he will
>     still be freed.

To take an example, even if the sun is shining, without the linking condition of a magnifying glass, it is impossible for the tinder to catch fire. Similarly, even though the Buddhas and Bodhisattvas of past, present, and future are always present, the deity's blessings and profound realiza-

---

* Lit. "a sadhana of minor activity," e.g., a practice for curing a sickness or for acquiring wealth, rather than for the major purpose of attaining enlightenment.

tion will not penetrate the disciples' streams of being in the absence of a teacher. There are stories from the past of ordinary disciples who, when accomplished knowledge holders actually showed them the yidam deity, had greater confidence in the yidam and thus, as a result of the connection going wrong, failed to obtain accomplishment.*

The teacher is the embodiment of all the Buddhas, the root of blessings, the source of accomplishment, the foundation of activities. Moreover, as far as we are concerned, the teacher is much kinder than all the Buddhas. Why is this? Because at this time, when we do not have the good fortune to see the Buddha in person or listen to him teach, our teacher is the dominant condition for the Buddha's activity penetrating us, the link through which we can actually see the Buddha in the absolute body (*dharmakaya* Buddha). In this respect, the teacher's kindness is inconceivable, and for this reason our teacher is definitely superior to all the Buddhas. As we read in the *Sutra of Immaculate Space:*

> Ananda, the Tathagatas are not visible to all beings, but spiritual friends, being fully visible, teach the Dharma and plant the seed of liberation. For this reason, consider the spiritual friend as more important than the Tathagatas.

This is particularly true here in the Mantra Vehicle, where all the deities of the mandala are embodied in the diamond master's body, speech, and mind, and it is on account of this that such teachers benefit beings. So if we disrespectfully scorn them, or respectfully make offerings to them, we will be doing the same to all the infinite deities of the mandalas. The benefits and dangers, therefore, are both much greater than in other vehicles. As the *Word of Mañjushri* says,

> Any being who in the future
> Shows contempt for a diamond holder
> Will have shown contempt for me:
> Therefore I have avoided contempt at all times.

And,

> In that form I will accept
> Offerings from other practitioners.

---

*They made the mistake, for example, of requesting empowerment from the yidam deity rather than from the teacher. They did not realize that the mandala of the deity that had been revealed to them was the teacher.

Pleasing such a teacher will purify
The obscurations of past deeds in their minds.*

Whether our teachers present in person are ordinary beings or emanations of Buddhas or Bodhisattvas, if we are able to pray to them considering them as the Buddha, there is absolutely no difference between them and the Buddha or Bodhisattva or yidam deity in person, because the source of blessings is devotion. So whichever profound practice we are undertaking, whether the generation phase or the perfection phase, we should begin by making the teacher's blessings the path. There is no more to it than that. But as long as we have not received the blessings, we will not be genuinely on the path. It is said that if disciples who keep the commitments give themselves wholeheartedly, with devotion, to an authentic diamond master, they will obtain the supreme and common accomplishments even if they have no other methods. But without devotion to the teacher, even if we complete the approach and accomplishment practices of the yidams of the six tantra sections, we will never obtain the supreme accomplishment. And we will be unlikely to accomplish many of the ordinary accomplishments either, such as those of long life, wealth, or bringing beings under one's power. Even if we do manage to achieve a little, it will have necessitated a lot of hardship and will have nothing to do with the profound path. When unmistaken devotion takes birth in us, obstacles on the path will be dispelled and we will make progress, obtaining all the supreme and ordinary accomplishments without depending on anything else. This is what we mean by the profound path of Guru Yoga.

Now in making devotional prayer the path, the objects of our prayer are the ones who actually bestow on us the greatest kindness—the teachers themselves. We can therefore meditate on them in any form.† Nevertheless, if we visualize our teacher in the form of the second Buddha, Padma Thöthrengtsel, who is the speech of all the Buddhas of the ten directions and three times appearing physically as a diamond master, all unfavorable circumstances and obstacles on the path will naturally be dispelled and we will accomplish the twofold goal in accordance with all our wishes. The dakini Yeshe Tsogyal speaks of this most essential and profound point as follows:

---

*In these two quotations it is the Buddha who is speaking, referring to teachers (diamond holders) of the future in whose form he will appear.
† In the form in which we see the teacher, or in the form of the deity.

In general terms, and for the people of Tibet in times to come,
The Lotus-Born is your predestined teacher.
To accomplish the Guru you should strive,
Perceiving your own teacher in the form of Padma.
Thus the blessings of compassion will flow the more abundantly.
Practice on the Teacher's Mind in sadhanas both long and short:
I promise, you cannot but accomplish Buddhahood in one life.

And according to his own diamond words,

For fortunate beings who have devotion
And yearningly pray to me,
By virtue of my special prayers of aspiration—
Cause and effect being connected—
My compassion is swifter than that of other Buddhas.

Again, in the *Secret Sayings* he says:

Attaining me, all other Buddhas you attain;
All other Buddhas do you see in seeing me,
For I am the embodiment of all the Sugatas.

And in Ratna Lingpa's *Prayer of Invocation for the Tenth Day:*\*

Pray with tears welling up in your eyes:
Blessings will flow like the main stream of a river.
When experiences blaze and blessings descend,
These are signs that I have come in person,
And at that moment, there is no doubt, I have arrived.
Now as I depart to the land of ogres,
I make a promise to the king and mantra practitioners,
To my children and disciples in Tibet,
That on every tenth day of the month
I myself will come to them.
The Lotus-Born lets no one down.
Cast away your doubts, my followers:
If you have a fit mind,
My children who diligently pray to me

---

\* This text is a treasure (*terma*) discovered by Ratna Lingpa, and therefore contains Guru Rinpoche's own words.

On this my day, the tenth of the month—
Even abandoned in cyclic existence, I'll be responsible for you.
Trust me wholeheartedly with body, speech, and mind.
To those of future generations who rely on me
And follow me, connected through prayers of aspiration,
In order to give them confidence and dispel their doubts,
I leave them this clear advice.
In truth, I do not depart or stay,
I am beyond coming and going,
Yet relatively, for those with habitual dualistic perceptions
I dwell in a celestial sphere.
Because their bodies are not purified
Of their tendencies to cyclic existence
And of the two obscurations, they will not see me.
When they purify their afflictive emotions and obscurations
They will see me, Padma, in person,
And be able to converse with me in words.
Even practitioners still on the path
Will meet me in experiences and in dreams.
In fact, those who, developing a virtuous mind,
Have given rise to boundless compassion
And remember me vividly for just an instant—
By doing so, they are meeting me.
For those who have a thought of devotion to me,
There is no break in the stream of my compassion.
Ultimately, for me there is no coming and going:
When someone purifies their evil deeds and twin obscurations,
At that moment they are meeting me.
Relatively speaking, from beings' point of view, it's true:
On account of my aspirations I dwell in the land of ogres;
Yet, because my compassion is unceasing,
If you have devotion, I am there by your side.
More than this I shall not say,
For that would be mere verbiage.
In essence, trust me with your heart and breath
And, whether your social status is high or low,
Depending on your devotion,
You will receive my blessings, there's no doubt.

For us red-faced people born in the dark kingdom,* the one who is much kinder than other Buddhas is Guru Rinpoche. When we meditate on him, practice his sadhana, and pray to him, it is as if we were meditating, practicing, and praying to the infinite Buddhas and the Three Roots. He has promised that he will constantly guide and bless us, and he will never let us down. That promise is a profound commitment made with his diamond speech. So pledge yourself to him with total conviction and heartfelt confidence.

## B. Different ways to practice

There are two parts: general principles in making devotion and respect the path, and specific points on the different stages of receiving blessings: the approach and so forth.

### 1. General principles in making devotion and respect the path

It is said in the writings of the great masters of the past that if you see your teachers as Buddhas, you will receive the blessings of the Buddhas. If you see them as Bodhisattvas, you will receive the blessings of Bodhisattvas. If you see them as accomplished beings, you will receive the blessings of accomplished beings. If you see them as ordinary beings—simply as good spiritual friends—then that is the sort of blessing you will get. While if you have no devotion at all, you will not receive any blessings at all.

For this reason, we should cultivate devotion, and there are four ways to do so. First, no other Buddha is greater than your own root teacher. The essence and embodiment of every one of the Three Jewels in the ten directions and three times is the teacher, and there is no end to the excellent qualities of the Three Jewels. Consider that the sublime beings who are working at present for the welfare of beings everywhere, the sun and moon, medicines, and even boats and bridges are manifestations of the teacher; that empowerments, transmissions, and instructions you receive from others, occasions when you are writing, reading, and studying, and

---

* I.e., the inhabitants of Tibet, on which, before the coming of Guru Rinpoche, the sun of the Buddhadharma did not shine.

even circumstances in which you can perform positive actions are all the miraculous display of the teacher. In short, decide that the teacher is the Buddha in person.

Second, think of all the countless Buddhas there have been in the past, of the Buddhas, Bodhisattvas, teachers, yidam deities, and so on at present dwelling everywhere in the ten directions, and of the former knowledge holders who were learned and accomplished. You can marvel at these inconceivable and innumerable beings, at their clairvoyance, miraculous powers, and other extraordinary qualities, and yet you do not have the good fortune to even meet them in a dream or hear them teach. Moreover, even if you were to meet them, they could not do anything more for you than do your teachers. Your root teachers are the ones who give you the pith instructions that constitute an unmistaken, complete method for attaining Buddhahood in a single body, in a single life. So even if they were to smash your body and vital force to dust, think that there is no way ever to repay their kindness.

Third, it will not do to think of your teachers when they are giving you teaching, offering you material gifts, and generally taking notice of you, but after a while to forget them. Nor merely when you are sick, in difficulty, or otherwise miserable, and not when you are comfortable and happy. Instead, remember your teachers again and again, and think of nothing else, even when you are moving around, walking, lying down, or sitting, and whether you are happy or suffering.

Fourth, when you are thinking of your teachers, do not just say "I take refuge" or recite one or two prayers and reckon that that will do. Instead, you should feel intense yearning, with your hair standing on end and tears welling up in your eyes—the sort of longing that can suddenly transform your awareness, make ordinary perceptions cease, and cause experiences to occur spontaneously.

When you have these four aspects together, you will have the sort of genuine devotion that allows blessings to penetrate your stream of being and is able to give rise to sudden realization.

Now there are four branches to applying devotion on the path. The first of these is never to think of anything as a fault in the teacher. If you see apparent faults in the teacher, you will be like Sangye Yeshe. Seeing Mañjushri as a lay practitioner with a wife and children, his faith wavered,[158] and this acted as an obstacle to his attaining the supreme accomplishment. It is your own impure mind that is responsible. How could there be a single fault in the Buddha? Let your teachers do what they are doing. Even if you see them doing such things as acting unchastely* or telling lies, train in thinking that these must be the best methods for benefiting beings. By using such skillful methods, they are certain to be maturing and liberating numerous beings, and they are therefore a hundred times, a thousand times more to be marveled at than others who observe strict vows. From the very fact that they are not doing it artfully or hypocritically, there can be no doubt that their conduct is that of a sublime being. In particular, if they should happen to scold you, it is to exhaust your evil deeds from the past; if they give you a beating, it is to drive out negative forces and obstacle makers. Think how immensely kind they are being in treating you lovingly and not dishonestly, like fathers with their children. If they seem not to take any notice of you and to be displeased with you, realize that it is because of your impure actions and obscurations, and make every effort to purify your obscurations and to do anything that will please them by serving your teachers' body, speech, and mind.

The second branch is to recognize that whatever your teachers do is a virtue, for as the accomplished beings of the past have said,

> These precious, authentic teachers—
> All that they do is excellent;
> Whatever they do is a virtue.
> Even if they are murderers or butchers,
> Be content, it is perfect;
> They surely hold beings with compassion.
> Even if they appear to have loose sexual morals,
> Good qualities are increasing, good qualities arise:
> It is a sign that they are uniting skillful means and wisdom.
> In fooling others with their lies,
> They're using a variety of gestures and means
> To guide all beings on the path to liberation.
> Even though they act as thieves, robbers, or gangsters,
> They are transforming others' property to accumulate merit
> And reducing people's poverty.
> In truth, when teachers like these
> Deliver a reprimand, it is a wrathful mantra:
> It is sure to dispel bad circumstances and obstacles.

---

*Tib. *mi tshang par spyod pa,* i.e., having sexual relations if they are monastics, or indulging in sexual misconduct if they are lay mantra practitioners.

When they give a beating, it is a blessing:
It gives rise to all accomplishments.
Beings who have devotion, be glad!

The third branch is to decide that you have to put an end to all your hopes and doubts. Do not be concerned that by meditating with devotion on your teachers you will please or displease them in this life, let alone entertain the hope that you will attain the supreme accomplishment. No matter whether or not they hold you with their compassion, no matter whether or not you attain accomplishment, there is nothing else for you to do than to have devotion.

The fourth branch is to always remain flexible and agreeable in your attitude to your teachers. Even in ordinary life, how much do respectable people put up with being polite and honest with their superiors, and that is only for this life, for a matter of months and years. Your teachers are the sources of all happiness, excellence, and good qualities, major and minor, in this life, the next life, and all your lives until you reach enlightenment. Therefore, you should be constantly adaptable in your wish to do everything you can, physically, verbally, and mentally, to serve them, including praying for their long life and the blossoming of their activities, for any Dharma qualities you obtain are entirely due to their kindness.

Use these four branches to train in developing devotion. For beginners it is difficult to give rise to uncontrived devotion right from the start and you have to create the foundation by deliberately arousing devotion. Later, develop the flow of devotion, getting used to it. Finally, when you gain the confidence of uncontrived devotion, you can be certain that your stream of being will inevitably be matured and liberated.

## 2. Specific points on the different stages of receiving blessings: the approach and so forth

There are two sections.

### a. IN GENERAL

To approach an authentic teacher, who is the source of all perfection and virtue and the root of the Diamond Vehicle path, and to then please that teacher with great respect, physically, verbally, and mentally, and thereby properly receive the maturing empowerments and liberating instructions and acquire the treasure of the teacher's mind, is the *approach*.

To one-pointedly put into practice the profound generation and perfection phases as instructed by the teacher and attain realization inseparable from the teacher's mind is the *accomplishment*.

Having obtained accomplishment—realization of the innate natural state that is one's own mind—to do whatever one can to benefit the doctrine and beings and especially to propagate the essential teaching of the Supreme Vehicle* is the *activity*.

It is by following these stages that one will fulfill the wishes of the knowledge holders of the past and hold their lineage; one will obtain accomplishment for oneself and benefit other beings, and by doing so one will join the ranks of the knowledge holders oneself.

### b. In particular

On the outer level, having gained the certainty that the triply kind teacher† is the embodiment of all refuges, to pray with intense yearning, faith, and devotion is the *approach*.

On the inner level, the Secret Mantra Vehicle method of purifying ordinary appearances, sounds, and thoughts, which are based on deluded attachment, into the great, infinitely pure display of the teacher's three secrets is the *accomplishment*.

On the secret level, to take the ultimate, absolute nature—the primal wisdom that is the essence of the empowerment—as the path and to grasp the ultimate accomplishment, the desired goal, is the *activity*.

One begins by clearly visualizing the support for empowerment,‡ according to the text. One then condenses the essential points of accumulation, purification, and increase by accumulating merit and purifying one's mindstream with the seven branches. With intense faith and devotion, one prays one-pointedly and invokes the teacher's mind by reciting the mantra. Finally one receives the blessings—the wisdom of the four empowerments—in the path empowerment, with the emanation and dissolution of rays of light. By the force of one's devotion, the support for empowerment melts into light and dissolves into one. The teacher's mind—the wisdom devoid of thought—blends indistinguishably with one's own mind, like water added to water, and one rests in evenness,

---

* "Supreme Vehicle" refers here to the Great Perfection.

† Tib. *bka' drin sum ldan,* the kindness of one's teachers is threefold by virtue of their bestowing empowerment, explaining or transmitting the tantras, and giving the pith instructions.

‡ The support for empowerment here is the teacher inseparable from Guru Rinpoche, from whom one receives empowerment.

maintaining, without tension or effort, the very nature of the Buddhas' wisdom, the great self-manifestation free of bias.

### i. Visualizing the object of prayer

Here, as regards visualizing the object of our prayer, there is effectively no difference between inviting our teachers from somewhere else (like a wisdom deity) and revisualizing them.* As we find in a sutra,

> For those who think of the Buddha,
> The Buddha will be present in front of them
> And will constantly bless them.

### ii. Accumulating merit with the seven branches

#### (1) Prostration, the antidote to pride

Imagine that you are emanating countless hundreds and thousands of bodies like your own, as numerous as the atoms in the universe, and that all beings, numerous as space is limitless, are also performing prostrations with you. How to do this is described in the *Sutra of Great Liberation:*

> With both hands joined above my head
> Like an opening lotus bud,
> And countless bodies amassed in clouds,
> I prostrate to the Buddhas of the ten directions.

So, joining your two hands like a lotus bud and placing them on your three centers,† perform the prostration by touching the ground with the five points of the body.‡ There are two ways of doing this: bowing down in what is known as a short prostration, and hitting the ground with one's body and stretching it out in what we call a full-length prostration. The first of these is the method of the common vehicle, while the second is the special method of the Mantra Vehicle as taught in the *Tantra of Stainless Parting* and other tantras. This is the prostration that my teacher taught and practiced; he said that it is more powerful in purifying obscurations and has greater benefits.

Inasmuch as the preliminary practices constitute a means to accumulate merit and purify obscurations, it is perfectly appropriate to combine

---

*I.e., simply reminding oneself of the teachers' presence.
† The crown, throat, and heart.
‡ The five points (Tib. *lus kyi ma lnga*) are the forehead, the knees, and the palms of the hands.

prostrations with the refuge practice. Nevertheless, since the actual instructions for doing prostrations are given at this point, the prostrations should be performed in association with the Guru Yoga and are a perfect branch of it.

As for the benefits of prostration, the *Transmitted Distinctions Regarding the Vinaya* declares:

> The beauty of a fine complexion, and noble speech,
> Power over your surroundings, the joys of gods and humankind;
> The company of sublime beings, great majesty,
> And wealth, the higher realms, and liberation you'll obtain.

and,

> A single prostration performed with great respect, pressing one's five
> limbs into the ground, is so powerful that one will obtain the royal
> state of a universal emperor as many times as the number of particles
> of dust beneath one's body down to the lowest depths of the earth.[159]

### (2) Offering, the antidote to miserliness

Arrange whatever material offerings you have, unsullied by such things as poor quality, impurity, and stinginess, and using them as a support for your concentration, mentally offer your own body, your wealth, and all the possessions of gods and humans—those that are owned and those that are not—and emanate infinite clouds of offerings arising from the display of concentration, as described in the life story of the sublime Samantabhadra.\* In the *Sutra of the Precious Lamp* we read:

> All kinds of flowers I spread and scatter,
> A myriad single blossoms and floral canopies,
> Flowers arranged, sent forth on beams of lights,
> And offered to the Buddhas and their heirs.
> Offerings beyond imagination held in my palm,
> And just as I offer them to a single Buddha,
> I offer them too to all the Buddhas, every one,
> Manifested with the sages' concentration.

As a result of such an offering, in our whole series of lives we will have an abundance of riches and be worthy of universal veneration.

---

\* See *The Words of My Perfect Teacher,* page 321, for the manner in which the Bodhisattva Samantabhadra made offerings.

### (3) Parting from negative actions, the antidote to hatred

With intense remorse at all the nonvirtuous actions that you have accumulated with your body, speech, and mind throughout your beginningless series of lives in cyclic existence until now—negative actions and downfalls such as shameful deeds that are naturally negative and those that violate edicts, and deteriorations and breaches of the commitments—part from them, keeping in mind the four powers. As you do so, imagine all your negative deeds and obscurations gathered in a black heap on top of your tongue. Rays of light from the body, speech, and mind of all the deities in the field of accumulation touch it and purify you as if washing away stains. The *Sutra Requested by Maitrimahasimhanada* declares:

> Whatever negative actions I have done unknowingly,
> I part from them.
> The wise, by parting from their faults,
> Do not abide with their deeds.

Parting from our faults delivers us from the deeds that obscure the higher realms and liberation and make us suffer in the lower realms; it gives rise to all the qualities that stem from virtue.

### (4) Rejoicing, the antidote to jealousy

Meditate with a feeling of tremendous gladness from the bottom of your heart, rejoicing at all the sources of good, untainted and tainted, accumulated in the past, present, and future by yourself and others, including the Buddhas' turning of the Great Wheel of the Dharma for the sake of sentient beings, the Bodhisattvas' infinite activities, and beings' positive actions consistent with ordinary merit and with liberation. The benefits of doing so are referred to in the *Condensed Transcendent Wisdom:*

> One may assess the weight of a billion Mount Merus,
> But not the merit of rejoicing.

Indeed, the merit of rejoicing is equal to that obtained from the source of good itself, and so cannot be measured.

### (5) Exhorting the teachers to turn the Wheel of Dharma, the antidote to bewilderment

In the presence of the Buddhas, Bodhisattvas, teachers, spiritual friends, and so forth who bear the enormous responsibility of others' welfare and who, weary and discouraged by beings' ungrateful behavior, would enter the happiness of nirvana without teaching, manifest countless thousands of billions of your own bodies making offerings of wheels, jewels, and so forth, and pray that they may constantly turn the Wheel of the Dharma to benefit beings with whichever teachings are appropriate. By doing so, you will purify obscurations arising from your having abandoned the Dharma, and in all your lives you will hold the sublime Dharma in your being and never separate from it

*(6) Praying not to pass into nirvana, the antidote to false views*

In the presence of all the teachers and Buddhas and Bodhisattvas in this and other Buddhafields who have completed their work benefiting beings and now wish to pass into nirvana, emanate numerous bodies like your own, praying as did the lay practitioner Chunda in the past, and imagining that they stay until cyclic existence is empty, working for the welfare of beings. Such a prayer will purify the negative deeds you have done that result in your having a short life and untimely death and that put others' lives in danger. You will attain infinite life.

*(7) Dedicating to enlightenment, the antidote to doubt*

Using your present positive action to symbolize all the sources of good accumulated by you and others in the past, present, and future, dedicate them all together—with compassion (dedicating them to beings' welfare) and with wisdom (dedicating them in order that they may attain the great enlightenment). Make the dedication in the same way as did Mañjushrikumara,* applying the seal of no concepts.

Since this kind of dedication is extremely important, we shall deal with it in some detail, in two main sections: (1) the reason dedication is necessary, and (2) the method for dedicating.

*(a) The reason one needs to dedicate*

Dedicating the sources of good that we have created to unsurpassable enlightenment is very important, for as *The Way of the Bodhisattva* points out, even though we may have accumulated merit, if we fail to dedicate it,

All the good works gathered in a thousand ages,
Such as deeds of generosity,

---

* Mañjushrikumara (Tib. *'jam dpal gzhon nu*), "Youthful Mañjushri," is one of the many names of the Bodhisattva Mañjushri.

And offerings to the Blissful Ones—
A single flash of anger shatters them.[160]

It only takes a single cause for exhausting merit—a surge of intense anger directed toward a special object, or similarly a wrong view—for one's store of virtuous deeds to be depleted. But by dedicating them to enlightenment, they will never be exhausted but grow greater and greater. This is further explained in the *Sutra Requested by Sagaramati:*

> Sagaramati, let us take an example. A drop of spit discarded on the sand will rapidly dry up. But if you spit into the ocean, as long as the ocean does not dry up, your spit will not dry up either. Sagaramati, it is the same with a source of good that you have produced. If you regret it, feel a sense of loss about it, disparage it, or dedicate it wrongly, it will be spent. But if you dedicate it to the oceanlike wisdom of omniscience, it will never be exhausted but grow ever greater.

Not only that, but such merit also necessarily and definitely becomes the cause of Buddhahood. In the *Sutra Requested by Gaganagañja* we read:

> Just as many rivers flowing from different directions
> Into the ocean all gain a single taste,
> Positive actions of different kinds
> Dedicated to enlightenment will also gain a single taste.

It is very important to affix the great seal of complete dedication to our sources of good, for as the sublime Nagarjuna says,

> No other treatises explain
> What you, the Bhagavan, have taught:
> To completely dedicate to all beings
> All one's meritorious deeds.

This extraordinary method of dedication is unknown to non-Buddhists and is a feature exclusive to Buddhism. If no such dedication is made, positive actions performed by those on the path of earnest aspiration* will mostly have no benefit, in the sense implied by the following quotation:

---

*Tib. *mos pas spyod pa'i dge ba.* This refers to the positive deeds of practioners on the paths of accumulation and joining who have not yet realized emptiness and who, being unable to genuinely practice the six transcendent perfections, merely aspire to do so. Such deeds, if not dedicated, tend to be rapidly exhausted.

Know that deeds are mostly beneficial,
Mostly nonbeneficial, or beneficial in every respect

Positive deeds performed from the eighth level up until the level of Buddhahood are all beneficial in every respect, as the *Four Hundred Verses on the Middle Way* explains:

When you, the Bhagavan, make a movement
It is never without reason:
Even the breaths you take
Are solely for beings' benefit.

When Bhagavan Buddhas breathe in and out, it is exclusively for others' benefit, so for them there is not an instant that is meaningless. Therefore, in order to make the positive actions we perform on the path of earnest aspiration meaningful, we must dedicate them completely.

### (b) The method for dedicating

This is divided into four: what is dedicated, the goal to which it is dedicated, for whose sake it is dedicated, and the way it is dedicated.

### (i) What one dedicates

Sources of good\*—which are what we are dedicating—are termed "good" because they give rise to happiness as their fully ripened effect, and "sources" because they are the causes of happiness, just as planting seed is the cause of a crop.

We can dedicate positive deeds regardless of when they are done, who does them, or what form they take,[161] as we find in the *Great Host Sutra*:

May all beings' positive deeds,
Those they have done, will do, and are doing now,
Become entirely good
On the same level as all the good there has been.†

Positive actions can be classified according to five groups of three criteria.

• First of all, classifying them in terms of three kinds of doer, there are positive actions performed by oneself, those done by others, and those that are done by both.

---

\*Tib. *dge ba'i rtsa,* also translated as "roots of virtue."
† "Good" in this case refers to the deeds and prayers of the great Bodhisattvas and ultimately to Buddhahood.

- Second, in terms of the three times, there are good deeds that have been performed in the past, those being performed at present, and those that will be performed in the future.
- Third, in terms of the three ways in which they are accomplished, there are good deeds performed with the body, with speech, and with the mind.
- Fourth, in terms of the actual action that is meritorious, there is virtue that arises from giving, from discipline, and from meditation.
- Fifth, in terms of the fully ripened effect, there are positive acts consistent with worldly ends, those consistent with liberation, and those consistent with omniscience.

All these five sets of three can be included in one's dedication. Of these, the most important is the merit that comes from meditation.

### (ii) The goal to which one makes the dedication

To dedicate to this life's goals with thoughts full of attachment or aversion—in order to defeat our enemies, say, or to gain something we desire—is wrong dedication. Dedicating in order to obtain happiness as a god or human in the next life is inferior dedication. Do not, therefore, dedicate with such ideas in mind. As we read in the *Ornament of True Realization,*

> Not including the three worlds . . .

And as already quoted, the master Ashvagosha says:

> All these sources of good that I have accomplished
> I dedicate as the cause of the state beyond the world,
> Without thoughts related to cyclic existence, or hopes
> Of any resulting fame, praise, or happiness, celestial or human.

The "state beyond the world" comprises the three levels of nirvana. Of them, the Listeners' and Solitary Realizers' nirvanas are inferior with respect to the Great Vehicle's nirvana, so we should not dedicate to these, for as the Buddha advises in the *Middle Sutra of Transcendent Wisdom,*

> Subhuti, you should dedicate this source of good only to the level of Buddhahood. Do not dedicate it to the levels of Listeners or Solitary Realizers, or to other levels.

Dedicate, therefore, only to the level of Omniscient Buddhahood, as in the *Prayer of Good Action:*

All of it I dedicate to enlightenment.

And in the *Sutra of Complete Dedication:*

These sources of good I dedicate to Buddhahood.

By dedicating to that end, we will incidentally reap all kinds of happiness in the meanwhile (a long life, good health, and happy circumstances—good family, wealth, and so forth), like the bran one gets as a by-product with the grain from a good harvest.

### (iii) For whose sake one dedicates

If we dedicate our merit to ourselves alone, or to a few people like our relatives and friends, even if it is an enormously positive action, its benefit will be diminished and it will be wasted, as the *Middle Sutra of Transcendent Wisdom* points out:

> Dedicate it for the sake of all sentient beings and not simply to your own gain, for you would then fall to the level of the Listeners and Solitary Realizers.

For this reason, we should dedicate it so that all beings, as numerous as space is vast, attain unsurpassable enlightenment, feeling for them an immense love and compassion, for in the countless times they have been our parents, they have shown us nothing but kindness. *The Way of the Bodhisattva* says:

> My body, thus, and all my goods besides,
> And all my merits gained and to be gained,
> I give them all and do not count the cost,
> To bring about the benefit of every being.

and,

> Directly, then, or indirectly,
> Do nothing that is not for others' sake.
> And solely for their welfare dedicate
> Your every action to the gaining of enlightenment.[162]

Even a small source of good dedicated in this way for the benefit and happiness of all sentient beings will grow bigger and bigger and result in the boundless accumulation of merit, because merit that is created with boundless beings in mind will be equally boundless, as the *Jewel Garland* points out:

> There's no measuring the extent of sentient beings,
> And likewise the benefit.[163]

All positive actions that are not thus nourished by bodhichitta are like the plantain tree: once they have yielded their respective fruits, they shrivel away. On the other hand, virtuous deeds impregnated with bodhichitta are like the wish-fulfilling tree: once they have borne fruit, rather than being spent, they continue to spread and grow more and more until the heart of enlightenment is reached. We have already cited *The Way of the Bodhisattva* on this:

> All other virtues, like the plantain tree,
> Produce their fruit, but then their force is spent.
> Alone the marvelous tree of bodhichitta
> Constantly bears fruit and grows unceasingly.[164]

Unless our good deeds are inspirited with this essential element, they will not become the cause of omniscience, for as *Ornament of the Sutras* explains,

> Because they are not completed by outer conditions*
> And the acts themselves are not perfect,
> Even though their intention is pure,
> They will not be transcendent discipline.

But a dedication underpinned by the extraordinary association of skillful means and wisdom will be a dedication that possesses the four excellent features, as the same text shows:

> Excellent aim and excellent reliance,
> Excellent means with determination to be free,
> And excellent application—with these
> One's path of aspiration is perfect.[165]

It is important to ensure that your attitude is correct in this respect.

### (iv) *The way to dedicate*

In absolute truth, all phenomena are devoid of any intrinsic nature, and therefore merit too cannot be objectified,† being entirely free of the

---

* "Outer conditions" here refers to the actions being done "for all sentient beings."
† Tib. *dmigs su med pa,* that is, it cannot be made an object (of one's mind, the subject) and conceptualized as a "solid" thing.

three concepts.* In relative, conventional truth, every aspect of a positive action—the agent who performs the action, the object of the action, and the action itself—is like a dream or a magical illusion: although it appears, it has no intrinsic nature. It is with this approach that the dedication should be made, for as we read in the *Middle Sutra of Transcendent Wisdom,*

> Subhuti, all phenomena are like a dream, like a magical illusion. Virtue too should be dedicated in the manner of its being like a dream.

And in the *Sutra Requested by Bhadra* we find:

> Not objectifying a giver,
> A recipient, or the gift itself,
> In this sameness,† for you, Bhadra,
> May giving be perfect and complete.

Similarly, in the *Sutra Requested by Druma:*

> Just as in the clear disc of a mirror
> One's whole face appears
> Without a face being there,
> Druma, know that all things are so.

It is not a good thing to have objectification and attachment, considering sources of good to be truly real. The *Transcendent Wisdom* tells us:

> It is hard enough for those with conceptual thoughts to have even a semblance of patience, let alone achieve perfect, unsurpassable enlightenment.‡

And the *Condensed Transcendent Wisdom:*

> Conceptualizing good deeds, the Buddha said,
> Is much the same as eating good food mixed with poison.

and,

> If attributes are absent, it is a dedication to enlightenment;
> If attributes are present, it is not a dedication to enlightenment.[166]

---

*Tib. *'khor gsum,* the concepts of subject, object, and action.
† "Sameness" in that the giver, the recipient, and the gift are all the same in being devoid of intrinsic nature.
‡ "Patience" in this case refers to the third kind of transcendent patience, the courage to confront and accept the teachings on emptiness and the profound truth.

We should therefore dedicate without any objectification and attachment, as the *Ornament of True Realization* affirms:

Absence of objectification,
Is the unmistaken characteristic.

Dedication is essentially a thought—that of transforming sources of good into the intention to gain enlightenment—to which is added the force of special words. The *Array of Qualities of Mañjushri's Buddhafield* states:

Everything depends on
The intention as a condition:
He who makes a prayer of aspiration
Will accomplish that very prayer.

What, then, is the difference between a dedication and a prayer of aspiration? Most scholars appear to maintain that these are two different names for the same thing. However, the tradition of our Omniscient Dharma King, Longchenpa, asserts that for a source of good that has already been produced, the words and prayer of aspiration together constitute a dedication, while to aspire to a source of good that has not yet been produced is a prayer of aspiration.

The fulfillment of the dedication depends on who performs it and where. If the dedication is made by someone with pure, superior motivation in a place where there is a support, imbued with blessings, of the Sugata's body, speech, or mind,* it will be fulfilled in accordance with his or her wishes:

If made before a stupa containing my relics,
It will be fulfilled, the Sugata declared.

Moreover, there are witnesses, who bring about the fulfillment of one's prayer exactly in accordance with its aspiration. *The Way of the Bodhisattva* speaks of them thus:

The Buddhas and the Bodhisattvas both
Have unimpeded vision, seeing everything:
All lies open to their gaze,
And likewise I am always in their presence.[167]

---

* I.e., in the presence of a statue or painting of the Buddha, of books containing his teachings, or of a stupa (representing the Buddha's mind).

Since they have unobstructed vision, the Buddhas and Bodhisattvas know our excellent thoughts and deeds, so with this in mind, you should maintain clear faith in the teacher and the Three Jewels, intense compassion for all sentient beings, and a strong desire to dedicate all sources of good to unsurpassable enlightenment. Without abandoning these three feelings, and keeping concentrated in your superior motivation, gather together all your own and others' virtuous deeds—past, present, and future—and offer the whole in the presence of all the Buddhas and Bodhisattvas in the ten directions. By freely donating them, dedicating them to the infinity of beings, your prayer will be fulfilled.

---

These seven branches for the accumulation of merit are mentioned again and again in the sutras, briefly or in detail, together with their benefits. Here is a passage from the *Sutra Requested by Shri Gupta:*

> For those who, thinking of the Buddhas of the ten directions,
> Fold their hands together
> And submit obeisance, make offerings,
> Rejoice in all merit,
> Purify their negative actions,
> And exhort, and pray,
> A heap of merit constantly arises
> Filling the whole of space.

### iii. The meaning of the Vajra Guru mantra, the essence of Guru Rinpoche

The mantra begins by expressing the seed syllables of the diamond body, diamond speech, and diamond mind: OM AH HUNG.

VAJRA means diamond: it is never changed by the elaborations of dualistic characterizing thoughts. It is present as the essential nature that is the all-pervading indestructible essence, awareness-emptiness. It is, therefore, the absolute body.

GURU means teacher. From that state, infinite clouds of Buddha forms and Buddhafields are arrayed, loaded with special qualities and endowed with the seven branches of union.* This is the body of perfect enjoyment.

---

*Tib. *kha sbyor yan lag bdun:* perfect enjoyment, union, great bliss, absence of intrinsic nature, total compassion, freedom from interruption, and absence of cessation.

PADMA, or "lotus," refers to the radiant awareness of discriminating wisdom—the diamond speech, great bliss—spontaneously appearing as a reflection or manifestation, miraculously born as the supreme lotus family. This is therefore the body of manifestation.

These three bodies being inseparable in the teacher, the great Diamond Bearer of Oddiyana, keep in mind his immense qualities as you pray from a state of yearning—the natural display, as devotion, of the basic nature of the mind free from all elaboration. Entreat him, "By the power of this prayer, may all the supreme and common accomplishments—SIDDHI—be now, at this very moment, bestowed in full on my mindstream—HUNG."

Reflecting like this on its meaning, recite the mantra, as the *Root Tantra of the Assembly of Knowledge Holders* advises:

> During the approach, visualize the teacher on the crown
>    of your head,
> Recite the mantra as a prayer.

This is an essential pith instruction.

As for the benefits of reciting the mantra, Guru Rinpoche himself said:

> The essence, the mantra that embodies the Sugatas,
> Is the practice that includes all the Buddhas.
> By reciting the *Siddhi* mantra one can traverse
> The fifteen levels and five paths and accomplish my level.
> It is the same as reading all the sacred teachings
> Of all the Buddhas of the past, present, and future.

and,

> Because of it, the phenomenal world will quake.
> Condensing the Buddhas of past, present, and future,
> It is inseparable from all the teachers.
> Because of it, haughty elemental spirits faint and tremble,
> The dakinis and Dharma protectors will gather like clouds,
> And all the hosts of dakas and dakinis
> Will be helpless but to come in person
> And bestow the supreme and common accomplishments.
> If there are no signs of this happening,
> I, Padma, have deceived beings.
> Therefore, fortunate children of the future,
> Keep it in your hearts. This is my pledge.

and,

> The twelve-syllable quintessence of the Lotus-Born
> Recited twelve hundred thousand times will render void
>    the seed of cyclic existence;
> Thirty-six hundred thousand times will place you in the ranks
>    of the knowledge holders;
> And ten million times will make you the equal of myself,
>    Padma.

### iv. Receiving the four empowerments

To repair any deteriorations and breaches of the commitments that may occur after we have entered the Secret Mantra Diamond Vehicle, to be empowered to practice the whole path (the generation and perfection phases, the Great Perfection, and so on), to avoid hindrances and deviations from the path, and to make all the special qualities grow more and more—all these depend on their root, the maturing empowerment. As it is said:

> Unless one has the support of the empowerment, one will not accomplish the secret mantras: One will be like a boatman without oars.

and,

> Without empowerment there is no accomplishment.
> One cannot obtain oil by pressing sand.

First we have to be admitted to the mandala and given empowerment by a qualified diamond master. This is the ground empowerment. Then, using the Guru Yoga and the mandala of the yidam, we receive the four empowerments by ourselves without depending on other conditions. This is the path empowerment. As the ultimate result, we receive the great rays of light empowerment* or empowerment of indivisible profundity and radiance, and we attain Perfect Buddhahood. This is the result empowerment. It is therefore extremely important, on account of its inconceivable

---

*The empowerment of great light rays (Tib. *'od zer chen po'i dbang*). According to the Sutra Vehicle, when a Bodhisattva is about to become a Buddha, light rays emanate from between the eyes of the myriad Tathagatas of the ten directions and vanish into the Bodhisattva's crown, and he attains Buddhahood. See Dudjom Rinpoche, *The Nyingma School of Tibetan Buddhism,* pages 142 and 912.

and profound significance in purification, completion, and maturation,*
to receive the path empowerment daily.

## C. The benefits and purpose of exerting oneself on the path in this way

There is an infinite number of teachings on this, among them this quotation from the *Tantra of the Jewel That Embodies All:*

> Better than meditating for a hundred thousand kalpas
> On one hundred thousand deities
> Is remembering one's teacher for a moment.
> The merit of this is infinite.

The *Tantra of the Array of Commitments* says:

> Better than meditating for one hundred thousand kalpas
> On Buddhas with all the major and minor marks
> Is thinking of one's teacher for a single instant.
> Better than a million recitations of the approach and
>     accomplishment
> Is a single prayer to the teacher.

In the *Array of the Sublime* we read:

> Those who visualize their gracious teachers
> On the crowns of their heads, in the centers of their hearts,
> Or in the palms of their hands
> Will hold even the accomplishment
> Of a thousand Buddhas.

And in the *Clarifying Lamp:*

> Fortunate disciple, far superior to the mass of merit that comes from the diamond body, speech, and mind of all the Bhagavan Buddhas—all those victorious, virtuous, transcendent Buddhas who dwell in the ten directions—is the merit of a single one of the master's pores.† Why is this? Fortunate disciple, bodhichitta is the essence of the Buddhas' wisdom.

---

*Tib. *dag rdzogs smin.* Through receiving empowerment one can purify obscurations, complete all the paths and levels, and mature one's being.

† "Merit" here refers to the merit of making offerings to a single one of the teacher's pores (compared to that of making offerings to the body, speech, and mind of all the Buddhas).

## II. Clarification of the points of the training in this case

Begin by arousing the mind intent on supreme enlightenment, thinking: "In order to establish all sentient beings who pervade space on the level of the union Vajradhara, I will practice the profound path of the Guru Yoga." Then, visualize everything you perceive around you, your whole environment, as the Unexcelled City of Lotus Light, whose attributes and arrangement are all perfect and complete, with yourself in the middle. If you visualize yourself in your ordinary form, your obscurations will not be purified and you will not receive the blessings. So, in order to be a fit receptacle for empowerment, to give rise to the primal wisdom of bliss-emptiness, and to make the auspicious connection for receiving guidance from the teacher, visualize a lotus, sun disc, and corpse piled one above the other, and upon this seat, the essence of awareness, the naturally radiant absolute body, the wisdom dakini in the form of Vajra Yogini, Tsogyal Khachö Wangmo.[168] She is a clear red in color, like a ruby, and has a semi-wrathful, extremely attractive expression. She is smiling, her string of teeth as white as moons, with the four shoots of her canine teeth slightly bared. Her three eyes full of devotion are staring longingly at the teacher's heart. She has the appearance of a fully bloomed young woman of sixteen years of age, with her swelling breasts and fully developed secret lotus. Of her two hands, the right one brandishes a copper curved knife with a *vajra* handle at the level of her right ear. With her left hand on her hip she carries a skull-cup filled with nectar to drink. She is trampling on the heart center of the corpse, symbolizing no-self, her two legs in the striding posture with the left leg slightly extended. Half of her hair, the color of the *zarma* flower,* is tied up and ornamented on top with a wish-fulfilling jewel blazing with light; the other half hangs loosely in separate locks. She is graced with a jewel crown embellished with bouquets of flowers, and adorned with the five bone ornaments (wheel, earrings, bangles, necklaces, and girdle), a short necklace of lapis lazuli, ruby, pearl, and other precious stones, and a long garland of many-colored flowers. Her earrings are circles of gold marked with a bell. Her gold bracelets and anklets have little bells that tinkle. Her silken headdress and scarves flutter and float around her. One cannot have enough of looking at her. Visualize her in a shimmering expanse of bright five-colored rays of wisdom light. Although

---

* The *zarma* flower is black.

she appears, she has no intrinsic existence, shining brilliantly like a rainbow in the sky.

Next, visualize in the sky in front of you, on a level with the crown of your head, a palatial expanse of intermingled five-colored rays of rainbow light, the natural radiance of the five wisdoms, and within it, a broad, elevated jeweled throne borne by eight great lions and covered with the finest celestial cloth. On this is a cushion consisting of a multicolored lotus with a hundred thousand petals in full bloom, a sun, and a moon, piled one above the other. Seated upon it is your kind root teacher, the embodiment of all the Buddhas, in the form and attire of Guru Padma Thöthrengtsel. His body is white tinged with red, like a conch shell coated with red varnish. Visualize him as a young boy of eight years, with the major and minor marks, dignified, beautiful, majestic, and blazing with light. He has a joyful face, with a semi-wrathful smile, and is staring at you with round, loving eyes. His right hand in the threatening gesture holds a golden five-pronged *vajra* just above the heart center. In his left hand in the gesture of equanimity he holds a skull-cup filled with wisdom ambrosia and the excellent vase of immortal life ornamented with a wish-fulfilling tree. In the crook of his left arm he is holding his consort Mandarava, hidden in the form of a three-pronged *khatvanga*. The latter is a staff made from a water tree* on top of which is a crossed *vajra,* the center decorated with a vase and three heads, nine iron rings on the prongs, and fluttering silk pennants embellished with a *damaru,* bell, and tinklers.

On his body he is wearing, as the innermost layer, the secret white diamond garment, then on top of it the dark blue long-sleeved gown of the Mantra Vehicle, followed by a red monastic robe figured with gold *patra* designs,† and outermost, a brocade cape the color of power.‡ On his head is the beautiful and lustrous Petaled Lotus Hat That Liberates on Sight. He is seated with his two feet in the royal posture, his dazzling form emanating infinite rays of the purest light. His body glows vividly with the majesty and splendor of the major and minor marks. His speech resonates with the soothing sound of the teachings and its sixty expressive qualities.

---

*Tib. *chu shing,* variously translated in other contexts as "bamboo," "plantain," "banana," etc., but referring in this case to the hard, black wood of the palm tree.
† The eternal knot and similar designs.
‡ I.e., red, the color of the activity of magnetizing or bringing under power.

His mind—clarity and depth inseparable—is refulgent with the primal
wisdom of knowledge, love, and power. With his one body, he pervades
every one of the Buddhafields in the ten directions; in each of his pores are
arrayed infinite Buddhafields, perfect and complete. Consider him like a
magical display actually embodying all the refuges, the Three Jewels and
the Three Roots.

---

EMAHO. One's perceptions are perfectly pure—the absolute
    Buddhafield, the Unexcelled,
Great Bliss, the city of Lotus Light, in the center of which
I am Tsogyal Khachö Wangmo,
Clear red, utterly beautiful with the major and minor marks,
    holding curved knife and skull,
Adorned with multicolored silks, and jewel and bone
    ornaments,
Standing in the striding posture on a seat of lotus, sun,
    and corpse,
And gazing longingly up into the sky.
In the sky in front, in an expanse of intermingled rainbow
    lights,
Is a seat of lotus (symbol of nonattachment), sun, and moon,
    and on it
My teacher in the form of the Lotus-Born (Padmasambhava),
His body white, tinged with red, radiant, majestic, a mass
    of glowing light.
He appears young, perfect with the major and minor marks,
    and semi-wrathful,
Wearing the lotus hat, secret garment, gown, Dharma robe,
    and brocade cape.
His right hand holds a vajra, his left a skull-cup and vase;
His two feet in the royal posture, he holds the khatvanga
    in the crook of his arm.
He whose majesty overawes all that appears and exists, Lord
    of all samsara and nirvana—
The nature of his body pervades all the Buddhafields,
Infinite pure lands are complete in the expanse of his body,
He is the Great Being who embodies all refuges.

---

With this visualization, ordinary thoughts should cease by themselves.

From your heart center imagine inconceivable light rays of devotion streaming forth into the palace of Lotus Light in the Unexcelled land of Chamara* and touching the heart of the Great Guru, the embodiment of all the Buddha families. Immediately, he knows that the time is ripe for blessing the minds of his fortunate disciples, and in an instant, he arrives, along with his retinue of thousands of millions of knowledge holders, dakas, and dakinis, like clouds gathering thickly in the sky or the swirling snow in a blizzard.

> HUNG. From the peak of the Glorious Copper-Colored
>     Mountain in the center of the isle of Chamara,
> The measureless palace of Lotus Light, Great Bliss,
> Noble Teacher, Manifesation Body of Oddiyana,
> With your hosts of knowledge holders, dakas, and dakinis,
> In order to bless us, holders of your lineage,
>     come I pray.
> OM AH HUNG VAJRA GURU PADMA THÖTHRENGTSEL
>     VAJRA SAMAYA DZA SIDDHI PALA HUNG AH

As you recite this, consider that he stays, inseparable from the meditation deity you have visualized.†

Next, manifest bodies as countless as the atoms in the universe, and together with all sentient beings, perform prostrations. Emanate and offer infinite clouds of outer, inner, and secret offerings. Regretting your negative acts as if you had drunk poison and vowing never to repeat them, acknowledge them and part from them. Rejoice with sincere delight at all marvelous deeds. Pray that the form body‡ may remain for as long as cyclic existence endures without passing into nirvana. Exhort the teacher to turn the Wheel of the Dharma unceasingly, teaching the Unsurpassable Profound Secret. Dedicate all your own and others' positive actions—

---

*Tib. *rnga yab*, the southwestern continent in the traditional Indian cosmology. Ngayab Zangdo Pelri, Chamara's Glorious Copper-Colored Mountain, is Guru Rinpoche's Buddhafield.

†Having invited the wisdom deity (Skt. *jñanasattva*, Tib. *ye shes sems dpa'*) from his Buddhafield, consider that he merges with the meditation deity (Skt. *samayasattva*, Tib. *dam tshig sems dpa'*, the deity you have created by visualization) and remains, so that what you have visualized in front of you is now truly Guru Rinpoche.

‡Tib. *gzugs sku* (Skt. *rupakaya*), i.e., the physical form of the teacher.

symbolized by this one—to unsurpassable enlightenment. Reflecting on the meaning of these, recite:

OM AH HUNG. To the embodiment of all refuges, Teacher
   inseparable from Oddiyana,
I submit obeisance with one-pointed respect in body, speech,
   and mind.
My body and possessions I offer as clouds of offerings,
   holding nothing back.
I acknowledge and part from my negative actions, downfalls,
   and deteriorations and breaches of the commitments.
I rejoice in all virtue, tainted and untainted.
I exhort you to turn the wheel of the teachings of the
   essential meaning.
I beseech you to remain forever without passing into nirvana.
This positive action and all sources of good
I dedicate that all beings may attain unsurpassable
   enlightenment.

In this way, accumulate merit as much as you can. Now, the entry of blessings into our stream of being depends entirely on the connection we make through our devotion, so we need to convince ourselves that our root teachers in fact embody all the infinite sources of refuge. Their body is the Sangha, their speech is the sublime Dharma, their mind is the Buddha, and thus they embody all the Three Jewels. Their body is the teacher, their speech is the yidam, their mind is the dakini, and thus they embody all the Three Roots. Their body is the body of manifestation, their speech the body of perfect enjoyment, and their mind the absolute body, and thus they embody all the three bodies. Because they are the embodiment of them all, in terms of their qualities, they are equal to the Buddhas; in terms of their kindness, they are far superior to any Buddha. So with this sort of complete confidence and certainty, your thoughts transformed by devotion, and with your mind and body aching unbearably from longing, develop yearning from the core of your heart, from inside your marrow, from the depth of your bones. Relying totally[169] on the teacher and unburdening all your hopes and expectations, pray as follows, considering that all beings, with you in the lead, are chanting with one voice:

KYEHO. Precious teacher, embodiment of all the Buddhas
Of past, present, and future—

Seeing you dispels the gloom of ignorance,
Hearing you cuts away the web of doubt,
Thinking of you transfers the realization of the mind lineage.
Your touch bestows blessings and accomplishments,
Your kindness is beyond all imagination,
Your qualities are as endless as space.
With intense, unbearable yearning
I pray to you, think of me with compassion.
My body, possessions, and sources of good
I offer you without attachment.
From now on and in all my lives,
I'll have no other refuge, guide, defender, or escort
Than you, my constant protector.
I entrust myself to you with body, speech, and mind;[170]
In happiness or pain, good times or bad,
Wherever you send me, high or low—Teacher, it is up
    to you.
In all my lives, since time without beginning,
I have been dominated by ignorance and delusion:
Jailed in the three worlds of cyclic existence,
I have been tortured by the three sufferings.
Unable to bear the burden of misery and pain,
From my heart I call out to you, Noble Teacher.
Though I want to be happy, I devote myself to deeds that lead
    to suffering.
Deceived by the demon in everything I perceive,
On account of my attachment, I wander, deluded by dualism.
For someone with my bad deeds and misfortune,
Who is there to afford protection other than you, my refuge
    and protector?
As I pray to you, Lord Teacher,
Hold me with compassion, you who are so kind.
Grant me your blessings, you who have ability and power.
Guide me, sublime Lord of All.
I beseech you, turn my thoughts to the Dharma.
Bestow on me the four empowerments,
Purify me of the four obscurations,
Help me attain the four bodies, I pray.
Transmit to me the blessings of the mind lineage.

Destroy the gloom of ignorance
And release the fetters of dualistic delusion,
Help me actualize the wisdom of omniscience,
Take me to the great exhaustion of phenomena beyond mind,
Grant me liberation in the great body of rainbow light,
The naturally accomplished youthful vase body.[171]

Say this prayer as many times as you can, with unwavering concentration. Then, visualize between the teacher's eyebrows a white eight-spoked wheel, its hub marked with the white syllable OM; on his tongue, a red eight-petaled lotus with a red syllable AH in its center; and in his heart center, a blue five-pronged *vajra* with a blue syllable HUNG in its center—all blazing with light. Consider that they represent the three diamonds of all the Tathagatas. From them, amid rays and large and small circles of rainbow light, all the blessings of the teacher's body, speech, and mind stream forth like countless specks of dust in a sunbeam. The qualities, blessings, and accomplishments of the body take the form of the Lotus-Born Guru, and in many different sizes—some as huge as Mount Meru, some as tiny as mustard seeds. The blessings of the teacher's speech are in the form of letters—the vowels and consonants, the Vajra Guru mantra, and Sanskrit and Tibetan letters, all in a variety of colors. The blessings of the teacher's mind take the form of symbolic attributes—*vajras*, skull-cups, long-life vases, *khatvanga*s, and so forth. As they dissolve into your respective centers, consider that you obtain all the empowerments, blessings, and accomplishments without exception.

From time to time, recognize the whole universe—the outer vessel—as the Palace of Lotus Light on Chamara's Glorious Copper-Colored Mountain, and all sentient beings—the inner contents—as groups of dakas and dakinis of Oddiyana. All sounds are the spontaneous sound of the Vajra Guru mantra. The thoughts that arise and dissolve are luminosity, great bliss, spontaneously arisen and spontaneously liberated. In this state of awakening recognition, recite the twelve syllables that are the essence of the Secret Mantra Vehicle—OM AH HUNG VAJRA GURU PADMA SIDDHI HUNG—accumulating as many recitations as you can, at least one hundred thousand for each syllable.

At the end of the session take the empowerments. From the syllables in each of the teacher's three centers, light rays of the same colors as their respective syllables emanate in an uninterrupted stream, like the smoke from sticks of incense, and dissolve into each of your respective centers.

Consider that the four obscurations are purified, that you receive the four empowerments, and so on, combining the visualization with the recitation of the text for taking the four empowerments:

> From the syllable OM in the teacher's forehead, there comes
> forth a ray of white light like a shooting star:
> It dissolves into my forehead, purifying the obscurations of
> the body and channels;
> I receive the body empowerment of the vase;
> My body is blessed as the manifestation of the diamond
> body;
> The good fortune for reaching the level of the body of
> manifestation is established in my being.
> From the syllable AH in his throat, there comes forth a ray
> of red light like a flashing lasso of lightning:
> It dissolves into my throat, purifying the obscurations of the
> speech and energies;
> I receive the secret speech empowerment;
> My speech is blessed as the manifestation of the diamond
> speech;
> The good fortune for reaching the level of the body of perfect
> enjoyment is established in my being.
> From the syllable HUNG in his heart, there comes forth a ray
> of dark blue light like a densely gathering cloud:
> It dissolves into my heart, purifying the obscurations of the
> mind and vital essence;
> I receive the mind empowerment of supreme knowledge that
> is primal wisdom;
> My mind is blessed as the manifestation of the diamond
> mind;
> The good fortune for reaching the level of the absolute body
> is established in my being.
> Again, from the teacher's heart, there comes forth a five-
> colored sphere, the essence of his mind, free from
> thoughts:
> It dissolves into my heart, purifying the two obscurations
> and all habitual tendencies;
> I receive the precious word empowerment;

I receive the blessing that the infinite ornaments—
the inexhaustible qualities and activities of all the
Buddhas—are complete in me;
The good fortune for reaching the essential body is
established in my being.

Again, give rise to intense devotion and pray as follows:

All-pervading lord, mighty embodiment of the four bodies,
Great treasure of knowledge, love, and compassion,
The thought of whom relieves the longing in my mind—
Incomparably kind teacher,
I pray to you from the depth of my heart.
Without my parting from you for an instant,
Bless me with your guidance,
And make me inseparable from you.

Consider that at this, the teacher's face joyfully breaks into a smile, his eyes filled with love and compassion, and he comes onto the crown of your head, where he immediately melts into light, dissolving upward from his throne and downward from the hair on his head to become a ball of light at the level of his heart. This passes through the crown opening on your head and dissolves into the middle of your heart:

The teacher melts into the essence of great bliss, becoming a sphere of five-colored light an inch in size, which dissolves into the middle of my heart: my mind becomes inseparable from the teacher's mind.

Remain in evenness for as long as you can, in the natural, innate state of luminosity beyond mind—awareness-emptiness, the nature of the absolute teacher watching itself.

As you arise from that state, again view all appearances as the multifarious expression of the teacher's body; all sounds as sound-emptiness, the spontaneous resonance of the channels; and all thoughts that arise as the spontaneous manifestation of the diamond wisdom.

Conclude by dedicating the merit and saying prayers for auspiciousness:

Precious, glorious root teacher,
Dwell on a lotus seat on the crown of my head.
Guide me with your great kindness,
And grant me the accomplishments of your body, speech,
    and mind.
With regard to the glorious teachers' lifestyles
May I never have even an instant's wrong view.
Through devotion—seeing everything they do as perfect—
May the teachers' blessings enter my mind.
All the positive deeds accumulated in the three times,
    symbolized by this one,
Unsullied by the stains of any selfish desire for personal peace
    and happiness,
I dedicate to the infinite hosts of beings, without a single
    exception,
As the cause for their attaining unsurpassable enlightenment.
In all my lives, may the feet of my teachers, the lords of the
    families,
Never cease to adorn the wheel of great bliss in my crown,
And through the path of devotion, may their minds and
    mine mingle as one.
Grant the good fortune that the twofold goal be
    spontaneously accomplished.

After this, continue with your everyday activities. With regard to your practice in between sessions, when you are walking, consider that the teacher is in the sky to your right and that you are circumambulating. When you are eating and drinking, consider that the teacher is in your throat and that you are making an offering of your food and drink, which has melted into nectar. Let everything you say become a prayer, and meditate that whatever you do, walking or sitting, is a service to the teacher. Whenever you have something new to enjoy, such as a new house or clothes, consider that they are a measureless palace or celestial garments, and offer them mentally or in reality to your teacher. When you go to sleep at night, after praying to be able to recognize luminosity, consider that the teacher on the crown of your head passes through the crown opening and comes to rest in your heart, which is now in the form of a four-petaled lotus.

Concentrate on the light from the teacher's body filling your body and the house with light, like a lamp held up in a dark room. Dissolving into the radiant, naked state of awareness-emptiness, fall asleep in this state without mental dullness and without being interrupted by other thoughts. If you wake up, stop the flow of thoughts and reflections—distraction, wildness, stupefaction, and so on—and concentrate solely on the teacher in your heart; then maintain the radiant state of luminosity. By doing so, you will gradually be able to recognize the luminosity of deep sleep and recognize your dreams. Again, when you get up in the morning, imagine the teacher passing up your central channel and out into the sky in front of your head, remaining there joyfully. Praying with devotion, resume the practice as described above.

Also, when you are ill, imagine your teacher, an inch in size, on the affected area. From the teacher's body nectar descends, washing away and purifying all disease. As for the illness itself, consider that it has occurred through the teacher's blessings as a skillful means purifying your negative actions and obscurations, and so meditate on illness with joy. If the manifestations of negative forces occur, consider them as the display of the teacher's activity exhorting you to virtue. In short, whenever you are comfortable and happy, this is due to the teacher's blessings. And when you are suffering, think of it as the teacher's compassion and use your difficulties to increase your devotion rather than looking elsewhere for things to be given up and antidotes.

When the time comes for you to die, mingling awareness and the absolute expanse of luminosity, remain in the state of evenness. This is the very best form of transference.* Alternatively, dissolve your mind, in the form of a ball of light, into the teacher's heart. By developing skill in this transference technique, you will be liberated. If you are unable to do that, you should recognize the deluded perceptions experienced in the intermediate state as having no intrinsic reality. Using devotion as the path, simply remember your teachers: through the power of their compassion, you will definitely be liberated in a pure Buddhafield.

Signs that your practicing the profound path has resulted in the blessings penetrating your mindstream may occur in reality, in experiences,

---

*Transference (Tib. *'pho ba*) is the practice at the moment of death by which a trained practitioner can direct his or her consciousness to the enlightened state or at least to a state in which further progress on the path is facilitated.

or in dreams. They are in general the signs described in the text of the practice for accomplishing the teacher.* More particular signs are: one has more devotion to the teacher than before; one is prepared to give one's life for the sake of the commitments; the perceptions of the eight ordinary concerns become hazy and unreal; one has relinquished the things of this life and therefore entertains little expectation or fear with regard to any of them; one's mind is rendered naked—clear and empty—and realization dawns transparently. These are the best and most reliable signs.

When we put all our energies into a practice,† it is quite common for bad deeds from the past to surface, so that all sorts of unwanted things happen to us: we fall physically ill, feel mentally anguished, experience the manifestations of negative forces and obstacle makers, fall victim to hostile people, bandits, and thieves, find ourselves subject to people's criticisms and false accusations, and so on. These are said to be signs that we are purifying ourselves, like the dirt that comes out when one washes a container. Therefore, when such things happen to you, don the great armor of diligence that renders the practice impervious to unpleasant circumstances.

Although it may happen that we get one or two good qualities here and there as signs of progress on the path, it can be hard to distinguish whether they are genuine signs or obstacles caused by demons. Even supposing they are genuine, the moment we attach any importance to them, they will turn into demonic obstacles, so get rid of all expectation, apprehension, and doubt, and do not be attached to good signs or frightened by bad ones.

It is said that while we are on the path, there are many mistakes we can make and ways in which we can go astray, but the principal errors are: to treat the teacher as an equal; to be lacking in pure perception with regard to one's spiritual brothers and sisters; to criticize other philosophical systems while being proud of one's own; to act hypocritically with regard to the commitments; to give the five poisons free rein; to have no respect for the law regarding actions and their effects; to air one's views and indulge in big talk about emptiness and so forth; to tell all and sundry about one's experiences; and to lie that one has sublime qualities that one

---

*Tib. *bla sgrub*, the lama sadhana of the main practice on the Three Roots.
† Lit. "when stone meets bone," a metaphor for unremitting perseverance in making the practice truly effective.

does not have. To make these the basis of one's practice is obviously the greatest error, yet even if the Buddha were to appear in person, it would seem difficult to block this perilous path onto which one can stray, for we ourselves* are blessed by demons, and beings in the decadent age have but little good fortune, so that there is much running after purely meaningless talk without understanding the real point of the Dharma. Even though we follow a teacher, train in acquiring good qualities, practice in retreat, and read many profound texts, it does not do the slightest bit of good to our minds and our characters get worse and worse. We grow ever more proud, the eye of pure perception grows dim, and we pass the time only in examining others' faults. People like us are impervious to the Dharma, we are breakers of the commitments, burdened with evil deeds from the past; we have truly been blessed by demons.

Our kind Teacher, the Buddha, summed up the Dharma as follows:

> Abandon all evildoing,
> Practice virtue perfectly,
> Completely subdue your mind:
> This is the Buddha's doctrine.

If we were to summarize the whole result of practicing the Dharma, it is that the mind has to be tamed. And yet nowadays there are practitioners who devote themselves principally to harming others for the sake of the Dharma, getting involved in disputes using the teachings as a pretext, tricking and deceiving people with the excuse that it is for the sake of beings—everything in fact that the Buddha taught as being at variance with the Dharma. Do not follow such ways.

In particular, there are the eight ordinary concerns, of which Nagarjuna said:

> You who know the world, take gain and loss,
> Or bliss and pain, or kind words and abuse,
> Or praise and blame—these eight mundane concerns—
> Make them the same, and don't disturb your mind.[172]

These eight ordinary concerns, not to speak of others, seem to stain even those who claim to be genuine Dharma practitioners without their noticing, so it is very important to remain thoroughly attentive.

---

*Dudjom Rinpoche is referring here to present-day teachers.

Moreover, there are six mistaken qualities we must avoid:

- mistaken patience, where we are unable to put up with difficulties in practicing the teachings but manage to put up with the most gruelling tasks in order to see through our projects for this life;
- mistaken aspiration, where we have no wish to practice the Dharma but are full of enthusiasm when it comes to achieving the eight ordinary concerns;
- mistaken enjoyment, where we have no taste for listening to the Dharma, reflecting on it, or meditating, but have plenty of appetite for material enjoyments;
- mistaken compassion, where we have no compassion when we or others perform negative actions, but feel compassion for people who are experiencing hardship for the sake of the Dharma;
- mistaken care, where we fail to introduce our dependents to the Dharma but help them succeed in this life;
- and mistaken rejoicing, where rather than meditate on joy with regard to people performing positive actions, we are delighted when our enemies meet with difficulties.

If we are always able to take the lowest seat,* there will be no way for pride and jealousy to creep in. And as long as pride does not arise, obstacles cannot occur. But the moment we start to feel proud and think, "Even my teacher is no better than I am," "Other practitioners do not know as much as I do," and so on, obstacles will happen.

In general, do not examine the faults of beings. Recognizing that they have been your mothers and thinking of their kindness, meditate on love and compassion. In particular, avoid looking for faults in those who have entered the gateway of the Dharma. Regard them as people in the same boat and reflect only on their good qualities, rejoicing at these and cultivating devotion. More especially, never look for defects in your teachers. Realizing that everything they do is full of excellent qualities, make an effort to train in devotion and pure vision. Take note also of this passage from the *Sublime Sutra of the Marks That Inspire the Development of Faith:*

> A greater fault than stealing the possessions of all the beings in a billion worlds and destroying all the stupas there are is criticizing a single Bodhisattva. If one scorns and insults a Bodhisattva, whatever

---

* "Taking the lowest seat" is a metaphor for humility.

the circumstances, one will be reborn in the Screaming Hell with a body five hundred leagues in size, with five hundred heads, each with five hundred mouths, each containing five hundred tongues, and each tongue plowed by five hundred plows.

In general, it is a boundless crime to criticize a sublime being; in this respect, Bodhisattvas are particularly dangerous objects, and Secret Mantra Vehicle practitioners even more so. We cannot know who is a sublime being or whether someone is inwardly a genuine practitioner. It is said that only a fully enlightened Buddha can judge; no one else can do so. If we speak badly of anyone or criticize them, we are sweeping away our own qualities. It is in the nature of things that by finding faults in others, we ourselves are destroyed. Change your attitude, therefore, and examine only your own faults.

The incomparable Dagpo Rinpoche* said:

> For beginners, it is not the time to struggle with afflictive emotions, but time to run away from them.

At present, we are not like those who have reached the stage at which they are able to take afflictive emotions on the path, so we need to be careful about things like getting angry, feeling jealous or proud, indulging in sex and drink, smoking, and lying around in a careless stupor. If we can do that, we are doing ourselves a good turn. When the scriptures speak of being able to take afflictive emotions as the path, they are referring to someone like the accomplished Indians and Tibetans of the past— someone who inwardly has truly reached the ultimate level of wisdom and outwardly can display miraculous powers. They are not talking about someone who, without having achieved complete control of his mind, is in fact recklessly indulging in afflictive emotions. It is extremely important not to misinterpret this point.

If you happen to come by things like food, clothes, and money, instead of pretending you do not need them, use as much as you do need to help you to practice, and give away whatever is left to fields such as the teacher and the Three Jewels. If you do not have such things, rather than making a lot of effort to seek wealth, invest in business, and so on, make do with what you have. It is said that anyone who practices the Dharma sincerely will have what he or she needs to live on provided by celestial beings.

---

*Gampopa, the author of *The Jewel Ornament of Liberation*.

Unless one can be content and not want more, being called a Dharma practitioner will in fact be a hollow deceit, so learn to be content with everything.

Constantly postponing things and remaining indifferent are enormous obstacles to any kind of virtuous practice. And if you make a lot of long-term plans, you will never incorporate the Dharma in yourself, so curtail your plans more and more. In particular, do not depend on a dry, intellectual understanding of emptiness: coarse behavior and crazy deeds in the name of the practice might fool a few people with impure deeds into thinking you are an accomplished being, but they are extremely destructive both for yourself and others, so it is very important to be careful. The scriptures say that an individual who has no experience or realization whatsoever cannot benefit beings even if he tries, and will harm himself besides. It is more productive simply to be diligent in one's own practice, as if one were protecting the sapling of a valuable medicinal tree from being cut. Someone who has attained the stage of warmth* but has not achieved stability might benefit others, but he will damage himself. Once one has attained the Bodhisattva levels,† one is able to benefit both oneself and other beings effortlessly.

In short, keeping your mind in tune with the Dharma, never displease the deities or your teachers. Try as much as you can to follow in some way the examples of the former knowledge holders and accomplished beings, and be diligent in the methods for spontaneously accomplishing the twofold goal.

This completes a brief explanation of the stages of the special preliminary practice that sows the seed of the extraordinary profound path in five sections.

———

Explaining and listening to these profound teachings is the occasion for both teacher and disciples to think of kindness. Reflect on the fact that by having the sublime Dharma to practice, we can make our human life meaningful and reduce existence to shreds, and this is all due to the kind-

———

*Tib. *drod*, the first of the four stages on the path of joining.
† The ten levels (Tib. *sa*, Skt. *bhumi*) on the paths of seeing and meditation. Bodhisattvas on these levels are able to truly benefit others because they have directly realized emptiness.

ness of the Buddhas and our teachers (who comprise the dominant condition), the sublime Dharma (the objective condition), our spiritual brothers and sisters (the immediately preceding condition), our parents (the concomitant condition), and the infinite host of loyal protectors who remove obstacles. How exceedingly kind they all are. Moreover, all these conditions occur because of kindness—because of the fact that the Buddha's teachings are still with us—so make a wish that the precious teachings may continue to endure for a long time. Finally, recognize that the teacher explaining the Dharma, the listeners, and the explanation itself appear but are all three devoid of intrinsic existence, like a magical illusion, and moved by intense compassion for beings who have not realized this, dedicate your sources of good to unsurpassable enlightenment. As disciples, pray from the depth of your hearts that the teachings may spread, that those who hold the teachings may flourish, and especially that the teachers may live long and turn the Wheel of the Dharma again and again.

The benefits of explaining and listening to the sublime Dharma are inconceivable. On the benefits of teaching the Dharma, the *Sutra Requested by Maitrimahasimhanada* says:

> The generosity of filling universes countless as the grains
>   of sand by the Ganges
> With gold and making gifts of them
> Is nothing compared to the benefit
> Of expounding a single verse in an evil age.

The *Root Tantra of All-Encompassing Awareness* says:

> Simply by hearing the names of the deities of the Secret Mantras, all the obscurations accumulated in ninety-three kalpas are exhausted. Each time the dharanis are recited, the benefits are immeasurable and boundless, so be diligent in teaching the Dharma.

The Great Omniscient One says:

> By teaching the Dharma with a clear mind directed toward liberation and without hoping or longing for gain, veneration, or fame, one will acquire memory, concentration, confidence, and complete freedom from afflictive emotions. One will hold the treasury of the Dharma, receive teachings from the Buddhas, and be praised and venerated by hosts of gods and humans. One will fulfill all their wishes for virtue and excellence. In all one's lives, one will remain

inseparable from the sublime Dharma. Having swiftly attained Buddhahood, one will bring beings to maturity with the rain of Dharma, and one will fulfill the aims of both oneself and others.

As for the merit acquired by those who listen to the Dharma, we can read in the *Sutra Requested by Narayana:*

> Fortunate disciple, when one has listened, one will gain knowledge. When one has knowledge, the afflictive emotions will be pacified. When the afflictive emotions have been completely pacified, demons will be unable to harm one.

The *Nirvana Sutra* has:

> From listening to the Dharma, faith takes birth. Through faith, one aspires to the six transcendent perfections and swiftly attains perfect Buddhahood. So the attainment of all virtue originates in listening.

This is just a summary of the infinite number of explanations to be found in the precious teachings the Buddha gave. And Longchenpa says:

> One has wisdom, concentration, the Stream of Dharma and other powers of retention,* and the eye of knowledge of what to avoid and what to adopt. One's virtue grows, while one's negative acts decrease. One is praised and venerated by all the world, including the gods. The darkness of ignorance is cleared away. After death, one takes miraculous birth in a lotus in a pure Buddhafield; one receives the teachings from the supreme manifestations of the Buddhas; having swiftly attained Buddhahood, one turns the sublime Wheel of the Dharma. These are some of the boundless benefits.

That those who listen to the teachings with faith derive such benefit is obvious enough, but even hearing the sound of the musical instruments summoning listeners to the teaching brings complete liberation from cyclic existence, as the *Sutra of the Gong* points out:

> The signal that the sacred teaching will begin—
> The beating of the drum or wooden gong—

---

*Tib. *gzungs.* The term "retention" includes not only Bodhisattvas' ability to remember the teachings, but also their ability to hold and transmit those teachings in an endless flow, in inconceivable ways and on a vast scale. The Stream of Dharma (Tib. *chos kyi rgyun*) is the name of a type of concentration that enables them to do this.

Will bring enlightenment to those who hear,
So what need mention they who come to listen there?

To sum up, for those who wish good for themselves there is nothing more important to do in this world than practice the Dharma. So, realizing that it is extremely difficult to meet with the teachings and that to do so has immense benefit, they should be diligent in using whatever means they can to teach the Dharma and listen to it. As we read in the *Sutra of the Inconceivable Secrets:*

> The coming of a Buddha in this world is rare indeed,
> It takes accumulation to find a human body.[173]
> Alas, those who have faith and listen to the Dharma
> Are hard to find, even in a hundred kalpas.

And the Great Omniscient One says:

> When we first enter the doctrine, we need to listen, because by recognizing the defects and advantages of samsara and nirvana, we start to adopt and avoid.* When we are training our minds we need to listen, because doing so removes our ignorance of things. While we are practicing we also need to listen, because when our virtuous activities stagnate, it helps us progress. Even when our minds are liberated we need to listen, because it stops the proliferation of doubts.

At present, from the moment we first set out on the path until we reach the end of it, listening is important in providing something to look up to,† because it turns our minds toward what the masters of the past practiced and increases our own experiences and realization. By being attached to the first teaching we receive, whatever it might be, thinking that it is sufficient, we will not get to the end of the path even if we practice in solitary retreat, because we will not be aware of the errors one can make on the path or know whether we are on the wrong path. We may appear to be practicing the Dharma, but we will not make any progress at all. To quote from the *Sutra of the Arborescent Array:*

> Fortunate disciple, if you wish to attain consummate Buddhahood, you must train in seeking to reach the other shore of the ocean of learning.

---

* I.e., adopt positive activities and avoid negative ones.
† Lit. "something or someone superior to oneself."

Therefore, in order to take the broad highway to liberation yourself, to ensure that the teachings endure for ages, and to bring beings to the glory and excellence of benefit and happiness, devote yourself to explaining and practicing this path, and spread the activities of the Universally Good Padmakara* to fill the whole of space.

---

*Tib. *kun bzang padma ka ra,* Guru Padmasambhava inseparable from the Buddha of the absolute body, Samantabhadra.

# Afterword

For every single one of the traditions of the profound and vast Dharma,
The text of the preliminary practice is the basic starting point,
The essence of the instructions, the greatest of wishing jewels.
Why would those with faith and fortune not use it as a crown?

This is the way ten million accomplished knowledge holders have taken,
There is no imagining a path more excellent than this,
So if you practice it properly, with diligence,
It is certain you will seize the great goal, the supreme everlasting state.

Though known as preliminary, it is the ultimate main practice,
Sufficient in itself, the main pillar of the path.
Without it, babbling on about profound, advanced practices like
    generation and perfection
Is like transferring consciousness into a headless corpse.

Many teachings you might have heard, but if they are not practiced,
Like the kimba fruit, they'll not release you when you are in need.*
You've relied on a mere understanding of the sublime Dharma—
Alas, friends, who has robbed you of your intelligence?

Bearing aloft the lamp of the sacred pith instructions,
Do not fall asleep on the bed of indolence,
But banish the darkness of existence with its hundreds of faults—
Now is the time to kindle the light of the twofold goal.

For you who do not make an effort to be diligent at once,
That archenemy, the Lord of Death, is here with mouth agape,
His fickle tongue swifter than the dance of lightning,
Impatient in his haste to snatch away a person's life.

---

*Despite its attractive appearance, the *kimba* fruit is bitter tasting, provides no nourishment, and may even be poisonous.

In a perfectly arrayed mansion of massive rocky mountains,
In delightful valleys and lonely forests,
The sage savors the nectar of concentration.
I urge you, seize the citadel of immortality and great bliss.

To clearly indicate the right path for achieving that,
I've used the instructions of the lineage teachers
That well explain the stages of the preliminary practice
And condensed the essential points of the profound meaning,
Arranging them in a way that is easy to understand.

I may not be so bright, but I'm unstained by inferior motives
And unsullied by any intellectual ambition,
And so, my sole, wholehearted wish being to benefit others,
I think I have nothing to regret in having expressed this with a pure,
    altruistic heart.

Nevertheless, for everything incorrectly explained I am to blame,
And I pray it will not lead to harsh retribution;
The parts that have been explained properly are so thanks to the
    kindness of my teacher:
Bless me that they are able to fulfill the sublime ones' aspirations.

By the merit I have obtained through these efforts
May all beings have the great good fortune
To hear, reflect, and meditate on this tradition of the supreme vehicle,
And spontaneously accomplish the perfect twofold goal according
    to their wishes.

May I too, without any selfish considerations,
Having committed myself as the guide of infinite beings,
Be the equal of the Bodhisattva Samantabhadra
And have mastery of the infinite great waves of activity.

With the victory banner of study and practice crowned
By that marvelous wishing jewel, the oral tradition of the
    profound secret,
Yielding a constant fine rain of the two accomplishments and
    everything desired,
May the three worlds be filled with fortune—benefit and happiness.

# Colophon

This easy-to-apply commentary, a series of complete instructions on the preliminary practice of the profound path, *Heart Essence of the Dakini,* entitled "A Torch of Perfect Explanation That Lights the Way to Freedom," was initially requested by my principal diamond disciple, Tulku Jigme Chöying Norbu Dön Thamche Drubpe De, who is the main holder of the doctrine of the Great Secret; with words of devotion, he presented an immaculate white silken ceremonial scarf and a precious mandala marked with auspicious signs. Along with this, I was persistently urged by the practitioner Trulshik Dorje, who said that it would be good to somehow write a clear and concise textbook so that the followers of our Dharma lineage would not need to look elsewhere for an introductory text. In reply to these and other repeated requests from numerous interested and intelligent disciples, I, Jigdrel Yeshe Dorje Gelek Nampar Gyalwa'i De, a tantric practitioner of royal descent who can claim to be a follower of the long tradition of the Great Master of Oddiyana, took as a basis the oral instructions of the Noble All-Pervading Lord, my sublime teacher, and clarified them using suitable sections from the excellent explanations of the learned and accomplished masters of the past. On the auspicious date of the Buddha's descent from the gods' realms, in the *prajña* part of the month of Ashvin in the Inexhaustible year (1946), when I was in my forty-third year, I composed this in the delightful monastery of the spontaneously arisen palace of the Arya at Puchu Terkyi Lhakang in the heart of a forested valley in the eastern region of Kongpo. May it be the foundation for vast benefit to the doctrine and beings.

SVASTI
Of all the paths so wondrous and profound this is the distilled essence,
    Essence that's the sappy marrow of instruction,
        For preliminary practices, a guide superlative!

Superlative disciples in all their multitude will find herein their joy,
  Joy great and inexhaustible:
    Of Dharma's gift a wellspring unexcelled!
Unexcelled is her sublime intent, and she is wisdom spotless and supreme,
  Supreme in clarity, Awareness-Holding Queen[174]—
    And perfect are her deeds, all glorious!
Glorious too the Master whose intent is of itself fulfilled:
  Fulfilled also the two accomplishments
    The wealth of which enriches wandering beings!
SARWADA KALYANAM BHAVATU

Chariot of the Path of Union
A Recitation Text for the Preliminary
Practice of the Profound and Secret
*Heart Essence of the Dakini*

Om svasti
Embodiment of the knowledge, love, and power of all the
    infinite Buddhas,
Gracious sovereign of the hundred Buddha families, lord
    of the mandala,
Glorious Teacher, Lotus Buddha,
I revere you as my crown jewel: grant your blessings.
Fortunate ones, I invite you into this chariot, an arrangement,
Clear and easily implemented, of the preliminary practice of the
    profound treasure,
The excellent path leading swiftly and easily to the union level
    of the four bodies.
Enter it now, with joy!

Those who have the fortune to encounter the profound path, and whose enduring good deeds have awakened as the wish to realize the union level of the four bodies in this life, should diligently and meticulously practice this very path from the beginning.

For this, there are two parts: the general preliminary practice for each session that makes one a fit vessel, and the specific preliminary practice that prepares one for the yogas of the two phases.

## I. General session preliminaries

Sit on a comfortable seat and observe the essential points of physical posture, keeping the body straight. Expel the three poisons with the stale air. Rest in relaxed awareness, turning the mind to natural concentration. Invoke in your mind the thought of the root teacher, the great being who embodies all the Buddhas, as follows:

In the sky in front of me, in an expanse of rainbow lights
and circles,
Upon a jeweled lion throne, lotus, sun, and moon,
Is my incomparably kind root teacher
In the form of the Lake-Born Diamond Bearer of Oddiyana,
Clear blue, holding vajra and bell, in the attire of the body of
perfect enjoyment,
United with his own radiance, the consort Great Bliss.
He is smiling happily, his body emanating rays of wisdom light.
He is the essential embodiment of all the infinite refuges.

Visualizing the teacher in this way, pray with intense devotion:

To the teacher I pray,
To the teacher, all-pervading absolute body, I pray:
Bless me that the darkness of ignorance be dispelled.
To the teacher I pray,
To the teacher, body of perfect enjoyment, I pray:
Bless me that the radiant light may shine from within.
To the teacher I pray,
To the teacher, compassionate body of manifestation, I pray:
Bless me with realization as vast as space.
To the teacher I pray,
To the teacher, precious Buddha, I pray:
Bless me that the twofold goal may be accomplished
spontaneously.

As a result of this fervent prayer:

The strength of my devotion inspires and delights the teacher,
And with a show of unbearable happiness,
He comes above the crown of my head, and as a cloud of
bodhichitta,
Confers the empowerment of the enthronement of wisdom:
In the great state of simultaneous realization and liberation
I am blessed.

Recite and concentrate on this, then rest in evenness for a while, in the
state of awareness without grasping. It is very important to do this practice
before each session as it is necessary for dispelling obstacles and for allow-
ing blessings to enter swiftly.

## II. Specific preliminary practices

This section has two parts: the common preliminaries that cultivate the field of one's mindstream with the four practices for turning the mind; and the uncommon preliminaries that sow the seeds of the profound path in five sections.

## A. The common preliminaries

It is extremely difficult to obtain a human birth like this, endowed with the freedoms and advantages. And once obtained, being impermanent, it quickly becomes subject to death. And having died, we will not become nothing, but will follow only our deeds, thus creating cyclic existence. Wherever we are reborn in cyclic existence, there is only suffering and nothing beyond. So think, "Now I must do whatever I can to be freed from this great ocean of suffering that is cyclic existence. To that end, from now on I will practice the authentic, sacred Dharma." And thinking, "Precious teacher, grant the blessing that I might be able to do that!" arouse intense faith and determination to be free:

> NAMO. Glorious embodiment of all the Buddhas and
>     Bodhisattvas of the three times,
> Endowed with knowledge, love, and power,
> Sole abiding refuge, kind teacher and lord,
> Dwell inseparably in the wheel of great bliss on the crown
>     of my head.
> As I pray to you, precious teacher,
> Bless me, incomparably kind lord.
>
> These freedoms and advantages are so difficult to find:
> May I make full use of this significant human body.
> As I pray to you, precious teacher,
> Bless me, incomparably kind lord.
>
> The perceptions of this life are just temporary conditions,
>     like a dream:
> May I be deeply mindful of impermanence and death.
> As I pray to you, precious teacher,
> Bless me, incomparably kind lord.
>
> The three worlds of cyclic existence are by nature suffering,
> So may I eradicate all attachment and clinging.

As I pray to you, precious teacher,
Bless me, incomparably kind lord.

Positive and negative actions ripen unfailingly:
May I be skillful and disciplined in adopting good
    and shunning evil.
As I pray to you, precious teacher,
Bless me, incomparably kind lord.

Keeping the meaning of these verses in mind, recite them as many times as possible.

## B. The uncommon preliminaries

There are five sections.

### *1. Refuge, the foundation of the path to liberation*

First, visualize the object of refuge.

The universe with its beings is a delightful pure Buddhafield,
In its center, the stainless, lovely lake of Dhanakosha.
In the middle is a jeweled lotus, petals unfurled,
With five branches, and on the pistil of the central branch
The embodiment of all the Buddhas, the teacher Thöthrengtsel
In the form of Nangsi Zilnön, He Whose Majesty Overawes
    Appearances and Existence,
Glowing with the splendor of the major and minor marks, majestic
    in an expanse of rays of rainbow light.
Above his head are the teachers of the knowledge holders'
    lineages—
The mind, symbol, and hearing lineages,
The prophesied lineage of the oral transmission, the lineage
    of empowerment and aspiration,
The lineage of teachings entrusted to the dakinis, and the authentic
    lineage of realization:
All are present, one above the other.
The branches of the lotus spread out in the four directions,
    and upon them,
To the right, is the Conqueror, King of the Shakyas,

Surrounded by the thousand Buddhas of the Buddhafields of the
  Fortunate Kalpa
And all the other Victors Gone to Bliss of all the times and
  directions.
To the rear, in the interstices of a beautiful lattice of five-colored
  lights,
Is the Excellent Speech, the sublime Dharma of transmission
  and realization, in the form of books,
Resonating with the sweet sounds of the vowels and consonants.
To the left are the Eight Bodhisattvas, Close Sons,
And around them, the Sublime Beings, the Sixteen Great
  Sthaviras, and so on—
All the Sanghas of Bodhisattvas, Listeners, and Solitary Realizers.
In front is Vajrakumara and his consort
Surrounded by the hosts of peaceful and wrathful yidam deities
  of the four or six tantra sections
And the dakas and dakinis of the three places.
Outside, all around and in between,
Are all the infinite hosts of loyal protectors of the three tantras,
Gathered like massing clouds.
All of these possess the activity of stirring the depths
  of cyclic existence
With the wisdom of knowledge, love, and power:
They are present as leaders guiding all us beings
And thinking of us with great compassion.

Visualizing this clearly, in their presence imagine that you and all other
sentient beings, with one voice, recite the following with complete trust
and great devotion physically, verbally, and mentally, going for refuge
until you reach the heart of enlightenment.

NAMO. I and the infinitude of those who have been my parents,
  numerous as space is vast,
Until the heart of enlightenment is reached,
Take refuge in the teacher, the Three Jewels.
Hold us with your love without separating from us
  for an instant.

Recite this as many times as you can.

## 2. Arousing the supreme bodhichitta, the essence of the path of the Great Vehicle

Appealing to the objects of refuge as your witness, recite:

All beings filling space have been my parents.
They wish for happiness, yet all they achieve is suffering.
How pitiful they are, wandering in cyclic existence with
 no chance of escape.
I must do everything I can to free them.
To that end I will drive myself with undistracted effort
And see the profound yoga through to completion.

Bringing to mind bodhichitta in aspiration and in action, recite as many times as possible:

Heed me, Protectors and your Children:
With the four boundless attitudes I will wholeheartedly take up
 the good of beings;
Holding bodhichitta, I will train in the six transcendent
 perfections.
May the twofold goal be spontaneously and gloriously fulfilled.

Do the mind training of equalizing and exchanging oneself and others, and imagine giving away your happiness and taking on others' suffering. At the end of the session:

From the objects of refuge a boundless nectarous stream
 of blessings
In the form of brilliant white rays of light issues forth.
They dissolve into me and everyone else and purify the
 obscurations of body, speech, and mind.
In an instant we melt into light and dissolve into the objects
 of refuge.
The surrounding objects of refuge melt in stages and are
 absorbed into the main deity;
The main deity is absorbed into the absolute space
 beyond concepts.

With this dissolution, rest in evenness.

## 3. Meditation and recitation on Vajrasattva, to purify negative actions and obscurations that act as unfavorable conditions

Visualize your root teacher in the form of Vajrasattva and consort actually present above the crown of your head. Developing intense shame and regret for the negative actions you committed in the past and vowing henceforth never to repeat them even if your life is at stake, imagine that the stream of nectarlike bodhichitta from the mantra garland in his heart purifies all your negative actions, obscurations, faults, and downfalls, with nothing left. Maintaining these essential points, the four powers, say:

Above my crown, on a lotus-and-moon seat,
Is the Teacher Vajrasattva, the color of crystal,
Smiling peacefully, youthful and radiant with the major and minor marks.
His right and left hands—means and wisdom—hold a vajra and a bell;
He sits cross-legged, in the complete attire of the body of perfect enjoyment.
On his lap is Topa, holding knife and skull, and embracing him.
In his heart is a moon disc with a HUNG surrounded by the mantra garland,
From which a stream of ambrosial bodhichitta flows down through the point of union,
Entering me by the crown opening and completely filling my body.
All deteriorations and breaches, negative actions, and downfalls are purified.
OM VAJRA SATTVA SAMAYA MANU PALA YA
VAJRA SATTVA TENOPA TISHTHA DRIDHO ME BHAVA
SUTOKAYO ME BHAVA
SUPOKAYO ME BHAVA
ANU RAKTO ME BHAVA
SARVA SIDDHIM ME PRAYACCHA
SARVA KARMA SUCHA ME
CHITTAN SHREYAM KURU HUNG
HA HA HA HA HO
BHAGAVAN
SARVA TATHAGATA VAJRA MAME MUÑCHA VAJRI BHAVA MAHA
    SAMAYA SATTVA AH

Recite this as much as you can. As you do so, consider that the whole of the inside of your body becomes white, filled to the brim by the flow of nectar; all your negative actions, obscurations and breaches are purified; your body and mind are pervaded by untainted bliss. This is the external way of purifying obscurations.

At the end, pray with intense devotion and yearning:

O Protector, in ignorance and confusion
I have transgressed and deteriorated the commitments.
My Teacher and Protector, give me refuge!
O supreme Diamond Holder,
Embodiment of great compassion,
To you, lord of beings, I go for refuge.
I acknowledge and part from all my deteriorations and breaches of
    the root and branch commitments of body, speech, and mind.
I beg you, cleanse and purify all the stains of my negative actions,
    obscurations, faults, and downfalls.

As a result of this prayer,

Vajrasattva smiles with pleasure and grants your prayer, saying:
    "Fortunate child, all your negative actions, obscurations, faults,
    and downfalls are purified!"
All negative actions and obscurations are purified; I become like
    a heap of crystal.
Again, Vajrasattva melts into white light
And blends into me, and I become Vajrasattva.
All that appears and exists is viewed as purified, as the infinite
    display.
OM VAJRA SATTVA HUNG

With this, consider that Vajrasattva on the crown of your head dissolves into you and that you transform into Vajrasattva. Viewing appearances, sounds, and thoughts as the play of the deity, mantra, and absolute nature, recite the quintessential mantra. This is the internal way of purifying obscurations.

At the end, even the conceptual elaborations of deity and mantra dissolve into radiant light: watch the true nature of the absolute Vajrasattva, awareness-emptiness, pure from the very beginning and free of all concepts of something to be purified and something that purifies. This is the secret, unsurpassable way of purifying obscurations.

## 4. Offering the mandala to gather the two accumulations, which are favorable conditions on the path

In the presence of the field of accumulation visualized in the same way as the object of refuge, using as a symbolic example the mandala that you actually set out, imagine that you are offering, externally, the array of the third-order Buddhafield of the World of Forbearance, comprised of a billion worlds; internally, your own body, your aggregates, elements, and senses-and-fields, along with all your possessions and merits past, present, and future; and secretly, the radiant absolute expanse, the spontaneously accomplished Buddhafield of the diamond essence, all the inconceivable aspects of the absolute nature whose nature is infinite visions of Buddha-bodies and spheres.

> OM AH HUNG. The glorious infinite array of the billionfold World of Forbearance,
> Along with my body, possessions, merit, and sources of good,
> All perfectly arranged as this beautiful mandala,
> I offer to the Three Jewels in order to complete the two accumulations.

Offer this as many times as you can. At the end, consider that the field of accumulation dissolves into you and all beings so that the two accumulations are completed.

## 5. Guru Yoga, the ultimate path of the bestowal of blessings

Begin by visualizing the support for empowerment:

> EMAHO. One's perceptions are perfectly pure—the absolute Buddhafield, the Unexcelled,
> Great Bliss, the city of Lotus Light, in the center of which
> I am Tsogyal Khachö Wangmo,
> Clear red, utterly beautiful with the major and minor marks, holding curved knife and skull,
> Adorned with multicolored silks, and jewel and bone ornaments,
> Standing in the striding posture on a seat of lotus, sun, and corpse,
> And gazing longingly up into the sky.
> In the sky in front, in an expanse of intermingled rainbow lights,
> Is a seat of lotus (symbol of nonattachment), sun, and moon, and on it

My teacher in the form of the Lotus-Born (Padmasambhava),
His body white, tinged with red, radiant, majestic, a mass
  of glowing light.
He appears young, perfect with the major and minor marks,
  and semi-wrathful,
Wearing the lotus hat, secret garment, gown, Dharma robe,
  and brocade cape.
His right hand holds a *vajra*, his left a skull-cup and vase;
His two feet in the royal posture, he holds the *khatvanga*
  in the crook of his arm.
He whose majesty overawes all that appears and exists, Lord
  of all samsara and nirvana—
The nature of his body pervades all the Buddhafields,
Infinite pure lands are complete in the expanse of his body,
He is the Great Being who embodies all refuges.

Having visualized this, so that your ordinary thoughts cease by themselves, recite:

HUNG. From the peak of the Glorious Copper-Colored Mountain
  in the center of the isle of Chamara,
The measureless palace of Lotus Light, Great Bliss,
Noble Teacher, Manifestation Body of Oddiyana,
With your hosts of knowledge holders, dakas, and dakinis,
In order to bless us, holders of your lineage, come I pray.
OM AH HUNG VAJRA GURU PADMA THÖTHRENGTSEL VAJRA
  SAMAYA DZA SIDDHI PALA HUNG AH

With this consider that blessings are bestowed and that the samaya and
wisdom deities remain inseparable.
  In order to accumulate merit, perform the seven branches:

OM AH HUNG. To the embodiment of all refuges, Teacher
  inseparable from Oddiyana,
I submit obeisance with one-pointed respect in body, speech,
  and mind.
My body and possessions I offer as clouds of offerings, holding
  nothing back.
I acknowledge and part from my negative actions, downfalls,
  and deteriorations and breaches of the commitments.

I rejoice in all virtue, tainted and untainted.
I exhort you to turn the wheel of the teachings of the essential
   meaning.
I beseech you to remain forever without passing into nirvana.
This positive action and all sources of good
I dedicate that all beings may attain unsurpassable
   enlightenment.

These seven branches include the three essential points of accumulation,
purification, and increase.

The entrance of blessings in one's mindstream depends exclusively on
the connection made through devotion, so develop the absolute certainty
that your root teacher, who is the embodiment of all refuges and, in terms
of qualities, the equal of the Buddhas, is much greater than them in terms
of kindness. Putting all your hope and trust in the teacher, pray one-pointedly as follows, again and again:

KYEHO. Precious teacher, embodiment of all the Buddhas
Of past, present, and future—
Seeing you dispels the gloom of ignorance,
Hearing you cuts away the web of doubt,
Thinking of you transfers the realization of the mind lineage.
Your touch bestows blessings and accomplishments,
Your kindness is beyond all imagination,
Your qualities are as endless as space.
With intense, unbearable yearning
I pray to you, think of me with compassion.
My body, possessions, and sources of good
I offer you without attachment.
From now on and in all my lives,
I'll have no other refuge, guide, defender, or escort
Than you, my constant protector.
I entrust myself to you with body, speech, and mind;
In happiness or pain, good times or bad,
Wherever you send me, high or low—Teacher, it is up to you.
In all my lives, since time without beginning,
I have been dominated by ignorance and delusion:
Jailed in the three worlds of cyclic existence,
I have been tortured by the three sufferings.

Unable to bear the burden of misery and pain,
From my heart I call out to you, Noble Teacher.
Though I want to be happy, I devote myself to deeds that lead
    to suffering.
Deceived by the demon in everything I perceive,
On account of my attachment, I wander, deluded by dualism.
For someone with my bad deeds and misfortune,
Who is there to afford protection other than you, my refuge
    and protector?
As I pray to you, Lord Teacher,
Hold me with compassion, you who are so kind.
Grant me your blessings, you who have ability and power.
Guide me, sublime Lord of All.
I beseech you, turn my thoughts to the Dharma.
Bestow on me the four empowerments,
Purify me of the four obscurations,
Help me attain the four bodies, I pray.
Transmit to me the blessings of the mind lineage.
Destroy the gloom of ignorance
And release the fetters of dualistic delusion,
Help me actualize the wisdom of omniscience,
Take me to the great exhaustion of phenomena beyond mind,
Grant me liberation in the great body of rainbow light,
The naturally accomplished youthful vase body.

This constitutes the external practice in the manner of prayer. Next, consider that the teacher's three places are marked with a white OM, a red AH, and a blue HUNG, blazing with light, representing the three diamonds of all the Tathagatas. From them, amid rays and circles of rainbow light, stream forth countless Buddha forms, syllables, and symbolic attributes, like specks of dust in a sunbeam. Consider that they dissolve into you, and that you receive all the blessings and accomplishments without exception. From time to time, recognize the environment as the palace of the Glorious Copper-Colored Mountain and its inhabitants as groups of dakas and dakinis of Oddiyana, all sounds as the spontaneous sound of the mantra, and all thoughts that arise and dissolve as spontaneously liberated, radiant light. In that state, recite one-pointedly:

OM AH HUNG VAJRA GURU PADMA SIDDHI HUNG

These twelve syllables are the essence of the secret mantras. At the end, take the four empowerments, applying the essential points of the visualization for each empowerment:

From the syllable OM in the teacher's forehead, there comes forth
 a ray of white light like a shooting star:
It dissolves into my forehead, purifying the obscurations of the
 body and channels;
I receive the body empowerment of the vase;
My body is blessed as the manifestation of the diamond body;
The good fortune for reaching the level of the body of
 manifestation is established in my being.
From the syllable AH in his throat, there comes forth a ray of red
 light like a flashing lasso of lightning:
It dissolves into my throat, purifying the obscurations of the speech
 and energies;
I receive the secret speech empowerment;
My speech is blessed as the manifestation of the diamond speech;
The good fortune for reaching the level of the body of perfect
 enjoyment is established in my being.
From the syllable HUNG in his heart, there comes forth a ray of
 dark blue light like a densely gathering cloud:
It dissolves into my heart, purifying the obscurations of the mind
 and vital essence;
I receive the mind empowerment of supreme knowledge that is
 primal wisdom;
My mind is blessed as the manifestation of the diamond mind;
The good fortune for reaching the level of the absolute body is
 established in my being.
Again, from the teacher's heart, there comes forth a five-colored
 sphere, the essence of his mind, free from thoughts:
It dissolves into my heart, purifying the two obscurations and all
 habitual tendencies;
I receive the precious word empowerment;
I receive the blessing that the infinite ornaments — the
 inexhaustible qualities and activities of all the Buddhas — are
 complete in me;
The good fortune for reaching the essential body is established
 in my being.

All this constitutes the internal practice in the manner of recitation, along with taking empowerment. Once again, give rise to intense devotion:

All-pervading lord, mighty embodiment of the four bodies,
Great treasure of knowledge, love, and compassion,
The thought of whom relieves the longing in my mind—
Incomparably kind teacher,
I pray to you from the depth of my heart.
Without my parting from you for an instant,
Bless me with your guidance,
And make me inseparable from you.

As a result of this prayer:

The teacher melts into the essence of great bliss, becoming a sphere of five-colored light an inch in size, which dissolves into the middle of my heart: my mind becomes inseparable from the teacher's mind.

Remain in evenness for as long as it lasts, in the natural, innate state of luminosity beyond mind—awareness-emptiness, the absolute-body teacher watching itself. This constitutes the secret practice of the absolute teacher free of conceptual elaboration in the manner of activities.

After that, as you arise from the session, again view appearances, sounds, and thoughts suddenly awakened as the teacher's three secrets.

Precious, glorious root teacher,
Dwell on a lotus seat on the crown of my head.
Guide me with your great kindness,
And grant me the accomplishments of your body, speech,
and mind.
With regard to the glorious teachers' lifestyles
May I never have even an instant's wrong view.
Through devotion—seeing everything they do as perfect—
May the teachers' blessings enter my mind.
All the positive deeds accumulated in the three times, symbolized
by this one,
Unsullied by the stains of any selfish desire for personal peace
and happiness,
I dedicate to the infinite hosts of beings, without a single exception,
As the cause for their attaining unsurpassable enlightenment.
In all my lives, may the feet of my teachers, the lords of the families,

Never cease to adorn the wheel of great bliss in my crown,
And through the path of devotion, may their minds and mine
   mingle as one.
Grant the good fortune that the twofold goal be spontaneously
   accomplished.

Concluding with these prayers of dedication, aspiration and auspiciousness, continue with your everyday activities. In between sessions, consider
that the first part of your food and drink is nectar, and that your clothes
are celestial garments, and offer them to the teacher on the crown of your
head. Whatever you perceive with the six senses, do not follow them with
ordinary thoughts but preserve the radiant awareness of them as deities,
mantras and wisdom. When you go to sleep at night, after praying to be
able to recognize luminosity, consider that the teacher on the crown of
your head passes through the crown opening and comes to rest in your
heart, which is now in the form of a four-petaled lotus. Concentrate on the
light from the teacher filling the whole of your body and, dissolving into
the radiant, naked state of awareness-emptiness, fall asleep in this state
without mental dullness and without being interrupted by other thoughts.
If you wake up, stop the flow of thoughts and reflections — distraction,
wildness, stupefaction, and so on — and maintain the radiant state of
luminosity. By doing so, you will be able to recognize the luminosity of
sleep and the dream state. Again, when you get up in the morning, imagine the teacher passing up your central channel and out into the sky in
front of your head, remaining there joyfully, and resume your practice as
described above.

Furthermore, when the time comes for you to die, mingling awareness
and the absolute expanse of luminosity, remain in evenness. This is the
very best form of transference. If you are unable to do that, remember the
three aspects of yogic perception in the intermediate state, and by that
means you will be liberated. So, maintaining constant devotion and keeping the commitments perfectly purely, be diligent in making the practice
of the two accumulations combined grow more and more. Exert yourself in this way, beginning with the four practices for turning the mind,
until you gain true experience in each of the stages of accumulation and
purification. In particular, practice the Guru Yoga with intense diligence,
convinced that it is the most extraordinary and profound essential point
of the path of the Diamond Vehicle, and considering it, therefore, as the
vital force of the main practice. Without the need to rely on the other

practices of the generation and perfection phases, you will certainly be liberated in Chamara, the Buddhafield of Lotus Light and, traversing the four knowledge-holder levels as if by magic, reach the level of the wisdom teacher, Samantabhadra.

The wise, if some there be, who wish for perfect freedom
From the burning torment of samsara's pit of fire,
And who rely on this sublime path, this king of forest trees,
Will find relief in its dense, cool shade—enlightenment.
By the power of deeds well done, may all beings filling space
Become the beneficiaries of this profound teaching,
And without ever turning back, joyfully and swiftly enter
That beautiful city, the Land of Lotus Light!

This "Chariot of the Path of Union," a recitation text for the preliminary practice of the general sections of Lama, Completion, and Mind of the new treasure, the profound and secret *Heart Essence of the Dakini,* is based on a previous, slightly unclear arrangement, which I intended to rearrange in a way that would be easy to recite and practice. Recently Tulku Jigme Chöying Norbu Dön Thamche Drubpe De from Kongyul Len Ri Sang Ngak Chödzong sent me a letter with the sincere request, "You must by all means complete this as it will surely be of immense benefit to all fortunate beginners practicing this path." Because of this, I, Jigdrel Yeshe Dorje, the shoot of the knowledge holders, composed this at the age of thirty-four on the tenth day of the wisdom side of full moon in the month Bhadrapada in the year of Ishva (1937), at the especially auspicious time of the close gathering, in the king of all the sacred practice sites blessed by the Great Teacher, the cave of Taktsang Senge Samdrup.

By this, may the activities of the profound path endure and spread to the ends of the universe, and may all those who make a connection with it gain the good fortune to be born at the feet of the Lotus-Born Teacher.

Sarwada mangalam

# Notes

1. In preparation for a teaching, one should have washed and put on clean clothes, while conducting oneself modestly and discreetly.
2. Tib. *mkha' snying nor bu.* This may mean the sun and moon, filling the palace with light. Alternatively it may refer to the Bodhisattva Akashagarbha's special ability to make everything beautiful.
3. Tib. *sib sib,* an expression used to describe softly falling rain or snow being absorbed.
4. "Superior" (Tib. *lhag*) means here that the teacher should have more knowledge than the disciple.
5. *Ornament of the Sutras,* XVIII, 10.
6. The trainings in discipline, concentration, and wisdom result in one becoming respectively disciplined (Tib. *dul*), peaceful (*zhi ba*), and perfectly peaceful (*nye bar zhi ba*).
7. *Fifty Verses on the Teacher,* 8 and 9.
8. Tib. *gdan,* lit. "seats," i.e., the different sitting postures for performing different activities.
9. Traditionally the arts and sciences (Tib. *rig gnas*) include medicine, astrology, grammar, logic, poetry, painting, music, and other subjects. A tantric master has had a first-class education and is a highly cultured individual.
10. This includes all aspects of the practice, including preparing mandalas and so forth.
11. Lit. "they are free from the path," i.e., they are not caught by attachment to the path.
12. Tib. *skyon can gyi bshes gnyen,* a friend full of defects, as opposed to a spiritual or virtuous friend (*dge ba'i bshes gnyen*).
13. The Tibetan word *rigs,* translated here as "family," has a number of meanings, including caste, race, class, type, and potential. In the present context its meaning is not confined to the individual's parentage, for it includes the notion of spiritual family. A disciple can be said to be of the Great-Vehicle family, meaning that he or she is born with the potential for developing the qualities of a Bodhisattva, while someone of the Listener family only has the potential to attain the level of Arhat. One from a bad or evil family clearly has little or no potential for spiritual growth.

14. Unless otherwise stated, all the quotations in this section are taken from the *Fifty Verses on the Teacher.*

15. The reason a master of the Diamond Vehicle might, for example, ask a monk to drink alcohol could be in order to help the monk cut his attachment to his vows and his pure observance of them. Drinking alcohol is normally forbidden because if one is drunk one risks breaking other vows.

16. Or even a cushion.

17. A bandage on an injured head, however, would be permissible.

18. Respectively Rigdzin Chenpo, Jetsun Dampa, or Pelden Lama.

19. I.e., within fifty miles.

20. Tib. *phan bde,* meaning temporary benefit and ultimate happiness, and therefore also translatable as "happiness and peace."

21. Tib. *rnal 'byor,* yoga, lit. "union (or integration) with the natural state."

22. Tib. *yan lag,* lit. "limbs," refers here to the scales on the underside of a snake adapted to locomotion. Unless one forcefully twists the snake they do not stand out. Similarly, one has to use forceful means in adopting the posture in order to create the right conditions for meditation.

23. The generation phase (*bskyed rim*) and perfection phase (*rdzogs rim*) that comprise the so-called main practice.

24. *Introduction to the Middle Way,* II, 7, last line. The quotation of this line on its own has necessitated modifying the verb. The entire verse reads:

    Common folk and speech-born Shravakas,
    And those established on the path of self-enlightenment,
    The Children of the Conqueror also—their final excellence
    And high rebirth derive from discipline alone.

25. In his *Guide to The Words of My Perfect Teacher,* Khenpo Ngawang Pelzang points out that discipline is the cause for obtaining the freedoms, positive deeds are the cause for obtaining the advantages, and that these primary causes have to be linked by a contributory cause, namely pure aspiration.

26. *The Way of the Bodhisattva,* IV, 17, 18.

27. *Letter to a Friend,* 59.

28. *The Way of the Bodhisattva,* IV, 20.

29. *The Way of the Bodhisattva,* IV, 15.

30. *The Way of the Bodhisattva,* I, 5.

31. Tib. *gsang sngags kyi de kho na nyid,* referring to the ultimate nature or natural state as realized in the Secret Mantra Vehicle.

32. Tib. *gtan 'dun gyi nor bu,* desired as a long-term investment, as a security.

33. Tib. *snying po len pa,* lit. "extract its essence."

34. *The Way of the Bodhisattva,* VII, 14.

35. *The Way of the Bodhisattva,* IV, 23. "Reprieve" refers here to the freedoms.

36. *Letter to a Friend,* 117 (last two lines).

37. Tib. *drang srong gi rgyal mtshan chen po,* "the great victory banner of the Sage" (i.e., the Great Sage, meaning the Buddha). This is the same as the "victory

banner of the doctrine" (Tib. *bstan pa'i rgyal mtshan*), a term used to describe the three Dharma robes: Buddhists who wear the monastic robes are said to fly the victory banner of the doctrine. Here, however, Dudjom Rinpoche is using the term to apply to anyone who is truly practicing the Buddhist teachings.

38. This is a treasure, or *terma*, a teaching given by Guru Rinpoche to Gyalse Lhaje (Prince Murub Tsenpo, the second son of King Trisong Detsen), and rediscovered by a reincarnation of the latter.

39. Alternative translation: they eventually have a phase of destruction and voidness or fusion with space. According to Buddhist cosmology, the universe goes through four phases: formation, duration, destruction, and voidness.

40. *Letter to a Friend*, 57.

41. Tib. *mi'am ci*, one of the eight classes of gods and spirits (*lha srin sde brgyad*), who take on human form and listen to the Buddha's teachings on earth.

42. Numerous explanations exist concerning the four ages from complete endowment through half-endowment and third-endowment (or alternatively through threefold endowment and twofold endowment) to the age of conflict, but they all involve a gradual decline from an age when beings have a complete set of qualities, which are progressively lost in the subsequent ages. One explanation is to be found in *Treasury of Precious Qualities*, page 394 (note 256).

43. The Tibetan makes use of a pun on the word "essence." To take the essence means "to make full use of," so this sentence means literally: "Take the essence of your possessions that do not have any essence."

44. *The Way of the Bodhisattva*, III, 12.

45. Tib. *rab tu byung ba*. This term is very often understood to mean taking monastic ordination.

46. *The Way of the Bodhisattva*, II, 58.

47. *Jewel Garland*, 278.

48. *Hundred Verses of Advice to the People of Tingri*, 29.

49. *Jewel Garland*, 317 (last two lines). There is a play on words in the Tibetan here (*'chi bdag rkyen*), with a reference to both the Lord of Death (*'chi bdag*) and the dominant condition (*bdag po'i rkyen*).

50. *Letter to a Friend*, 55.

51. *The Way of the Bodhisattva*, II, 39.

52. *The Way of the Bodhisattva*, VIII, 31 (last three lines).

53. *The Way of the Bodhisattva*, IV, 16.

54. *The Way of the Bodhisattva*, VI, 59.

55. *The Way of the Bodhisattva*, II, 62.

56. *The Way of the Bodhisattva*, IV, 12 (second half), 13, 14.

57. *Letter to a Friend*, 104. This verse has been interpreted differently by various commentators.

58. *Hundred Verses of Advice to the People of Tingri*, 18.

59. *The Way of the Bodhisattva*, I, 28.

60. The Archer in this quotation is the great Indian master Saraha, referring to himself in the realizational songs from which these two quotations have been taken.

61. *Letter to a Friend,* 68.

62. *The Way of the Bodhisattva,* II, 36.

63. The traditional arithmetic described here can be best conveyed by the table below. On this basis, the lifetime in the Reviving Hell, for example, would be equivalent to 50 x 360 x 500 x 360 x 500 (where the traditional calendar year contains 360 days) or 1,620 billion human years. See also *The Words of My Perfect Teacher,* pages 64 and 65. For the last two of the eight hot hells, the *Treasury of Abhidharma* mentions that the life spans there are half an intermediate kalpa in the Hell of Intense Heat and a whole intermediate kalpa in the Hell of Ultimate Torment.

64. The life span in the Hell of Burst Blisters is twenty times that in the Hell of Blisters; the life span in the Hell of Lamentation is twenty times that in the Hell of Burst Blisters; and so on.

65. *The Way of the Bodhisattva,* VII, 12.

66. *Letter to a Friend,* 83, 84.

67. *Letter to a Friend,* 86.

68. *Letter to a Friend,* 92.

69. *Letter to a Friend,* 96 (last line).

70. *Letter to a Friend,* 89, 90.

71. *Letter to a Friend,* 69.

72. Lit. "concentration that has a taste."

73. *Letter to a Friend,* 74. "Kamaloka god" is a god in one of the six gods' realms of the world of desire. "Avici" is the Sanskrit name for the Hell of Ultimate Torment.

74. *Sublime Continuum,* IV, 53bc.

75. Lit. "One cannot fix a date, saying, 'I shall be liberated at such-and-such a time.'"

76. Tib. *snying po med pa,* lit. "devoid of essence."

77. Khenpo Shenga points out in his commentary on the *Treasury of Abhidharma* that a lie that is not understood by the other party constitutes the negative action of worthless chatter.

| No. of human years | equivalent to one day in (god realm) | Lifetime in god realm |
|---|---|---|
| 50 | 4 Great Kings | 500 years |
| 100 | Heaven of the 33 | 1,000 |
| 200 | Free of Conflict | 2,000 |
| 400 | Joyous | 4,000 |
| 800 | Enjoying Magical Creations | 8,000 |
| 1,600 | Mastery over Others' Creations | 16,000 |

78. In his *Guide to The Words of My Perfect Teacher,* Khenpo Ngawang Pelzang notes that this does not mean eating the food of anyone in general who is a Dharma practitioner but rather eating the provisions of someone practicing intensively in retreat with the result that they run out prematurely and thus prevent him or her from completing the intended period of practice.

79. *Jewel Garland,* 14–16.

80. Tib. *nyid kyi lta ba,* explained by Lobzang Palden Tenzin Nyentrak in his commentary on the *Jewel Garland* as the view that scorns the karmic law of cause and effect.

81. The ten Dharma activities (Tib. *chos spyod bcu*) are: copying the scriptures, making offerings (i.e., venerating the Three Jewels), giving generously to others, listening to the teachings, reading them, committing them to memory, explaining them to others, performing the daily recitations of prayers and scriptures, reflecting on the meaning of the teachings, and meditating on them.

82. *The Way of the Bodhisattva,* I, 19.

83. *Sublime Continuum,* I, 60cd, 61ab.

84. *The Way of the Bodhisattva,* VII, 42.

85. *Letter to a Friend,* 30, 31.

86. *Letter to a Friend,* 52.

87. *Six Aspects of Taking Refuge* (Tib. *skyabs 'gro yan lag drug pa*) by the great Indian master Vimalamitra.

88. *Seventy Stanzas on Refuge.*

89. *Sublime Continuum,* I, 20–21.

90. *Sublime Continuum,* I, 22.

91. *The Way of the Bodhisattva,* II, 26.

92. Tib. *yang dag dge bsnyen,* also translatable as "perfect *upasakas.*" An *upasaka* or "follower of virtue" is anyone who has taken refuge in the Three Jewels and the term is therefore used for lay practitioners who have not taken further monastic vows. In this context the meaning is not restricted only to lay practitioners.

93. Buddhist monastic robes were originally made by dyeing patches of cloth that had been thrown away and stitching them together. This tradition persists in modern ready-made robes, which have a patch from an old robe sewn on, or whose design reproduces the patchwork impression.

| equivalent to one day in (hell realm) | Lifetime in hell realm |
| --- | --- |
| Reviving | 500 years |
| Black Line | 1,000 |
| Crushing | 2,000 |
| Screaming | 4,000 |
| Great Screaming | 8,000 |
| Hell of Heat | 16,000 |

94. *Letter to a Friend*, 2. Kangyur Rinpoche, in his commentary, refers to "base materials such as wood or stone." Wooden or stone statues, however crudely carved, should be respected and venerated just as much as the most skillfully fashioned gold images.

95. *Six Aspects of Taking Refuge*.

96. *Six Aspects of Taking Refuge*.

97. *Six Aspects of Taking Refuge*.

98. The *Tale with a Sow* (*Sukarikavadana-sutra*) tells the story of a dying god's distress when he sees that he is going to take birth in the womb of a sow. Indra advises him to take refuge in the Three Jewels. This he does, and then dies. He is immediately reborn in the Tushita heaven.

99. *Ornament of the Sutras*, X, 7–8.

100. Devadatta, who was Buddha Shakyamuni's cousin, was responsible for causing a Tathagata to bleed when, in a failed attempt to kill the Buddha by crushing him under a huge rock, he injured the Buddha's foot. He also created a split in the Sangha by creating a new monastic order, with five new rules which he knew the Buddha would not adopt. Finally, he incited the prince Ajatashatru to kill his father, King Bimbisara. The two of them thus committed three of the five crimes with immediate retribution (see above on page 123).

101. *Jewel Garland*, 5.

102. *Sublime Continuum*, I, 156.

103. Tib. *'dod pa'i dad pa*, also called "yearning faith."

104. Tib. *cang shes*, lit. "all-knowing." Implied in this term is the fact that the deer are tame.

105. With the refuge tree next to your pillow.

106. For example, to think "The Three Jewels have no compassion" is to abandon the Dharma, and must be avoided at all costs.

107. *The Way of the Bodhisattva*, I, 15, 16.

108. *The Way of the Bodhisattva*, V, 23.

109. *Letter to a Friend*, 13.

110. *Letter to a Friend*, 8.

111. Giving with improper intention includes doing so in order to harm others or to become famous, or to gain higher rebirth and wealth in the next life. An improper gift would be one that harms others. An improper recipient would be someone who is not benefited by the gift. An improper manner of giving is any manner that is not kind and joyful. Of the four proper aspects of generosity, proper intention refers to bodhichitta, proper gift refers to one's inner and outer possessions, proper recipient refers to the four "fields," and the proper manner of giving to giving respectfully and gently. See also *The Jewel Ornament of Liberation*.

112. The four virtues in discipline (Tib. *tshul khrims yon tan bzhi*) are (1) to take vows properly from someone else and (2) with perfectly pure motivation,

(3) to repair breaches should they occur, and (4) to be respectfully mindful of one's vows in order to avoid breaking them.

113. The seven kinds of ordination for individual liberation (Tib. *so thar ris bdun*): male and female lay practitioners (*upasaka*s), male and female intermediate ordinees (*shramanera*s), fully ordained monks and nuns (*bhikshu*s and *bhikshuni*s), and probationer nuns.

114. See the chapter on discipline in *The Jewel Ornament of Liberation*, where Gampopa quotes from *The Bodhisattva Levels:* helping others usefully, relieving the pain of those who suffer, giving instruction to those who do not have sufficient knowledge, acknowledging other people's help and helping them in return, protecting others from danger, consoling those who suffer, giving everything necessary to those in need, gathering disciples, introducing them to the path according to their respective attitudes, making others rejoice on account of one's excellent qualities, correctly destroying negativity, using magical displays to frighten others away from evil, and inspiring others. (As presented by Gampopa these appear to number thirteen rather than eleven: it is probable that four of them are paired to make eleven in all.)

115. An alternative translation is "those who harm us by thwarting our projects and so forth."

116. *The Way of the Bodhisattva*, VI, 1 and other verses at the beginning of the chapter on patience.

117. The five ideas (Tib. *'du shes lnga*) are those mentioned in *The Bodhisattva Levels:* (1) those who harm us are to be cherished; (2) they are mere phenomena; (3) they are impermanent; (4) they suffer; and (5) we should take responsibility for them. The nine considerations or points to be understood through analysis (*brtga pa dgu*) are introduced by Shantideva in *The Way of the Bodhisattva*, VI, verses 31, 42, 43, 44, 67, 48, 107–8, 119, and 112, respectively: (1) those who harm us are not masters of themselves; harm done to us is the fault of (2) our past actions, (3) our body, and (4) our mind; (5) no one in particular is at fault; (6) those who harm us are helping us; (7) they are being very kind to us; (8) our patience delights the Buddhas; and (9) it brings us enormous benefits. These five ideas and nine considerations are explained in detail in the chapter on patience in *The Jewel Ornament of Liberation*.

118. "Virtue" (Tib. *dge ba*) refers here to anything conducive to attaining happiness, whether in the higher realms of cyclic existence or in liberation from cyclic existence.

119. Tib. *sems gnas thabs dgu*, also called nine stages of settling the mind: focusing the mind, maintaining concentration, revitalizing concentration, firmly settling the mind, taming the mind (or mastering concentration), pacification, complete pacification, one-pointedness, and settling in equanimity. See also Takpo Tashi Namgyal, *Mahamudra*, page 47.

120. Tib. *yid byed bdun:* (1) discernment of the characteristics (of suffering and peace), (2) interest, (3) detachment or separation (from the afflictive emotions of the desire realm), (4) joy (at freedom from such afflictive emtions and at the minor bliss attained), (5) examination as to whether one is free of afflictive emotions, (6) application (of antidotes), and (7) the experience of the result of the latter.

121. The ten powers of perceptual limitlessness (Tib. *zad par gyi skye mched bcu*), also called the ten limitless *ayatana*s, concern the four elements (earth, water, fire, and wind), the four colors (blue, yellow, white, and red), infinite space, and infinite consciousness. Through concentration, the specific quality of any one of these ten can be transferred to the others. Thus the solidity of earth can be transferred to water, so that it can be walked upon.

   The eight kinds of perceptual domination (Tib. *zil gyis gnon pa'i skye mched brgyad*), also called the eight dominant *ayatana*s, comprise four kinds of ability to control shapes (as large or small) while remaining visible or invisible and four powers over the colors (blue, yellow, white, and red) of outer phenomena.

   The eight perfect freedoms (Tib. *rnam thar brgyad*) comprise three in performing miraculous manifestation and transformations (form beholding form, nonform beholding form, and beholding beauty); four with regard to the subtle mental perceptions of the four formless states of infinite space, infinite consciousness, utter nothingness, and neither existence nor nonexistence; and the perfect freedom of cessation. See *Treasury of Precious Qualities,* pages 341–43.

122. Tib. *gzhan don bcu gcig:* using whatever means are appropriate to help those who need befriending, those who do not know how to help themselves, those who have helped one, those who are afraid, those who are in misery and pain, those who are destitute, those who need somewhere to stay, those who wish to get on well with others, those who are engaged on the right path, those engaged on the wrong path, and those who can only be convinced by means of miracles.

123. *Sublime Continuum,* I, 77. Although there is a great difference between a Buddha's activities and those of a Bodhisattva, ordinary beings are unable to see any difference.

124. *Ornament of the Sutras,* XVII, 7.

125. *Ornament of the Sutras,* XVII, 14.

126. *Ornament of the Sutras,* XX, 28, 29.

127. *Ornament of the Sutras,* XVII, 15. This quotation defines the six transcendent perfections by explaining their Sanskrit etymology.

128. *Ornament of the Sutras,* XVII, 74.

129. *The Way of the Bodhisattva,* VIII, 120.

130. *The Way of the Bodhisattva,* VIII, 129.

131. *The Way of the Bodhisattva*, VIII, 131.
132. To take Shantideva's analogy of preparing for the journey and actually setting out, losing the aspirational bodhichitta is equivalent to tearing up one's travel tickets.
133. *The Way of the Bodhisattva*, V, 11.
134. *The Way of the Bodhisattva*, I, 6.
135. *The Way of the Bodhisattva*, I, 18 and 19.
136. *The Way of the Bodhisattva*, I, 12.
137. Tib. *mchod sdong*, lit. "offering tree," can mean a shrine or stupa to which the faithful make offerings. The Bodhi tree is also referred to as "the great offering tree."
138. *The Way of the Bodhisattva*, I, 9.
139. Tib. *don yod*, lit. "meaningful" or "significant," i.e., it benefits beings (even if it does not appear to be a positive action).
140. *The Way of the Bodhisattva*, I, 36.
141. These similes are to be found on page 352 et seq. of *The Flower Ornament Scripture*, Vol. 3, translated by Thomas Cleary, Boston: Shambhala, 1987. This work is a translation from the Chinese of the *Avatamsaka Sutra*.
142. Tib. *chos bzhi*, lit. "four things" or "ways" (Skt. *dharmas*).
143. Tib. *mtshams med du: kha'i las*, lit. "actions for which there is no interval between the action and its resultant suffering," i.e., the five crimes with immediate retribution (*mtshams med lnga*). See page 123.
144. The hundred-syllable Heruka mantra reads OM VAJRA HERUKA SAMAYA MANU PALA YA, VAJRA HERUKA TENOPA TISHTHA DRIDHO ME BHAWA . . . SARVA TATHAGATA VAJRA MAME MUŃCHA VAJRI BHAVA MAHA SAMAYA HERUKA AH.
145. We have reproduced the mantra here slightly differently from its usual Tibetan transliteration in order to follow more closely its sense in Sanskrit.
146. I.e., fulfill all my wishes.
147. Tib. *jo wo je lha gcig*. Atisha Dipamkara (982–1054), who was known throughout Tibet as Jowo Je (Lord), was, for his disciples, the unique refuge (*lha gcig*).
148. Tib. *zlas nyams* (transgression by association) and *zhor nyams* (incidental transgression).
149. *Jewel Garland*, 212.
150. The term "alternative" (Tib. *gzhan*) is that used in the Kalachakra tantra, as explained by Jamgön Kongtrul in his *Treasury of Knowledge*. See *Myriad Worlds*, page 148.
151. Their names in English are literally Yoke Bearer (Tib. *gnya' shing 'dzin*), Plow Bearer (*gshol mda' 'dzin*), Forest of Acacia Trees (*seng ldeng can*), Lovely to Behold (*lta na sdug*), Horse's Ear (*rta rna*), That Which Bows Down (*rnam 'dud*), and Rim (*mu khyud 'dzin*).
152. The shapes of these continents are said to reflect the appearance of their respective inhabitants when seated cross-legged.

153. The thirty-two weaknesses of womankind (Tib. *bud med kyi skyon sum cu rtsa gnyis*) may refer to thirty-two kinds of sickness to which women are prone and which interfere with spiritual practice.

154. Tib. *yongs 'dus sa brtol,* also translatable as the "all-gathering earth-piercing," another name for the wish-fulfilling tree, whose roots are in the realm of the demigods.

155. *The Way of the Bodhisattva,* IX, 34.

156. *Introduction to the Middle Way,* I, 16.

157. Tib. *mthong brgyud,* lit. "seeing lineage." How to perform the mandala offering can only be learned by seeing a practical demonstration given by one's teacher, or a fellow practitioner, who has in turn learned it properly by receiving the visual transmission from his or her teacher.

158. Lit. "he had a faithless thought" (or thought of nondevotion).

159. Lit. "down to the mighty golden ground"—the foundation of the universe.

160. *The Way of the Bodhisattva,* VI, 1.

161. In other words, whether in the past, present, or future, whether by oneself or someone else, and whether they are simply a good thought or an apparently insignificant positive deed.

162. *The Way of the Bodhisattva,* III, 11, and V, 101.

163. *Jewel Garland,* 187 (last two lines).

164. *The Way of the Bodhisattva,* I, 12.

165. *Ornament of the Sutras,* XIV, 9. "Excellent aim" refers to interest in the aim of the Great Vehicle, "excellent reliance" to reliance on the two accumulations of merit and wisdom, "excellent means" to the different means used to overcome defects in meditation, and "excellent application" to constant diligence in the practice.

166. The presence or absence of attributes (*mtshan ma*) here refers to attributes being apprehended (*'dzin pa*) or not.

167. *The Way of the Bodhisattva,* V, 31.

168. Tsogyal Khachö Wangmo (Tib. *mtsho rgyal mkha' spyod dbang mo*), lit. "Celestial Queen, Sea of Victory."

169. Lit. trusting that "whatever I do, you know."

170. Tib. *glo snying brang gsum,* lit. "with all three—lungs, heart, and chest."

171. Tib. *gzhon nu bum pa'i sku,* the inwardly radiating absolute body (*dharmakaya*), which is hidden like a lamp inside a jar.

172. *Letter to a Friend,* 29.

173. "Accumulation" (Tib. *tshogs*) refers not only to the accumulation of merit, but the coming together of all the conditions necessary for taking a human birth.

174. Rigdzin Wangmo, the name of Dudjom Rinpoche's *sangyum* who had the Tibetan text printed. As his tantric consort, she is here referred to as "Wisdom Supreme" (*shes rab*).

# Glossary

ABHIDHARMA (Skt.), *chos mngon pa.* One of the *three baskets;* the branch of the Buddha's teachings that deals mainly with psychology and logic.

ABSOLUTE BODY, *chos sku,* Skt. *dharmakaya,* lit. "Dharma body." The emptiness aspect of Buddhahood; also translated as body of truth, absolute dimension.

ACCOMPLISHED BEING, *grub thob,* Skt. *siddha,* lit. "one who has attained the accomplishments." Someone who has attained the fruit of the practice of the *Secret Mantra Vehicle.*

ACCOMPLISHMENT. (1) *dngos grub,* Skt. *siddhi.* The result (and goal) of spiritual practice. Common accomplishments include supernatural powers, which a Bodhisattva may use to benefit beings. The principal goal, however, is the supreme accomplishment, which is enlightenment. (2) *sgrub pa.* In the context of the recitation of mantras, *see approach and accomplishment.*

ACCUMULATIONS, *tshogs,* the accumulation of merit and accumulation of wisdom.

ADAMANTINE, *see diamond.*

ADOPTION AND AVOIDANCE, *blang dor,* the adoption (or acceptance) of positive actions and avoidance (or rejection) of negative actions, distinguishing right and wrong.

AFFLICTIVE EMOTIONS, *nyon mongs pa,* Skt. *klesha.* Mental factors that influence thoughts and actions and produce suffering. For the three and five principal afflictive emotions, *see three poisons* and *five poisons.*

AGGREGATES, *see five aggregates.*

AJATASHATRU, *ma skyes dgra,* "Future Foe" (lit. "unborn enemy"). An Indian prince named for the hatred that he felt while in his mother's womb for his father, King Bimbisara, whom he subsequently murdered. He later became a disciple of Buddha Shakyamuni.

AKASHAGARBHA, *nam mkha'i snying po,* "Essence of Space." One of the *Eight Great Close Sons.*

**AMITABHA,** *'od dpag med,* "Boundless Light." The Buddha of the lotus family.

**ANANDA,** *kun dga bo,* "Ever Joyful." Buddha Shakyamuni's attendant and close disciple for twenty-five years. Renowned for his retentive memory, it was he who, having heard almost every word the Buddha had spoken, recited the sutra section of the teachings at the First Buddhist Council.

**ANCIENT TRANSLATIONS,** *snga 'gyur.* The first teachings translated from Sanskrit and propagated in Tibet, those of the Ancient Tradition, as distinct from the teachings of the New Tradition that were translated and propagated from the 10th century onward.

**ANGULIMALA,** *sor phreng,* "Finger Necklace," named for the garland he strung together of the fingers from the 999 people he murdered before he met the Buddha and regretted his violent deeds.

**APARACHAMARA,** *rnga yab gzhan,* "Other Yak Tail." The subcontinent situated to the east of our southern continent, *Jambudvipa.*

**APARAGODANIYA,** *ba lang spyod,* "Bountiful Cow." The western continent in the ancient Indian cosmology.

**APPROACH AND ACCOMPLISHMENT,** *bsnyen sgrub.* Two steps in practices involving the recitation of a *mantra* in a *sadhana.* In the first, practitioners *approach* the deity that they are visualizing by reciting the deity's mantra. In the second they are familiar enough to identify themselves with the deity. *See also deity.*

**ARHAT** (Skt.), *dgra bcom pa,* lit. "one who has vanquished the enemy" (the enemy being afflictive emotions). A practitioner of the Basic Vehicle (that is, a *Listener* or *Solitary Realizer*) who has attained the cessation of suffering, i.e., nirvana, but not the Perfect Buddhahood of the Great Vehicle.

**ASANGA,** *thogs med,* "Unimpeded." The great 4th century Indian master and father of the vast activity tradition whose disciples established the Chittamatra or Mind-Only school of Mahayana Buddhism. His writings include the five great treatises that he received from *Maitreya.*

**ASHVAGOSHA,** *rta dbyangs,* "He whose voice is a horse's neigh." An important Indian Buddhist writer of the 1st–2nd century, also known as Aryashura.

**ASHVAKARNA,** *rta rna,* "Horse's Ear." The fifth of the seven golden mountain ranges surrounding Mount Meru.

**ATISHA,** *jo bo a ti sha,* "Sublime Lord." The great Indian master and scholar Dipamkara (982–1054), who spent the last ten years of his life in Tibet propagating the teachings on refuge and bodhichitta and contributing to the translation of Buddhist texts. His disciples founded the Kadampa school, which emphasized the teachings on the mind training.

**AVALOKITESHVARA**, *spyan ras gzigs dbang phyug*, "The Lord Who Gazes Down [compassionately on the world]." One of the *Eight Great Close Sons,* and the Bodhisattva who incarnates all the Buddhas' compassion, he is considered to be the principal Bodhisattva protecting the people of Tibet, where he is known as Chenrezi.

**BASIC VEHICLE**, *theg dman,* Skt. *hinayana.* Lit. "lesser vehicle" (in relation to the Mahayana or Great Vehicle): the vehicle of the *Listeners* and *Solitary Realizers* that leads to the state of *Arhat.*

**BASKET**, *sde snod,* Skt. *pitaka.* A collection of scriptures, originally in the form of palm leaf folios stored in baskets. The Buddha's teachings are generally divided into three baskets: *Vinaya, Sutra,* and *Abhidharma.*

**BENEFIT AND HAPPINESS**, *phan bde.* The temporary benefit of happy states in cyclic existence and the ultimate happiness of nirvana. This expression is therefore sometimes translated as "happiness and peace."

**BHADRA**, *bzang po,* "Good." The name of a disciple whom the Buddha taught in a sutra bearing his name.

**BHAGAVAN** (Skt.), *bcom ldan 'das.* An Indian term of veneration for someone of high spiritual attainment, used in Buddhism as an epithet of the Buddha. In its Tibetan translation, which might be conveyed in English as "Transcendent, Virtuous Conqueror," it is defined as "he who has overcome (*bcom*) the four demons, who possesses (*ldan*) the six excellent qualities, and who does not dwell in either of the two extremes of samsara and nirvana but has gone beyond them (*'das*)."

**BODHISATTVA** (Skt.), *byang chub sems dpa'.* A follower of the Great Vehicle whose aim is enlightenment for all beings.

**BODY OF MANIFESTATION**, *sprul sku,* Skt. *nirmanakaya.* The aspect of Buddhahood that manifests out of compassion to help ordinary beings.

**BODY OF PERFECT ENJOYMENT**, *longs spyod rdzogs pa'i sku,* Skt. *sambhogakaya.* The spontaneously luminous aspect of Buddhahood, only perceptible to highly realized beings.

**BRAHMA**, *tshangs pa.* Lit. "pure": the name given to a number of gods in the *world of form.*

**BRAHMIN** (Skt.). A member of the priestly caste in Indian society.

**BUDDHA** (Skt.), *sangs rgyas.* One who has dispelled (Tib. *sangs*) the darkness of the two obscurations and developed (Tib. *rgyas*) the two kinds of omniscience (knowing the nature of phenomena and knowing the multiplicity of phenomena).

**BUDDHAFIELD,** *sangs rgyas kyi zhing khams.* A pure land or world manifested by a Buddha or great Bodhisattva through the spontaneous qualities of his realization, in which beings can progress toward enlightenment without falling back into the lower realms of cyclic existence. Also, any place whatsoever, when it is perceived as a pure manifestation of spontaneous wisdom.

**BUDDHAGUHYA,** *sangs rgyas gsang ba,* "Secret Buddha." An 8th century Indian master of the *Diamond Vehicle* whose disciples included Vimalamitra and a number of Tibetans.

**CAPABLE ONE,** *thub pa,* Skt. *Muni.* An epithet of the Buddha Shakyamuni, often translated as Mighty One. He was called "capable" because, when he was a Bodhisattva and there was none who had the courage to tame the most unfortunate beings, with extremely gross views, afflictive emotions, and actions, he, our kind Teacher, was the only one, of all the 1,002 Buddhas of this Excellent Kalpa, who had the strength or capacity to vow to benefit them.

**CENTRAL CHANNEL,** *rtsa dbu ma,* Skt. *avadhuti.* The central axis of the subtle body. Its exact description varies according to the particular practice. It represents nondual wisdom.

**CHAMARA** (Skt.), *rnga yab.* The Indian word for a fan or fly whisk, traditionally made from a yak's tail; an emblem of royalty. The name of the southwestern subcontinent or island in the Indian cosmology.

**CHANDRAGOMIN,** *go mi dge bsnyen,* "The Layman Moon." A 7th century Indian master and proponent of the Chittamatra system, famous for his debate with the Madhyamika master Chandrakirti (author of *Introduction to the Middle Way*) and for his having observed the eight *upavasa* vows for lay practitioners (usually lasting for twenty-four hours) for the rest of his life.

**CHÖGYAL PAKPA,** *chos rgyal 'phags pa blo gros rgyal mtshan.* The influential Sakya master Chögyal Pakpa Lodrö Gyaltsen (1235–1280), who was Sakya Pandita's nephew. As well as being the fifth leader of the Sakya school, he was the spiritual advisor of the Mongol emperor Kublai Khan, and played an important political role in Tibet.

**CIRCUMAMBULATION,** *skor ba.* An act of veneration that consists of walking clockwise, concentratedly and with awareness, around a sacred object, e.g., a temple, stupa, or sacred mountain, or the residence, and even the person, of a spiritual master.

**CLOSE SONS,** see *Eight Great Close Sons.*

**COMMITMENT,** *dam tshig,* Skt. *samaya,* lit. "promise." The sacred link between master and disciple, and also between disciples, in the *Diamond Vehicle.* The Sanskrit word *samaya* can mean: agreement, engagement, convention, precept, boundary, etc. Although there are many detailed obligations, the most essential commitment on the part of the disciple is to consider the teacher's body, speech and mind as pure.

CONQUEROR, *rgyal ba,* Skt. *Jina,* also Victorious One. A general epithet for a Buddha.

CONSORT. (1) *yum,* feminine deity represented in union with a male deity (*yab*). She symbolizes wisdom, which is inseparable from skillful means (symbolized by the male). They also symbolize the space of emptiness inseparable from awareness. (2) *gsang yum,* lit. "secret mother." The wife of a great lama.

CONSTITUENTS, *khams,* Skt. *dhatu.* (1) The eighteen elements or constituents that encompass all knowable phenomena: the six sense objects (forms, sounds, smells, tastes, physical sensations, and mental phenomena), six sense organs (eye, ear, nose, tongue, body, and mind), and the six corresponding sense consciousnesses. (2) The five elements: earth, water, fire, wind, and space.

CROWN OPENING, *tshang pa'i bu ga,* Skt. *brahmarandhra,* lit. "aperture of Brahma." The crown opening is the term used in the anatomy of the subtle body to indicate the point on the top of the head where the central channel (Tib. *rtsa dbu ma*) ends.

CYCLIC EXISTENCE, *'khor ba,* Skt. *samsara,* lit. "wheel." The endless round of birth, death, and rebirth in which beings suffer as a result of their actions and afflictive emotions.

DAKINI (Skt.), *mkha' 'gro ma,* lit. "moving through space." The feminine principle associated with wisdom and with the enlightened activities of the teacher. This term has several levels of meaning. There are ordinary dakinis who are beings with a certain degree of spiritual power, and wisdom dakinis who are fully realized.

DAMARU (Skt.), a small hand-drum consisting of two bowl-shaped drums fixed back to back, with a double thong acting as the beater when the drum is twisted rapidly back and forth. *Damaru*s are sometimes constructed from the tops of two skulls and therefore described as "skull-drums."

DEEDS, *las,* Skt. *karma.* Also translated in this book as "actions," or as "past deeds." Implied in the use of this term is the force created by a positive or negative action which is then stored in an individual's stream of being and persists until it is experienced as pleasure or pain (usually in another life), after which the deed is said to be exhausted. Although the Sanskrit term *karma* simply means "action," it has come to be widely used to signify the result produced by past deeds (Tib. *las kyi 'bras bu*), which is sometimes wrongly equated with destiny or fate, that is, with something beyond one's control. In the Buddhist teachings, the principle of *karma* covers the whole process of deeds leading to results in future lives, and this is taught as being something that is very definitely within one's control. *See also law of cause and effect.*

**DEGENERATE AGE,** *snyigs dus,* Skt. *kaliyuga.* A period in which beings have shorter life spans, their afflictive emotions increase, they themselves are particularly difficult to help, wars and famines proliferate, and wrong views are widespread.

**DEHA,** *lus,* "Body." The subcontinent situated to the south of the eastern continent, *Purvavideha.*

**DEITY,** *lha,* Skt. *deva.* This term designates a Buddha or wisdom deity, or sometimes a wealth deity or *Dharma protector,* as distinct from a nonenlightened god in the world of desire, the world of form, or the formless world.

**DEMIGODS,** *lha min,* Skt. *asura.* Also called jealous gods. A class of beings whose jealous nature spoils their enjoyment of their fortunate rebirth in the higher realms and involves them in constant conflict with the gods in the god realms.

**DEMON,** *bdud,* Skt. *mara.* In the context of Buddhist meditation and practice, a demon is any factor, on the physical or mental plane, that obstructs enlightenment. *See also four demons.*

**DETERMINATION TO BE FREE,** *nges 'byung.* Also translated as "renunciation." The deeply felt wish to achieve liberation from *cyclic existence.*

**DEVADATTA,** *lhas byin,* "Divine Gift." A cousin of the Buddha, whose jealousy prevented him from deriving any benefit from the teachings.

**DHANAKOSHA,** "Treasury of riches." The lake in the land of Oddiyana in which Guru Rinpoche was born.

**DHARMA** (Skt.), *chos.* The Buddha's doctrine; the teachings transmitted in the scriptures and the qualities of realization attained through their practice. Note that the Sanskrit word *dharma* has ten principal meanings, including "anything that can be known." Vasubandhu defines the Dharma, in its Buddhist sense, as the "protective dharma" (*chos skyobs*): "It corrects ( *'chos*) every one of the enemies, the afflictive emotions; and it protects (*skyobs*) us from the lower realms: these two characteristics are absent from other spiritual traditions."

**DHARMA PROTECTOR,** *chos skyong,* Skt. *dharmapala.* The Dharma protectors fulfill the enlightened activities of the teacher in protecting the teachings from being diluted and their transmission from being disturbed or distorted. Protectors are sometimes emanations of Buddhas or Bodhisattvas, and sometimes spirits, gods, or demons who have been subjugated by a great spiritual master and bound under oath.

**DIAMOND,** *rdo rje,* Skt. *vajra,* lit. "lord of stones." On account of the diamond's seven characteristics (it cannot be cut, it is indestructible, true, hard, enduring, unimpeded, and invincible), the terms "diamond" and "adamantine" are used to represent the unchanging, indestructible nature of reality and to thus qualify an enlightened being's body, speech, mind, wisdom, concentration, posture, and so forth. In this book, the symbolic implement of the same name, originally a weapon used by Indra, is denoted by its Indian name, "*vajra.*"

DIAMOND BEARER, *rdo rje 'chang.* See *Vajradhara.*

DIAMOND BEING, *see Vajrasattva.*

DIAMOND BROTHERS AND SISTERS, *rdo rje spun grogs.* Men and women who have received *empowerment* together from the same *diamond master.*

DIAMOND HOLDER, *rdo rje 'dzin.* One who holds the transmission and realization of the *Diamond Vehicle.* Vajradhara ("Diamond Bearer") is also known by this name.

DIAMOND MASTER, *rdo rje slob dpon,* a master of the *Diamond Vehicle.*

DIAMOND POSTURE, *rdo rje dkyil krung,* Skt. *vajrasana.* Meditation posture with the legs crossed and the feet resting on the thighs.

DIAMOND VEHICLE, *rdo rje theg pa,* Skt. *vajrayana.* The vehicle based on realization of the diamondlike nature of the mind. Synonymous with *Secret Mantra Vehicle.*

DOWNFALL, *ltung ba.* A fault due to the transgression of a rule (monastic or other).

DUALISTIC, *gnyis 'dzin,* lit. "grasping at (or apprehending) two." The concept of "I" and "other," or of an apprehending subject and an apprehended object.

EIGHT GREAT CLOSE SONS, *nye ba'i sras chen brgyad.* The principal Bodhisattvas in Buddha Shakyamuni's retinue: Mañjushri, Avalokiteshvara, Vajrapani, Maitreya, Kshitigarbha, Sarvanivaranaviskambhin, Samantabhadra, and Akashagarbha. Each fulfills a particular role to help beings. Symbolically they represent the pure state of the eight consciousnesses.

EIGHT ORDINARY CONCERNS, *'jig rten chos brgyad.* The normal preoccupations of unrealized people without a clear spiritual perspective. They are: gain and loss, pleasure and pain, praise and criticism, fame and infamy.

EIGHTY GREAT ACCOMPLISHED BEINGS, *grub chen brgyad bcu.* (1) Eighty (or eighty-four) great accomplished beings (Skt. *mahasiddhas*) of ancient India whose lives have been recounted by Abhayadatta. See *Buddha's Lions* (Emeryville, Dharma Publishing, 1979). (2) The eighty siddhas of Yerpa in Tibet, disciples of Padmasambhava who attained the supreme accomplishment.

EMPOWERMENT, *dbang bskur,* Skt. *abhisheka,* lit. "transfer of power." The authorization to hear, study, and practice the teachings of the *Diamond Vehicle;* this takes place in a more or less elaborate ceremony in which the diamond master introduces the disciple to the mandala of a deity.

**EMPTINESS,** *stong pa nyid,* Skt. *shunyata.* The absence of true existence (in the sense of any permanent, independent, and single entity) in all phenomena.

**ENDURING DEEDS,** *las 'phro,* sometimes translated as "residual karma." The effects of actions performed in the past that have yet to be exhausted. In the West, the phrase "a person's karma" has come to be used to convey the idea of the person's destiny or luck, this being, of course, related to his or her enduring deeds. *See also deeds.*

**ENLIGHTENMENT,** *byang chub,* Skt. *bodhi.* Purification (*byang*) of all obscurations and realization (*chub*) of all qualities.

**ESSENTIAL BODY,** *ngo bo nyid kyi sku,* Skt. *svabhavikakaya,* the fourth body, which is the very essence or aspect of inseparability of the *absolute body,* the *body of perfect enjoyment,* and the *body of manifestation.*

**ETERNALISM,** *rtag par lta ba.* The belief in an eternally existing entity, such as a soul. Considered an extreme philosophical tendency.

**EVENNESS,** *mnyam pa nyid,* also sameness, equality: all things equally have the nature of emptiness.

**EVERYDAY ACTIVITIES,** *spyod lam.* This term covers a wide range of meanings, including general conduct and the four everyday activities (*spyod lam rnam pa bzhi*) of moving around, sitting, lying down, and walking. However, in this context "everyday" does not mean "ordinary," implying that one can forget what one has been meditating on during the session, for it is important to understand that everything one does in the postmeditational period, in between sessions, should still be carried out with a continued awareness of the practice. In a retreat situation, organized into several practice sessions per day, the "everyday" activities in the periods between sessions often include daily prayers, study, and other virtuous activities, in addition to taking meals, washing, and so forth, and even these are transformed into the practices of offering, purification, and so on.

**EXCELLENT SPEECH,** *gsung rab,* Skt. *avacana.* The Buddha's teachings. *See also Twelve Branches of Excellent Speech.*

**FIELD,** *zhing.* A term used to refer to the object of an action (for example, the recipient of one's generosity, or the victim of one's aggression). The relative importance of that object has an influence on the result of the action. In general, positive actions performed in relation to "great" fields, such as sublime beings or one's parents, have immeasurably greater positive results than ordinary actions, while negative actions so performed result in terrible suffering in the hells. *See also four fields.*

**FIVE AGGREGATES,** *phung po lnga,* Skt. *panchaskandha.* The five psychophysical components into which a person can be analyzed and which together produce the illusion of a self. They are form, feeling, perception, conditioning factors, and consciousness.

**FIVE FAMILIES**, *rigs lnga,* Skt. *pañcakula.* The Buddha, Vajra, Jewel, Lotus, and Action families. The five Buddha Families represent the true nature of all things. For example, the Five *Conquerors* are the true nature of the five aggregates, their Five *Consorts* the true nature of the five elements, the five wisdoms the true nature of the *five poisons,* and so on.

**FIVE PATHS**, *lam lnga,* the paths of accumulating, joining, seeing, meditation, and no more learning. These comprise five different sections of the path to enlightenment, which follow one after the other.

**FIVE POISONS**, *dug lnga.* The five afflictive emotions of bewilderment, attachment, hatred, pride, and jealousy.

**FIVE WISDOMS**, *ye shes lnga.* Five aspects of the wisdom of Buddhahood: the wisdom of the absolute space (Tib. *chos dbyings kyi ye shes*), mirrorlike wisdom (*me long gi ye shes*), the wisdom of equality (*mnyam nyid kyi ye shes*), discriminating wisdom (*so sor rtog pa'i ye shes*), and all-accomplishing wisdom (*bya ba grub pa'i ye shes*).

**FORM BODY**, *gzugs sku,* Skt. *rupakaya.* The body of form comprises the **body of perfect enjoyment** and the **body of manifestation** together.

**FORTUNE**, *skal ba,* also translated as destiny, luck, merit. In understanding this term it should not be forgotten that an individual's "luck" (or lack of it) in the present life is the result of positive (or negative) deeds he or she has performed in past lives. The "fortunate beings" to whom Dudjom Rinpoche addresses this work are not merely lucky to be disciples receiving teaching. It is because of the spiritual studies and practice they have undertaken in previous lives, and the connections they have made with the lineage masters of the present teaching, that they are now able to fulfill their "destiny" to continue to progress spiritually. Those of evil destiny, with little or bad fortune, do not have such luck, as a result of their previous negative actions and meager stock of positive ones.

**FOUR BODIES**, *sku bzhi.* The **three bodies** together with the **essential body.**

**FOUR BOUNDLESS ATTITUDES**, *tshad med bzhi.* Boundless love, compassion, joy, and impartiality, applied to all sentient beings without distinction.

**FOUR DEMONS**, *bdud bzhi.* The demon of the aggregates, the demon of afflictive emotions, the demon of the Lord of Death, and the demon of the sons of the gods (or demon of distraction). *See also* **demon.**

**FOUR EMPOWERMENTS**, *dbang bzhi,* the vase empowerment, the secret empowerment, the wisdom empowerment, and the precious word empowerment.

**FOUR FIELDS.** Fields with excellent qualities, for example, the Three Jewels; beneficial fields such as one's parents and other beings who help one; those who suffer (fields of suffering), such as the sick, orphans, and other beings without protection; and enemies and others who have harmed one (fields of harm).

**FOUR JOYS,** *dga' ba bzhi.* Four increasingly subtle experiences of bliss beyond ordinary feelings, connected with the practice of the channels and energies related to the third, or wisdom, empowerment.

**FOUR OBSCURATIONS,** *sgrib pa bzhi.* Obscurations related to deeds, obscurations related to afflictive emotions, conceptual obscurations, and obscurations of habitual tendencies. *See also obscurations.*

**FOUR TANTRA SECTIONS,** *rgyud sde bzhi.* Kriyatantra, Upatantra (Ubhayatantra or Caryatantra), Yogatantra, and Anuttarayogatantra.

**GAGANAGAÑJA,** *nam mkha' mdzod,* "Sky Treasure." A great Bodhisattva.

**GANDHARVA** (Skt.), *dri za,* lit. "one who feeds on smells." A kind of spirit that feeds on scents. *Gandharva*s are also classed as inhabitants of the lowest gods' realms, where they are renowned for their musical skills. The name is also used for beings in the intermediate state: since they inhabit a mental body, they feed not on solid food but on odours.

**GARUDA** (Skt.), *mkha' lding.* A mythological bird, master of the skies. It traditionally preys on the *naga*s.

**GENERATION PHASE,** *bskyed rim,* Skt. *utpattikrama.* The meditation associated with sadhana practice in which one purifies oneself of one's habitual clingings by meditating on forms, sounds, and thoughts as having the nature of deities, mantras, and wisdom. *See also perfection phase.*

**GLORIOUS COPPER-COLORED MOUNTAIN,** *zangs mdog dpal ri.* A *Buddha-field* manifested by *Padmasambhava,* to which he departed when he left Tibet and where he is now still said to be.

**GODS,** *lha,* Skt. *deva.* A class of beings who, as a result of accumulating positive actions in previous lives, experience immense happiness and comfort, and are therefore considered by non-Buddhists as the ideal state to which they should aspire. Those in the *world of form* and *world of formlessness* experience an extended form of the meditation they practiced (without the aim of achieving liberation from cyclic existence) in their previous life. Gods like Indra and others of the *six classes of gods of the world of desire* possess, as a result of their merit, a certain power to affect the lives of other beings and they are therefore worshipped, for example by Hindus. The same Tibetan and Sanskrit term is also used to refer to enlightened beings, in which case it is more usually translated as "deity."

GREAT MASTER, *slob dpon chen po*. This epithet usually refers to *Padmasambhava, Guru Rinpoche.*

GREAT OMNISCIENT ONE, *kun mkhyen chen po*. The name usually used to refer to Longchen Rabjam (*Longchenpa*).

GREAT PERFECTION, *dzogs pa chen po*, also called Atiyoga. The highest of all the vehicles leading to enlightenment, by which it is possible to attain Buddhahood in a single lifetime. "Perfection" means that within the mind all the qualities of the three bodies are naturally present: its nature is emptiness, its natural expression is clarity, and its compassion is all-encompassing. "Great" refers to the fact that this perfection is the natural condition of all things.

GREAT VEHICLE, *theg pa chen po*, Skt. *mahayana*. The vehicle of the Bodhisattvas, referred to as great because it aims at full Buddhahood for the sake of all beings.

GURU RINPOCHE, *gu ru rin po che*, lit. "Precious Teacher." The name by which *Padmasambhava* is most commonly known in Tibet.

HABITUAL TENDENCIES, *bag chags*, Skt. *vasana*. Habitual patterns of thought, speech, or action created by one's attitudes and deeds in past lives.

HIGHER REALMS, *mtho ris*. The gods' realms, the demigod realm, and the human realm.

INDIVIDUAL LIBERATION, *so sor thar pa*, Skt. *pratimoksha*. The collective term for the different forms of Buddhist ordination and their respective vows, as laid down in the *Vinaya.*

INDRA, *brgya byin*, "He who is honored with a hundred gifts." The ruler of the Heaven of the Thirty-Three.

INTERMEDIATE ORDINEE, *dge tshul*, Skt. *shramanera*. An intermediate ordination between lay followers who take the four basic vows and fully ordained monks and nuns. Although this level of ordination may serve as a novitiate until the ordinee is ready or old enough to take full ordination, it is incorrect to refer to *shramanera*s as novices because some *shramanera*s remain so all their lives without passing to higher ordination. This is the case with most nuns in Tibet, where the lineage for fully ordained nuns has been lost and full female ordination is only possible by taking the *bhikshuni* vows in another country whose lineage has continued unbroken.

INTERMEDIATE STATE, *bar do*. The term used for the various stages of experience between death and the next rebirth, with a wider interpretation that includes the various states of consciousness in life.

ISHADHARA, *gshol mda' 'dzin,* "Plow Bearer." The second of the seven golden mountain ranges surrounding Mount Meru.

ISHVARA, *dbang phyug,* "the Mighty Lord." An all-powerful god.

JAMBUDVIPA, *'dzam bu gling,* "Land of the Jambu Tree." The southern continent in the ancient Indian cosmology, the world in which we live.

JETARI, "He who is victorious over the enemy." A 10th century Indian master, the teacher, among others, of *Atisha Dipamkara.*

KALPA (Skt.), *bskal pa.* A unit of time (of inconceivable length) used in Buddhist cosmology to describe the cycles of formation and destruction of a universe, and the ages of increase and decrease within them.

KAMALASHILA. An 8th century Indian master and exponent of the Yogacharya Madhyamika school. He was a disciple of Shantarakshita and accompanied the latter when he was invited by King Trisong Detsen to establish the Dharma in Tibet and found the monastery of Samye.

KAMBALA. A 10th century Indian *mahasiddha* (great accomplished being), also known by the name of Lawapa.

KANAKAMUNI, *gser thub,* "Golden Capable One." The fifth of the thousand Buddhas in this Fortunate Kalpa.

KASHYAPA, *'od srung,* "Guardian of Light." The sixth of the thousand Buddhas in this Fortunate Kalpa.

KAURAVA, *sgra mi snyan gyi zla,* "Companion of Unpleasant Sound." The subcontinent situated to the west of the northern continent, *Uttarakuru.*

KHADIRAKA, *seng ldeng can,* "Forest of Acacia Trees." The third of the seven golden mountain ranges surrounding Mount Meru.

KHATVANGA, a special trident with a variety of symbolic ornaments.

KNOWLEDGE HOLDER, *rig 'dzin,* Skt. *vidyadhara.* One who through profound means holds the deities, mantras, and the wisdom of great bliss.

KRAKUCCHANDA, *'khor ba 'jig,* "Destroyer of Cyclic Existence." The fourth of the thousand Buddhas in this Fortunate Kalpa.

KSHITIGARBHA, *sa'i snying po,* "Essence of Earth." A Bodhisattva, one of the *Eight Great Close Sons.*

KURAVA, *sgra mi snyan,* "Unpleasant Sound." The subcontinent situated to the east of the northern continent, *Uttarakuru.*

LAW OF CAUSE AND EFFECT, *las rgyu 'bras.* Lit. "action, cause, result." In the context of the Buddhist teachings, the process by which every action inevitably produces a corresponding effect, usually in a subsequent lifetime. See also *deeds.*

LESSER VEHICLE, *theg dman,* Skt. *hinayana.* See *Basic Vehicle.*

LEVELS, *sa,* Skt. *bhumi.* See *ten levels.*

LIBERATION. (1) *thar pa:* freedom from samsara, either as an *Arhat* or as a *Buddha;* (2) *bsgral las byed pa:* a practice performed by a fully realized being in order to liberate the consciousness of a malignant being into a Buddhafield.

LINEAGE, *brgyud.* The process by which the Buddhist teachings have been transmitted from master to disciple in a continuous line from their original source until the present day, either from the teacher's mind to the disciple's mind (in the mind lineage of the Conquerors), or through symbolic gestures (in the symbol lineage of the knowledge holders), or by the disciple's hearing the master's words (in the hearing lineage of ordinary beings), or by the teachings being transmitted to a disciple before being hidden as treasure to be rediscovered later by an incarnation of that disciple (in the treasure lineage).

LISTENER, *nyan thos,* Skt. *Shravaka.* A follower of the *Basic Vehicle* whose goal is to attain liberation for himself or herself as an *Arhat.*

LONGCHENPA, *klong chen rab 'byams pa* (1308–1363). Also known as the Omniscient Sovereign or King of Dharma: one of the most influential spiritual masters and scholars of the Nyingmapa school. He wrote more than 250 treatises covering almost all of Buddhist theory and practice up to the *Great Perfection,* including the *Seven Treasures (mdzod bdun),* the *Nyingtik Yabzhi (snying tig ya bzhi),* the *Trilogy of Rest (ngal gso skor gsum),* the *Trilogy of Natural Freedom (rang grol skor gsum),* the *Trilogy of Dispelling Darkness (mun sel skor gsum)* and the *Miscellaneous Writings (gsung thor bu).* See Dudjom Rinpoche, *The Nyingma School of Tibetan Buddhism.*

LOWER REALMS, *ngan song.* The hells and hungry spirit and animal realms.

MAITREYA, *byams pa,* "Love." One of the *Eight Great Close Sons* who, as the future Buddha, presently resides in the Tushita heaven.

MAITRISIMHANADA, *byams pa seng ge'i sgra,* "Lion's Roar of Love." The name of a Bodhisattva disciple of Shakyamuni Buddha.

MAJOR AND MINOR MARKS, *mtshan dpe.* The thirty-two major marks and eighty minor marks of excellence that charaterize a Buddha's physical form.

MANDARAVA. A dakini, daughter of the King of Zahor, in India. She was one of the five principal disciples and *consorts* of *Padmasambhava* and one of the main holders of his teaching.

**MAÑJUSHRI,** *jam dpal,* "Gentle and Glorious." The Bodhisattva who embodies the Buddhas' knowledge and wisdom.

**MAÑJUSHRIKIRTI,** *jam dpal grags pa,* "He who is as famous as Mañjushri." Said to have been the eighth king of Shambhala, who arranged the Kalachakra teachings into their present form in the Kalachakra tantra.

**MAÑJUSHRIMITRA,** *jam dpal bshes gnyen,* "He whose Friend is Mañjushri." An important Indian master in the lineage of the **Great Perfection.**

**MANTRA** (Skt.), *sngags.* A manifestation of supreme enlightenment in the form of sound: a series of syllables that, in the *sadhanas* of the **Secret Mantra Vehicle,** protect the mind of the practitioner from ordinary perceptions and invoke the wisdom deities. The Sanskrit word is explained as meaning "that which liberates the mind."

**MARA** (Skt.), *bdud.* Demon, the tempter in general, that which makes obstacles to spiritual practice and enlightenment. *See* **demon.**

**MERIT,** *bsod nams,* Skt. *punya.* The first of the two accumulations. "Merit" is also sometimes used loosely to translate the Tibetan terms *dge ba* (virtue, positive action) and *dge rtsa* (sources of good for the future).

**MERU, MOUNT,** *ri rgyal po ri rab.* The immense mountain, wider at the top than at the bottom, that forms the center of the universe around which the four continents of the world are disposed, according to the ancient Indian cosmology.

**MINDSTREAM,** *rgyud,* lit. "continuity," also translated as stream of being, mind, continuum, being. This term denotes that aspect of an individual that continues from one moment to the next and from one lifetime to the next, and which therefore includes the individual's stock of positive and negative deeds, and positive and negative habitual tendencies.

**NAGA** (Skt.), *klu,* a serpentlike being (classed in the animal realm) living in the water or under the earth and endowed with magical powers and wealth. The most powerful ones have several heads. In Indian mythology they are preyed on by the *garuda*s.

**NAGARJUNA,** *klu sgrub,* "He whose accomplishment is related to the *naga*s." The great 1st–2nd century Indian master and father of the profound view tradition who rediscovered the Buddha's teachings on Transcendent Wisdom (*Prajñaparamita*) in the realm of the *naga*s and composed numerous treatises that became the basic texts for the proponents of the Madhyamika or Middle-Way philosophical system.

**NANDA,** *dga' bo,* "Joyful." A cousin of Buddha Shakyamuni who, despite his attachment to his wife, eventually overcame his desire and became an Arhat.

**NARAYANA,** *sred med bu,* "Free of Craving." One of the eight Guardians of the World. An incarnation of Vishnu, a warrior of great strength.

**New Tradition,** *gsar ma pa.* The followers of the *tantras* that were translated and propagated from the 10th century onward by the translator Rinchen Zangpo and others. It designates all the schools of Tibetan Buddhism except for the Nyingmapa, or Ancient Tradition.

**New Translations.** *See New Tradition.*

**nihilism,** *chad par lta ba.* The view that denies the existence of past and future lives, the principle of cause and effect, and so on. One of the extreme views refuted by the proponents of the Middle Way.

**Nimindhara,** *mu khyud 'dzin,* "Rim." The outermost mountain range surrounding Mount Meru.

**nirvana** (Skt.), *mya ngan las 'das pa,* lit. "beyond suffering" or "the transcendence of misery." While this can be loosely understood as the goal of Buddhist practice, the opposite of samsara or cyclic existence, it is important to realize that the term is understood differently by the different vehicles: the nirvana of the Basic Vehicle, the peace of cessation that an Arhat attains, is very different from a Buddha's "nondwelling" nirvana, the state of perfect enlightenment that transcends both samsara and nirvana.

**Nishkalankashri,** *snyogs med dpal,* "Unsullied Glory." *See Nishkalankavajra.*

**Nishkalankavajra,** *snyogs med rdo rje,* "Unsullied Diamond." Indian author and translator (into Tibetan) of a number of treatises on tantra, including a mandala-offering ritual.

**obscurations,** *sgrib pa,* Skt. *avarana.* Factors that veil one's Buddha-nature. *See also two obscurations, four obscurations.*

**Oddiyana,** *o rgyan.* A dakini land which is the birthplace of *Padmasambhava.* According to some it is located between present-day Afghanistan and Kashmir. The use of "Oddiyana" coupled with titles such as "Great One," "Second Buddha," and "Great Master" invariably refers to *Padmasambhava.*

**ogre,** *srin po,* Skt. *rakshasa.* A kind of malignant spirit that feeds on human flesh. (Sometimes translated as "cannibal," although *rakshasa*s are not known to eat their own kind.)

**omniscience,** *thams cad mkhyen pa,* a synonym of Buddhahood.

**Omniscient Dharma King,** *kun mkhyen chos kyi rgyal po,* Kunkhyen *Longchenpa.*

**Omniscient Dharma Lord,** *kun mkhyen chos rjes,* Kunkhyen *Longchenpa.*

**Padma Thöthrengtsel,** *padma thod phreng rtsal,* lit. "Padma garlanded with skulls." One of the names of *Padmasambhava.*

**PADMASAMBHAVA OF ODDIYANA,** *o rgyan padma 'byung gnas.* The Lotus-Born Teacher from Oddiyana, often known as Guru Rinpoche. During the reign of King Trisong Detsen in the 8th century, the Great Master subjugated the evil forces hostile to the propagation of Buddhism in Tibet, spread the Buddhist teaching of the Diamond Vehicle in that country, and hid innumerable spiritual treasures for the benefit of future generations. He is venerated as the Second Buddha whose coming was predicted by the first one, Buddha Shakyamuni, to give the special teachings of the Diamond Vehicle.

**PANDITA** (Skt.). A scholar, someone learned in the five traditional sciences (crafts, medicine, philology, logic, and philosophy). The term is used to refer primarily to Indian scholars.

**PARTING,** *bshags pa,* lit. "splitting" or "laying aside." This term, which has often been translated as "confession," includes two aspects: openly and remorsefully acknowledging (or confessing) one's faults and misdeeds, and resolving not to repeat them. It is because of this resolution (which is not included in the usual meaning of the word "confession") that one is able to lose the habitual tendencies to commit negative actions and that one is therefore able to purify and free oneself from the negative consequences of one's past deeds, parting from them so that they are no longer an impediment to one's spiritual progress. This process requires that the four powers be properly employed (see the chapter on the practice of Vajrasattva): one does not part from one's negative deeds simply by ignoring and forgetting them.

**PATH OF ACCUMULATING,** *tshogs lam.* The first of the *five paths,* according to the Bodhisattva vehicle. On this path one accumulates the causes that will make it possible to proceed toward enlightenment.

**PATH OF EARNEST ASPIRATION,** *mos spyod kyi lam,* comprises the paths of accumulating and joining. The level of earnest aspiration is a sort of prelevel before one reaches the first of the ten Bodhisattva levels. Practitioners on the paths of accumulating and joining have not yet realized emptiness and cannot therefore practice the six transcendent perfections in a truly transcendental way. Their practice is more a question of willingness than of the genuine practice of a mature Bodhisattva.

**PATH OF JOINING,** *sbyor lam,* the second of the *five paths.* On this path one connects oneself to or prepares oneself for seeing the two kinds of no-self on the *path of seeing.*

**PATH OF MEDITATION,** *sgom lam,* the fourth of the *five paths,* during which a Bodhisattva traverses the remaining nine of the ten levels.

**PATH OF NO MORE LEARNING,** *mi slob pa'i lam,* the last of the *five paths,* the culmination of the path to perfect enlightenment—Buddhahood.

PATH OF SEEING, *mthong lam,* the third of the *five paths,* the stage at which a Bodhisattva in meditation gains a genuine experience of *emptiness* and attains the first of the ten bodhisattva levels.

PERFECTION PHASE, *rdzogs rim,* Skt. *sampannakrama.* (1) "with characteristics" (Tib. *mtshan bcas*): meditation on the *channels and energies* of the body visualized as a diamond body; (2) "without characteristics" (Tib. *mtshan med*): the meditation phase during which the forms visualized in the *generation phase* are dissolved and one remains in the experience of emptiness.

PITH INSTRUCTIONS, *man ngag,* Skt. *upadesha.* Instructions that explain the most profound points of the teachings in a condensed and direct way for the purposes of practice.

POSITIVE ACTIONS CONSISTENT WITH ORDINARY MERIT, *bsod nams cha mthun gyi dge ba'i las,* positive actions that are not backed by bodhichitta and which therefore are not a direct cause that leads to Buddhahood. Such actions result in higher rebirth, but they contribute in only a limited way to liberation from cyclic existence.

PRIMAL WISDOM, *ye shes,* Skt. *jñana.* The knowing (*shes pa*) that has always been present since the beginning (*ye nas*); awareness, clarity-emptiness, naturally dwelling in all beings.

PROFOUND INSIGHT, *lhag mthong,* Skt. *vipashyana.* The perception, through wisdom, of the true nature of things.

PURE PERCEPTION, *dag snang.* The perception of all the world and its contents as a pure Buddhafield, as the display of the Buddha bodies and wisdoms. Pure perception is fundamental to the practice of the *Diamond Vehicle.*

PURVAVIDEHA, *lus 'phags po,* "Majestic Body in the East." The eastern continent in the ancient Indian cosmology, named for the appearance of the beings living there.

RAKSHASA (Skt.), *srin po,* a kind of malignant spirit or ogre that feeds on human flesh.

RENUNCIATE, *dge sbyong,* Skt. *shramana,* lit. "one who trains in virtue." A general term for someone who has renounced worldly life and taken monastic ordination.

ROOT DOWNFALL, *rtsa ltung.* The breaking of a vow the observance of which is fundamental to successfully accomplishing the path. Its definition is as follows: if the vow is kept it is the root that gives rise to all the excellent qualities of the path and result; if it is not kept it becomes the cause of lower realms and the root of suffering, and as a result one falls further and further down in subsequent lives.

**ROOT TEACHER,** *rtsa ba'i bla ma.* (1) The principal, or first, spiritual teacher from whom one has received empowerments, commentaries, and pith instructions. (2) The teacher who has introduced one to the nature of the mind.

**SADHANA** (Skt.), *sgrub thabs.* The method for accomplishing the level of a particular *deity,* for example, the lama, *yidam,* or *dakini.*

**SAGARAMATI,** *blo gros rgya mtsho,* "Ocean of Intelligence." The name of one of the Buddha's Bodhisattva disciples.

**SAGE,** *drang srong,* Skt. *rishi.* A hermit or saint; in particular the famous sages of Indian myth, who had enormous longevity and magical powers. The Buddha is sometimes referred to as the Great Sage.

**SAMANTABHADRA** (Skt.), *kun tu bzang po,* "Universal Good." (1) The original Buddha (*Adibuddha*), the source of the lineage of the tantra transmissions of the Nyingma school; he who has never fallen into delusion, the absolute-body Buddha, represented as a naked figure, deep blue like the sky, in union with Samantabhadri, as a symbol of awareness-emptiness, the pure, absolute nature ever present and unobstructed; (2) the Bodhisattva Samantabhadra, one of the eight principal Bodhisattva disciples of Buddha Shakyamuni, renowned for the way in which, through the power of his concentration, he miraculously multiplied the offerings he made.

**SAMSARA** (Skt.), *'khor ba.* See *cyclic existence.*

**SANGHA** (Skt.), *dge 'dun.* The community of Buddhist practitioners. The use of this term varies: it may include only *sublime beings,* who have attained the path of seeing, or the monastic community, or the disciples of a particular teacher.

**SARAHA,** *sa ra ha.* An Indian *mahasiddha* (great accomplished being), author of three cycles of songs of realization (*doha*).

**SECRET MANTRA VEHICLE,** *gsang ngags kyi theg pa.* A branch of the **Great Vehicle** that uses the special techniques of the tantras to pursue the path of enlightenment for all beings more rapidly. Because these practices are based on the realization of the diamondlike nature of the mind, this vehicle is also known as the **Diamond Vehicle.**

**SENSE OF DECENCY,** *khrel yod.* Also modesty, consideration of others. To be ashamed because of what others might think if one commits negative actions. This is one of the *seven noble riches.*

**SENSE OF SHAME,** *ngo tsha shes.* Also conscientiousness, honesty. To be ashamed of oneself if one commits negative actions. This is one of the *seven noble riches.*

**SENSES-AND-FIELDS,** *skye mched,* Skt. *ayatana.* The sources of consciousness. The six sense organs (eye, ear, nose, tongue, body, and mind) and their corresponding sense objects (forms, sounds, smells, tastes, physical sensations, and mental phenomena).

**SEVEN BRANCHES,** *yan lag bdun.* A form of prayer comprising seven parts: prostration, offering, confession, rejoicing, requesting the teachers to turn the wheel of Dharma, requesting them not to pass into nirvana, and dedication of merit.

**SEVEN NOBLE RICHES,** *'phags pa'i nor bdun.* Faith, discipline, generosity, learning, a sense of decency, a sense of shame, and wisdom.

**SEVEN-POINT POSTURE OF VAIROCHANA,** *rnam snang chos bdun.* The seven points of the ideal meditation posture: legs crossed in the diamond (vajra) posture, back straight, hands in the gesture of meditation, eyes gazing along the nose, chin slightly tucked in, shoulders well apart "like a vulture's wings," and the tip of the tongue touching the palate.

**SHAKYAMUNI,** *sha kya thub pa,* "Capable One of the Shakyas." The seventh of the thousand Buddhas in this Fortunate Kalpa. The Buddha of our time, who lived around the 5th century B.C.

**SHAMEFUL DEEDS,** *kha na ma tho ba,* lit. "that which cannot be mentioned" or "cannot be praised." This term covers every kind of action that results in suffering and not only the most serious kinds of wrongdoing. Shameful actions are divided into those that are naturally negative and those that are negative in that they involve breaches of vows.

**SHANTIDEVA,** *zhi ba lha,* "Peaceful God." The great 7th century Indian poet and *mahasiddha* (great accomplished being), author of the famous poem on the practice of bodhichitta, *The Way of the Bodhisattva* (*Bodhicharyavatara*).

**SHATHA,** *g.yo ldan,* "Land of Deceit." The subcontinent situated to the north of the western continent, **Aparagodaniya.**

**SHIKHIN,** *gtsug tor can,* "He Who Bears the Crown Protuberance." The second of the thousand Buddhas in this Fortunate Kalpa.

**SHRI SINGHA** (Skt.), "Glorious Lion." An important master in the lineage of the Great Perfection; teacher of Jñanasutra, **Vimalamitra,** and **Guru Rinpoche.**

**SIX CLASSES OF GODS OF THE WORLD OF DESIRE,** *'dod khams kyi lha,* Skt. *kamalokadeva.* Four Great Kings, Heaven of the Thirty-Three, Heaven Free of Conflict (Yama), the Joyous Realm (Tushita), Enjoying Magical Creations, and Mastery over Others' Creations.

**SIX KINDS OF PRETERNATURAL KNOWLEDGE,** *mngon par shes pa drug.* (1) The knowledge and ability to perform wonders appropriate to the needs of beings, such as the miraculous multiplication of objects; (2) the clairvoyance of the divine eye (the knowledge of births and deaths of all beings); (3) the clairaudience of the divine ear (the ability to hear all sounds throughout the three-thousand-fold universe); (4) the knowledge of one's own and others' past lives; (5) the knowledge of the minds of others; (6) the knowledge of the exhaustion of stains, i.e., that one's own deeds and emotions have been brought to exhaustion.

SIX ORNAMENTS, *rgyan drug,* the six great Indian commentators of the Buddha's teachings: Nagarjuna, Aryadeva, Asanga, Vasubandhu, Dignaga, and Dharmakirti.

SIX REALMS OF EXISTENCE, *'gro drug.* Six modes of existence caused and dominated by a particular mental poison: the hells (anger), and the hungry-spirits realm (miserliness), animal realm (bewilderment or ignorance), human realm (desire), demigod realm (jealousy), and *god* realm (pride). These correspond to the deluded perceptions that are produced by beings' past actions and are apprehended as real.

SIX TANTRA SECTIONS, *rgyud sde drug.* Kriya, Upa, Yoga, Mahayoga, Anuyoga, and Atiyoga.

SIX TRANSCENDENT PERFECTIONS, *pha rol tu phyin pa drug,* Skt. *sad paramita.* Generosity, discipline, patience, diligence, concentration, and wisdom.

SIXTEEN STHAVIRAS (Skt.), *gnas brtan bcu drug.* Sixteen Arhats, close disciples of the Buddha, to whom he entrusted the preservation and propagation of his teachings after he passed into nirvana.

SKILLFUL MEANS, *thabs,* Skt. *upaya.* Spontaneous, altruistic activity born from wisdom.

SOLITARY REALIZER, *rang sangs rgyas,* Skt. *pratyekabuddha.* The term applied to followers of the **Basic Vehicle** who attain liberation (the cessation of suffering) on their own, without the help of a spiritual teacher. Although some Solitary Realizers with sharp intellects remain alone "like rhinoceroses," others with dull minds need to stay in large groups, "like flocks of parrots." Solitary Realizers' practice consists, in particular, of meditation on the twelve links of interdependent origination.

SOURCE OF GOOD, *dge rtsa.* A positive or virtuous act that serves as a cause propelling its perpetrator toward happy states.

SPIRITUAL COMPANIONS, *chos grogs.* Students of the same teacher, or with whom one has received teaching. It is considered vital to have harmonious relations with such people, particularly in the Diamond Vehicle.

SPIRITUAL FRIEND, *dge ba'i gshes gnyen,* Skt. *kalyanamitra.* A synonym of spiritual teacher.

STREAM OF BEING, *rgyud. See* **mindstream.**

STUPA (Skt.), *mchod rten,* lit. "support of offering." A symbolic representation of the Buddha's mind. The most typical Buddhist monument, which often has a wide square base, a rounded midsection, and a tall conical upper section topped by a sun and moon. Stupas frequently contain the relics of enlightened beings. They vary in size from tiny clay models to the vast stupas at Borobudur in Indonesia and Bodha in Nepal.

SUBAHU, *lag bzang,* "He who has good arms." The name of one of the Buddha's disciples.

SUBHUTI, *rab 'byor,* "Greatly Endowed." One of the Buddha's foremost disciples, renowned for his understanding of emptiness.

SUBLIME BEING, *'phags pa,* Skt. *arya.* Usually someone who has attained the *path of seeing:* in the Great Vehicle, a Bodhisattva on one of the ten bodhisattva levels; in the Vehicles of the Listeners and Solitary Realizers, a Stream-Enterer, Once-Returner, Nonreturner, or Arhat.

SUDARSHANA, *lta na sdug,* "Lovely to Behold." The fourth of the seven golden mountain ranges surrounding Mount Meru.

SUDHANA, *nor bzang,* "Excellent Treasure." Named for the treasures that appeared when he was born. The Bodhisattva whose spiritual journey is recounted in the *Sutra of the Arborescent Array (Gandavyuha Sutra).*

SUGATA (Skt.), *bde bar gshegs pa,* lit. "one who has gone to bliss." An epithet of a Buddha.

SUMERU (Skt.), *ri rab.* See **Meru, Mount.**

SUPERIOR MOTIVATION (or intention or attitude), *lhag bsam.* In the context of the Great Vehicle, a good heart, the altruistic attitude of bodhichitta.

SUSTAINED CALM, *zhi gnas,* Skt. *shamatha.* The basis of all concentrations, a calm, undistracted state of unwavering concentration.

SUTRA (Skt.), *mdo.* (1) A scripture containing the teachings of the Buddha; (2) the Sutra-pitaka (*mdo sde*), the one of the **three baskets** that deals with meditation.

TAINTED (ACTION), *zag bcas.* An action performed with the **three concepts** of subject, object, and action, and therefore tainted by afflictive emotions, so that it results in cyclic existence.

TANTRA (Skt.), *rgyud.* Any one of the texts on which the **Diamond Vehicle** teachings are based. They reveal the continuity between the original purity of the nature of mind and the result of the path, which is the realization of that nature.

TARA, *sgrol ma,* "She who liberates," "the Savioress." A female bodhisattva manifesting in many forms, of which the best known are Green Tara and White Tara who, according to legend, appeared from two lakes formed by the tears of **Avalokiteshvara** and are thus associated with the compassion of all the Buddhas.

**TATHAGATA,** *de bzhin gshegs pa,* "one who has gone to thusness." A Buddha; one who has reached or realized thusness, the absolute nature.

**TATHAGATAGARBHA,** *de bzhin zhegs pa'i snying po,* lit. "essence of the Tathagatas." A synonym of the Buddha-nature present in every single sentient being.

**TEN DIRECTIONS,** *phyogs bcu.* The four cardinal points, the four intermediate points, and the zenith and nadir.

**TEN LEVELS,** *sa bcu,* Skt. *dashabhumi.* The ten stages of realization by which a sublime Bodhisattva progresses toward enlightenment, beginning with the first level on the *path of seeing.* The nine other levels occur on the *path of meditation.* The eighth, ninth, and tenth levels are termed the three pure levels, or great levels.

**TEN TRANSCENDENT PERFECTIONS,** *pha rol tu phyin pa bcu.* The *six transcendent perfections* together with transcendent means (*thabs*), aspirational prayer (*smon lam*), strength (*stobs*), and primal wisdom (*ye shes*). Each of these ten is practiced predominantly on one of the ten bodhisattva levels, generosity on the first level, discipline on the second, and so forth.

**THREATENING GESTURE,** *sdigs mdzubs,* Skt. *tarjani mudra.* A symbolic gesture or mudra, pointing with the forefinger and little finger.

**THREE BASKETS,** *sde snod gsum,* Skt. *tripitaka. See **basket.***

**THREE BODIES,** *sku gsum,* Skt. *trikaya.* The three aspects of Buddhahood: the *absolute body, body of perfect enjoyment,* and *body of manifestation.*

**THREE CENTERS,** *gnas gsum,* the forehead or crown center, throat or speech center, and heart center.

**THREE CONCEPTS,** *'khor gsum,* lit. "three spheres." Subject, object, and action, perceived as having real and independent existence.

**THREE DIAMONDS,** *rdo rje gsum,* the diamond body, diamond speech, and diamond mind. *See **diamond.***

**THREE JEWELS,** *dkon mchog gsum,* Skt. *triratna.* Collectively, the object of refuge of all Buddhists. The *Buddha, Dharma,* and *Sangha.*

**THREE LEVELS OF ENLIGHTENMENT,** *byang chub gsum.* The enlightenment of the *Listeners, Solitary Realizers,* and *Bodhisattvas.*

**THREE POISONS,** *dug gsum.* The three afflictive emotions of bewilderment, attachment, and aversion. *See also **five poisons.***

**THREE ROOTS,** *rtsa gsum,* the teacher or lama, root or source of blessings; the *yidam,* source of accomplishments; and the *dakini* (or *protectors*), source of activities.

**THREE TIMES,** *dus gsum,* Skt. *trikala.* Past, present, and future.

**THREE TRAININGS,** *bslabs pa gsum,* Skt. *trishiksa.* The threefold training in discipline, concentration, and wisdom.

**THREE WORLDS,** *khams gsum.* The *world of desire,* the *world of form,* and the *world of formlessness.* Alternatively (Tib. *'jig rten gsum, sa gsum, srid gsum*): the world of *gods* above the earth, that of humans on the earth, and that of the *naga*s under the earth.

**THUSNESS,** *de bzhin nyid,* Skt. *tathata.* The absolute nature of things, emptiness, the absolute space free from elaboration.

**TRANSCENDENT PERFECTION,** *pha rol tu phyin pa,* Skt. *paramita.* A term used to describe the practice of a Bodhisattva, combining skillful means and wisdom, the compassionate motivation of attaining enlightenment for the sake of all beings, and the view of emptiness. *See six* and *ten transcendent perfections.*

**TREASURE,** *gter ma.* Teachings that were hidden, along with statues and other objects, by *Padmasambhava, Yeshe Tsogyal,* and others in earth, rocks, lakes, and trees, or even in more subtle locations such as space or mind for the sake of future generations, and then rediscovered in miraculous ways by incarnations of Padmasambhava's disciples, the treasure discoverers.

**TREATISE,** *bstan bcos,* Skt. *shastra.* A commentary on the Buddha's teachings. The term *shastra* does not necessarily apply to a commentary on one particular teaching (a named sutra, for example) but includes works by both Indian and Tibetan masters that provide condensed or more accessible expositions of particular subjects.

**TUSHITA HEAVEN,** *dga' ldan,* lit. "The Joyous." One of the realms of the gods in the *world of desire,* in which Buddha *Shakyamuni* took a final rebirth before appearing in this world. The future Buddha, *Maitreya,* is currently in the Tushita heaven teaching the Great Vehicle.

**TWELVE BRANCHES OF EXCELLENT SPEECH,** *gsung rab yan lag bcu gnyis.* The twelve types of teaching given by the Buddha, corresponding to twelve kinds of text: condensed (*mdo sde,* Skt. *sutra*), melodious (*dbyangs bsnyan, geya*), prophetic (*lung bstan, vyakarana*), verse (*tshigs bcad, gatha*), spoken with a purpose (*ched brjod, udana*), conversatory (*gleng gzhi, nidana*—questions, talks, etc.), concerning his past lives (*skyes rab, jataka*), marvelous (*rmad byung, adbhutadharma*), establishing a truth (*gtan babs, upadesha*), biographical or "expressing realization" (*rtogs brjod, avadana*), historical (*de ltar byung, itivrittaka*), and very detailed (*shin tu rgyas pa, vaipulya*).

**TWENTY-FIVE DISCIPLES,** *rje 'bang nyer lnga.* The greatest Tibetan disciples of *Padmasambhava.* All of them attained the supreme accomplishment. The most famous were King *Trisong Detsen, Yeshe Tsogyal,* and *Vairotsana.* Many of the great masters of Tibetan Buddhism are emanations of the Twenty-Five Disciples.

**TWO ACCUMULATIONS**, *tshogs gnyis.* The accumulation of merit (Tib. *bsod nams*) and the accumulation of wisdom (Tib. *ye shes*).

**TWO GOALS**, *see twofold goal.*

**TWO KINDS OF OBSCURATION**, *see two obscurations.*

**TWO OBSCURATIONS**, *sgrib gnyis.* The obscurations of afflictive emotions and conceptual obscurations. *See also* **obscurations.**

**TWOFOLD GOAL**, *don gnyis.* One's own goal, benefit, or welfare (*rang don*) and that of others (*gzhan don*). Often understood in the ultimate sense of the goal for oneself being achieved by the realization of emptiness, the *absolute body* (*dharmakaya*), and the goal for others by compassion manifesting as the *form body* (*rupakaya*).

**UDUMBARA** (Skt.). The udumbara flower is said to blossom only once in a kalpa and is therefore used in Buddhist teachings as a symbol of exceptional rarity.

**ULTIMATE EXCELLENCE**, *nges legs.* The lasting happiness of liberation and omniscience, i.e., Buddhahood.

**UNION (LEVEL OF)**, *zung 'jug gi go 'phang,* the level of *Diamond Bearer* (Vajradhara), "union" referring to the union of the *absolute body* (*dharmakaya*) and the *form body* (*rupakaya*).

**UNIVERSAL GOOD**, *see Samantabhadra.*

**UNIVERSAL MONARCH**, *'khor lo sgyur ba'i rgyal po,* Skt. *chakravartin.* (1) A king ruling over a world system; (2) an emperor.

**UNTAINTED**, *zag med.* Uncontaminated by negative emotions, including concepts due to the afflictive emotion of ignorance.

**UPASAKA** (Skt.), *dge bsnyen.* A layman who has taken refuge in the Three Jewels and keeps one or more of the basic precepts.

**UTPALA** (Skt.), a kind of blue lotus flower.

**UTTARAKURU**, *sgra mi snyan,* "Unpleasant Sound." The northern continent in the ancient Indian cosmology, named for the sound beings hear when they are about to die.

**UTTARAMANTRINA**, *lam mchog 'gro,* "Land of Great Progress." The subcontinent situated to the south of the western continent, *Aparagodaniya.*

**VAIROCHANA**, *rnam par snang mdzad,* "Illuminator." One of the five Tathagatas, the Buddha of the Buddha family.

**VAJRA** (Skt.), *rdo rje,* lit. "lord of stones," a diamond. The symbolic implement (representing skillful means) held by tantric deities and used in tantric rituals.

Originally a stone thrown by Indra as a weapon (hence "Indra's thunderbolt"). In Buddhism it represents the unchanging, indestructible nature of reality, which has seven characteristics: it cannot be cut, is indestructible, true, hard, enduring, unimpeded, and invincible. This diamondlike nature gives its name to the *Diamond Vehicle*. See also *diamond*.

**VAJRA YOGINI**, *rdo rje rnal 'byor ma*, "She who practices the adamantine union with the natural state." A female form of Buddha in the *body of perfect enjoyment*.

**VAJRADHARA**, *rdo rje 'chang*, "Diamond Bearer." In the New Tradition (which follows the tantras translated and propagated in Tibet from the 10th century onward) he is the primordial Buddha, source of all the tantras. In the Ancient Tradition (which follows the teachings introduced to Tibet by the great master *Padmasambhava* in the 8th century), Vajradhara represents the principle of the Teacher as enlightened holder of the teachings of the *Diamond Vehicle*.

**VAJRAKUMARA**, *rdo rje gzhon nu*, "Diamond Prince." Another name of the wrathful deity Vajrakilaya (*rdo rje phur ba*), who is related to the Buddhas' activity.

**VAJRAPANI**, *phyag na rdo rje*, "Vajra Bearer." One of the *Eight Great Close Sons*, the manifestation of the Buddha's power. Also known as the Lord of Secrets (Tib. *gsang ba'i bdag po*).

**VAJRASATTVA**, *rdo rje sems dpa'*, "Diamond Being" or "Diamond Hero." The deity most widely practiced for purification in the *Diamond Vehicle*.

**VAJRATOPA**, *rdo rje snyems ma*, "Diamond Proud." The consort of *Vajrasattva*.

**VEHICLE**, *theg pa*, Skt. *yana*. A means for travelling the path to liberation.

**VICTORIOUS ONE**, *rgyal ba*, Skt. *Jina*. A general epithet for a Buddha.

**VIDEHA**, *lus 'phags*, "Majestic Body." The subcontinent situated to the north of the eastern continent, *Purvavideha*.

**VIMALAMITRA**, *dri med bshes bnyen*, "Stainless Friend." An Indian master who held an important place in the lineages of the *Great Perfection*. He went to Tibet in the 8th century, where he taught extensively, and composed and translated numerous Sanskrit texts. The quintessence of his teaching is known as the *Vima Nyingtig*.

**VINATAKA**, *rnam 'dud*, "That Which Bows Down." The sixth of the seven golden mountain ranges surrounding Mount Meru.

**VINAYA** (Skt.), *'dul ba*, lit. "taming." One of the three baskets; the section of the Buddha's teaching that deals with discipline, and in particular with the vows of monastic ordination.

**VIPASHYI**, *rnam par gzigs*, "Perfect Insight." The first of the thousand Buddhas in this Fortunate Kalpa.

**Vishnu,** *khyab 'jug.* An important Hindu god.

**Vishvabhu,** *thams cad skyob,* "Protector of All." The third of the thousand Buddhas in this Fortunate Kalpa.

**Wheel of Dharma,** *chos kyi 'khor lo,* Skt. *dharmacakra.* The symbol of the Buddha's teaching. To turn the wheel of the Dharma means to teach the Dharma. During his lifetime, the Buddha gave three major series of teachings, which are referred to as the first, second, and third turnings.

**wheel,** *'khor lo,* Skt. *cakra.* One of the centers of energy at different points on the *central channel,* from which radiate the small subtle channels going to all parts of the body. Generally there are considered to be four or five of these wheels.

**wish-fulfilling jewel,** *yid bzhin nor bu,* Skt. *chintamani.* A fabulous jewel found in the realms of the gods or *naga*s that fulfills all wishes.

**wish-fulfilling tree,** *dpag bsam gyi shing.* A magical tree which has its root in the realm of the demigods but bears its fruit in the realm of the gods of the Thirty-Three.

**world of desire,** *'dod khams,* Skt. *kamaloka* or *kamadhatu.* The first of the three worlds, comprising the hells, and the realms of the hungry spirits, animals, humans, demigods, and the *six classes of gods of the world of desire.*

**World of Forbearance,** *mi mjed 'jig rten,* Skt. *saha.* Our universe, which is the Buddhafield of Buddha Shakyamuni.

**world of form,** *gzugs khams,* Skt. *rupadhatu.* The second of the three worlds, comprising the twelve realms of the four concentrations and the five pure abodes.

**world of formlessness,** *gzugs med khams,* Skt. *arupyadhatu.* The third of the three worlds, at the peak of existence. It comprises the spheres of infinite space, infinite consciousness, utter nothingness, and neither existence nor nonexistence.

**wrong view,** *log lta,* Skt. *mithyadristi.* A false belief, particularly a view that will lead one to courses of action that bring more suffering. *See also* **eternalism** and **nihilism.**

**yaksha** (Skt.), *gnod sbyin.* A class of powerful spirits who, despite their Tibetan name of "harm-doers," are as often beneficent as malignant.

**Yeshe Tsogyal,** *ye shes mtsho rgyal,* "Wisdom Sea of Victory," **Padmasambhava**'s mystic **consort** and greatest disciple. She served him perfectly and helped him to propagate his teachings, in particular by concealing spiritual treasures to be rediscovered later for the sake of future disciples.

**YIDAM**, *yi dam,* Skt. *devata, istadevata.* A deity representing enlightenment, in a male or female, peaceful or wrathful form, that corresponds to the practitioner's individual nature. The yidam is the source of accomplishments.

**YOGA** (Skt.), *rnal 'byor,* lit. "union (Tib. *'byor*) with the natural state (*rnal ma*)." A term for spiritual practice.

**YOGI** or **YOGINI** (Skt.), *rnal 'byor pa.* A person practicing a spiritual path.

**YUGANDHARA**, *gnya' shing 'dzin,* "Yoke Bearer." The innermost mountain range surrounding Mount Meru.

# Bibliography

## Works Cited in the Text

Accomplishment of Wisdom, ye shes grub pa, Jñanasiddhi, a general commentary on tantra by Indrabhuti.

Analysis of Actions, *see* Sutra on the Analysis of Actions.

Approach to the Absolute Truth, don dam bsnyen pa, Paramarthaseva, a tantra treatise.

Array of Qualities of Mañjushri's Buddhafield, 'jam dpal zhing gi yon tan bkod pa, Mañjushri-buddhaksetra-gunavyuha-sutra, part of the Pagoda of Precious Jewels (Ratnakuta).

Array of the Sublime, *see* Great Array of the Sublime.

Bodhisattva Levels, byang sa, Bodhisattvabhumi-shastra, a treatise by Asanga.

Clarifying Lamp, sgron gsal, Pradipoddyotana, a commentary on the Guhyasamaja Tantra.

Close Mindfulness Sutra, dran pa nyer ba'i bzhag pa'i mdo, Saddharma-smrityupasthana-sutra.

Commentary on the Ornament of True Realization, mngon rtogs rgyan 'grel, Abhisamayalankara-vrtti.

Compendium of the Buddhas' Wisdom, mdo dgongs pa 'dus pa, a tantra, one of the four root "sutras" of Anuyoga.

Condensed Transcendent Wisdom, sdud pa, Prajñaparamita-sañcayagatha, one of the Prajñaparamita sutras.

Diamond Daka, rdo rje mkha' 'gro, Vajradakaguhya-tantraraja, a tantra.

Diamond Necklace, bshad rgyud rdor phreng, an explanatory tantra.

Discourse on Impermanence, mi rtag pa'i gtam, Anityartha parikatha.

Display of the Perfected Wheel, 'khor lo chub pa rol pa, a tantra.

Distinguishing the Middle from Extremes, dbus mtha' rnam 'byed, Madhyantavibhaga, one of the five treatises of Maitreya-Asanga.

Ear Ornament Sutra, snyan gyi gong rgyan, another name for the Avatamsaka (or Great Host) Sutra.

Essence of the Sun Sutra, nyi ma'i snying po'i mdo, Suryagarbha-sutra.

Fifty Verses on the Teacher, bla ma lnga bcu pa, Gurupañchashika, a treatise by Ashvagosha.

Flower Chapter, me tog gi tshoms.
Four Hundred, *see* Four Hundred Verses on the Middle Way
Four Hundred Verses on the Middle Way, dbu ma bzhi brgya pa, Madhyamaka-catuhshataka, a treatise by Aryadeva.
Gathering of the Glorious Ones, dpal ldan 'dus pa, a tantra.
Glorious Tantra of the Gathering of Secrets, dpal gsang ba 'dus pa'i rgyud, Shri Guhyasamaja Tantra.
Golden Garland of Pledges, tha tshig gser phreng, a teaching given by Guru Rinpoche to Gyalse Lhaje and hidden as a treasure.
Great Array of the Sublime, a ti bkod pa chen po, a tantra of the Great Perfection.
Great Commentary on Transcendent Wisdom in Eight Thousand Verses, brgyad stong 'grel chen, Astasahashrika-prajñaparamita-vyakhyabhisamayalamkara-loka, a treatise by Haribhadra.
Great Host Sutra, phal po che'i mdo, Avatamsaka-sutra (also known as the Flower Ornament Scripture).
Heaped Lotuses, padma spungs pa, a tantra.
Hevajra Tantra, rgyud brtags gnyis, Hevajra-tantra in Two Chapters.
Highest Expression of Truth, nges brjod bla ma.
Hundred Parables on Action, las brgya pa, Karmashataka, a sutra.
Hundred Verses of Advice to the People of Tingri, ding ri brgya rtsa ma, a treatise by Padampa Sangye, translated as *The Hundred Verses of Advice* by the Padmakara Translation Group, Shambhala Publications, 2005.
Intentionally Spoken Chapters, ched du brjod pa'i tshoms, Udanavarga, a sutra.
Introduction to the Middle Way, dbu ma la 'jug pa, Madhyamakavatara, a treatise by the 7th century Indian master Chandrakirti, translated under the same title by the Padmakara Translation Group, Shambhala Publications, 2002.
Jewel Garland, rin chen phreng ba, Ratnavali, a treatise by Nagarjuna.
Lamp for the Path, lam sgron, Bodhipathapradipa, a treatise by Atisha.
Letter to a Friend, bshes pa'i springs yig, Suhrllekha, a treatise by Nagarjuna, translated as *Nagarjuna's Letter to a Friend* by the Padmakara Translation Group, Snow Lion Publications, 2005.
Magical Display of Indestructible Reality, sgyu 'phrul rdo rje, a tantra.
Mandala Sutra, mandala gyi mdo.
Middle Sutra of Transcendent Wisdom, yum bar ma, Pañchavimshatisahasrika-prajñaparamita.
Net of Magical Display, sgyu 'phrul drva ba, Mayajala tantra.
Nirvana Sutra, mya ngan 'das mdo, Mahaparinirvana-sutra.
Ornament of the Essence, snying po rgyan, a tantra.
Ornament of the Indestructible Essence, rdo rje snying po rgyan, a tantra.
Ornament of the Sutras, mdo sde rgyan, Mahayana-sutralamkara, one of the five treatises of Maitreya-Asanga.
Ornament of True Realization, mngon rtogs rgyan, Abhisamayalankara, one of the five treatises of Maitreya-Asanga.

Pagoda of Precious Jewels, dkon mchog brtsegs pa, Ratnakuta (also called the Jewel Mound Sutra).

Prayer of Good Action, bzang spyod smon lam, Bhadracarya-pranidhana (the final section of the Sutra of the Arborescent Array).

Prayer of Invocation for the Tenth Day, tshes bcu bskul thabs, a treasure discovered by Ratna Lingpa.

Root Tantra of All-Encompassing Awareness, kun 'dus rig pa'i mdo, one of the root tantras (or "sutras") of Anuyoga.

Root Tantra of the Assembly of Knowledge Holders, rig 'dzin 'dus pa rtsa ba'i rgyud.

Sayings on Impermanence, mi rtag pa'i tshoms.

Secret Sayings, gsang thems, or Secret Guide to Accomplishing the Guru (bla ma sgrub pa'i gsang them gnad yig).

Self-Arisen Awareness, rig pa rang shar, one of the seventeen tantras of the Great Perfection.

Series of Lives, skyes rabs, Jataka.

Seven-Point Mind Training, blo sbyong don bdun ma, a treatise by Chekawa Yeshe Dorje.

Seventy Stanzas on Refuge, skyabs 'gro bdun cu pa, Trisharana-saptati, a treatise by Chandrakirti.

Six Aspects of Taking Refuge, skyabs 'gro yan lag drug pa, Sadangasharana, a treatise by Vimalamitra.

Six Prerequisites for Concentration, bsam gtan chos drug, Dhyanasaddharma-vyavasthana, a treatise by Avadhutipa.

Source of Nectar Tantra, bdud rtsi 'byung ba'i rgyud.

Sovereign Array of Sublime Qualities, 'phags pa yon tan bkod pa'i rgyal po, Sarva-dharma-guna-vyuharaja sutra.

Story of Sangharakshita, dge 'dun srungs kyi rtogs brjod, the 67th chapter of the Bodhisattvavadana-kalpalata (byang chub sems dpa'i rtogs pa brjod pa dpag bsam gyi 'khri shing) by Kshemendra.

Story of Shrona, gro bzhin skyes kyi rtogs brjod, the 20th chapter of the Bodhi-sattvavadana-kalpalata (byang chub sems dpa'i rtogs pa brjod pa dpag bsam gyi 'khri shing) by Kshemendra.

String of Lives, skyes pa rabs kyi rgyud, Jatakamala, a treatise by Aryashura.

Sublime Continuum, rgyud bla ma, Uttaratantrashastra, one of the five treatises of Maitreya-Asanga.

Sublime Sutra of the Arborescent Array, 'phags pa sdong po bkod pa'i mdo, Arya Gandavyuha sutra, the final chapter of the Great Host Sutra (Avatamsaka Sutra).

Sublime Sutra of the Marks That Inspire the Development of Faith, 'phags pa dad pa'i stobs bskyed pa la 'jug pa'i phyag rgya'i mdo, Arya-shraddhabaladhanavatara-mudra-sutra.

Supreme Victory Banner Sutra, mdo rgyal mtshan dam pa, Dhvajagra-sutra.

Sutra of Advice to the King, rgyal po la gdams pa'i mdo, Rajavavadaka-sutra.

Sutra of Complete Dedication, yongs su bsngo ba'i mdo, Parinatacakra-sutra.

Sutra of Extensive Play, rgya cher rol pa'i mdo, Lalitavistara-sutra.

Sutra of Great Liberation, thar pa chen po'i mdo, Mahamoksha-sutra.

Sutra of Immaculate Space, nam mkha' dri ma med pa'i mdo.

Sutra of Manifest Enlightenment, mngon par byang chub pa'i mdo, Abhisambodhi-sutra.

Sutra of Perfect Renunciation, mdo sde mngon par 'byung ba, Abhiniskramana-sutra.

Sutra of Precious Space, nam mkha' rin po che'i mdo.

Sutra of the Arborescent Array, *see* Sublime Sutra of the Arborescent Array.

Sutra of the Buddha's Treasure, sangs rgyas mdzod kyi mdo, Buddhadharma-koshakara-sutra.

Sutra of the Fortunate Kalpa, mdo sde bskal bzang, Bhadrakalpika Sutra.

Sutra of the Gong, gandi'i mdo, Gandi-sutra.

Sutra of the Immaculate, dri ma med pa'i mdo, Vimalaprabha-pariprccha-sutra.

Sutra of the Inconceivable Secrets, gsang ba bsam gyis mi khyab pa'i mdo, tathagata-acintya-guhya-nirdesha-sutra, part of the Pagoda of Precious Jewels (Ratnakuta).

Sutra of the King of Concentrations, ting 'dzin rgyal po, Samadhiraja-sutra.

Sutra of the Miracle of Decisive Pacification, rab tu zhi ba rnam par nges pa cho 'phrul gyi mdo, Prashanta-vinishcayapratiharya-samadhi-sutra.

Sutra of the Precious Lamp, dkon mchog ta la la'i mdo (also, dkon mchog sgron me'i mdo), Ratnolka sutra.

Sutra of the Sublime Essence, snying po mchog gi mdo.

Sutra of the Teaching on the Four Powers, chos bzhi bstan pa'i mdo, Caturdharma-nirdesha-sutra.

Sutra of the Ten Qualities, chos bcu pa'i mdo, Dashadharmaka-sutra.

Sutra on the Analysis of Actions, las rnam par 'byed pa'i mdo, Karmavibhaga.

Sutra Remembering the Three Jewels, dkon mchog rjes dran.

Sutra Requested by Bhadra, bzang pos zhus pa'i mdo, Bhadra-paripriccha-sutra.

Sutra Requested by Brahma, tshang pas zhus pa'i mdo, Brahma-pariprccha-sutra.

Sutra Requested by Druma, ljon pas zhus pa'i mod, Drumakinnararaja-pariprccha-sutra.

Sutra Requested by Gaganaganja, nam mkha' mdzod kyi mdo, Gaganaganja-paripriccha-sutra.

Sutra Requested by Maitreya, 'phags pa byams pas zhus pa'i mdo, Maitreya-paripriccha-sutra.

Sutra Requested by Maitrimahasimhanada, byams pa seng ge'i sgra chen pos zhus pa'i mdo (also called byams pa senge'i mdo), Maitrimahasimhanada-sutra.

Sutra Requested by Narayana, sred med kyi bus zhus pa'i mdo, Narayana-pariprccha-sutra.

Sutra Requested by Putri Ratna, bu mo rin chen gyis zhus pa'i mdo, Mahayano-padesa-sutra.

Sutra Requested by Ratnacuda, gtsug na rin chen gyis zhus pa'i mdo, Ratnacuda-pariprccha-sutra, part of the Pagoda of Precious Jewels (Ratnakuta).

Sutra Requested by Sagaramati, blo gros rgya mtshos zhus pa'i mdo, Sagaramati-paripriccha-sutra.

Sutra Requested by Shri Gupta, dpal sbas kyis zhus pa'i mdo, Shrigupta-paripriccha-sutra.

Sutra Requested by Subahu, lag bzang gis zhus pa'i mdo, Subahu-paripriccha-sutra.

Sutra That Inspires an Altruistic Attitude, lhag bsam bskul ba'i mdo, Adhyashayas-añcodana-sutra.

Tale with a Sow, phag gi rtogs brjod, Sukarikavadana-sutra.

Tantra of Perfect Union, yang dag par sbyor ba zhes bya ba'i rgyud chen po, Samputa.

Tantra of Secret Union, snyoms 'jug gsang ba'i rgyud.

Tantra of Stainless Parting, dri med bshags rgyud, also called Tantra of Stainless Confession.

Tantra of Supreme Wisdom, ye shes dam pa'i rgyud.

Tantra of the Array of Commitments, dam tshig bkod pa'i rgyud, Samaya-viyuha.

Tantra of the Emergence of Chakrasamvara, sdom 'byung, Samvarodaya Tantra.

Tantra of the Jewel that Embodies All, kun 'dus rin po che'i rgyud.

Tantra of the Song of Vajrasattva, rdo rje sems dpa' glu'i rgyud.

Tantra of the Sublime Wish-fulfilling Secret, gsang ba yid bzhin mchog gi rgyud.

Tantra of the Three Verses on the Wisdom Mind, dgongs pa tshigs gsum pa'i rgyud.

Tantra That Drives Back Armies, dpung rnam par bzlog pa'i rgyud.

Tantra That Establishes the Three Commitments, dam tshig gsum bkod pa'i rgyud.

Three Stages, rim gsum, Mayajalopadesakramatraya, a commentary on the Guhya-garbha Tantra by Vimalamitra.

Transcendent Wisdom, yum, Prajñaparamita, a sutra.

Transcendent Wisdom in Eight Thousand Verses, brgyad stong pa, Astasahashrika-prajñaparamita, one of the Prajñaparamita sutras.

Transmitted Distinctions Regarding the Vinaya, lung rnam 'byed (dul ba rnam par 'byed pai lung), Vinayavibhaga, a sutra.

Treasury of Abhidharma, chos mgnon pa'i mdzod, Abhidharmakosha, a treatise by Vasubandhu.

Treasury of Songs of Realization, do ha mdzod, Dohakosha, a compilation of Saraha's songs of spiritual realization.

Vajrapañjara Tantra, gur, a tantra.

The Way of the Bodhisattva, spyod 'jug, Bodhicharyavatara, a treatise by Shanti-deva, translated under the same title by the Padmakara Translation Group, Shambhala Publications, 1997, 2006.

Well-Explained Reasoning, rnam bshad rigs pa, Vyakhya-yukti, a shastra by Vasubandhu.

White Lotus Sutra of Compassion, rnying rje pad ma dkar po'i mdo, Karuna-pundarika-sutra.

Word of Mañjushri, 'jam dpal zhal lung, a tantra treatise.

## SECONDARY SOURCES

### Tibetan Commentaries

Jokhyab Pema Trinle Nyingpo (jo khyab padma 'phrin las snying po). lam rim ye shes snang ba'i brjed byang, a subcommentary on Jamgön Kongtrül's commentary of the discovered treasure, lam rim ye shes snying po.

Khenpo Shenga (gzhan phan chos kyi snang ba). bstan bcos bzhi brgya pa zhes bya ba'i tshig le'ur byas pa'i mchan 'grel, a commentary on *Four Hundred Verses on the Middle Way.*

Khenpo Shenga (gzhan phan chos kyi snang ba). chos mngon pa'i mdzod kyi tshig le'ur byas pa'i mchan 'grel shes bya'i me long zhes bya ba, a commentary on *Treasury of Abhidharma.*

Khenpo Shenga (gzhan phan chos kyi snang ba). dbus dang mtha' rnam par byed pa'i tshig le'ur byas pa zhes bya ba'i mchan 'grel, a commentary on *Distinguishing the Middle from Extremes.*

Khenpo Shenga (gzhan phan chos kyi snang ba). theg pa chen po mdo sde'i rgyan ces bya ba'i mchan 'grel, a commentary on *Ornament of the Sutras.*

Lobzang Palden Tenzin Nyentrak (blo bzang dpal ldan bstan 'dzin snyan grags). rgyal po la gtam bya ba rin po che'i phreng ba'i rnam bshad snying po'i don gsal pa zhes bya ba, a commentary on Nagarjuna's *Jewel Garland.*

Mipham Gyamtso ('ju mi pham rnam rgyal rgya mtsho). theg pa chen po mdo sde'i rgyan gyi dgongs don rnam par bshad pa theg mchog bdud rtsi'i dga' ston ces bya ba, a commentary on *Ornament of the Sutras.*

Mipham Gyamtso ('ju mi pham rnam rgyal rgya mtsho). theg pa chen po rgyud bla ma'i bstan bcos kyi mchan 'grel mi pham zhal lung, a commentary on the *Sublime Continuum.*

### Translated texts

Aryashura. *Fifty Stanzas on the Spiritual Teacher,* with a commentary by Geshe Ngawang Dhargey. Dharamsala: LTWA, 1992.

Dilgo Khyentse and Padampa Sangye. *The Hundred Verses of Advice.* Translated by the Padmakara Translation Group. Boston: Shambhala Publications, 2005.

Dudjom Jigdral Yeshe Dorje. *The Pearl Necklace: A Supplication to the Series of Successive Lives of His Holiness Dudjom Rinpoche* (from *Wisdom Nectar: Dudjom Rinpoche's Heart Advice*). Translated by Ron Garry. Ithaca: Snow Lion Publications, 2005.

Dudjom Rinpoche. *The Nyingma School of Tibetan Buddhism.* Translated by Gyurme Dorje and Matthew Kapstein. Boston: Wisdom Publications, 1991.

Gampopa Seunam Rinchen. *Le Précieux Ornement de la Libération.* Translated by Christian Bruyat and the Padmakara Translation Group. Saint Léon-sur-Vézère, France: Editions Padmakara, 1999.

sGam.po.pa. *The Jewel Ornament of Liberation.* Translated by H.V. Guenther. London: Rider and Company, 1959.

Jamgön Kongtrul Lodrö Tayé. *The Treasury of Knowledge, Book One: Myriad Worlds.* Translated by the Kalu Rinpoche Translation Group. Ithaca: Snow Lion Publications, 2003.

Longchen Yeshe Dorje, Kangyur Rinpoche. *Treasury of Precious Qualities.* Translated by the Padmakara Translation Group. Boston: Shambhala Publications, 2001.

Patrul Rinpoche. *The Words of My Perfect Teacher.* Translated by the Padmakara Translation Group. Boston: Shambhala Publications, 1998.

Takpo Tashi Namgyal. *Mahamudra: The Quintessence of Mind and Meditation.* Translated by Lobsang P. Lhalungpa. Boston: Shambhala Publications, 1986.

# Index

*Page numbers in boldface indicate the main explanation
or definition of a term or subject.*

absolute body, 18, 19, 52, 90, 237, 257,
    261, 268
  mandala, 220
  mind of the teacher, 265
  enlightened mind, 32
  result of accumulation of wisdom,
    217, 218
accomplishment, 245
*Accomplishment of Wisdom,* 37, 144
accumulation of merit, 217, 228, 229, 232.
    *See also* two accumulations
accumulation of wisdom, 218, 228, 232.
    *See also* two accumulations
actions
  cause and effect of, 117–19
  indeterminate, 130
  negative, 119–24 (*see also* ten negative
    actions)
  positive, 126–28 (*see also* ten positive
    actions)
  results of, 125–26, 128–30
activity, 245
Ajatashatru, 152, 308n100. *See also*
    Darshaka
Akashagarbha, 60
*Analysis of Actions,* 114
Ananda, 237
Angulimala, 203
animals, 107–8
approach, 244, 245
*Approach to the Absolute Truth,*
    21, 219
Arhat, 123
*Array of Qualities of Mañjushri's
    Buddhafield,* 256
*Array of the Sublime,* 260
Ashvagosha, 74, 227, 252
aspiration, mistaken, 274
Atisha, 140, 206, 219, 311n147
Avalokiteshvara, 163

bodhichitta
  in action, 170, 172
  in aspiration, 170, 171
  benefits of, 189–93
  categories of, 170
  decline of, 188
  definition of, 169
  exchanging oneself and others, 187
  precepts, in action, 175
  precepts, in aspiration, 173
  training in, 193–95
Bodhisattva, 130, 172, 177, 178, 180, 181,
    203, 257
  negative deeds against a, 123, 191–92,
    274–75
  practice of, 186
  vow, 189, 196, 207
*Bodhisattva Levels,* 170, 177
body of manifestation, 52, 144, 161, 163,
    220, 258, 265, 268
body of perfect enjoyment, 32, 52, 144, 161,
    211, 220, 257, 265, 268. *See also* eight
    jewel ornaments; five silken garments
Brahma, 75, 76, 88, 89, 97, 113, 129, 150, 189
Buddhaguhya, 220

care, mistaken, 274
carefulness, 39, **174**
Chandragomin, 67
Chögyal Pakpa Rinpoche, 221
Chunda, 249
*Clarifying Lamp,* 260
*Close Mindfulness Sutra,* 97, 105, 112, 125
*Commentary on the Ornament of True
    Realization,* 38
commitments, 26, 27, 124, 201, 204, 206,
    207, 238, 259, 272
compassion, 169, **171**, 172, 186, 194, 196,
    197, 227, 249
  mistaken, 274

*Compendium of the Buddhas' Wisdom,* 14, 15, 34

concentration, 49, 112, 113, 114, **179**, 182, 183, 185, 207, 228, 247
   categories of, 179–80
   conditions for, 49, 179

*Condensed Transcendent Wisdom,* 60, 152, 248, 255

confession. *See* parting (from negative actions)

Copper-Colored Mountain, 264, 267

crimes with immediate retribution, 33, 61, 152, 204. *See also* five crimes with immediate retribution

criticism, results of, 26, 123, 274, 275

Dagpo Rinpoche, 275

Darshaka, 203

dedication of merit, 180, 185, 213, 227, 231, **249–57**
   four excellent features of, 254
   and prayers of aspiration, 256

demigods, **111**, 112

demon, 156, 272, 273, 278

Devadatta, 21, 152, 308n100

devotion
   four branches of applying, 242–44
   four ways to cultivate, 241–42

Dhanakosha, Lake, 158

*Diamond Daka,* 33

*Diamond Necklace,* 27

diligence, 50, 70, 91, **178**, 182, 183, 185, 228, 272
   categories of, 178–79

disciples
   bad, 24–26
   good, 23–24

discipline, 63, 64, 128, 143, **176**, 182, 183, 185, 189, 228
   categories of, 176–77

*Discourse on Impermanence,* 73

*Display of the Perfected Wheel,* 34, 42

*Distinguishing the Middle from Extremes,* 49, 50, 127

Dudjom Lingpa, 160

*Ear Ornament Sutra,* 147

eight (offering) goddesses, 225

eight auspicious objects, 226

eight auspicious symbols, 226

Eight Great Close Sons, 32, 163

eight jewel ornaments (of the body of perfect enjoyment), 210

eight kinds of perceptual domination, 180, 310n121

Eight Knowledge Holders, 162

eight ordinary concerns, 2, 70, 135, 272–74

eight perfect freedoms, 180, 310n121

eight perfect qualities (of water), 158, 222–24

eight perverse acts, 124

eight states of lack of opportunity, 59–60

eight subcontinents, 223

eight types of mental application, 49, **50**, 179

eleven ways (of benefiting beings through discipline), 177, 309n114

eleven ways (of benefiting others through concentration), 180, 310n122

enjoyment, mistaken, 274

*Essence of the Sun Sutra,* 151

exchanging oneself and others, **187**, 196, 197

faith, 23, 24, 152, **153–58**, 166, 192, 232, 245, 257, 278
   as antidote to laziness, 50
   categories of, 153
   as cause of bodhichitta, 169
   lack of, 25, 26, 157, 191, 242
   as motive for taking refuge, 140
   and the precious human body, 60, 61, 64
   similes of, 156, 157

*Fifty Verses on the Teacher,* 10, 19, 26, 30, 339

five bone ornaments, 261

five circumstantial advantages, 61

five crimes that are almost as grave, 123

five crimes with immediate retribution, **123**, 124, 209

Five Excellent Ones of Sublime Nobility, 162

five faults in meditation, **49–50**, 179

five ideas (in developing patience), 178, 309n117

five individual advantages, 60–61

five objects of desire, 96

five offerings, 229

five silken garments (of the body of perfect enjoyment), 210

*Flower Chapter,* 64

four (great) continents, 223

four black actions, 174

four boundless attitudes, **170–72**, 195, 230

four concentrations, 114, 179

four empowerments, 259, 268

Four Great Kings, 75, 76, 88

Four Hundred. See *Four Hundred Verses on
the Middle Way*
*Four Hundred Verses on the Middle Way,* 23,
110, 130, 251
Four Noble Truths, 131–34
four powers (in purification), 203–6, 248
four principles of a renunciate, 183
four ways of attracting disciples, 185–86
four white actions, 174

Gaganagañja, 231
Gampopa. *See* Dagpo Rinpoche
Garab Dorje, 161, 162
*Gathering of the Glorious Ones,* 223
generosity, 70, **175**, 182, 183, 185, 186, 218,
228, 277
categories of, 175–76
*Glorious Tantra of the Gathering of Secrets,* 32
gods
in form and formless worlds, 112–13
in world of desire, 60, 101, 108, 111–12,
114, 129
*Golden Garland of Pledges,* 71
*Great Array of the Sublime,* 12
*Great Commentary on Transcendent Wisdom
in Eight Thousand Verses,* 59
*Great Host Sutra,* 251
Guru Nangsi Zilnön, 159
Guru Rinpoche, 241, 258, 259
Great Master, 12, 71, 92, 114, 118, 142,
144, 162, 214
Great Master of Oddiyana, 283
Lake-Born Diamond Bearer, 51
Lotus-Born Guru, 239, 267
mantra of (*see* Vajra Guru mantra)
Oddiyana, Diamond Bearer of, 258
Padma Thöthrengtsel, 238, 262
Padmasambhava, 160
Gyalse Lhaje, 71
Gyurme Ngedön Wangpo, 160

*Heaped Lotuses,* 186
Heaven of the Thirty-Three, 112
hell(s)
cold, 101–3
Diamond, 201, 204
ephemeral, 104
hot, 99–101
neighboring, 103–4
span of life in, 101, 102, 104, 306nn63–64
of Ultimate Torment, 25, 26, 33, 35, 37,
42, 100, 202
*Hevajra Tantra,* 172

*Highest Expression of Truth,* 18
humans, 109–11
*Hundred Parables on Action,* 38, 117, 126
hundred-syllable mantra. *See under*
Vajrasattva
hungry spirits, 105–7

Indra, 75, 76, 88, 89, 97
*Intentionally Spoken Chapters,* 76, 77, 79
*Introduction to the Middle Way,* 63, 228
Ishvara, 75, 89

Ja, King, 162
Jambudvipa, 66, 223
Jampel Shenyen. *See* Mañjushrimitra
Jetari, 220
jewel, wish-fulfilling, 5, 67
*Jewel Garland,* 66, 81, 125, 127, 129, 132, 153,
217, 253

Kalachakra (mandala offering tradition),
220
Kamalashila, 229
Kambala, 220
karma. *See* actions
khatvanga, 159, 160, 262, 267
Kshitigarbha, 32
Kunga Nyingpo, 11

*Lamp for the Path,* 140
laziness, 50, 73, 91, 178, 188
antidotes to, 50
*Letter to a Friend,* 135, 147, 174, 175, 203, 273
on the defects of cyclic existence, 97, 105,
106, 107, 108, 112, 113
on impermanence, 74, 81, 93
on the precious human birth, 63, 69
lineage teachers, 159–61
lineages, different categories of, 161–62
Longchenpa, 278
Great Omniscient One, 19, 24, 42, 44,
62, 69, 80, 90, 174, 277, 279
Omniscient Dharma King, 12, 256
Omniscient Dharma Lord, 154

*Magical Display of Indestructible Reality,* 17
Maitreya, 192, 193, 203
mandala
accomplishment, 220, 229
offering, 220, 222, 230
mandala offering
benefits of, 228, 229
as best of all offerings, 218

mandala offering (*continued*)
    different kinds of, 220, 221
    in Mantra Vehicle, 219
    materials, 221
    visualization of, 229–31
    *See also* thirty-seven-element mandala
*Mandala Sutra,* 228
Mandarava, 262
Mañjushri, 192, 242
Mañjushrikumara, 249
    *See also* Tikshna Mañjushri
Mañjushrikirti, 220
Mañjushrimitra, 161
masters. *See* teachers
Meru, Mount, 74, 223, 248
    as center of the mandala, 219–21, **222**,
        230, 231
    as simile, 83, 97, 154, 163, 203, 267
    top of, 226
*Middle Sutra of Transcendent Wisdom,* 4,
    127, 172, 252, 253, 255
mindfulness, 5, 39, 41, **50**, 173, 174

Nagarjuna, quotations from, 99, 180,
    217, 236, 250. See also under *Jewel
    Garland; Letter to a Friend*
Nanda, 203
Narayana, 89
*Net of Magical Display,* 11
nine considerations (in developing
    patience), 178, 309n117
nine methods of settling the mind, 179,
    309n119
nine modes of expression (of the peaceful
    deities), 210
*Nirvana Sutra,* 78, 92, 147, 152,
    278
Nishkalankashri, 220
Nishkalankavajra, 220

offerings, 2, 30, 247, 249. *See also* five
    offerings; mandala offering
*Ornament of the Essence,* 206
*Ornament of the Indestructible Essence,* 31,
    32, 36, 42
*Ornament of the Sutras,* 9, 151, 182, 183,
    184, 185, 254
*Ornament of True Realization,* 169, 170,
    252, 256

Padampa Sangye, 132, 195
    *Hundred Verses of Advice to the People
    of Tingri,* 81, 93

Padma Thöthrengtsel. *See under* Guru
    Rinpoche
Padmasambhava. *See under* Guru Rinpoche
*Pagoda of Precious Jewels,* 192
parting (from negative actions), 202, 203,
    206–8, 212, 214, 248
patience, **177**, 182, 183, 185, 228
    categories of, 177–78
    five ideas in developing, 178
    mistaken, 274
    nine considerations in developing, 178
Pokhong Tulku. *See* Gyurme Ngedön
    Wangpo
*Prayer of Good Action,* 252
*Prayer of Invocation for the Tenth Day,* 239
profound insight, 179, 218
prostration, 246, 247
purification, 201–14
    benefits of, 207
    signs of, 214
    *See also* parting (from negative actions);
        Vajrasattva

Ratna Lingpa, 239
refuge, 139–52
    benefits of, 150–52
    objects of, 141–45
    practice of, 158–66
    precepts of, 146–49
    reasons for taking, 139–41
    visualization of, 158–65
    vow, 146
rejoicing, 248
    mistaken 274
*Root Tantra of All-Encompassing Awareness,*
    277
*Root Tantra of the Assembly of Knowledge
    Holders,* 235, 258

Sagaramati, 250
Samantabhadra, Bodhisattva, 230, 247, 282
Samantabhadra, the primordial Buddha,
    161, 162
Samantabhadri, 161
samaya. *See* commitments
Sangye Yeshe, 242
Saraha, 82, 236. See also *Treasury of Songs of
    Realization*
*Sayings on Impermanence,* 75
Seas of Enjoyment, 222, 223
*Secret Sayings,* 239
*Self-Arisen Awareness,* 23, 24
*Series of Lives,* 110

seven branches (of accumulation of merit), 232, 233, 245, **246–57**
seven branches of union, 257
seven factors (of concentration), 179, 310n120
seven golden mountain ranges, 222, 311n151
seven kinds of ordination for individual liberation, 176, 309n113
seven noble riches, 16, 90, 156, 229
*Seven-Point Mind Training,* 187
seven precious attributes (of royalty), **224–25**, 229
seven semiprecious articles, 226
seven sets of qualifications of a diamond master, 12–19
*Seventy Stanzas on Refuge,* 150
Shakyamuni, Buddha, 66, 75, 91
  Bhagavan, the, 21
  Lion of the Shakyas, 163
  Lord of the Shakyas, 75
shameful deeds, 119, 124, 248
Shantideva, quotations from. See under *Way of the Bodhisattva, The*
Shri Singha, 160
six classes of beings, sufferings of, **98–113**, 132
six kinds of preternatural knowledge, 145
six mistaken qualities, 274
Six Ornaments (of Jambudvipa), 162
*Six Prerequisites for Concentration,* 49
six stains, 4
six transcendent perfections, 172, **175–85**, 195, 278
  categories of, 182
  characteristics of, 181
  definitions of, 184
  in the mandala offering, 228
  practicing, 184
  reasons for number, 182
  reasons for order, 183
Sixteen Great Sthaviras, 163
sixteen serious faults, 124
*Source of Nectar Tantra,* 43
*Sovereign Array of Sublime Qualities,* 13
stale air, expelling, 51
*Story of Sangharakshita,* 104
*Story of Shrona,* 104
*String of Lives,* 3
Subahu, 173
Subhuti, 123, 252, 255
*Sublime Continuum,* 113, 132, 143, 145, 153, 180
*Sublime Sutra of the Arborescent Array,* 15

*Sublime Sutra of the Marks That Inspire the Development of Faith,* 274
Sucharita, 220
Sudhana, 192
suffering
  four great rivers of, 109–10
  similes of, 114
  three kinds of, 113–14
  truth of, 132
*Supreme Victory Banner Sutra,* 151
sustained calm, 179, 218
*Sutra of Advice to the King,* 84
*Sutra of Complete Dedication,* 253
*Sutra of Extensive Play,* 75, 78, 87, 88, 224
*Sutra of Great Liberation,* 246
*Sutra of Immaculate Space,* 237
*Sutra of Manifest Enlightenment,* 67
*Sutra of Perfect Renunciation,* 97, 224
*Sutra of Precious Space,* 60
*Sutra of the Arborescent Array,* 9, 29, 65, 66, 69, 191, 192, 279
*Sutra of the Buddha's Treasure,* 20
*Sutra of the Fortunate Kalpa,* 182
*Sutra of the Gong,* 278
*Sutra of the Immaculate,* 152
*Sutra of the Inconceivable Secrets,* 156, 190, 279
*Sutra of the King of Concentrations,* 74, 174
*Sutra of the Miracle of Decisive Pacification,* 123
*Sutra of the Precious Lamp,* 156, 158, 247
*Sutra of the Sublime Essence,* 171
*Sutra of the Teaching on the Four Powers,* 203
*Sutra of the Ten Qualities,* 157
*Sutra on the Analysis of Actions,* 118
*Sutra Remembering the Three Jewels,* 145
*Sutra Requested by Bhadra,* 255
*Sutra Requested by Brahma,* 189
*Sutra Requested by Druma,* 255
*Sutra Requested by Gaganagañja,* 250
*Sutra Requested by Maitreya,* 43
*Sutra Requested by Maitrimahasimhanada,* 248, 277
*Sutra Requested by Narayana,* 278
*Sutra Requested by Putri Ratna,* 88
*Sutra Requested by Ratnacuda,* 44, 64
*Sutra Requested by Sagaramati,* 250
*Sutra Requested by Shri Gupta,* 70, 257
*Sutra Requested by Subahu,* 5
*Sutra That Inspires an Altruistic Attitude,* 147

*Tale with a Sow,* 150
*Tantra of Perfect Union,* 31, 41

*Tantra of Secret Union,* 35
*Tantra of Stainless Parting,* 207, 246
*Tantra of Supreme Wisdom,* 32
*Tantra of the Array of Commitments,* 260
*Tantra of the Emergence of Chakrasamvara,* 146
*Tantra of the Jewel That Embodies All,* 260
*Tantra of the Song of Vajrasattva,* 208
*Tantra of the Sublime Wish-fulfilling Secret,* 19
*Tantra of the Three Verses on the Wisdom Mind,* 208
*Tantra That Drives Back Armies,* 35
*Tantra That Establishes the Three Commitments,* 26
Tara, 6
teachers
    connection with disciples, 27, 237, 265
    devotion to, 32, 43, 52, 238, **241–44**
        (*see also* faith)
    following one's, 29–44
    importance of, 9, 235–38
    qualifications of, 9–19
    wrong kinds of, 20
teachings
    giving, 2–3
    receiving, 2–6, 276–79
ten advantages, 60
ten Dharma activities, 307n81
ten negative actions, 119–28
ten positive actions, 127–29. *See also* ten Dharma activities
ten powers of perceptual limitlessness, 180, 310n121
ten principles, 10, 11–12
thirty-seven-element mandala, 221, 231
    visualization of, 222–27
three defects of the pot, 3–4
Three Jewels, 141, **142**, 144–52, 165–67, 263, 265
    six features analogous to those of a jewel, 145
Three Roots, 203, 241, 263, 265
*Three Stages,* 37
three trainings, 10
    relationship to transcendent perfections, 183
Tikshna-Mañjushri, 6
*Transcendent Wisdom,* 9, 156, 255
*Transcendent Wisdom in Eight Thousand Verses,* 123
*Transmitted Distinctions Regarding the Vinaya,* 65, 132, 247

*Treasury of Abhidharma,* 79, 101, 102, 103, 107, 119, 120, 121, 122, 221
*Treasury of Songs of Realization,* 96
Tsogyal Khachö Wangmo, 261
two accumulations, 43, 92, 150, 152, **217–18**

Udayana, 203
udumbara (flower), 21, 61, 71
Uttarakuru, the northern continent, 79, 223

Vairochana, seven-point posture of, 50
Vajra Guru mantra, 267
    meaning of, 257
Vajra Yogini, 261
Vajradhara, 11, 32
    union, 261
Vajrakumara, 163
Vajrapani, 162
*Vajrapañjara Tantra,* 33
Vajrasattva, 161, 162, 200, **204**, 207, 208, 210, 213
    hundred-syllable mantra, 204, 206, 208, 210, 222
    six-syllable mantra, 213
    visualization of, 210
Vajratopa, 210
vigilance, 39, 41, **50**, 173, 174
Vimalamitra, 162
    *Six Aspects of Taking Refuge,* 139, 148, 149
Vishnu, 75, 89
vows, 119, 124, 141, 150, 176, 177, 201, 202, 207

*Way of the Bodhisattva, The,* 130, 133, 145, 227, 233, 309n117
    on bodhichitta, 170, 173, 177, 186, 189, 190, 191, 192
    on dedicating merit, 249, 253, 254, 256
    on the defects of cyclic existence, 96, 98, 105
    on impermanence, 80, 82, 83, 87, 89, 91
    on the precious human birth, 63, 64, 65, 67, 68
*Well-Explained Reasoning,* 4
*White Lotus Sutra of Compassion,* 68, 152
wisdom, 153, **180**, 181–85, 218, 232, 249, 258
    and accumulating merit, 227, 228
    categories of, 181
wish-fulfilling jewel, 5, 67
*Word of Mañjushri,* 237

Yeshe Tsogyal, 51, 160, 238

# The Padmakara Translation Group

The Padmakara Translation Group is devoted to the accurate and literary translation of Tibetan texts and spoken material into Western languages by trained Western translators, under the guidance of authoritative Tibetan scholars, principally Taklung Tsetrul Pema Wangyal Rinpoche and Jigme Khyentse Rinpoche, in a context of sustained study and discussion.

## TRANSLATIONS INTO ENGLISH

*The Adornment of the Middle Way.* Shantarakshita and Mipham Rinpoche. Shambhala Publications, 2005.

*Counsels from My Heart.* Dudjom Rinpoche. Shambhala Publications, 2001.

*Enlightened Courage.* Dilgo Khyentse. Editions Padmakara, 1992; Snow Lion Publications, 1994, 2006.

*The Excellent Path of Enlightenment.* Dilgo Khyentse. Editions Padmakara, 1987; Snow Lion Publications, 1996.

*A Flash of Lightning in the Dark of Night.* The Dalai Lama. Shambhala Publications, 1993. Republished as *For the Benefit of All Beings.* Shambhala Publications, 2009.

*Food of Bodhisattvas.* Shabkar Tsogdruk Rangdrol. Shambhala Publications, 2004.

*A Guide to The Words of My Perfect Teacher.* Khenpo Ngawang Pelzang (trans. with Dipamkara). Shambhala Publications, 2004.

*The Heart of Compassion.* Dilgo Khyentse. Shambhala Publications, 2007.

*The Heart Treasure of the Enlightened Ones.* Dilgo Khyentse and Patrul Rinpoche. Shambhala Publications, 1992.

*The Hundred Verses of Advice.* Dilgo Khyentse and Padampa Sangye. Shambhala Publications, 2005.

*Introduction to the Middle Way.* Chandrakirti and Mipham Rinpoche. Shambhala Publications, 2002.

*Journey to Enlightenment.* Matthieu Ricard. Aperture, 1996.

*Lady of the Lotus-Born.* Gyalwa Changchub and Namkhai Nyingpo. Shambhala Publications, 1999.

*The Life of Shabkar: The Autobiography of a Tibetan Yogin.* SUNY Press, 1994; Snow Lion Publications, 2001.

*Nagarjuna's Letter to a Friend.* Longchen Yeshe Dorje, Kangyur Rinpoche. Snow Lion Publications, 2005.

*The Nectar of Manjushri's Speech.* Kunzang Pelden. Shambhala Publications, 2007.

*The Root Stanzas on the Middle Way.* Nagarjuna. Editions Padmakara, 2008.

*Treasury of Precious Qualities.* Longchen Yeshe Dorje, Kangyur Rinpoche. Shambhala Publications, 2001, 2010.

*The Way of the Bodhisattva (Bodhicharyavatara).* Shantideva. Shambhala Publications, 1997, 2006.

*White Lotus.* Jamgön Mipham. Shambhala Publications, 2007.

*Wisdom: Two Buddhist Commentaries.* Khenchen Kunzang Pelden and Minyak Kunzang Sönam. Editions Padmakara, 1993, 1999.

*The Wish-Fulfilling Jewel.* Dilgo Khyentse. Shambhala Publications, 1988.

*The Words of My Perfect Teacher.* Patrul Rinpoche. International Sacred Literature Trust—HarperCollins, 1994; 2d edition, AltaMira Press, 1998; Shambhala Publications, 1998.

*Zurchungpa's Testament.* Zurchungpa and Dilgo Khyentse. Snow Lion Publications, 2006.

*Ekajati.*

*Rahula.*

*Dorje Lekpa.*

*Shenpa Marnak.*